HEROES OF
COASTAL
COMMAND
1939 – 1945

Andrew D. Bird is one of Britain's respected military historians and his previous books include *A Separate Little War: The Banff Coastal Command Strike Wing Versus the Kriegsmarine and Luftwaffe 1944-1945,* and *Coastal Dawn: Blenheim's in Action from the Phoney War Through the Battle of Britain.* He lives in Berkshire.

Also by Andrew D. Bird

*A Separate Little War: The Banff Coastal Command Strike Wing
Versus the Kriegsmarine and Luftwaffe 1944-1945*

*Coastal Dawn: Blenheim's in Action from the Phoney War Through the
Battle of Britain*

HEROES OF
COASTAL
COMMAND
1939 – 1945

ANDREW D. BIRD

FRONTLINE
BOOKS

Frontline Books, London
Published in Hardback in 2018 by Frontline Books, an imprint of
Pen & Sword Books Ltd, an imprint of Pen & Sword Books Limited,
47 Church Street, Barnsley, S. Yorkshire, S70 2AS
www.frontline-books.com

A CIP catalogue record for this book is available from the British Library

ISBN 9781526710697

Text and plates designed and typeset in the UK
Printed and bound by TJ International Ltd, Padstow, Cornwall

*This book is dedicated in memory of the indomitable
men and women of Coastal Command
especially those who made the ultimate sacrifice
and to the ones they left behind*

Contents

Foreword

As a very junior maritime navigator in an RAAF P-3 Orion squadron in the early 1980s I had the fortune to meet a few of the surviving Royal Australian Air Force aircrew from Coastal Command and their Pacific War peers. Their recollections of their wartime experiences, and memories of lost comrades, had not dimmed over the decades. Thus, when Andrew Bird invited me to write the foreword to this book, I felt deeply honoured both to recognise his work and to honour, in a small way, those who have gone before in maritime military aviation.

Andrew's expertise in this field is well known and his earlier books, *A Separate Little War* and *Coastal Dawn*, shows his exceptional talent and his empathy for the subject. With his trademark thoroughness, Andrew has painstakingly researched this new work, which continues the story of the somewhat underplayed histories of Coastal Command; he has started to place Coastal Command on the same pedestal that, quite rightly, Fighter and Bomber Commands are to be found. After all, it was the war at sea that truly frightened Prime Minister Winston Churchill.

Certainly not a dry recitation of facts, Andrew has captured the stories with a genuinely fresh approach of those flying a great variety of missions over the seas. Each chapter is a stand-alone tale of the exploits of a great variety of aircrew, be they chasing U-Boats or striking at surface shipping. The inclusion of relatively unknown Blenheim and Hampden flights neatly balances those of the better-known Catalina and Beaufighter sorties. Most would be familiar with the classic anti-U-Boat missions, but the coverage of weather reconnaissance sorties and flag-dropping flights over Paris gives a much broader view of the many and varied roles Coastal Command aircrew undertook during the Second World War.

The characters, like the whole of the Royal Air Force, come from all over the Commonwealth and Occupied Europe. With so many heading from Australia and New Zealand to the shores of Britain, I am pleased that he has broadened their wartime lives to include parts which pre-, and in some cases, post-date their time in Coastal Command. The subtle recognition of the role that families often played, and impact of their losses, brings the humanity of the War and, in particular, the maritime war to the fore. Seeing these men as sons, brothers and husbands adds poignancy to their tales.

Heroes of Coastal Command is impeccably researched and superbly written in an engaging style and in part on a genuinely fresh approach to events. This captivating new research and well considered revisionism is an opportunity to better understand what the maritime aircrews did to preserve our world.

Air Commodore John Meier,
Director General History and Heritage, Royal Australian Air Force,
27 November 2017.

Author's Note

So as not to cause any confusion, I have used German ranks, rather than the English translation. I have also called German air and ground units by their German terminology. All times have been converted to British Double Summer Time (BDST), the time zone used by Coastal Command during operational sorties. Since 1916 when the British Summer Time Act was passed establishing British Summer Time (BST) had been an hour ahead of GMT. In 1940 however, the clocks were not put back by an hour at the end of Summer Time and continued to advance by one hour each spring and put back by an hour each autumn, until July 1945. During these summers, therefore, operating on BDST, Britain was two hours ahead of GMT. French time, usually an hour ahead of UK time, was therefore an hour behind BDST. So, when Operation Squabble took place in Paris at a local time of 11.27 hours, on Friday 12 June 1942, the BDST time was 12.27 hours. Confusingly most contemporary accounts mistakenly refer to the British time zone in use at BST rather than the correct BDST.

Equally, so as not to cause confusion, I have used their common names where they are known or surnames rather than nicknames, although they are referenced when the person is first introduced, and ranks given are those that pertained at the time. I have standardized references to aircraft Bristol Beaufighter in the first instance then referred to as Beaufighter, Consolidated Liberator to Liberator and Short Sunderland to Sunderland.

Chapter 1

Wing Commander 'Jack' Davenport AC, DSO, DFC*, GM – 455 Squadron

Air Marshal Sir Arthur Harris had been Air Officer Commanding-in-Chief RAF Bomber Command for exactly three months and eight days as he descended down the long steps into the 'Hole', as the Operations Room was known at RAF High Wycombe. He expected all those who were to attend the early morning conference to be there. Wednesday 8 April 1942 was no different, the commander-in-chief's senior staff stood around the planning table which Harris referred to as the High Alter. There was a deathly silence as he entered the room, took off his cap, sat down, and took out and lit one of his American cigarettes.

'What did the Hun do last night?' he enquired.

The intelligence officer rattled off the answer then handed him a list of priority targets, most of which had come from the Air Ministry in London, staff officers of a lower rank still wet behind the ears, and whom Harris had an utter distrust and dislike; why was it their role to try and tell him his job, however indirectly?

Harris studied the list through his half-rimed tortoiseshell glasses, then, after conferring with Air Vice Marshal Robert 'Sandy' Saundby, his senior air officer, announced that the night's raid would be directed at Hamburg. He turned to the chief weatherman and grilled him. On this occasion it was straightforward enough: the weather looked promising, but changeable, he told him, forecasting cloudy skies, clearing over the target. Harris was satisfied with that.

Next came the allocation of aircraft. The figures showed there would be a record number of 272 available, of which there would be only seven Lancasters, the remainder consisting of 177 Wellingtons, twenty-two

Stirlings, thirteen Manchesters, twelve Halifaxs, and forty-one Hampdens, including ten from 455 Squadron. Crews were not expected to fly two nights in a row and, fortunately, the Essen operation had been scrubbed on Easter Monday, 6 April, because of bad weather.

The past three months had been a time of assessment, retraining and experimentation. Much of the Command's hopes had rested on the Avro Manchester bomber, but the Rolls-Royce Vulture engines had proved to be underpowered and completely unsuitable for the airframe. The other main aircraft which Bomber Command expected to be able to rely upon, the Handley Page Hampden, had also been found to be inadequate. It would be an estimated six months before Harris would see suitable numbers roll off the Avro production line of the four-engine Lancaster to give him the strike force he needed.

But, at least two Hampden squadrons were potentially going to Air Marshal Philip de la Ferté Joubert's Coastal Command. Negotiations had already begun at the Air Ministry, Saundby had informed him; and that night's raid against Hamburg would see one of those squadrons – the Australian 455 Squadron – with only twenty-one days remaining in Bomber Command.

Some 150 miles north, in the largely flat Nottinghamshire countryside, the crews of 455 Squadron were readying themselves for another day. RAF Wigsley airfield was just only three months old, built as a satellite for the much larger RAF Swinderby a few miles down the road and, although it lay to the west of Lincoln, it was in the middle of nowhere. For the officers of Wigsley the nearest decent public house was in the adjacent Harby village.

It was partly this reason that 21-year-old Pilot Officer Jack Davenport found he had to venture out into the surrounding towns of Newark or Lincoln whenever he wanted a night out. The son of a sheep wool trader[1] from Sydney, the state capital of New South Wales, Davenport tended to spend his time when not flying or operations socialising in the Officers Mess or playing draughts and shove ha'penny. He reckoned it was a pretty good place to unwind in between the intensity of flying his first initial fifteen combat operations over Occupied Europe. In any case, he did not own a car, wasn't one for drinking endless pints of beer and, in the cold spring days, it made sense to him to stay routed near to his companions.

By 10.00 hours he and the other officers in the squadron had breakfasted and taken a long ride to the southern side of the airfield. Davenport, with Pilot Officer Alan Bowman his navigator, reported into the flight hut, where the news had already arrived that they would be flying that night, and to Hamburg. Take-off was due at 21.00 hours.

Davenport had joined the squadron in March. He was a tall, broad-shouldered man, sociable and thoughtful. His face had a clear completion, with a thin pencil moustache above a mouth that was always ready to crease into a big smile. His father had hailed from Adelaide with an English-born father, William, who died leaving his mother widowed. In due course, after Prince Alfred College, he attended the well-respected School of Mines and Industries and began working at William Haughton & Co., a wool-broking and shipping agent that had sites throughout Australia, Europe, Canada and London. It was in Adelaide he met Davenport's mother, Grace Hutton. However, their future lay in Sydney where his father took up a new position with William Haughton. Grace's brother and her mother followed. The New South Wales capital was vibrant, but the wool-broker encountered difficulty in insuring the cargo and his father's career was short-lived. The Davenports moved into the hotel business in Sydney's Haymarket area where trade was brisk. Jack was born on 9 June 1920 and entered into the harsh realities of life with a father medically unfit to work due to a serious bout of pleurisy. Brief sojourns to Coogee, and Coonamble were not successful, but Davenport's time in the central-western plains sparked a real enthusiasm for the bush that remained with him. Treasuring the poetry of Banjo Patterson and Henry Lawson, and with a nudge of encouragement would recite Lawson's 'The Teams.'

The metropolis of Sydney drew them back, and the years that followed were some of the most difficult for Davenport's family. Roy's fortunes fluctuated until work ceased due to a crippling bladder infection made him bed-bound. Grace cared for her ill husband and despite the difficulties raised three boys, Phil, Jack and Keith. Her independent spirit and quiet dignity assured the family stayed together as she fought to make ends meet. There were occasions when the Davenports had no idea where the next meal would come from. Grace often went hungry herself, so her boys could eat, even if it was only bread and dripping. The constant caring for her ill husband and looking after three very active boys, making ends meet, and a succession of shared houses and cramped rooms with family and friends, wore her down and in 1928 she pleaded to her sister and Phil was whisked off on an extended visit to Adelaide.

Roy recovered enough to enter the workplace but as the depression gained momentum the family came face to face with the bailiffs in Sydney. Jack and Keith tussled with the bailiffs and fought them off using broom handles until Grace's mother intervened.[2] However in a few days, shortly after Phil returned from Adelaide, the family was evicted. After a spell living in Roscoe Street, Bondi Beach, and tending a boarding house, the Davenports moved into a flat in Tamarama. Phil started at Sydney Boys

High School in 1931, the many upheavals and struggles with poverty saw Jack, like Phil leave school to seek employment without his leaving certificate.[3]

The years of poverty left a scare; Jack wanted a job that offered security after leaving school in 1935 and began working in a warehouse. Five years on, by the time war broke out, he was working at the Commercial Bank of Australia in the Sydney branch as a savings bank ledger keeper with a gross salary of £70, paid fortnightly, and from there he would see the commercial aeroplanes of Qantas fly over daily. By May 1940, having reached the age of twenty, promotions had seen him rise to general bank ledger keeper with a yearly income of £170. Assessed as a good type with ambition, Jack took the generous extended military leave offered by the bank and, on 5 July 1939, Corporal Anthony Nugent induced Jack into A Company 30th Battalion, New South Wales Scottish Regiment, which was affiliated with the Black Watch whose striking tartan formed part of its battledress.[4]

Jack regularly attended Millers Point drill hall and training camps. His competence was noted by his commanding officers and he rose through the ranks. In mid-1940 Sergeant Jack Davenport's name was listed as being selected to train recruits for the 7 Division AIF. The continuous balling of recruits became mundane and being 'air minded' applied to join the Royal Australian Air Force (RAAF) in spring 1940, about two weeks after his brother Phil. He had decided that he wanted to become a pilot, unfortunately, interrupted schooling meant he did not have the right qualifications, but Jack was not the only one. To address this the RAAF devised weekend tutoring to provide trainees with consistent technical knowledge. Commonly known as the 'twenty-one lessons,' Jack got up to scratch on navigation, mathematics, aerodynamics, King's regulations, administration, law and Morse code.[5]

As 1940 drew to a close, the Davenport boys Phil, Jack and Keith, welcomed in the New Year together. Six days later Jack reported to 2 Recruitment Centre, Woolloomooloo at 08.30 hours. After all the formalities were completed Jack and his colleagues arrived at Bradfield Park still wearing civilian clothes. He was told he could be aircrew - wireless operator/air gunner. 'But I insisted that my mind was set on being a pilot, they said if I did well in on my wireless operator's course I'd be able to re-muster as a pilot,' he said. Showing the kind of grit and determination that would stand him in good stead later, he attained first place in his course exams. 'I did well and was remustered.'[6]

Narromine in western New South Wales beckoned. Unusually, Jack volunteered to be a bomber pilot, rather than a fighter pilot as was the preference of most. 'You were flying with somebody else for whom you were responsible and who had some responsibility towards you.' Jack made his first solo flight in a Tiger Moth on 19 March 1941 after 29 hours dual and 25.10 hours solo; Canada was confirmed as his next destination to complete his pilot's training. When he left on 20 May 1941, it was the first time he had left the east coast shores. Destined for Alberta, he joined 31 Course, flew over the rivers, lakes and the snowy mountains of the province, then finally he crossed the Atlantic, to Greenock on the *Umtalia* in mid-September 1941, with his wings on his tunic and a commission.

During his three-week stay at the transit base in Bournemouth,[7] he met Pilot Officer Alan Bowman, a fellow Australian. Like Jack he had served in the Territorials during the interwar years and was a white-collar worker, and they soon became good friends. Davenport was posted to 2 Central Flying School in Church Lawford, Warwickshire, however he managed to swap from becoming an instructor with one of his new friends, who was married and had children, and posted to Bomber Command. An amicable agreement was reached with their commanding officer and four days later Jack was posted to 14 (Bomber) Operational Training Unit (OTU) Cottersmore, Rutland, and it was there that he joined his first crew. 'There was pressure to crew up,' he said. Pilots and crew had all assembled in a large room at the station and been told to sort themselves out. Amazingly, this method more often than not proved successful. It certainly did for Davenport, who immediately teamed up with his colleague navigator Alan Bowman, a Queenslander of Boonah who had worked as a shipping clerk for ten years before enlisting in the air force in October 1940, and his wireless operator/air gunner Les Jonas; and so began the job of converting onto the Handley Page Hampden twin-engine bomber.

The Hampden came into service in September 1938, and since then had played second fiddle to the Vickers Wellington. Despite its speed and manoeuvrability it could not sustain heavy punishment and its armament could not ward off Luftwaffe fighters. In December 1939, at a meeting chaired by Air Chief Marshal Edgar Ludlow-Hewitt, and his senior staff, with Air Vice Marshal Arthur Harris, who was at that time 5 Group Commander, Ludlow-Hewitt said: 'We believe that the Hampden can know longer realistically operate by day and will now operate solely under the cover of darkness.' Harris concurred: 'twenty-one have been lost to fighters since the start of the war, one to friendly fire'.

Certainly, Jack Davenport thought it was a lovely aircraft, good to fly, but was aware there were lots of hazards and disadvantages – as he was soon to discover. Davenport was confronted on 9 December with the loss of Pilot Officer Osbourne Fisher and Sergeant Kenneth Thornton, killed when their Hampden veered off to port straight after take-off, ploughing into fields near Bottom Farm, Melton Mowbray. Five days later his friend Pilot Officer Anthony 'Tony' Webb, a member of the Royal Air Force who, like Jack, had trained at Fort Macleod, was killed practising single engine flying. It was impossible to forget, however, and the next day he cycled to see Tony's wife Joan, who lived nearby, and between flying practice he comforted her, returned Tony's bike and helped arrange the funeral. 'It was sad saying farewell to Tony for the last time,' he entered in his diary on Sunday 16 December 1941.

Six weeks before the end of Jack's operational training, he was allocated an old Hampden that was no longer in good enough condition to carry out operations and was therefore on the books at Cottersmore for trainee crews.

Davenport duly took off, knowing that his final assessments were due within a few weeks, Jack put the Hampden into a climb. Reaching a sufficient height, he executed a steep turn and then another the opposite way. The pressure on the elderly airframe caused the complete nose Perspex to dislodge and crack. As the cold air rushed into the aircraft, Jack yanked the stick to regain control, only to hear Sergeant Les Jonas in the mid-upper turret call out, 'Turn the heating on it's freezing back here!' A moment later the Hampden was in a vertical spin plunging earthwards. Jack couldn't get a response from the aileron and he thought the right rudder had been torn off. He had to admit they were in trouble and calmly told Bowman and Jonas to 'bail out, I repeat bail out.' Jonas jumped, however the centrifugal forces had pinned Bowman squarely to the floor and was unable to retrieve his parachute from the stowage compartment. He remained stuck and disorientated until 4,000 feet when Jack finally regained partial control 'using bags of rudder and aileron'. But, 'owing to the rudder locking on she span again the same way and I thought I'd "had" it.' Alan grabbed his parachute pack and instinctively clipped it on, ready to jump. He then caught sight of movement, 'Jack's feet were still working away on the rudder peddles.' There was still an outside chance of saving the aircraft.

Miraculously at 1,500 feet, the Hampden finally responded to Jack's attempts to stabilise it and came out of the spin. Davenport felt the plane come to a halt, then both engines picked up. It was in pretty poor shape, with no Perspex, bomb doors wrenched off, no brake pressure, the rear escape hatch open and damage externally around the cockpit. Having survived this ordeal, Jack tried to locate Jonas before landing. It wasn't the gentlest of landings, but fortunately Handley Page's airframe held what remained together and Davenport and Bowman scrambled out.

The following day, Davenport was told to take another Hampden up and fly a test flight ready for a night flight. He did not dwell on his harrowing brush with death the day before. 'We just got on with things,' he said.

Four months later, he was preparing to fly to Hamburg again in a Hampden, and with him were Bowman, and Sergeants Ernest 'Smithy' Smith and Clifford 'Harry' Harrison. His first 'op' with 455 Squadron had been on 30 March – a leaflet drop over Paris – and now he was about to take part in his eighth. Thirty finished operations constituted a completed tour, so he and his crew still had some way to go. They needed to have excellent responses and iron determination. Jack Davenport had both.

On the morning of 8 April, Smithy and Harry checked the guns and the swivel ratchet mechanism to make sure it was well lubricated, and that the radio set functioned, while Davenport made sure the aircraft was performing correctly. All seemed as it should. Then Harry was pulled from the op replaced by Sergeant Clifford Marshall as the gunner. Later in the afternoon came the briefing. All pilots and navigators arrived at Wigsley's briefing room. Here there was a large map and an assortment of photographs relating to the target – Hamburg – and details of what times they should be over the target. Wing Commander Grant Lindeman from Sydney spouted further details: the bombing course and the best possible height to attack. Intelligence warned about flak positions, and in between a briefing by the Met Officer. The end of the briefing the men trooped up the road to the Mess and the operational meal: bacon and real eggs, a mug of strong tea. Now they had to wait for night to come.

Darkness descended. The truck took them down to the airfield, where Davenport and Bowman met their two crewmen and were taken out to their aircraft. The boys left behind on the truck who had yet to reach their aircraft gave them a quick goodbye and someone said, 'Have a good time. See you all later.' At F-Freddie Jack clambered into the cockpit and 'Taff', one of the RAF ground crew, put Jack's safety harness over his shoulders and remarked: 'Don't worry you'll be okay. You always come back.' Up to now the Ynysybwl-born Welshman has been right. The engine run-up prior to take-off had been normal, all gauges were correct, and the chocks were cleared. Davenport then perambulated around the perimeter and waited for Pilot Officer Harold 'Mick' Martin, who haled from Edgecliff a small suburb on the Eastern side of Sydney, to take off on the main runway. Martin's Hampden D-Dog gradually lifted from the ground and cleared the hedgerow, at 21.40 hours. The control caravan flashed a green Aldis light and Davenport, with Bowman and Smithy in the nose and

Marshall in the rear cabin, opened the throttles and gradually sped across the concrete, and climbed into the air.

It was now some fifteen days since Jack's first fresher sortie to Paris, he and his crew were considered experienced as he formatted on Squadron Leader Philip 'Mickey' Moors *J-Johnny*, who had only been with them for four weeks, arriving from 25 OTU. Moors, however, had already finished one tour of ops with 50 Squadron. His trio crossed the English coast near Happisburgh, Norfolk, and out over the sea, aiming to rendezvous with the rest of the bombers when they were eighty miles from the German coast.

Seven hours and fifteen minutes later, Davenport touched *F-Freddie* back down again having diverted to Coningsby. They had encountered heavy weather which had caused static, icing and spasmodic electrical storms. Before reaching the primary target his starboard engine had coughed and spluttered. Nevertheless, he told his crew 'we're pressing on'. Though the left engine's temperature gauge was fluctuating, *F-Freddie* joined the other 271 other aircraft converging on Hamburg.

The warning siren rang out in Hamburg city streets that hostile aircraft were in the area. 12.30 hours, wooden benches in shelters became full as people dragged themselves from their slumber to take shelter. Elsewhere, other Hamburgers were showing a similar reluctance to go to the shelters. Suddenly, they heard the faint thrum of enemy aircraft grow nearer and nearer.

Above, heavy cloud over the target interfered with the approach of the bombers, as did flak and searchlights. Despite his eagerness to get in and out of the target area Davenport had made nine dummy runs over Hamburg. Unable to pinpoint the target his navigator called out, Bombs gone.' Their landmine and a pair of 250lb bombs from 3,000 feet, fell away through cloud. Rid of its load Jack guided *F-Freddie*, towards Wilhelmshaven through violent electrical storms over the North Sea. Making landfall near Skegness there was still something not right with the radial engine and Jack arranged to land at Coningsby thirty-one miles nearer than Wigsley. 'Weather conditions en route were unfavourable, static and icing being experienced. Cloud over the target interfered with operation, and flak opposition was not intense,' Bowman told the Coningsby intelligence officer, during debriefing.

The next day, Thursday 9 April 1942, Jack, Alan, Smithy and Marshall returned to base and their camera was whisked off for the film to be processed. Women wearing the blue uniform of the Women's Auxiliary Air Force sat in silence marrying up images of last night's raid on Hamburg. After a brief moment another pair of monochrome photographs were placed under the viewfinder. Studying the images taken from *F-Freddie* the WAAF didn't recognise the street layout, and after consultation realised that they were of Hamm, 202 miles southwest of Hamburg. Davenport was suddenly called to St Vincents Hall, a Victorian mansion near Grantham serving as 5 Group HQ to discover: 'It was a very good photograph of Hamm, but you were meant to be going to Hamburg, and an explanation of how you got to Hamm would be in order,' the senior intelligence officer demanded. Jack was dumfounded. 'I thought I'd won the 5 Group best photograph of the month competition!' he said.

An intensive run of operations continued. Essen Market Square, Germany, was the main target on 10/11 April. Jack dodged flak and searchlights and at one point swooped down to fifty feet to take a pop at a searchlight battery shouting 'Take that you bastards,' over the intercom. Reaching Essen they dropped their bombs on the first run and headed home. Jack Davenport had finally touched down at Wigsley at 03.25 hours, safely as it turned out. Jacks colleague Flying Officer Seth Manners who he had paired with at Cottesmore on training flights had not return. Nothing had been heard since take-off at 21.43 hours, confirmation came in August 1942 in a communique from the International Red Cross Society Geneva that they had been shot down, along with Flying Officer Robert Roberts all Australian crew Keck, Hill, Wright and Canning in *D-Dog*.

Sorties continued leading up to and after their official notification at midday on Sunday 17 April from Air Vice Marshal John Slessor, who had taken over as commander of 5 Group, about their imminent departure to Coastal Command. Eight days later, on 25 April, an intense evening party started at RAF Wigsley that culminated in the Sergeants Mess. The nucleolus of founding fathers said farewell including 'Mick' Martin and Lindeman's navigator, Robert 'Bob' Hay who were being posted to 50 Squadron. Both would go onto play a prominent role with the famous 617 Squadron in Operation *Chastise* and beyond the dams raid.

Despite some extremely sore heads in the morning, eighteen Hampdens departed Wigsley. Pilot Officer John Bunbury swung very badly but, apart from that, did not have too much trouble taking off. Then off went Jack, with Alan, Smithy, plus two airmen Grieg, and Garbutt. 'I grasped the brake lever firmly and pushed the throttles to full, then I let off the brakes and the old Hampden slowly got its tail up, and after about thirty seconds lumbered into the air and we were off to Leuchars, Fifeshire, in Scotland' said Davenport.

Lindeman had successfully retained Jack Davenport and his crew pleading directly with the Commander-in-Chief. 'Retain services of Davenport to help form squadron for new task. Together with ten junior crews' said a cablegram addressed to Grant Lindeman from Coastal Command HQ Senior Air Staff Officer. 'It is of such importance that 455 and 144 Squadrons to be taken off line.' It was he said going to be based at Leuchars, and Brian Reynolds was Station Commander. There was a great deal of urgency, SASO told him. It was essential to get the squadron there right away then get cracking with the training.

When Philip Joubert de la Ferté took over in June 1941 as Air Officer Commanding-in-Chief Coastal Command, he had been keenly aware that his new command was starved of resources and rarely received the column inches nationally or regionally in the press or on the radio, or even internally within the RAF. After the breakout from Brest of the *Scharnhorst, Gneisenau, Prinz Eugen* that became known as the Channel Dash Joubert recognised the immediate need to develop the commands torpedo capability in European waters.

English Electric Company[8] supplied fourteen modified Hampden Torpedo-Bomber's (TB) to the Australians. The results of the first trials by them at Royal Naval Air Station at Crail had not prompted despair. Lindeman found 42 Squadron based at Leuchars had ineffective techniques so, assisted by Lieutenant Commander Roger Harland a torpedo and electronics specialist, within a few weeks Lindeman and Wing Commander James McLaughlin CO of 144 Squadron began developing tactics. 'From the Hampden trials,' wrote Reynolds to Joubert, 'it would appear that very little latitude can be allowed in the height and speed at the time of release.' Special altimeters may be fitted at Leuchars, but he suggested on advice of RN officer Harland, the practical dropping speed should be 120 mph at 80 feet. Meanwhile the crews honed their new skills, dropping dummy torpedoes, and simulating attacks on Royal Navy ships.

Sunday 3 May, saw Jack Davenport complete lectures at Crail then attend a briefing on bombing Gossen airfield near Kristiansund in southern Norway. At roughly 01.00 hours Davenport flew his Hampden over the target at 4,500 feet delivering four canisters of incendiaries and two 250 lb. bombs. It was only when they taxied and came to a halt that they discovered a 20mm cannon had gone through the port flap.

After this rather uneventful journey the following day Jack was made deputy flight commander of A Flight. With it came responsibilities, despite whatever shortcomings there might have been. Finally, in July 1942 A and B Flights were declared operational. Russia beckoned in the September. Operation *Orator* defending Convoy PQ18 in the Barents Sea against German destroyers was successful. They'd not sailed from their Norwegian lairs and 455 Squadron returned to Scotland by sea in late

October. 455 endured another year flying Hampdens before converting to the Bristol Beaufighter.

Group Captain Athol Richards[9] Acting Air Officer Commanding RAAF Overseas Headquarters had been pressing Coastal Command HQ persistently to re-equip the squadron with Beaufighter Mk TF Xs since 28 August 1943. He received a memorandum on the 23 November stating that with effect from 15 December the Fighter type would be arriving at Leuchars. There the Adjutant William Branch wrote. 'It's two years and five months since 455 Squadron received its first Hampden.'

It's CO Wing Commander Robert 'Bob' Holmes was repatriated to Australia on 5 December after a tenure of ten months being replaced by Davenport. Over the following days Leuchars became a whirlwind of activity as the transformation took place. There was a great deal to do on the station and beyond this self-contained brick village. Wing Commander Jack Davenport and Sheila McDavid wed on 8 January 1944.[10]

A new chapter in the 455 story begins.

After a blissful week on honeymoon in the Scottish Highlands Jack and Sheila journeyed back to Leuchars,[11] where Jack resumed command of 455 Squadron. Progress was being made with his flight commanders Lloyd Wiggins, Colin Milson and his navigation officer, who had organised the training programme.

'The standard of results is a little higher than expected 26 days into training,' wrote the navigation officer. Coastal Command HQ charted progress on the Beaufighter training and on 1 March 1944 the new Commander-in-Chief Sholto Douglas who had arrived at Eastbury Park in the January from the Middle East told SASO Air Commodore Aubrey Ellwood[12] to declare them operational.

Monday 6 March, Colin Milson was sent that afternoon on the squadron's first sortie – an anti-shipping patrol off the Norwegian coast in the vicinity of Egero Light. Fourteen vessels steaming north were spotted, ten were merchantman. There were four escorts, some four Messerschmitt 109 single-engine fighters from Jagdgeschwader 5, the 'Eismeer Wing' based near Stavanger, further along the Norwegian coast, with a Blohm Voss flying boat in the vicinity too. Milson's anti-flak Beaufighters attacked from the seaward side in the face of heavy opposition, whilst 489 Squadron Beaufighters made good run-ins dropping torpedoes on the mark, whilst one was being chased by an Me 109. With it bearing down on him, the pilot lifted the nose and sought cloud cover.

Flight Sergeant John 'Tiger' Payne was desperately trying to fly *G-George* as he ran in towards his chosen target with Messerschmitt

20mm cannon and machine gun fire kicking up sea spray. Payne finally managed to shake the pair off, whilst Milson, with his experience in the Mediterranean on Beauforts, evaded the enemy fighters only for his Beaufighter to be holed by flak. Before 18.39 hours, all eight Beaufighters from 455 Squadron had safely made it back to Leuchars, including Payne. None of them had returned unscathed; all had battle damage of various degrees. The tough and charismatic Colin Milson was recommended for a Bar to his DFC, for his leadership on the mission.

Davenport's first Beaufighter sortie was five days afterwards with his navigator 35-year-old, Flying Officer Ralph Jones, known to the aircrew as 'Gramps.' In poor visibility they groped their way along the Norwegian coast from Obrestad Light sighting nothing and on the 26th he and New Zealander John 'Johnny' Dinsdale CO of 489 Squadron were informed again by the station Met Officer that the weathers unsuitable for flying sorties. They'd managed to get off the ground for five sorties but encountered bad weather on all. Lack of sightings gave 18 Group no results. It was decided at Coastal Command HQ that the Australians and New Zealanders should transfer to Langham on the north coast of Norfolk.

At Langham was Group Captain Arthur Clouston, a New Zealander who had travelled to England, joined the RAF, and become a test pilot at RAE Farnborough, Hampshire. He had had a busy aviation career as a junior officer and awarded the AFC in 1938. Winning many acclaimed trophies in his DH. 88 Comet (G-ACSS) around the globe before going back into the service. Clouston may have been a 43-year-old Flight Lieutenant, but he rose through the officer ranks and by 1943 was commanding 224 Squadron on anti-submarine missions in the Bay of Biscay. Tangling with Junkers 88s, Clouston was awarded a DFC and DSO for his actions before taking over as Station Commander. He was unusual among high placed officers in that he had operational combat experience from the current conflict.

On arrival in April 455 Squadron and 489 Squadron would officially be known as the Langham Wing, unofficially the Anzac Wing. Davenport's adjutant Branch hastily oversaw the arrival of beds and accommodation for aircrew and hundreds of groundcrew. Chairs and tables were purloined from nearby RAF Bircham Newton's married quarters. 'You'll be kept very busy,' said Clouston. Coastal Command HQ kept both squadrons active with furious exchanges between ships and Beaufighters along the European coast, and three days after D-Day Jack's immediate DSO was gazetted. It was also his 24th birthday.

July and August where lean. Ultra decrypts from the Government Code and Cypher School at Bletchley Park confirmed what Davenport,

Dinsdale and their aircrews knew, the Germans were protecting their convoys more heavily with flak-ships and sailing only at night. It was imperative that as far as possible every anti-shipping strike should have the greatest possible chance of success and Sholto Douglas issued, 'Make sure there is never any respite for the enemy.'

Saturday, 9 September 1944, was another big day for Langham. Fourteen of 455's aircrew would be involved with three squadron planes used twice. The previous afternoon Flight Lieutenant's John Pilcher DFC and his navigator Samuel 'Ted' Drinkwater carried out a flying test in the squadron's *B-Beer*. Whilst his navigator checked his radio set, Pilcher made sure the aircraft was performing correctly.

In the early hours of the 9th, after the 'ops' meal at the mess, came the briefing. All pilots and navigators stepped into the briefing room that were on the Mayfly list. A large map of the Scandinavian coastline and strike photographs filled the main wall. White tapes indicated their routes out and back. Davenport talked about their ETA and the Intelligence Officer warned them about new anti-aircraft positions on flak-ships that had been noted by the North Coates Wing. A briefing from the Met Officer followed, then Jack Davenport ended it with 'Good Luck.'

As aircrew truck took them down to the airfield again, Pilcher and Drinkwater where taken to their aircraft, but during the run-up of the engines prior to take off it became clear there was something not right. A loose engine cowling, so two airmen approached from the rear and hastily secured the catches. Quickly the eight Beaufighters are on the move, led by Pilcher in *B-Beer* and followed by Flying Officer Thomas Higgins in *C-Charlie*. Behind Higgins came the next trio Flying Officer Lloyd Farr DFC in *N-Nuts* and Flight Sergeant Ray Dunn *M-Mother*, with a four-minute gap before the next foursome are airborne. The first deviation from the planned reconnaissance took place within fifteen minutes when *N-Nuts* returned to base at 05.39 hours with technical trouble. The electrical wires that had been plugged into the rear motor of the rockets had come loose for some inexplicable reason on the portside.

At 06.45 hours with zero visibility in driving rain and hail, unable to distinguish the other planes with their wing and taillights on at 300 feet, Pilcher called up on the R/T 'Return to base independently.' It continued to rain with intermittent lightning. New Zealander Warrant Officer Donald 'Don' Tunnicliffe, part of the inner formation of nine TorBeaus of 489 Squadron, was manoeuvring his aircraft straight towards sea level rather than turning blind to avoid collision. Levelling out at twenty feet on Tunnicliffe then turned on a reciprocal course for base. White-capped seawater was spraying the TorBeau, however, there was a noise similar to the tearing of Irish linen, Tunnicliffe instinctively pulled up – the sea had pummelled his undercarriage doors.

Pilcher was unable to contact Flying Officer Arthur Jones in *T-Tommy* since aborting the sortie he had just vanished. Unaware of the abort message Jones had carried on with the search for enemy shipping along the Dutch coast. He had found a convoy, with his navigator Alex Jones plotting course, position and then sent a sighting report back.

At around 08.15 hours, in *T-Tommy*, Jones navigator, Alex said, 'Fifteen minutes to go until we're at Langham.' Arthur Jones touched back down at 08.30 hours and clambered out. There was roughly five hours before the next sortie took off. Flight Sergeant Allan Ibbotson tracked the convoy identifying six merchantmen, with a further six unidentifiable. *X-X-Ray* reached Langham at 16.00 hours, after a largely uneventful journey and were greeted by their groundcrew.

The relay continued to the Dutch coast. Beaufighter *J-Johnnie* thundered down the runway taking to the skies at 16.59 hours. Crewed by Flying Officer William 'Bill' Stanley[13] of Northbridge New South Wales, with his navigator Flying Officer Ken Dempsey from Preston, Victoria, the pair set off on their second sortie a special reconnaissance from Terschelling to Den Helder.

It was a short trip, low over the foreboding seascape, the forecast had not been good and en route had lived up to expectations, but around 16.55 hours, Stanley encroach nearer Ijmuiden and the flak unit on Fort Island, part of Marine-Flakabteilung 816, spotted them. As *J-Johnnie* turned hard to starboard over the installations below, a single line of tracer came racing towards them and a moment later it struck the Beaufighter. Instantly the oil pressure gauge needle for the port engine dropped to zero. Stanley automatically feathered the engine, whilst making adjustments to the flying trim and the remaining engine. Stanley called to his navigator 'there were a few expletives,' Ken Dempsey recalled,[14] and at 18.25 hours the navigator sent out a distress call requesting that air sea rescue be alerted.

Langham airfield immediately went on standby. The fire tender and ambulance were placed by their crews at the edge of the NE/SW runway that would be used for the emergency, unless there was a change in wind direction. Word spread and soon a cluster of concerned men and women in uniform had assembled.

Out over the North Sea, Stanley nursed his Beaufighter back about 220 miles to Langham. As *J-Johnnie* approached, the flying control officer Alexander Donley ordered Stanley to make a glide approach for landing.

'The silly beggar didn't know that this was a difficult manoeuvre in a Beaufighter,' said Stanley. Electing to make a single engine approach, correcting the drift with his rudder. A hundred yards from the runway his undercarriage locked, but he had forgotten to adjust the flaps. 'I'd forgotten to check, and my speed was rather to high,' said Stanley. The Beaufighter slammed onto the concrete, the force ripping off both undercarriage legs. The Beaufighter became airborne, gliding fifteen yards. The aircraft looked to be in a good position to make a perfect belly-landing when Stanley instinctively pushed the nose down, not realising his undercarriage had broken off. The Beaufighter crumpled heavily into the ground again and swung ninety degrees to the right as it skidded along, finally coming to a halt. Stanley felt the plane stop. However, seconds later, disaster struck. The starboard engine's remaining fuel ignited, flames pulsated into the air spreading instantly to the mainplane and port engine. Flames engulfed the aircraft.

Wing Commander Jack Davenport, who had been watching from the control tower, ran down the tower's steps and jumped into an Air Force blue two-seater Morris 'Tilly'. Blasting his horn, the men and women running towards the crash on foot quickly parted as the vehicle bounded over the grass. In a matter of seconds Davenport was speeding alongside the fuel-fed inferno stopping yards from the plane.

Inside *J-Johnnie* Dempsey managed to open his blister and scramble clear, leaping through flames and bellowing smoke, but the cockpit was completely surrounded by flames. Stanley could not get out, his feet were trapped. The force of the second impact had pushed the instrument panel back, completely wedging him in his pilot's seat, unable to move. Cursing to himself, Dempsey ran to the nose of the Beaufighter in a crouching stance, amid exploding 20mm cannon shells and burning fuel, but was held back by the furious flames and intense heat which took his breath away.

With 20mm shells discharging all around, Jack scrambled through the flames onto the port wing, negotiating the forward fuselage. He sat astride the canopy and pulled open the Perspex hatch. Then hanging down headfirst, he got a firm grip of Stanley's flying jacket and pulled, but nothing happened. 'He wouldn't budge,' remembered Davenport. He wrestled with Stanley, trying to release him as the intense temperature weakened the aircraft's structure. The mainplane, suddenly collapsed under Jack's bodily weight but he continued to fight to save his comrade. 'Grabbing him with a great heave, with strength that I probably didn't have, I pulled him out of his flying boots which were caught up.' Thence out of the cockpit dragging the badly burnt and dazed Stanley down onto the wing root, Davenport then cradles him through the inferno and walks away from the wreck to the waiting medical staff.

Despite the pain and severe burns to his face, hands, and body, Stanley insisted on seeing Jack before he left for the station sick quarters as 'he thought that I had been badly burnt but I reassured him that mine were only slight burns of no consequence.' In the ambulance the Australian pilot insisted on giving his commanding officer a report of their findings and said: 'there's a convoy moving down the coast near Ijmuiden'.

Dempsey agreed, but all his notes had been destroyed in the fire.

Meanwhile, nine miles away at Little Snoring,[15] groundcrew had hurried over to Flying Officer Tommy Thompson's aircraft *A-Apple* which had been diverted from Langham where Stanley's plane blocked the runway, as had Flying Officer Steve Sykes machine twenty minutes earlier. Thompson switched off his engines. He clambered out feeling utterly wretched. Remembering the sight of a tall plume of thick black acrid smoke rising from Langham's main runway. A jeep drove out to meet him and take him and his navigator, Warrant Officer Ivor Gordon, to flying control before flying back to Langham at 21.00 hours that evening.

Jack Davenport tried to underplay his injuries to his men, although he had sustained burns to his own face, eye brows, hair, and hands, with further burns to his legs sustained when the mainplane caved in. When Warrant Officer Noel Turner enquired as to his health, Davenport told him, 'only my battledress jacket has been singed'. After a brief assessment made by the station medical officer regards the injuries to Stanley, in September 1944, RAF Ely Hospital had a state-of-the-art Burns Unit, and he was driven there at speed with a lighted sign with 'Priority.' 'Although the patient's injuries are severely extensive, I do not believe them life threatening, although he may not be able to continue flying,' was RAF plastic surgeon, George Morley's prognosis. At Ely, two nurses immersed Stanley in a saline bath. Treatments included a combination of M and B powder, prontosil and a dressing of tulle gras and moist saline dressings to prepare the surface for skin grafting.[16]

On the afternoon of 10 September, Davenport was at Ely – looking troubled. A sister found him, 'Are you alright sir?' she asked. Davenport nodded but said nothing more. Perhaps it was the near loss of two members of his squadron the day before and just needed a moment of contemplation after seeing the young flying officer or the ward full of young men burned beyond recognition, or badly mutilated by wounds. For one so young the burden of command was immense.

'If it hadn't been for Jack the fire tender and blood wagon would have arrived to remove nothing more than a well cooked crisp,' Turner told Clouston, who submitted an immediate recommendation for the George Medal,[17] a non-operational decoration that like the George Cross, recognized acts of great valour, courage and self-sacrifice of the highest order. 'Thoroughly deserves the medal,' Coulson scrawled in pencil on the Honour and Awards Form sent to Coastal Command's No. 16 Group's HQ.

Davenport was always a very visual commanding officer, and a man who led by example. He liked his pilots, and navigators to share the same attitude and be committed to their tasks. And, made a point of drinking with his blokes in the mess, and participating in sports 'Aussie Rules' was a favourite at Langham of Jack's. He would also stand up for his men and women on the squadron and would back them to the hilt against any outside pressure, or if they found themselves in trouble. In saving 'Bill' Stanley, he had proved again what he had pledged that as their commanding officer, he would honour this commitment, even if it meant at the expense of his own life.

Jack endeared himself to the British and Australian public when it was announced that 'one of the most daring of Coastal Command's ace ship-busters,' was 'the only pilot in the Royal Australian Air Force to be awarded the George Medal as well as the DSO and DFC and Bar in this war'.

After an arduous journey to London six months after the Second World War ended, his wife Shelia accompanied Jack to his investiture ceremony at Buckingham Palace on 16 October 1945. 'It was quite an event. The Palace of course is absolutely grand, the decorations and the curtains … and the carpets, including the works of art hanging on the walls,' remembered Davenport.

King George VI stood on a small podium, and one by one the recipients were called forward, presented to the King. It was then Jack Davenport's turn he moved forward, the King took his medal from a cushion, which a junior officer held, and pinned it on the left breast of Jack's uniform. King George VI was impressed by the Australian's attitude, bravery and imperturbability when he gave this award to Davenport. All this had been achieved before he was twenty-five.

Chapter 2

Wing Commander Edric 'Sam' McHardy DSO, DFC* CdeG Someone on my Shoulder

Another of Coastal Commands youthful pilots, was twenty-four-year-old Wing Commander Edric 'Sam' McHardy, DFC and Bar, a lithe, fair-haired New Zealander, five feet thee inches tall and twelve stone, who was uniformly known as 'Sam', although know one seem to know exactly why.

McHardy had been flying Coastal Commands fighters since their inception into the service in October 1939. He had been in the thick of most anti-shipping strikes, and in the first week of D-Day made no fewer than six missions against enemy shipping. For McHardy even when off duty it was hard to resist dropping by the Operations Room to await the return of his crews.

In sharp contrast to some of his contemporaries, McHardy had had a far more emotionally satisfying life. He had grown up in a large loving and close family on a farm near the Rangitiki River, two miles from the town of Ashhurst on New Zealand's North Island. There were five children three boys, Jock, Sam, Harold, and two girls, Bunty and Mary. 'I was four when the local doctor arrived with his black bag to see my mother. Hiding in the garden whilst he was in the house, then shortly after his visit it was announced, our youngest brother Trevor had joined the McHardy family,' said Sam, 'an expanding family now with four boys and two girls'.[18]

His father Alexander, and his mother, who had been twenty-years-old when they married lived, with their children in a great house named *Siberia*. Before going to school McHardy's days consisted of walkabouts in the bush with his father and farm labourers, who felled swathes of trees for lumber and construction. Joining in when the hay-making season arrived, reaping oats and barley using a large elderly steam-powered British-built traction engine, that puffed and chugged away with big belts attached to a machine that filled bags with grain. At five Sam was sent to school in a two-room country school in Ashhurst, walking the two miles every day, here he stayed until 1927, when his grandfather, Leslie McHardy, had become ill. Alexander McHardy relocated the family to Hawkes Bay onto the Blackhead Sheep and Cattle Station, twenty-eight miles from Waipawa. It had been in a rough state but had been greatly improved since 1886 and these pastures now held roughly 30,000 sheep on over 17,000 acres.

The family prospects seemed good. Sam and his two younger brothers, after months with a governess, were sent to Hereworth Prep School in Havelock North. After three enjoyable years Sam joined Wanganui Collegiate School going into Hadfield, one of the three boarding houses. 'Typical, unsatisfactory school Sunday Service at 10.30 a.m., and at 6.30 p.m., with a good sermon from the Reverend on the "Inequality of the World"[19] and "Austerity"', scribbled McHardy in his school diary. Despite the struggle when the depression hit, the McHardys pulled through to recover, with Sam joining the workforce in a junior position to learn the basics about sheep actually working with them in ancient communal ways before he graduated to a shepherd. He acquired a horse called Sam and a border collie named Mac, gradually taking over the mantle from their junior shepherd. Conditions were harsh, particularly when wearing oilskins, leggings and boots in relentless wet weather conditions, McHardy was becoming frustrated and occasionally in tears when ewes he tended gave birth to stillborn lambs and skinning dead lambs to use the coat on an orphan lamb to get it adopted. It was all about endurance. Digging in. Holding on.

After a year of farming at Blackhead McHardy became restless[20] as his lambs were bred and sold for meat and looked at widening his horizons. May 1938, Sam went to the countries capital, Wellington, with his eldest sister Mary in their Morris Eight. It had been agreed that Sam would join the navy, unfortunately their aptitude test had already been held. Disappointed, they strolled to the Merchant Marine office which could only offer him a job as a Bell Boy. 'Why don't you walk around to the Air Force office it can't do you any harm,' said Alexander Hawkins.[21]

There was nothing else to do, so Sam and Mary walked around to the Air Force office, after a quick selection board of very senior officers, he was whisked into a side room, coughed once, and was presented with a bundle of official papers for his parents to sign.

'Well, I suppose we will have to sign,' said his father.

19

In June, after swearing allegiance to King George VI, Sam was accepted and given a short service commission in the Royal Air Force, and finally left New Zealand on Thursday 2 February 1939, aboard the passenger liner *RMS Tainui*. Sam was one of fifteen young men who had been given a four-year short service commission. The eighteen-year-old had left his girlfriend on Wellington quayside along with his family, sailed via Pitcairn Island, Panama and Jamaica, arriving in England at Southampton on 15 March. Now the possibility of actually getting into one of the new monoplane fighters was within touching distance.

A little over three hours later, Sam made his way to a very grey city of London. 'It was depressing and lonely,' Sam wrote in a letter home. There Sam and his fellow New Zealanders trooped along to New Zealand House, 415 The Strand. McHardy spoke with Patricia who made arrangements for him to get to 10 Elementary & Reserve Flying Training School (E&RFTS) at Yatesbury in Wiltshire. Unfortunately for McHardy he found the course had already started and went straight into lectures. Here he came face to face with a former colleague of Flying Officer Louis 'Buster'[22] McHardy, Sam's uncle who had died in an Avro Tutor with Jack Markby piloting the plane. Flight Lieutenant Christopher Birks whisked Sam out[23] of the lecture.

'McHardy we are going flying right now, understand?'

'Yes, sir,' replied the bemused New Zealander, as he followed the flying instructor in white overalls. Sam asked him for an explanation. 'When I saw your name and details I requested the CO make you one of my pupils, as your uncle and I were great friends and we had flown together previously before the accident.'

'How did it happen?'

'Just minutes after take-off, from Hucknell, Markby failed to complete a spin, and went into the ground near Bulwell Hall golf course's seventh tee, which absolutely horrified the nearby golfers,' said Birks. 'Right let's get you kitted out.' Sam with Birks' help, grabbed a flying suit, gloves, helmet, goggles, and a parachute then signed some forms. Sam waddled out onto the tarmac like a penguin. There before them stood a row of de Havilland Tiger Moths. Birks showed Sam how to fit himself into the front seat and strap up. His first lesson was about to begin.

'I don't want you to do anything initially. All right?'

Thirty minutes later they curved in to land and taxied in. Sam entered in his log: 'Air Experience: Effect of Controls, Taxying and handling of engine.'

By 24 March, Sam McHardy had 'gone solo,' and was still alive after amassing six hours of instruction. He had grown to enjoy the experience, receiving his A Licence in April. Early May saw his course finish and assessments given out. Sam had completed roughly forty-five flying hours and now his logbook bulged at the foot of the appropriate page with the award of 'Exceptional'.

'Hope that my future flying will live up to it,' he scrawled in a note to his parents. McHardy kept a group photograph of his pilots' course at 10 E&RFTS taken the first week of May. The name of each written in white, but McHardy one day wrote 'KIA' – killed in action – above those he knew had already been lost.

On Friday 12 May, McHardy arrived at Uxbridge and was fitted out with all his uniforms by Gieves tailors. McHardy's last dining-in night was 26 May – he had been posted to his course at Sealand in northeast Wales. Before leaving, his course members attended one of the last RAF Hendon Air Displays watching the highly experienced Squadron Leader Edward 'Teddy' Knowles put a Hawker Hurricane through its paces.

Four days later, McHardy was at Sealand and issued with an airman as his batman. 'I had not anticipated such a luxury, life as a pilot officer was on the up and up,' said Sam. James 'Jimmy' Leggate[24] was McHardy's Flight Commander and flying instructor and after four hours dual with Leggate he soloed in an ageing Hawker Hart. Sam had fallen in love with the Hart – it was a joy to fly – but despite his continued 'above average' assessments McHardy was not one of the chosen fifteen officers selected for single-engine aircraft and was one of the remaining twenty-seven to fly Oxfords and destined for heavy bombers. A meeting concluded with Leggate coming up against a bureaucratic brick wall, unable to change the outcome for McHardy.

McHardy walked into the Blossoms Hotel in Chester that evening with Maurice Baird, a former labourer living on Howon Street in Foxton North Island. With the economic depression, any labouring jobs were overwhelmed with applicants and Baird volunteered for the Air Force. It was not until April 1938 that he was accepted for a short-term commission and arrived in March with fellow Kiwi, McHardy, both ending up on the same course. On this occasion both missed the 22.00 hours curfew as they enjoyed a late drink for another thirty minutes.

A taxing time for McHardy and Baird followed. Leggate's temper, never the most even at the best of times, exploded. Loosing his rag on this occasion, 'both confined to base for ten days' – and every half-an-hour McHardy and Baird had to appear in front of the Provost Marshal[25] firstly in mess kit, then civilian suit, best RAF uniform, the process was repeated until 22.00 hours over the next ten days. 'We certainly became more discrete about where we did our late carousing after this treatment,' said McHardy.

Sunday 3 September, whilst cleaning down a Hawker Hart on the tarmac, he and his fellow pupils were summoned to the Officers Mess. They heard Neville Chamberlain make his fateful announcement that Britain was at war with Germany. McHardy stood at ease with the others, listening in silence. The war had started, but everything was very quiet, no bombs or wail of an air siren droning out. 'Carry on,' said Reginald Brichett Chief Ground Instructor. The assembled group discussed the inevitable, but they were hardly ready for Armageddon as they stepped out back to their bi-planes.

With this announcement his instructor Leggate was post away from the unit, his place being taken by Flight Lieutenant Eric Michelmore. With no twin-engine Oxfords available, McHardy continued flying the obsolet bi-planes until Thursday 2 November when Pilot Officer Sam McHardy received his wings, his final assessment once again being marked 'Exceptional'. Then, a little over nine months later McHardy, Baird and five others found themselves joining a new squadron forming at Hendon, No. 248 Squadron.

They reached North London the following day, and promptly met by their commander, Wing Commander George 'Hutch' Hutchinson. So that made seven pilots but where were the others going to come from? Twenty-one were needed, and if the operational order for the formation of the squadron was to be taken to the letter, then they had to reach eight complete crews by the end of November, 1939.

McHardy found himself posted to 'A' Flight with Flight Lieutenant Allan Pennington-Legh as his Flight Commander, a twenty-six-year-old, who had previously lived in Sunderland Avenue Paddington, before joining the Air Force.

Patrick Woodruff, a Canadian of Edmonton, who had enlisted in the RAF in 1937, was running a conversion course for the new arrivals. McHardy was ahead of the queue, his three endorsements from Sealand saw to that. 'With Woodruff's tuition, accumulated roughly two hours of dual on our short-nosed Bristol Blenheim under his guidance,' wrote McHardy,

Despite the lack of air gunners and navigators, McHardy carried out ferry flights with Pennington-Legh to Kemble in the squadron's Miles Magister to pick up new Blenheims. He also practiced radio transmissions and scrambles. McHardy flew again around midday on 18 January when 'B' Flight was ordered to provide cover for an RAF communications aircraft as far as the English coast. A lack of co-ordination meant they never found the plane and returned to Hendon.

The trials and training continued, with 248 Squadron converting to the long-nose Blenheim Mark VI fighter, joining Fighter Command. Air

Chief Marshal Sir Hugh 'Stuffy' Dowding the first Commanding-in-Chief of Fighter Command since 1938 submitted figures to Marshal of the Royal Air Force Cyril Newall Chief of the Air Staff on the strength of his force numerically including these long range fighters under the opuses of 'Trade Protection'. Then during the last week of February 1940 Dowding had a change of face[26] oversaw the transition of four Blenheim squadrons, 248, 235, 236 and 254, to Coastal Command. Thoroughly happy to have passed them on to help Air Chief Marshal Sir Frederick Bowhill, the C-in-C of RAF Coastal Command maintain surveillance from The Skagerrak to the Spanish coast and support the East Coast convoys, North Sea fishing fleets and British Naval vessels as they became mission ready.

Their new Air Officer Commanding signalled a change of venue, to North Coates in Lincolnshire. At roughly 15.30 hours, 'B' Flight tore off in to the air for their new base. Sandwiched in the Blenheim's fuselage were tools, kit, ground or aircrew, 'it was a real busman's holiday,' wrote Chiefy Cartwright in a letter home. Fortunately, the weather remained reasonably good for the flight of nearly one and a half hours. They all landed by 17.00 hours, with Woodruff in the dual Blenheim touching down last – the Canadian duly bought the drinks in the North Coates' Officers Mess that evening.

On 5 March their commander, Wing Commander George 'Hutch' Hutchinson, required Pennington-Legh's and Roger Morewood's flights to be in the air quickly. The loudspeaker blared and McHardy and his fellow 'A' Flight pilots sprinted across the intervening twenty-five yards of the airfield to their aircraft and took off within minutes.

In sections of three, Hutchinson was at the head, McHardy was tucked tightly in on the portside with Australians Charles Bennett on starboard and Lewis Hamilton following behind as 'arse-end Charlie' protecting their rear. Pilot Officer's Arthur Bourgeois, Sydney Gane, and Arthur Garrad made up the second section. Climbing through the early morning haze, at 3,000 feet they emerged into clear skies and levelled out at 7,000 feet.

'Follow my lead,' said Hutchinson over the R/T. He began a series of dives and climbs, managing to dive down to 3,000 feet. After several manoeuvres, Hutchinson carried out yet another that got McHardy in a position where the orange glow of the morning sun was directly in his eyes.

'McHardy I want you as tight to me as a maiden's arse,' said Hutchinson over the R/T.[27]

'I'm close all right,' replied McHardy as he watched his leader's plane.

There was a sudden clunk. McHardy and Hutchinson separated from the section, and McHardy's aircraft lurched down towards the ground, whilst Hutchinson's Blenheim shot upwards. Regaining control both re-joined the formation after this incident. McHardy safely made it back but landed with his undercarriage retracted. Both men inspected their aircraft: 'there was a split along the leading edge of Hutchinson's tailplane and a large dent on McHardy's starboard wing tip, on the belly-landed Blenheim. Hutchinson said nothing and just walked away to his office in Hanger 2.

Such were the frustrations of trying to perfect and maintain the tight figure 'Vic' formations that they were being so assiduously trained in. McHardy's incident was forgotten within three days. Hutchinson was waved off and replaced by Squadron Leader Victor Streatfield who had been at Gosport since the latter part of 1938 attached to an Artillery Co-operation Unit, having previously served in Egypt.

The new mark of Blenheims did not arrive in any numbers until 24 April, by which time 16 Group had ordered 248 Squadron to Thorney Island then onto Gosport all within five days. This did not affect their operational availability because the new Blenheims would need a number of modifications to receive the gun pack before they could be flown with the squadron. Of the ordinary Blenheims ten were completely new and eight were hand-me-downs from various RAF units.

Those who were struggling more for hours on the long-nose more than others tended to use Woodruff's dual Blenheim more, while Sam McHardy and Maurice Baird, both of whom were progressing well, continued to increase their hours on the type using squadron aircraft when they became available. So it was that by the end of the first week at Thorney Island, McHardy had managed roughly a dozen low-level cross-country and navigational flights over the English Channel towards Guernsey and Jersey.

Pilot Officer Alfred 'Al' Smitz[28] originally from Rangoon, Burma, joined the squadron as Gunnery Officer, posted in from the British Air Forces in France. The mid-height, square-jawed twenty-nine-year-old, put 'A' and 'B' Flight's through their paces against towed drogues, ground targets and mock aerial duals against Beauforts of 42 Squadron at Thorney Island. On the morning of 6 May at 05.00 hours, McHardy and the pilots of 248 Squadron woke at Gosport to the sound of a hunting horn[29] and Smitz banging on their doors. Minutes later pyjama-clad pilots were hastily putting on flying gear over their sleeping garments and running for their Blenheim fighters as air gunners scrambled hurriedly to their individual machine, and the ground crew pulled away the chocks.

The twin-engine Blenheim's having taken off, 'B' Flight formed up into two sections of three, in a figure 'V', and flew towards Ford Naval Air station to intercept an aircraft. Eventually 'B' Flight did sight a Beaufort, which they attacked. Morewood with Pilot Officers Anthony Holderness, Frank Elger, Gordon 'Barry' Atkinson, Maurice Baird, and Archibald 'Eddie' Hill, attacked from the port quarter, there were benefits to this kind of exercise and it was already self-evident that more drogue training was necessary. But time was running out.

Streatfield, received the news by telephone from 16 Group '235 Squadron operating under 11 Group's sector controllers in the southeast need urgent replacements,' said Air Vice-Marshal John Tyssen. McHardy and Morewood were selected having completed gunnery courses at Ford with an above average score. 'There was little doubt,' wrote Streatfield, 'these were my two best pilots at this precise time.' McHardy, along with John Morris and Corporal Peter Neale, arrived at Bircham Newton around midday, on Saturday 11 May. Parking his Blenheim fighter at an empty dispersal, he strode out to meet Morewood who had his dog at his side. A black cocker spaniel called Andrew, the dog was rarely from his master, except when Morewood was flying, although on this occasion the dog had made the two-hour journey in the long-nose Blenheim.

After formalities McHardy, Morris, Morewood and Ernest Leathem entered the Mess at Bircham Newton and met Wing Commander Ralph MacDougall who in turn introduced them to Pilot Officers William 'Bill' Bain, and Henry 'Hal' Randall of 254 Squadron also on detachment. 'Our third pilot, Sergeant Albert Tubbs, is in the Senior Non-Commissioned Officers Mess,' said Randall. Both then helped 248's pilots get suitable quarters, which were at a premium. Having been given two rooms to share, McHardy darted about, familiarising himself with the station. A pre-war airfield that, beyond the red brick buildings, painted with camouflage, were hangars and dispersal areas. Blenheims of 235 Squadron were parked off the perimeter track near the main hangars. On a few of the aircraft day-to-day servicing was taking place where they were parked, and occasional shouts could be heard. The squadron offices were in front of one of the hangars, a temporary wooden building that smelt of fresh paint and wood preserve. The interior had a row of three rooms and a large area given to an eclectic mix of couches and chairs. A chalk board indicated that Randall, Bain and Tubbs were on a mission with Robert Patterson to go off at 19.30 hours. Five hours later at 22.30 hours, 'Patterson's plane crashed on landing; undercarriage collapsed. The three fellows got away with cuts and bourses,' wrote McHardy.[30]

After a brief interlude at Manston, McHardy, Morewood and their aircrew were on readiness in the early hours of Monday 13 May,[31] at Bircham Newton. At 08.56 hours, McHardy, Morris and Neale sprinted to their Blenheim. McHardy and Morris jumped up onto the wing and hurriedly clambered through the hatch, Morris went forward into the nose, whilst McHardy fastened his parachute harness, and plugged his flying helmet leads in. Pre-flight checks were done, Neale and Morris declared all their systems were okay, a thumbs up to the ground crew and away.

Speeding off in a pair with Morewood, McHardy heard the controller telling them 'Den Helder – Buster'. Heading out to sea at top speed, they had been sent to patrol over two destroyers bombarding enemy positions on the Zuider Zee. McHardy set course, flew out over the coast at Cromer and out to sea, changing track to bring him and Morewood over the boats at 3,000 feet. Circling, McHardy watched the coloured tracer arcing out from Den Helder and Texel across the sky. He then saw straight ahead the thin shape of German twin-engine Messerschmitt 110s, named the 'Zerstörer' (Destroyer) some five of them in line-astern.

Switching the gun button to 'fire' and pulling the ring sight into position McHardy realised that he was now level with the lead Me 110. He curved towards the nearest Messerschmitt so that he could get a short burst off, however this was counteracted by one turning directly towards him, with another behind him. Pulling the control column back McHardy managed to get away from the pulsing 20 mm cannon and machine-gun fire into a cloud. Edging out from his protective layer McHardy looked for a target, he saw his friend Morewood diving down towards the deck then spotted a German plane to starboard and went after it. McHardy curved around, opened fire with his four Browning machine guns in a head-on attack and, moments later, the Me 110 banked away and L -Leather turned right and the sky was suddenly empty.

Sweat rings under the armpits on his light blue shirt showed McHardy anxiety, but with a feeling of elation he now headed back for home. On the ground his elation extended to the mechanics and armourers who saw his guns had been fired – the tell-tale red patches that keep the dust and grim away had been shot through and streaks of smoke ran underneath the fuselage from the planes gun pack. 'We stood and waited, anticipating the worst, then a slightly jaded S-Sugar flying low from the east with its port engine horribly misfiring. It staggered over the boundary hedge and touched down,' McHardy wrote. 'Morewood emerged with his long handle-bar moustache glistening with sweat after the hot confines of his oxygen mask and had a thrilling story to tell.'[32]

With the situation worsening ingenuity and the make-do-and-mend attitude at Coastal Command HQ at Eastbury Park ensured that makeshift replacements were available as one of 235 Squadron flight commanders departed on fourteen days leave. Allan Pennington-Legh of 248 Squadron temporarily replaced Richard Cross,[33] and brought with him Alfred Fowler in a second Blenheim. On their arrival they were immediately placed at readiness and sat around the dispersal.

Across the Channel the German *Blitzkrieg* was rolling through the continent at speeds the British, French and Dutch had not anticipated. On 18 May, as troops and civilians from Europe began seeking refuge in Britain fleeing from the carnage, RAF squadrons provided air cover. McHardy, Pennington-Legh, and Fowler were scrambled and ordered to patrol over HMS *Arctic Hunter* with its cargo of refugees. With the Germans enjoying their turkey shoot in aerial battles, never had so many different types of aircraft been seen over the Continental skies since the First World War. Inevitably, mistakes were made.

By the time Pennington-Legh, was nearing Zeebrugge, McHardy and Fowler were several miles behind unable to use their super-charged boost as their 100-octane fuel was required for Dowding's Spitfires, Hurricanes and Boulton Paul Defiants not Blenheims. Finding *Arctic Hunter* amongst what seemed thousands of ships was impossible then red and green flares blossomed in the sky receiving the correct recognition signal, the three Blenheims began circling. At that moment McHardy spotted a twin-engine bomber – a Junkers 88 he recognised with its distinctive black crosses and swastika attacking a stranded ship.

The Junkers 88 pilots were finding that it was very difficult to hit the stationary Italian cargo ship *Foscolo* whose cargo was being salvaged, six miles off the coast of Zeebrugge. Disabled four days previously by the Luftwaffe, they had come back to complete the job. At what was judged the right height the Junkers began their dive, aiming for the largest ship. In a classic 'staircase' attack they hurtled towards it, the planes' distinct twin Jumo engines thrumming. The bombs hit the water and sending huge fountains of spray into the air, but none seem to have hit the cargo ship.

McHardy, Pennington-Legh and Fowler attacked. McHardy however, drew level with one of the enemy aircraft, but at the same moment the German dived towards the sea. Following him down, McHardy could see an airman crouched in the upper gun position, looking back at him. McHardy managed to stay on his tail and get a deflection shot off as the pair raced over the sea the enemy bomber filled his ring sight, McHardy pressed the firing button and felt the Blenheim shudder and rattle as the four machine-guns fired. Pennington Legh, who as his flight commander swung in front of him, opening fire on the Junkers. The rear gunner opened fire at him, but on Alan's third burst from astern the Junkers pulled away, his Blenheim became enveloped in Jumo engines' exhaust smoke. Although he was not sure whether he had hit it or not, he then heard over the R/T 'Enemy coming down!'

In what seemed seconds, they were amongst them. McHardy and Pennington-Legh became embroiled in a dogfight, Pennington-Legh's first, and two aircraft were diving down on the Blenheims. Forgetting the Junkers 88, McHardy began a wheeling climbing turn to creep up underneath the fuselage of one of the enemy planes. Unseen, he fired. As he came out of the steep climb the twin-engine fighter lost height rapidly and began turning and weaving so that McHardy was initially unable to get a clear shot. They had fallen so low that they sped over the masts and funnels of ships hoping to shake off the pursuer.

Its gunner returned fire. Red flashes of tracer arced lazily towards the Blenheims starboard engine then accelerated, hammering into the Bristol built radial engine. With no immediate sign of damage McHardy followed him, when the aircraft filled McHardy's sight, he opened fire with his four Browning machine guns. There was a belch of smoke, and to his satisfaction watched the aircraft crash into the sea off Nieuport at 16.30 hours. He disengaged and saw his fellow men still in combat.

Pennington-Legh had managed to carry out an evasive manoeuvre away from the second twin-engine fighter and now found himself engaged in a fierce melee with a single attacker, but he managed to dodge the fire and get on the tail. Pennington-Legh put a sequence of short well-aimed bursts saw the first belch of white smoke, then black smoke burst from the aircraft and it began to fall. A white parachute blossomed and floated down with survivor, Jean Bot, towards De Panne, in Belgium.

There was no point in hanging around. McHardy was out of ammunition as was his gunner twenty-one-year-old Glaswegian, William Heaviside, who had joined the Royal Auxiliary Air Force in 1937. His navigator, Spires, got his bearings and soon the English coastline appeared ahead of him. Keeping Margate on their left they continued towards Felixstowe all three eventually landed at Bircham Newton at 17.30 hours. 'Caught two Germans near the Belgium and French coast,' wrote McHardy to his mother the next day, his excitement still profound, 'Penny and I bagged one each, so my own private score stands at one – definitely.'[34] Although later confirmed as two French Potez 631 twin-engine fighters. Jean Bot was one of the lucky ones – in fact, one of only a dozen aircrew from his unit ACII that remained alive.

After ten days of battle McHardy, Morewood, Pennington-Legh, and Fowler left 235 Squadron on 19 May – to be sent north, out of the fray, to Scotland. As preparations got underway for an evacuation called Operation *Dynamo*, Pennington-Legh and McHardy found themselves congregating again with 'A' Flight of 248 Squadron at Montrose in Angus. Sharing Montrose was one of the Auxiliary Air Force squadrons, 602,[35] or at least a detachment. It had originally been formed at Renfrew on 15 September 1925 equipped with Airco DH.9 As. Now, sixteen years later, their pilots had the ultra-modern machine, the Supermarine Spitfire Mk1, under the leadership of Renfrewshire farmer, Squadron Leader George Pinkerton.

On 16 October 1939, Pinkerton as a Flight Lieutenant in 602, shared in the destruction of an Junkers 88 of Stab I./KG30 with Archibald McKellar and Paul Webb. It had been targeting HMS *Southampton* in the Firth of Forth but had been hit by anti-aircraft fire. Flying on one engine, it was engaged by McKellar, Pinkerton and Webb. The Junkers streaked across the sky over Edinburgh, with the three Spitfires in its wake. Webb, lost contact in the chase along the Fife coast, as McKellar and Pinkerton spasmodically opened-up with their eight Brownings, then its pilot, Hauptmann Helmut Pohle, tried to escape by gaining height. Pinkerton was now beginning to tire of this game. He opened fire. Bullets shattered the Perspex canopy and splinters spitting around the cabin maimed Pohle, August Schleicher, and killed Kurt Naake. Then McKellar's fire ruptured the port fuel tanks and the Junkers plummeted from the sky hitting the water with a great burst of white foam near Crail.

Back at Montrose, 248 Squadron's six Blenheims were dispersed around one end of the airfield. Elsewhere were the Spitfires of 602 Squadron, as well as a Tiger Moth and a Miles Master advance trainer that was primarily used as an introduction to the Spitfire. Pinkerton's 602 Squadron's 'A' Flight from Montrose and 'B' Flight from Dyce were sent to Drem, in East Lothian, a busy grass airfield east of Edinburgh, in preparation to enter the fray. The mantle of responsibility for the defence of northeast Scotland had been handed over to 248 Squadron which transferred to Fighter Command.

Within days they were flying missions. Sam McHardy was one of three sent on an offensive patrol over the North Sea on 28 May, checking the sea-lanes, and convoys of merchant shipping plying back and forth. One naval corvette had identified a Heinkel 115 floatplane, clearly watching the convoy with interest, just staying out of range of the corvette's main guns. McHardy arrived on the scene and saw the outline of the floatplane. But he was too far away to engage, and the Heinkel from Luftflotte 5 turned away and vanished into cloud.

But McHardy wasn't going to give up. Leaving Gane and Garrad over the convoy he climbed up towards the cloud base and stalked the Heinkel through the cloud, but to his amazement it escaped. Somewhat bewildered, he called up Gane and Garrad over the R/T, and together the three dashed back towards Dyce.

He learnt from Sydney Gane what had happened. The Heinkel had swooped out of the clouds at the rear of the convoy and made off towards Norway. Unfortunately, neither himself nor Arthur Garrad had managed to chase the floatplane down. So, after six miles, they returned to cover the convoy. Low on fuel Arthur's navigator had signalled the corvette of their imminent departure. Later that day, at 22.00 hours, McHardy bade farewell to the rest of 602 Squadrons 'A' Flight.

On 17, June the French asked for an armistice whilst Erwin Rommel's men speedily advanced into Cherbourg and other German forces pushed on to the Swiss border. Armistice terms negotiated on 21 June were signed the next day at Compiègne in the railway wagon in which Germany signed the First World War cease-fire.

For Britain and its Commonwealth, the future outlook was very bleak indeed. Without France, Streatfield told his senior pilots, the next battlefield would be on a Napoleonic scale, 'be prepared for you or the man standing either side of you to die,' said Streatfield.

Later, on the evening on 30 June, with finally a brief moment to himself, McHardy wrote to his mother Olive: 'Just a brief line to tell you I am alive and well.' He neglected to say that since 603 Squadron's 'A' Flight had returned under Squadron Leader George Denholm, commonly known as 'Uncle George' by his youthful pilots. McHardy's commanding officer received a telegram: '248 are not required to participate in intercepting enemy aircraft, over the Scottish mainland on receipt of Yellow and Red warnings … signed Air Vice Marshal Richard Saul.' It was perhaps not surprising, therefore, if Streatfield was feeling a bit tetchy.

Wednesday 3 July, six Spitfire pilots greeted McHardy cheerfully, including Denholm, after he had successfully shot down a Heinkel off Peterhead. 'We shot down a Hun,' my dear Sam,' Denholm told him, 'and now we are going to get bestially drunk tonight.' On 12 July lunch at the crew room dispersal was interrupted by an air raid warning, everyone dived for cover as Heinkels launched the first major blitz on Aberdeen. They stood down later, not having flown. Pilot Officer James Caister of 603, who had shared the downing of a Heinkel that had taken part in the attack, enquired if McHardy and Pennington-Legh wanted to join them for drinks a couple of miles down the road 'Fortunately the natives were still friendly,' remarked McHardy. The partly-built ice ring in Anderson

Drive had been bombed-out, so were buildings nearby. Afterwards, back at the mess, his fellow officers, envious of his combat missions and tally, questioned him again. His spell at Bircham Newton turned out to be quite a refreshing interlude in what had become a dull life on 248 Squadron, with continual convoy protection carried out from Dyce. Between sorties McHardy schooled new SNCO pilots who had arrived with minimal flying time and only roughly five hours air-to-air and air-to-ground gunnery. None had ever flown over water, used an oxygen mask nor completed the shipping recognition paper. He gave each one roughly ten hours of extra 'tuition,' taking them to shoot at a wreck and practice formation flying over water and evasive technics to give the youngsters some tactical nous.

As the day fighters were getting all the accolades, Bowhill at Eastbury Park Northwood, London was still intently watching the movement of his 'fighter' squadrons as they flittered between Coastal and Fighter Command and once again 248 came back into the fold, although this time Bowhill promptly relocated them. There was no let-up from Sumburgh in the Shetlands when they moved there in mid-July. Having finally moved airfields, Streatfield was told by Coastal Command that the Blenheims were needed as bombers as well as reconnaissance aircraft. 'A' Fight recorded a success on 3 August when 'Gane found a U-Boat he peeled down and dropped his four 250 lb bombs from 700 feet,' penned McHardy in his diary. A few days after, McHardy flew a convoy patrol and tried to intercept a German raider from Luftflotte 5. The other pilots commiserated with him after he had touched down.

Air Vice Marshal Charles Breese AOC 18 Group offered a means of getting 248 Squadron more directly involved with the battle. Furthermore, it was a tactical approach that had been tried and tested previously in the Battle of Norway – raid the enemy's ports. The weeks went by and the word 'Trondheim' began to feature and there began the loss of McHardy's colleagues.

Maurice Baird had been woken at 04.30 hours with a cup of tea. He met Sergeant Douglas Burton another Kiwi from Opunake, a small town on the southwest coast of Taranaki, who had reported for duty on the 19th, from 106 Squadron at Finningley. Burton had layers on, wearing battle-dress, shirt and roll-neck sweater. Outside, it was chilly as they stepped out to the operations tent to find their Air Gunner Stanley Wood and, observer Sergeant Richard Copcutt. Here they bumped into Pilot Officer John Dodd and Archibald 'Eddie' Hill. It was the last time they saw the pair as both their aircraft malfunctioned. For Baird, Burton, Copcutt and Wood in *X-X-Ray* it was a monotonous journey across the North Sea and

Maurice was glad to see a Dornier 18. He called up 'Tally-Ho,' on the intercom, turning towards the enemy.

Locked in combat, twisting and turning until astern of the floatplane Maurice watched the Dornier fill his ring sight. He closed nearer, now he was firing, the guns shaking the aircraft as he watched the trail of bullets hit their target. There was a puff of smoke, as he sped underneath.

He pulled hard and then began climbing back up towards the Do 18 to reengage, but the puff of dark smoke and debris bursting into the air that he had witnessed meant the Dornier fell away, the trail of smoke thickening. Maurice had his first victory. A joyous Baird got Copcutt to send a message at 09.30 'shot down enemy plane.'

But he had been guilty of watching his victims clambering into their dinghy and not keeping an eye on his back, a cardinal sin. Suddenly Messerschmitt fighters were all over them. Maurice was conscious that he must continue to twist and turn continually. Wood suddenly opened fire with the Vickers machine-gun which made Maurice turn even tighter, and then moments later, shouted 'I've been hit in one foot!' Burton felt unprepared for this; no one had warned him of the difficulties of trying to navigate – plot your position and give course instructions – whilst Baird was taking evasive action. With his compasses swinging, Maurice flew towards Haugesund where centuries ago Vikings had their royal seat, rather than flying back out towards the North Sea. He inched down lower towards the water, thereby giving some protection, but his efforts did not seem to be working. Thirty-seven miles west of Haugesund, Oberleutnant Werner Petermann, good-looking with light blue eyes and chestnut hair, had turned twenty-four in January. He had been born in Altenburg in central Germany and had joined the Luftwaffe in 1936, as an officer cadet. After completing his training as a Jagdflieger he was posted to Jagdgeschwader 77 in July 1940 and assigned to their 5 Staffel operating from Kristiansand.

This was Petermann's fifth opportunity to engage a Blenheim, and he followed the weaving X-X-Ray ever-lower getting on its tail and opening fire. After another burst the mid-upper gunner fell silent and then started firing again, but now the Blenheim began to smoke. With a sense of satisfaction, Heinrich now prepared to give the Blenheim the killer burst into the starboard engine and in moments it was on fire.

Baird was loosing the battle. He limped on, but the dense smoke entered the fuselage and cockpit impeding his visibility. For Whetstone-born Copcutt, grappled with the sliding port and starboard sliding windows to extract the smoke, but it laid like a blanket. Baird needed to ditch very quickly, especially as the controls had become heavy in his hands. Over the R/T Baird shouted, 'pre-pare to ditch'. There was no reply. Using hand gestures Burton Wood, and Copcutt got ready to ditch, Wood clutching the dinghy pack. Suddenly the aircraft slammed into the water and stopped abruptly, knocking Burton and Copcutt unconscious.

Somehow, Maurice extracted himself through the roof. While Wood scrambled out and inflated the dinghy, with no sign of either Burton or Copcutt, Baird clambered back into the plane located Burton and dragged him to the escape hatch aft of the gun turret, then made a desperate attempt to locate his regular observer Copcutt but with the machine now sinking lower in the water it was clear Baird only had minutes left. Shouting 'Copcutt, Copcutt,' he heard nothing and went about lifting Burton out and lowering down to Woods below. Maurice then slid down himself. Safely reaching the dinghy, Woods pushed off, and both men paddled away as their Blenheim finally disappeared beneath the waves. Maurice and Wood heroically battled against the tidal flow as Burton lay unconscious the trio's ordeal was over when a Heinkel 59 floatplane found them. Plucking them to safety the Luftwaffe crew landed them at Stavanger quayside. Under armed guard the three survivors then mustered in the dockyard before being led off. Baird badly bruised, Burton bruised and slightly injured was admitted to Stavanger, Wood with a bullet lodged in his foot was transferred to Oslo hospital for treatment then onto a Prisoner of War Camp. It had been a miserable day. Burton's last message was 'somewhat corrupt and uncertain - believe crew in dinghy,' wrote an administrator in pencil on a cablegram to the New Zealand Air Force HQ in London.

Meanwhile, Pennington-Legh had been posted to Skitten which meant promotion for Sam McHardy to Flying Officer and he took over 'A' Flight. His office in his new role was every primitive – a bell tent, furnished with a chair, trestle table and a bucket filled with sand as a substitute for a fire extinguisher. Nor were there any toilets nearby or at the dispersal, as the aircrews risked missing the occasional scramble if they walked to the only brick building, and most went in the sand dunes, between the edge of the airfield and the beach.

By the afternoon of Sunday 3 November, the rain had stopped and the sky in the Shetlands had begun to brighten into cobalt blue. At roughly 10.11 hours, Blue section was ordered off to intercept an unidentified plot. McHardy, Gordon Atkinson and Arthur Garrad took-off, with Sam leading. Once again McHardy thought it would be a trainee pilot in an Oxford that had got lost. However, they saw nothing, but were asked to continue with the patrol out towards Rattray Head. They did as they were ordered and Garrad immediately saw a Heinkel 111 ahead and below at around 4,000 feet one mile away. He called up Atkinson and McHardy on the R/T, and they manoeuvred into line astern and turned in towards the enemy. McHardy made sure his ring sight had clicked into place, he switched his gun button to 'fire,' and heard the excited Garrad call 'Tally-Ho,' as he pounced on the enemy. McHardy and Atkinson made beam attacks. Sam called, 'Blue Two come in!' Turning to starboard, McHardy looped around to come in from astern with Gordon, as the Heinkel seemingly turned towards Norway. Now behind the Heinkel, McHardy pressed the gun button and pumped his remaining rounds into the enemy aircraft. To his amazement dense smoke appeared from the port engine. Then just as suddenly the aircraft rapidly made for the low cloud base near the sea with Atkinson giving chase. The Heinkel's pilot dived into the layer of cloud as a piece of the port engine cowling sheared off and plummeted towards the sea. It emerged through the cloud close enough for Atkinson to see it tumble into the water.

McHardy, out of ammunition, and with the Heinkel 111 having disappeared, headed back towards the Shetland coast, repeatedly calling up Atkinson and Garrad over the R/T, but with no response. Making a good landing, when he finally stopped and pulled out his leads and released his harness, he jumped down onto the ground, and dashed over to Gordon Atkinson to learn if he had any success. Fortunately, he had managed to continue to attack despite the Heinkel's gunner hitting the oil cooler, which removed cowling gills.

'A probable,' McHardy concluded.

'Anyone see what happened to Anthony?'[35] enquired Streatfield. No one had. After searches which lasted until 15.00 hours, it was accepted that the nineteen-year-old, who had kept the squadron entertained with his superb trumpet playing, emulating Louis Armstrong when performing in 'Two-Four-Eight' jazz trio.

Inevitably, McHardy penned three letters that evening to Anthony's parents Arthur and Sadie in Hampshire, his navigator Ernest Bayliss of the same parish, and Harold Moynham's their air gunner a bright Londoner from Tooting who had been aircrew on McHardy's Blenheim on quite a few occasions since arriving in late July.

McHardy and 248 Squadron continued to patrol the sea-lanes and meet any Luftwaffe attacks on Allied shipping until they returned to the mainland in January 1941. 'There was a string of commanding officers James Coats, Leslie King and Stewart 'Billy' Wise as 248 began converting to Bristol Beaufighters,' wrote McHardy. As it was, the atmosphere in 248 had changed a great deal in recent months. The pilots and aircrews hardly needed any more disruption, when it was announced that McHardy was leaving.

So it was on Monday 21 July 1941, McHardy was back in familiar surroundings flying a requisitioned Blenheim that had been allocated to 404 Squadron from Bircham Newton into his new base of Castletown. 'It was great to be reunited with 'Woody' Woodruff again,' recalled McHardy, 'I'd learnt that he had been at Catfoss, in East Yorkshire as an instructor. It was Woody's job to make sure the Blenheim crews coming through training were fit to be sent to operational squadrons.' Now the pilots and aircrew of Woodruff's Canadian squadron found themselves with a Kiwi as 'B' Flight commander who had recently collected his DFC from Buckingham Palace. Most found him easy going enough and appreciated that although he was their flight commander, he was also willing to join in the party antics.

Rough details of training were mapped out with Woodruff, much of which was riding on the assumption that Air Vice-Marshal Reginald Marix the forty-two-year-old AOC of 18 Group could help them achieve a move to Dyce because of the extremely poor facilities at Castletown.

Frontline duties commenced with a move to Skitten roughly five miles northwest of Wick on 22 September when 18 Group issued Woodruff with instructions to send his fighters out to sea to protect a convoy. McHardy had returned to the old routine of readiness and convoy patrols along the coastline and in between there had been a chance to practise.

Marix advised the squadron to fly low-level training with flights routed out over John O'Groats and over the area east and west of Pappa Westray. Navigational, air-to-air, air-to-cloud firing commenced at Dalcross after Woodruff, McHardy and Flight Lieutenant Iain Watson negotiated with Douglas Howard at 19 OTU Kinloss to use this facility. Final approach training against a marker and simulated bomb dropping was carried out over Loch Shin. Marix warned Woodruff and both flight commanders not to fly anywhere near naval ports or other likely defended spots. Night flying was also to be carried out at Dalcross.

It was typical of McHardy that he insisted on flying the first dual training sorties with Sergeant Gordon Bell[36] and McLean, determined to judge for himself whether they were capable of going solo. He was also flying with his new crew – his usual navigator had arrived Sergeant Robert 'Bob' Sims, with whom he had regularly flown with on 248 Squadron, however his air gunner Bowe was straight out of gunner school.

They flew to the Highlands, to Loch Shin, Lairg village lying at the south-eastern end, the loch was surrounded by low and high ground, and it looked to be ideal. Furthermore, the water was calm because the loch was narrow. As they approached, McHardy dropped low following the contours and then roared over the loch at 200 mph, and as close to fifty feet as he and Sims could judge, his navigator stood next to McHardy watching the altimeter. They carried out a number of dummy runs, by which time the small population of Lairg was watching from the shore. Trying a final run over the blue water McHardy then turned on a heading for Skitten.

By the afternoon of 1 October, with most, if not all of the crews having now received some sort of training, with Sam trying to teach them the rudimentary dog-fighting, Woodruff informed Group Captain Cecil Rickard of 18 Group that the squadron was considered operational. However, the focus of the day, was to be to make sure that six Blenheims had been equipped with the newly installed two machine-guns in their turrets. One flight was then to fly immediately to Sumburgh. McHardy the 'B' Flight Commander, and his flight were detailed to travel to the Shetlands. While all the Blenheims had been fitted with the two 0.303 machine guns, it did not mean that they were operationally ready. Fine-tuning on harmonization had to be done. Mechanical checks, particularly on their two Bristol engines, were necessary with the aircraft consistently exposed to the coastal elements.

Despite whatever short comings there might have been, on Friday 3 October, Captain Grieg Lund from the Norwegian Administration at the Air Ministry gave a lengthy lecture on their impending missions off Norwegian coastal waters and fjords to McHardy, Kenneth Hay-Roe, Pilot Officer's John Inglis, and Dunlop with Sergeants Bell, Leighton, MacKay, Barber and 'B' Flight's navigators, and Iain Watson with his 'A' Flight pilots and navigators. Driving rain prevented 'B' Flight carrying out the planned dawn take-off so it was not until 11.00 hours that McHardy and his pilots finally got going.

On the tenth day of October, McHardy with seven Blenheims commenced missions from Sumburgh and was impressed by the hospitality he and his men received. By 14.40 hours, the nineteen-year-old James MacKay from Ottawa was in the air on convoy protection duty, but his Wireless Transmitter failed, MacKay flew into Sumburgh and immediately swapped aircraft. He was sent into the air again at 16.00 hours. Edwards navigation brought them back over the convoy and they continued to shadow until a Catalina replaced them. MacKay, Edwards and Pearce reported to McHardy 'we saw nothing'. It was wearisomeness protecting them but the merchant ships that made up the 'OA' for 'Outbound Convoy,' were only protected by just one naval corvette with just one four-inch gun and four anti-aircraft guns. Convoys continued to progress leisurely towards their destination on thirteen consecutive days with McHardy's men buzzing overhead, occasionally planes were identified as German, clearly watching the two or four columns of merchant shipping on their designated trade route.

Reconnaissance missions off Norway had negative results until 16 October when intelligence had reported movement of an enemy convoy and shortly before 11.55 hours from a single Blenheim from 'B' Flight, piloted by twenty-two-year-old, Gordon Bell originally from Orpington in Kent. His father Robert a film projectionist had immigrated with his wife and three sons to Canada in March 1920, settling in Edmonton. Accepted into the Royal Canadian Air Force in 1940 a little over a year later he completed his training and was posted straight to 404 Squadron. Bell now found himself fourteen miles from Haugesund.

In excellent visibility, with binoculars Sergeant John Matkin could see shapes in the water ahead. 'Four merchantmen, escorted by one destroyer,' remarked Matkin over the R/T. Bell climbed to 500 feet, increased revs and boost, then pushed the nose forward and dived with the air speed creeping up to 260 mph, the convoy drawing ever closer.

'Right stand by Matkin and Mullen's.'

'Ready.'

Suddenly ahead heavy and light anti-aircraft guns opened up, Bell made sure the gun button was set to 'fire' and pressed the button, the Blenheim vibrated as machine-gun bullets sprayed the decks of two merchantmen, somehow Bell, Matkin and Mullen's managed to get past the flak unscathed. Now it was time to head for home. Gordon Bell finally touched down at Sumburgh at 13.40 hours safely. As Bell's crew were clambering from their Blenheim, Dunlop's crew, which had landed ten minutes earlier, was undergoing its debrief with the squadron Adjutant Raymond Crimp and the station commander. Both then congratulated Bell and his aircrew upon hearing of their success 'you've completed the first action against the enemy by this squadron,' said Crump. Feeling pretty cheerful they trooped off to the Flight Office, they found Sergeants Irvine Barber, Ernest Gillam and Jonathan Shaw busily getting ready, grabbing sheepskin Irvin flying jackets, boots, helmets goggles and parachutes to scramble after Sam McHardy. Barber, a twenty-year-old Canadian had a 'press on' spirit and an aptitude to learn that McHardy liked in his pilots. The son of a Lead Burning foreman, Barber had joined the Royal Canadian Air Force just as soon as he turned nineteen and after six months training out in Canada, had travelled from Halifax Nova Scotia to Britain, arriving in early in 1941. While some men could find themselves caught up at the Personnel Reception Centre in Uxbridge or further training. Barber was within four days posted to 404 Squadron in Scotland.

Oval faced with striking blond hair, Barber was tall and muscular, despite him trying to grow a wispy moustache he looked younger than he was. Coming onto the squadron Barber had had the least training in the entire Canadian squadron, but he had done very well in the short time given him, having arrived with less than forty-five hours twin-engine flying training.

At 14.40 hours, Barber had set off towards Norway to search between Bergen and Haugesund, but found nothing out at sea, so, disappointed, had returned to Sumburgh, landing at 18.05 hours. McHardy had landed five minutes before Barber and had sighted three U-Boats and a merchantman. McHardy then flew with Sims and Bowes on an escort mission. It was his last as a flight leader, as Coastal Command HQ at Eastbury Park, Northwood and 18 Group notified Sam McHardy of his promotion on 17 October to squadron leader. Sam was greatly relieved that his efforts had been rewarded. 'I thought this was nice,' said Sam. 'I am going to enjoy this.'

Enjoyment was short lived as 'B' Flight lost its first aircrew. McHardy pointed out, 'there were so few pilots, eight to be exact, together with the same number of navigators and air gunners, it really seemed like a large family than anything else, and therefore three deaths at once seemed very personal indeed.' Sam bade farewell to Barber, Gillam, and Shaw at 15.40 hours. They scrambled into the air ten minutes later, going to protect another convoy roughly twenty miles south of Peterhead the easternmost point in mainland Scotland.

They had encountered a weather front that progressively got worse. Barber had headed back to the Shetlands, with Gillam giving him co-ordinates for Sumburgh airfield. However, due to the intensity of the rain, Barber flew straight across the airfield twice without spotting it, and Sumburgh watch office lost contact whilst the Blenheim was reported to be circling near Lerwick to the north. The incident saw McHardy flying out at 23.50 hours to Lerwick twenty-five miles away with his aircrew and Gordon Bell after reports from the ground controller of Barber's last known position Bell threw out parachute flares and flame floats whilst McHardy circled and called on the R/T to the Canadian. With no response on the R/T or visually being able to see anything on the sea's surface or in the harbour in deteriorating conditions, after forty-five minutes McHardy touched down at Sumburgh.

Sam returned disappointed in losing a promising, bright, and intelligent chap who no doubt would have gone onto gain a commission. Ernest

Gillam, the navigator on Barber's plane, had joined from 248 Squadron on 31 July, was experienced and proven to be good at his job. The surviving three had signalled their position, but by the time a naval launch found the position in daylight, the Blenheim had disappeared along with its crew. 'We never found out what actually happened to them,' wrote McHardy.

At the mess on 5 November, the pilots began to gather. Bell, Brown, Lacy and Mackay had breakfast. Bell left at 05.55 hours, then at forty-minute intervals Brown, Lacy and MacKay, finally racing down the runway at 07.35 on his ninth mission. It was a long trip flying a reconnaissance route starting at Bergen to Trondheim. Roughly four hours later they began arriving back – only one had been lost from 'B' Flight – James MacKay, with navigator William Pearce and Thomas 'Pop' Hedefine. 'It was sad to know that some of these young blokes, like James MacKay were not coming back,' wrote Adjutant Raymond Crump, 'when four days previously we had lost Robert Leighton and two aircraftsmen with Inglis and Corporal Holmes injured in a collision it was a massive loss.'[37] It was a sobering day. McHardy had only just assembled the 'B' Flight burial party for Leighton's burial in Lerwick Cemetery when confirmation came through of MacKay's loss. The North Sea had claimed another three victims.

By the middle of November, Sam had added roughly another fifty hours on Blenheim fighters. His aircrews were making daily forays to Norway, but their frustration was growing, as they had seen nothing significant to attack. Their flight commander got them off the mark on 19 November when two small vessels had been spotted north of Stadlandet. 'I stayed close to the sea for the run-in then popped up. Sparks flickered as the decks were raked with bullets,' said McHardy on the debriefing report. Heaving *A-Apple* into a climb McHardy spotted a Radio Detection Finding station on the headland nearby. He pulled even wider then turned in, diving with a prolonged machine-gun burst and sowed the ground in front, creeping towards the building. 'In the middle of the strafing a person in uniform dashed out and dived head-first over the adjacent cliff edge. Can only assume they knew there was a ledge on the far side or they had a fall of hundreds of feet into the sea,' said McHardy.

So it was that at 05.00 hours, the pilots of 'A' Flight at Dyce awoke to the sound of being told, 'Were off to Sumburgh to join McHardy today 1 December!' All crews reported to the Briefing Room. Patrick Woodruff announced the immediate move to Sumburgh, stressing the importance of the flight being operational within five days. In the interim, 'B' Flight was to continue flying missions off the Norwegian coast.

'A' Flight with engines fuelled, then flew on over to the Shetland Isles. On the fifth day at their new posting, Pilot Officer Robert 'Bob' Schoales of Fort William in Ontario had flown out in *V-Victor* to search a designated section of the Norwegian coast. With his navigator Rogers taking regular drift readings for wind variations and checking the compass, they found themselves approaching the coast with some fifty miles to go. Minutes later without warning there was a violent jolt, the port engine airscrew stopped. Initially it looked unlikely that Schoales would make it home but, amazingly, he was able to continue flying the aircraft, and flew back towards Sumburgh. At around 14.15 hours, in *V-Victor*, Schoales navigator Rogers said, 'Position given to controller, dispatching escorts, Bob.'

McHardy asked Pilot Officer Edward 'Ed' Pierce to commence a search. The twenty-seven-year-old heard the 'B' Flight Commander, tell him 'watch out for a Catalina and good luck.' The son of an Englishman, Edward had been born in Leigh-on-Sea in Essex and after leaving school with a clutch of exam results became a clerk. He moved to Wimbledon in southwest London before emigrating to the United States in 1938. Good-looking, charming and a decent sportsman, Edward lodged on North Ridgewood Road in New Jersey whilst employed as a grain agent in April 1940 before moving to Winnipeg to be a grain exporter.

With the whole of Europe under the Jack Boot, Pierce joined the Canadian Air Force and completed his pilot training in Canada. By the time he was awarded his wings and a commission in early 1941, Pierce looked set to be posted to either Coastal or Bomber Command. After a brief stay at the transit base in Uxbridge he was posted along with several sergeant pilots, including Robert 'Bob' Schoales to 404 Squadron.

At 14.40 hours, Pierce in *Z -Zebra* was flying very low on a course to intercept *V-Victor*. Pierce sighted the Blenheim at 14.54 hours. Schoales by now low on fuel, radioed Pierce to say they had roughly an hour's worth of fuel left when he suddenly saw one of their own Catalina's. 'Signals and pleasantries exchanged at 15.00 hours, the lead twin-engine Blenheim fighter was identified as the object of our search,' wrote Flight Lieutenant Thomas piloting the flying boat.[38] In line astern formation they turned for home twenty-five minutes later at Skerries east of the main Shetland Isles Thomas left for Sullom Voe. Schoales and his crew touched back down at 15.47 hours, exhausted. There to greet them as they clambered out was McHardy. 'So we realised then,' said Schoales, 'this Kiwi was a good egg.' Four minutes later Pierce's Blenheim landed.

After dinner in the Officers Mess, they all decided to celebrate Schoales return. Wing Commander John Twigg and Flight Lieutenant Joseph Edmond of 314 Squadron had attended a court martial on the station with McHardy and Woodruff didn't join them, preferring to return to Sullom Voe for their own Officers Mess dance. The rest of 404 Squadron headed off to the bar in high spirits yelling, 'Four-Oh-Four Squadron!' at the tops of their voice.

They had downed a number of pints when the barman called time – the barrels were empty! They moved onto whisky. By midnight McHardy thought perhaps they should be getting to bed. Shepherding the drunks to their beds, he couldn't help wondering how anyone was going to make a pre-dawn reconnaissance.

He was awoken at 04.30 hours, with the news that visibility was down to less than half-a-mile. 18 Group stood them down so the flight lieutenants of 'A' and 'B' Flight hastily arranged lectures. For McHardy his two flights at the beginning of December would be his only ones, as he received a transfer signal of the 'immediate' variety Woodruff and the Adjutant advised him to proceed with all speed. Pilot Officer Norman Taylor flew into Sumburgh in an Oxford. He had come to collect McHardy for this urgent appointment at Hatston Naval Air station slightly northwest of Kirkwall, Orkney. McHardy was introduced to David 'Corky' Corkhill and his pilot, seconded to 819 Squadron flying Fairey Swordfish torpedo bombers, both were under the instructions from Rear Admiral Sir Harold Burroughs to fly McHardy out to Scapa Flow. Corkhill and his pilot, an accomplished Supermarine Walrus crew, took off with Sam McHardy bound for HMS *Kenya*. Within half an hour the Walrus was alongside, and Corkhill had clambered out up onto the upper wing and hooked his aircraft to a crane that had been lowered by the light cruiser. Hoisted aboard, Corkhill said farewell, and McHardy was ushered into the Wardroom to meet Burroughs. 'I was given a sealed envelope, by Burroughs,' recalled McHardy, in which 18 Group informed me that I was to become "Air Force Coordinator" for a secret mission' codenamed Operation *Archery*.

Vice-Admiral Lord Louis Mountbatten had taken over as head of Combined Operations, the headquarters in Richmond Terrace combined all three services Army, Navy and Air Force to plan and execute hit-and-run raids on occupied Europe. Mountbatten wanted to make an immediate impact, and so a raid was conceived on German positions on the small island of Vågsøy that lay on the northern side of the mouth of Nordfjord between Bergen and Trondheim. The island was situated at the entrance to a system of fjords that were being used as anchorages for naval and transport ships. On the south-eastern side was the island's administrative centre, Måløy, where coastal batteries and fortifications had been identified by aerial reconnaissance which had flown by Squadron Leader Neil 'Nebby' Wheeler. Rapidly the planning progressed and McHardy was asked to coordinate with Brigadier Charles Haydon the commander of the Special Services Brigade tasked with commanding the non-naval aspect of the raid. He also had to liaise with Cecil Rickard of 18 Group and ultimately Group Captain Alfred 'Fred' Willets who was the Assistant Adviser Combined Operations – Air Forces. 'Burroughs was overall in charge for this combined mission,' said McHardy, 'I would dine in the evening with him, Haydon and the other staff officers including the former Norwegian actor Captain Martin Linge, and Lieutenant Colonel John Durnford-Slater.'

Operation *Archery* saw 575 troops being sent, mostly 3 Commando, although there were elements of 2 and 6 Commando and a handful of 4 Commando to provide battlefield first aid. Linge was to lead a dozen from the Norwegian Independent Company No. 1 who had trained under British instruction in bases the length and breath of British Isles for this there first major raid their task would be supported by aircraft from Bomber and Coastal Command. After meticulous planning, a dress rehearsal for the raid itself 'a tactical exercise' was carried out on 11 December, using an island near Scapa Flow. McHardy had to use as far as possible, the radio signals, codes and emergency procedures for an aircraft ditching that they would be using on the actual operation. It was precisely the dry run operation Burroughs had outlined.

The air element of Blenheims, Beaufighters and Hampdens scrambled into the air. Sergeants John Campbell and Lloyd Bolli were in the first at 21.30 hours and searched for any sign of enemy aircraft. Much needed direction, support and purpose were given by eight individual sorties flown throughout the day by the Canadian's. With Schoales and Woodruff flying a second sortie, as the light closed in McHardy on board HMS *Kenya* advised 'Ed' Pierce in *Z-Zebra* and Philip Foster flying *L-Leather* to put down at Wick. 'That evening the mood in the Wardroom aboard HMS *Kenya* was one of success, my R/T between ship and aircraft had functioned properly,' wrote McHardy.

Whilst final considerations were being weighted up for Operation *Archery*, on board HMS *Kenya*, the convoy made for an anchorage near Sullom Voe. 413 Squadron's Flight Lieutenant Alexander Meikle was earmarked to provide weather reports on his return from a mission. 'The weather was not at all decent, visibility was four miles falling to zero in the snow, wind speed was 28 knots, sea extremely rough, frequent snow, opaque ice at low level. Snow and ice continues to Shetland Isles,' reported Meikle. Postponed initially for twenty-four hours, it gave valuable time to repair the former Belgium ferries HMS *Prince Charles* and HMS *Prince Leopold* that suffered flooding in bow compartments. This, noted Burroughs, 'should have been foreseen.'[39] That same night, Christmas Eve, McHardy, Linge and other staff officers got ashore and were entertained by Twigg and officers of 413 Squadron, 'the merriment continued into Christmas Day, helping with the serving of the traditional lunch in the airmen's mess,' wrote Twigg.

Everyone was in a buoyant mood as they headed back to the light cruiser. Durnford-Slater and Commander John Lowe had overseen the mend of both troop transport ships and with renewed impetus, at 16.00 hours, on Friday 26 December the task force sailed. At first light the next morning having endued rough seas they rendezvous with HMS *Tuna* and were guided into position by its doused light.[40]

05.30 hours. Aircrew of 50 Squadron, Bomber Command at Wick, felt a sense of relief edged with trepidation in the knowledge that they were taking the fight to the enemy in Norway. Many of the crews had flown over German-held territory before, but 305 miles over sea was tedious in their Hampden's. Others saw it as quite some adventure however, McHardy was surprised to hear a number of aircrew suddenly realise that everything was under a blanket of snow. At 08.58, McHardy gave them the green light. They were confident that they were going to hit their mark – the German coastal battery at Måløy.

Their commanding officer, Wing Commander Russell Oxley, had told them at the mission briefing that they should attack from low level, dropping their 250lb. bombs from between 100 and 150 feet. By the time Pilot Officer John 'Johnnie' Day[41] navigator and bomb aimer, picked out the aiming point, Hampden *A-Apple* was flying straight and level through a virtual wall of flak. Bursts shaking the plane when suddenly a cannon shell burst caught the Perspex nose and underside where Day was lying. His lower torso caught the impact and managed to call out 'Bombs away!' over the intercom. Pilot Officer Norman Goldsmith took immediate evasive action to take the machine away from the flak. Day had felt as if he had been rugby tackled and had the wind knocked out of him. He felt no pain but had no control over his legs. Relieved he was still alive, he muttered into the microphone, 'I am hit,' then gave the course 'steer 230'. Now out of harm's way Sergeant Nairn 'Robbie' Robinson left his wireless operators position crawled forward to apply a tourniquet and administer a shot of morphine with the help of Sergeant Alexander 'Baldy' Waldie. For Day, the exhilaration had now been replaced by one of gloom, being diminished of his navigational responsibilities of getting the boys home. There was no question of going to Wick, so, undeterred, Goldsmith headed for Sumburgh, which was reached after roughly eight hours in the air.

One of the seven 50 Squadron Hampden's with smoke bombs was going in from South Vågsøy. It was piloted by Sergeant Reginald 'Reggie' Smith a Rhodesian had attended Plumtree School in the province, becoming part of the thriving Lloyd House just after New Year's Day in 1933. Studying hard Smith passed his Matric six years later and left school at sixteen to enter the Rhodesian Civil Service Law Department. Despite enjoying his job, like many Rhodesians with war looming in Europe, Smith felt compelled to volunteer for the Air Force. February 1940 saw Smith start his training in Southern Rhodesia. Flying over the vast open countryside and in clear skies it ensured Smith passed out 'above average.' He sailed to England in 1941 as a qualified pilot; having crewed up and been through OTU he and his crew were posted to 50 Squadron.

'We had done quite well,' reported Smith[42] 'we turned and flew up the coast and came under heavy anti-aircraft fire.' His bomb aimer Pilot Officer Robert Watson lined up to drop their load of phosphorus smoke bombs fifty yards ahead of the advancing commandos. Then a sense of horror as Smith's aircraft disintegrated around him. Anti-aircraft fire directed from Måløy hit the Hampden as Watson released their load; the explosive shock wave sent one phosphorus smoke bomb careering away from its intended target and slammed in to a Landing Craft Ship about to disgorge thirty commandos, twenty were immediately enveloped in a white phosphorus shower of burning particles. Despite this set back, Durnford-Slater pressed on, having seconds earlier fired a red star shell indicating 'cease naval bombardment' as the Hampdens flew in. As their smoke screen hung in the air sporadic small arms fire could be heard.

'It was a terrible sight, seeing remnants of the Hampden hit the water's surface,' wrote McHardy. Smith used his strength to clamber out of the stricken bomber before it finally submerged, half way down the fuselage Sergeant Derek 'Sandy' Bell was climbing out of the hatch when the fuselage went down – taking him down with it. The twenty-three-year-old, from South Shields had joined the Air Force in the summer of 1938 as an aircraftsman later mustering as an air gunner. After completing the course, he joined 23 Squadron and was credited with the destruction of a Heinkel with his pilot Raymond 'The Dook' Duke-Woolley on 18 June 1940. Now, Smith and his remaining aircrew 'paddled in icy cold temperatures with only the buoyancy of their Mae West's keeping their heads above water,' Russell Oxley later wrote in his *Letts* diary, 'with no dinghy they held onto each other.' Smith asked Watson and Sergeant John Williams if they could swim, both shook their heads sadly confessing they could not swim. Smith was the only able swimmer, so the other two had to clutch the trailing mangle on his Mae West. Smith struck out for the shore through the freezing water.[43]

McHardy picked up radio chatter from his vantage point on *Kenya's* bridge and heard that there might be survivors in the water from the

Hampden.[44] He quickly scribbled a note and gave the position to a naval lieutenant. A Signal to HMS *Prince Leopold* read 'at the earliest opportunity look for airmen in water.' On the bridge Lieutenant Kennedy Brown searched with a pair of binoculars for twenty minutes 'something down there in water. Could be them?'[45] Commander John Lowe called 'Stop' engines. In the stillness of the fjord voices could be heard shouting for help. Carefully, with reduced power Lowe and Brown guided the helmsman who edged HMS *Prince Leopold* closer. The men came into view again both heard the faint cry that came down wind to them.

'Over here, we're over here!' yelled Smith.[46]

'Here! Here! We're here!' Watson shouted, his voice cracking with the bitter cold.

A whaler was launched, water sheeting over the bows drenched naval rating, James Waugh, as it plunged into the water. With the help of Gerard McGuckin and Fredrick Pearson, the airmen were plucked out of the water. Watson was heaved aboard, sprawling awkwardly half over the side 'his legs frozen as stiff as tree trunks', followed by the other two. Both Watson and Williams were laying back, their faces pale blue and strained. Reaching HMS *Prince Leopold* sickbay, both the navigator and wireless operator were found to be dead from exposure and cold as they had been in the water for roughly forty minutes.[47] Smith's circulation had been kept going through the energy and exercise in swimming in a desperate attempt to keep his crewmen alive. In trying to save his friends, he had saved himself.

In the midst of all the activity McHardy from the bridge watched the Beaufighters and Blenheims and caught sight of Messerschmitts and Heinkels as they came into attack. 'Bandits coming in from the east,' he warned the aircrews of both types of planes, which turned to meet the new attack.[48] 'McHardy directed and controlled every phase of the air battle, warning, advising, instructing,' wrote Burroughs, 'we all felt pretty safe on the ship.'

Woodruff circled above, 'catching glimpses of smoke rising as buildings were blown up, and tiny figures scampering across snow covered roads and fields exchanging fire.' The air fighting continued: 'there was the clatter of machine gun fire overhead which heralded a fight going on with two Blenheim fighters and two Messerschmitts,' wrote McHardy in his diary, 'I called up on R/T warning the pilot what was happening.'

Flight Lieutenant Kenneth Illingworth,[49] a twenty-four-year-old scholar from University of London Queen Mary's College, came from Skipton, West Yorkshire. His father John had been a serving officer in the Prince of Wales's Own (West Yorkshire) Regiment acting as a Traffic Officer in June

1918.[50] Unfortunately, he was killed whilst marshalling by the roadside when an enemy air-burst shell blast lifted him of his feet. Illingworth was one-year-old, his mother Muriel brought up her son alone near Mill Bridge, schooling him nearby. Anxious to see something of the bustle of London Kenneth gained a scholarship and worked toward his degree. However, the war intervened and found himself being interviewed by an RAF recruitment officer during the summer recess in 1939 and was commissioned as a pilot officer that December.

Twenty-five months after joining an operational squadron and surviving clashes over Norway, where they flew so low they almost touched the water to evade Messerschmitt 110s, then Dunkirk and the skies of southern England during the Battle of Britain and having already won the DFC, Illingworth was now in a desperate melee near Måløy with Me109s. Arthur Clarke flinched as a cannon shell fragment hit his torso 'it was quite gruesome,' said John Pate the navigator, 'I lifted him from the turret and laid him on the fuselage floor to bandage the wound and make Clarke comfortable.'

Illingworth was weaving *A-Apple* as around them two Messerschmitt fighters took it in turns to sweep down upon them. Pate scrambled into the tractor seat of the gun turret and got the two machine-guns firing but with no apparent effect. One German fighter attacked. Coming within point-blank-range he opened fire, cannon and machine-gun rounds punching holes in the fuselage and mainplane 'Ken, I'm hit,' Pate said, as Clarke, lying prone on the floor, received further wounds.

In the cockpit, Illingworth was still desperately trying weave out of the line of fire but over the intercom he heard someone shout they had been hit when more tracer sped past the Perspex. Quickly looking around, he realised it was meant not for him but another Blenheim, that piloted by John Roche. He tried to climb to help out Roche, but the Blenheim was losing height, smoke trailing behind. Roche struggled to keep height, with the starboard engine on fire everything rushed towards him in what must be the last moments before hitting the water.

In *A-Apple*, Illingworth turned sharply to bring his belly-mounted gun pack into play. As the second Me109 came in on the beam he turned inside it, his tactics and skill continued to deny the German a kill and suddenly his pursuer was gone. Despite the severe pain from his wounds Clarke managed to tug the limp body of Pate out of the turret, and tended to his wounds, although weak from his own injuries. Illingworth already had the bearings worked out for the route home. He kept a reserve 1:500 scale map stuffed in his left flying boot for such emergencies, which thankfully were rare. The sky deepened in colour as the light faded as Illingworth's course got him closer to the Shetland Islands. He reckoned he was doing rather well.

'Any one awake?' Illingworth said into the intercom.[51]

Clarke had managed to plug his microphone leads into a vacant socket and in a weak voice replied, 'Still Living!' Illingworth needed to let the airfield know a battle-scared Blenheim was approaching. 'I'll have a crack at it,' Clarke replied to Illingworth's request. Crawling on his stomach, he negotiated the main centreplane dragging himself past Illingworth who gleefully gave a thumbs-up. The wireless had miraculously survived the air fighting and Clarke was able to let the controller know. 'Thank God for that,' said Illingworth.

With the airfield in sight he selected the 'under carriage down' lever, but a red warning light flashed on the instrument panel – the undercarriage was not locked! It was clear that Kenneth Illingworth's plane may not survive a forced landing. Somehow, though he managed to put it down adjacent to the runway, and the next moment it was grinding its way across the grass until finally it halted.

Illingworth escaped with minor cuts and bruises in the forced landing. A doctor and two male nurses hurried to the Blenheim where Illingworth helped them tend the badly injured Pate and Clarke before they were transferred to the Gilbert Bains Hospital in Lerwick.[52] Kenneth visited the following day and passed on the best wishes of Roderick McConnell[53] the newly installed commanding officer of 254 Squadron after the tragic demise of Wing Commander George Bernard-Smith his aircrew and passengers prior Operation *Archery*.

Meanwhile, McHardy watched the commandos bring back prisoners, and had gathered roughly eighty Norwegian recruits, as well as the capture of complete German naval codebooks. Amongst the losses was Martin Linge,[54] devastating to the fledgling Norwegian Company No. 1. HMS *Kenya* and the rest of the force left with the area and headed for home. From Scotland these Norwegians were sent to London, and to the London Reception Area in the Royal Patriotic School for a medical and clearance.

McHardy was debriefed at Scapa Flow. The raid had been pretty successful, four factories destroyed, ammunition and fuel stores and the telephone exchange blown up, and roughly one-hundred German soldiers killed and ninety-eight captured. Hatston Naval Air station[55] beckoned for McHardy, flying the short distance in a Walrus before being packed off to Sumburgh. McHardy arrived back on base and took great delight in unpacking and sending his battledress to be laundered; by and large he found the spirits to be good too. John McCutcheon, and Pierce had claimed two probable's on the Vågsøy mission.

On the 16 January, McHardy took off on a patrol in *X-X-Ray* to photograph the composition of German convoys near Bergen. After exhausting the roll of film in the camera, the aircrew continued the patrol and after three-quarters-of-an-hour McHardy saw a Heinkel 115 floatplane[56] about 1,000 feet above his Blenheim some two miles away. Gaining height using full throttle, he called up his air gunner, Bowe, on the intercom to be ready, and manoeuvred astern of the Heinkel. 'I was aware there was a considerable amount of cloud which the nimble 115 could escape into,' wrote McHardy, 'so I attacked on the seaward side – starboard quarter opening fire at 500 yards closing to within 100 yards with a long burst as the enemy swung off to port pretty sharpish.' Chasing after the enemy at 150 yards fired a two-second burst from astern, then Bowe gave short bursts as they broke away. The Heinkel then climbed for the cloud with McHardy wheeling round to get astern again until it was directly in front of him at 'roughly less than 75 yards.' He pressed down on his gun-button and dispensed his remaining rounds at the machine. Bits of aircraft began flying off, smoke burst from the port engine and then a great lick of smoke from the fuselage, before it entered dense cloud. 'Claimed it as a probable, then celebrated with John Inglis in the Officers Mess drinking Crème de menthe[57] the only drink we had left,' McHardy later wrote.

Sunday 1 February was notably quiet in 'B' Flight's offices. As McHardy was sitting at his desk catching up on office work he got word over the telephone of an unidentified aircraft out at sea, south of Sumburgh. Shortly afterwards, the controller said the plane was now thought to be a Catalina flying boat from Sullom Voe. But moments later came a roar of engines and machine-gun fire. Scrambling to take cover, McHardy dived headlong into the adjutant's office to take cover behind a large steel safe, only to find the space already taken by fellow pilot, Donald MacKenzie! Venturing outside, McHardy saw a weathered Junkers 88 dropping a stick of bombs from roughly 100 feet. Vast explosions followed, and huge plumes of smoke began rising from the airfield's intersecting runways. In response to this there was neither anti-aircraft fire nor any fighters of their own. The Junkers circled around then flew in firing, when suddenly there was a loud crack, and a brief moment later the offices tacked onto the side of the main hanger construction – a long row of rooms on the ground floor and another set, with a slight pitched roof above – collapsed in a huge cloud of smoke. Sam McHardy watched in horror and ran to give a hand as the 88 disappeared out of sight.

Searches began straight away for trapped people and retrieval of salvageable items. Flight Lieutenant Terrance Kirk, 404 Squadron's Medical Officer, rushed over to him: 'It's good of you to help, Sam!' and 'we don't know how many.' Men removed beams and masonary as others struggled to reach those caught in the strafing, with reassurances when found injured were carefully extracted. AC1 David 'Dave' Clarke and 18-year-old AC2 Norman Leitch were lifted out with bullet wounds to the upper torso and abdomen. Kirk and three medical orderlies tried to stem the loss of blood with field dressings as McHardy and the engineering officer helped lift the stretchers onto an Ambulance – but both succumbed to their wounds. A dozen had been injured, and seven Blenheim fighters had temporarily been rendered unserviceable. For the time being at any rate, six less RAF aircraft for the Germans to worry about attacking merchantman plying trade between Norway and Dutch ports.

There was, of course, the loss of the two airmen, notification that they had died was sent to their next of kin, with funerals taking place on Thursday 5 February. Rain clouds covered the sky, and there was a strong gale blowing, as McHardy led the funeral procession with 'B' Flight officers, senior non-commissioned officers and airmen into Lerwick Church. It was bitterly cold as McHardy left - his RAF greatcoat collar turned up to afford some protection against the elements as he marched back to RAF Sumburgh. Later, in his office, the New Zealander would make arrangements for Norman Leitch body to be shipped back to North Tyneside for burial at Wallsend as expressed by his parents. That evening, with at last a few moments to himself, McHardy wrote home. 'Dear Mother,' he began. 'Just another brief line to tell you that I am alive and well.' Finishing with 'Your ever-adoring son, Sam,' he had signed off after just a few lines with a 'P.S. Much prefer you nicknaming me Sam to my christened Edric.'

Chapter 3

Flying Officer Lloyd Trigg VC DFC
Consolidated Courage

The time was 04.43 hours; the date was 13 August 1943.[58] A short way off to the port side of the Sunderland Flight Lieutenant John Pare saw an object in the water. 'Dinghy,' yelled Flying Officer Graham Godden. About thirteen hours had lapsed since Flight Sergeant Charlie Watkinson, flying Sunderland *H-Harry*, had first sighted the dinghy. On board *H-Harry*, navigator Flying Officer Patrick Dempsey called to Watkinson, 'sharks circling the dinghy and some swimming under it.' He then settled down, worked out the co-ordinates and radioed base. Watkinson gave the signal: 'OK starting first run.'

Aft of his position Gunter and Gillham heaved the Lindholme Gear cylindrical containers out of the starboard bomb door. Dempsey saw them splash down next to the five figures and took some snaps for the squadron album.

Sitting huddled in the dinghy, Oberleutnant zur See Klemens Schamong[59] and the others, had been caught out by the speed with which the Sunderland had come at them – and by the low level of the approach. 'Suddenly,' recalled Schamong, 'the speeding white shape was thundering like a four-engine demon towards our small inflatable at a height of about 100 feet'.

Moments later, the Lindholme Gear hit the water, less than ten feet away, drenching them all. The wash battered the dinghy, but as the water subsided, it was clear that they were still afloat. For Schamong and his six men, it was with heartfelt relief.

'Poor buggers', thought Watkinson as they left the dinghy, which was being buffeted by high waves, as the flying-boat flew on towards the Gambia border and their Bathurst base.[60]

Pare arrived at 01.10 hours and the square search began; 100 miles in one direction and then *F-Freddie* moved up ten miles and came back again carrying on these runs until they found traces of the aircraft or survivors. Rather than feeling tense, at his navigator's station on board *F-Freddie*, Reginald Saffier was excited with the chase. 'I learnt early on to keep cool,' he said, 'and we were headstrong to think we'll find them OK.'[61] Their confidence had not been dampened by Flight Lieutenant Francis Johnston's earlier failure.

So, Pare began his twenty-second run, and on this occasion he managed to line up the aircraft perfectly on track and at the right height. It was then 04.43 hours and at last something was sighted in the water. 'Dinghy', Pare shouted on the R/T, 'prepare to drop flame floats and marine markers'. In the rear turret Sergeant Arthur Dumont saw red flashes illuminate the darkness below then sway like a clock's pendulum, 'Nice cluster Godden,' said Dumont. Two minutes had passed since the sighting and the dropping of the pyrotechnics. 'We could see the water lashing the occupants in the dinghy,' recounted Dumont, 'all the illumination brought home the perils of ditching in the sea'. They stayed over the dinghy. Saffier sent the signal 'Confirm dinghy sighted. Seven occupants on board,' then sent another to HMS *Clarkia*, which was co-operating with them in the search. Saffier, quickly wrote their reply down saying, 'We are six miles south'.

Saffier said, 'Better turn right, Skip, Navy not too far away'.

'How did that happen?' Pare asked Saffier as they banked steeply and changed course, following the co-ordinates to the correct crossing point to lead the hound to the fox.

'Don't know, Skip. Pretty rough down there in the drink?'

'Specially if you're in a tin can.'

Briefly, they lost sight of the Flower-class Corvette, but soon after Pare saw the vessel on the starboard side once more. As they continued, a message was flashed from HMS *Clarkia*, which read; 'We're peddling as fast as we can,' to which Pare reply 'there is no other place we'd rather be'.[62]

Heading 148 degrees, Captain Stanley Darling, an Australian Naval Officer seconded to the Royal Navy, guided his Corvette to the dinghy aided by the Sunderland. Reaching the dinghy at 06.31 hours.

'What's your message? Sir.'[63]

Send, 'Am stopping to pick up survivors numbering seven.'

Able Seaman Ernie Todd flashed it, and saw a brief acknowledgement from above, before the meaning struck home. He lowered the lamp and looked down as men were being hauled up the scramble nets, and then looked ahead across the sea checked his watch, twenty-three minutes before sunrise.

From the bridge Darling slid down the ladder on to the main deck to greet the flyboys. A torrent of short sharp words carried along on the breeze, 'Germans!' then 'quick two of you go grab a .303 rifle,' from the Chief Petty Officer. Darling walked towards the seven men. One stepped forward and saluted and stuck out his right hand, 'Oberleutnant zur See Clemens Schamong,' Darling responded and asked, 'Sprechen Sie Englisch?'

In *H-Harry*, Pare circled waiting for a response. Precisely ten minutes later a message was flashed. Saffier couldn't believe what he was writing down: 'Seven occupants in dinghy are GERMAN, survivors from a U-Boat attacked and sunk by Liberator *D-Dog* on 11 August 1943'.

Back at Bathurst Bay, Pare found the realization that eight men would not be returning to their homes very hard to come to terms with. For so long he had been focusing on destroying enemy shipping and U-boats in his mind's eye: he had not really thought of the human cost, which was now stacking up.

The seemingly endless war at sea continued and, up until Wednesday, 7 July 1943,[64] 200 Squadron had been muddling through with the first American-built aircraft to see operational service with the Royal Air Force, the Lockheed Hudson. It had been three years and one month since the squadron had taken delivery of their aircraft. Two arrived on 1 June, both from 206 Squadron. That was a start. Ground and aircrew joined this new outfit, the only real indication of what they had been formed to do came from the ex-206 Squadron crews kicking their heels around in the Bircham Newton Officer's Mess living up to their motto 'nought escapes us.'

'Coastal Command,' said John 'Johnny' Walker.

'I don't fancy searching for a speck in the ocean,' replied Trinidadian John Carrington, who had been studying at Cambridge University before joining the RAF.

'You'll get used to it,' said the tall Irishman, his crew standing alongside of him at the bar.

Another Hudson arrived from 233 Squadron late in the afternoon. Australian Wing Commander Douglas Candy[65] supposed that he would be told eventually as the amount of men and women arriving was extraordinary. Four more Hudsons arrived, borrowed or purloined from a number of different 16 Group squadrons, which made seven in all – enough for crews to get in the air for familiarization flights. Now four days later, on the first Saturday in June, Candy received a note from Coastal Command Headquarters detailing the transit of 200 Squadron on 12 June, to Gibraltar, via way of Malta to Gambia, from where it would begin its intended role in anti-submarine and convoy cover in the South Atlantic.

By the late afternoon of 18 June, five crews had reached Jeswang, in Gambia. Candy realised that a talk was in order. Assembling the nineteen of them together in a brick building reputedly used by Latvian Herbert Cukurs, Candy gave a speech that was short and to the point. 'You're here to do a special job, to stop German U-Boats attacking our convoys,' he told them, 'all I can tell you is you will have to know every ship outline there is, and you will probably never see the enemy, but on that one occasion you do you'll give them a bloody nose. Discipline is absolutely essential as is no fraternization with the local women.'

Candy insisted on flying the first training sortie over undulating pastures and dense forest canopy that surround the area. Over the following days, Jeswang and Bathurst became a whirlwind of activity as a transformation took place then, on 30 June, the squadron flew its first operational sortie.

Convoy protection became the normal routine, the task would be carried out month after month. Squadron commanders changed in the interim. Candy gave way to Benjamin Dias and, by September 1942, Wing Commander William Ingle[66] had taken over command from Dias. He arrived and sorted out the flights, which required a degree of tact, empathy and diplomacy. The jigsaw was nearly complete, and it was no small achievement when Ingle's crews peaked at 172 sorties. Meanwhile, memos and papers on rotation of aircrew and new groundcrew were going back and forth over precise allocations in the Hudson Communications aircraft to Gibraltar, concerning the proposed allocation of the Consolidated Liberator aircraft for the squadron; each Liberator required a team of nearly fifty to get it airborne, of which eight were the aircrew.[67]

Nonetheless progress was being made. Lloyd Trigg,[68] a twenty-nine-year-old New Zealander, was imbued with the same kind of 'press on regardless' spirit that Ingle liked in his pilots. The eldest son of Merthyr Tydfil-born Frank Trigg, a veteran of the First Boar War who had immigrated to Australia in 1900, then worked his passage to New Zealand's harsh Northland. Lloyd's mother, Cecelia White, was just twenty-six when she married and only twenty-nine when her son the eldest of three had been born. Frank became the community storekeeper and ran a billiard saloon in the remote settlement of Victoria Valley north of Mangamuka Range. Here the couple lived with their three sons and daughter until Frank died, aged forty-eight in 1929. Cecelia sold the store and the family moved to Princes Street in Mairtown, Whangarei, and Lloyd was enrolled at Whangarei High School. The redheaded youngster Lloyd Trigg was quick at processing information and made rapid decisions. This aided him when witnessing a collision, aged twelve: 'I yelled at our bus driver to stop', there had been a collision, and a truck had tumbled off the road and into the river, 'jumping out of the bus I immediately slithered down the river bank, wrenched open the driver's door and hauled the truck driver out of the submerged cab,' he told his head teacher.[69]

Sadly, the Trigg youngsters lost their mother in 1932, but fortunately a housekeeper took them in. Thereafter Lloyd responded by trying even harder to succeed at Whangarei High School. He became a very competent violinist whether playing solo or in the school orchestra, played rugby for the 1st XV and took up long distance running. Trigg qualified for university, aiming to become a teacher. But the Depression struck New Zealand and he went to work on a mixed sheep station in Wairarapa.

There aged twenty-four, he became infatuated with Nola McGarrie. 1938 saw the couple marry into a struggling economy. Through enterprise and hard work to sustain an income Trigg combined farming, selling and servicing German-manufactured farming machinery for Booth MacDonald when the couple returned to Victoria Valley. It was true money was short, but they recovered. Lloyd had gradually taken over the mantle from the owners of the property; by the time war was declared, they had two sons, John and Waynn and the family prospects seemed good.

As a farmer he was out on the plains most days and caught sight of commercial planes fly over, which captured his imagination as they'd done when he was a child. Lloyd volunteered for the Air Force: 'I was completely intrigued by the mystery of flight,' he told Nola. Life in this green outback was a remote existence – he had never been further than the country's capital Wellington, in his life, but equally, like many young New Zealanders, felt compelled to play his part and do his duty for their mother country, Britain.

Despite volunteering, it was not until 17 June 1941 that he was called up, and even then, he was considered at the age of twenty-seven too old to be trained as a combat pilot. Fortunately, his sharpness of mind and physical fitness got Lloyd through Levin, and then moved to Harewood for Elementary Flying Training School (EFTS). In September he embarked for Canada, to complete his pilot training under the Empire Training Scheme. After an exceptional run of 'above average' assessments Trigg was awarded his pilot's wings on 16 January 1942 and was commissioned a pilot officer. Canada and the United States were a strong contrast to Victoria Valley. Time passed in a blur on No.31 General Reconnaissance School with lectures and instruction on instruments and navigation as Trigg converted onto the Lockheed Hudson. Finally, he crossed the Atlantic to Liverpool on the *Athlone Castle* in October 1942, with his wings on his dark blue tunic and a promotion to Flying Officer.

Lloyd marked time at Bournemouth, being entertained by host families at weekends, courtesy of the Isles Dominion Hospitality Scheme. His leave was taken in London where he toured the Tower of London and saw bomb damage. He also managed a brief trip to the glorious Welsh Valleys to see distant relatives. Caught up in transit he was quickly posted to 200 Squadron, in West Africa arriving in January 1943.

Teaming up with navigator, Ivan Marinovich,[70] a Yugoslav whose parents Lovre and Mary settled in Auckland after Archduke Franz Ferdinand was assassinated. Marinovich was a wine producer with his parents in the Oratia Valley. Volunteering at twenty-two, for the Air Force as a pilot his training was terminated on Thursday 31 July 1941 after a flight of fifty minutes when assessed as below average. Ivan was at EFTS for another two months after he was remustered onto the navigational course.

Eventually with a bit of trial and error Trigg had a complete crew for the Hudson and they began flying missions from Yundum. It was a mundane routine of convoy protection, flying sweeps back and forth over the merchantmen and their Royal Navy escort. Except in March, when two U-boats[71] were sighted off the West African coast when Trigg was airborne on two separate occasions. Reacting quickly, Trigg attacked as the submarines submerged. His prompt acted earned him the Distinguished Flying Cross. Apart from this flurry little changed as the crew rotated except the number of vessels and weather pattern.

It was just as well for Trigg and his crewmates got on as they were then ordered to be one of three crews to be sent to the Bahamas to convert[72] onto the B-24 Liberator at 111 OTU Nassau. Leaving the West African shores from Accra, Ghana, on 4 May in a laden Curtis C-46 Commando. Captain Edward McInnis (USAAF) with Trigg as co-pilot,[73] gradually lifted off the ground, flying a route encompassing the Ascension Islands, Brazil, Trinidad, and Puerto Rico into the United States. At Nassau, their third C-46 pilot, Earl Lancelet, clambered from the sun-bleached plane, attired in shorts and baseball cap and cheerfully said farewell before charting his flight back to Miami.[74]

Training started on 12 May and by the end of Wednesday, 5 June, the crewing for Lloyd Trigg's was more or less complete. There were as prescribed eight airmen to crew the Liberator. The Navigator on Lloyd Trigg's crew was thirty-one-year-old Marinovich. His regular the pair had entered the hanger and immediately found a fellow Kiwi. 'I'm looking for a wireless operator. You look intelligent,' Trigg said to Arthur Bennett. Bennett had already learnt to fly and had his 'A' Licence but selected to be trained as an air gunner. Because of his high exam pass marks, Bennett was told to re-muster for wireless operator. Another Flight Sergeant, Lawrence

Frost[75] had been a hardware assistant at Briscoe & Company in Auckland swapping to the hardware of .50 calibre machine-guns. Posted to Canada for training in October 1941, Frost finally received his WAG chevron, as they were commonly known in early May 1942. It was a long journey, to England via Buffalo New York, where he met an acquaintance, Dorothy Swetlin of Cleveland Ohio,[76] who was flattered by his attention. Joining 200 Squadron, in Yundum on New Year's Day in 1943,[77] Frost immediately began flying operationally on the unit's Hudsons but found he was continually flying with different aircrew. 'I had no consistency except with Gilbert Johnston until Soper from 'Trigger's' crew said they had a spare place,' he wrote in a letter home. The rest of the crew included another New Zealander, Terrence 'Terry' Soper of Takaka a small settlement at the far northern end of the Southern Island. He heeded the call, like his father Algernon in the First World War, who had fought with the Canterbury Mounted Rifles in Egypt. Completing his instructional course he passed out as a WAG in Canada, briefly joining Ferry Command crewing planes between Montreal and Newfoundland before the posting to 200 Squadron. Other nationalities included George Goodwin,[78] a commissioned Pilot Officer, the youngest of all the crew at twenty and Lloyd Trigg's co-pilot. His father had emigrated to America from Holland but died two years after his son was born in 1924, the Goodwin's then entered Canada. Despite money being scarce at home in Erickson, British Columbia, his mother provided the maternal stability for George, as a youngster to be good academically and excel in all school and field sports at Creston High School. Now wearing Canadian Air Force dark blue uniform Goodwin found himself finishing his course at 111 OTU, in overall fourth place. Squadron Leader Aubrey Easton noted: 'Exceptionally keen officer and pilot – Intelligent.' The other two were English and Irish, but they all got along well enough and would fly this new machine together.

Flight Sergeant Richard Bonnick[79] of Kingsbury, Surrey, had chosen to be aircrew and a WAG. After leaving school aged seventeen, he decided to join the RAF. His mother, Jessie, worried that it would be initially too dangerous. But hearing that her son had gained promotion and qualified as a wireless operator/air gunner she was pleased. Receiving a letter whilst at Nassau. 'Dear Mother . . . I have been impressed by my first flight, and was struck by its speed and ruggedness . . . Don't worry everything okay'

The fourth officer on the crew John 'Johnny' Townsend[80] BEM was a Flying Officer originally a contracts assistant for a leading commercial photographer in Birmingham. With uncertainty in the air in 1939, Townsend was one of those mobilised when Sunday, 3 September dawned, he was employed on 'D' Flight at Cardington, Bedfordshire as an aircraftsman. A change of task was needed and by 29th, he was back with his wife Ruby at Highgrove Farm Gloucestershire, nestling quietly in the famous Cotswold Hills.

After months of training Townsend was quickly posted to a gunnery school and then onto 410 Squadron.[81] During his time as a Flight Sergeant with 410, he survived a crash as a WAG. In poor visibility the Boulton Paul Defiant descended through a copse of trees whilst flying operationally on Monday 8 December 1941 at Drem. They were so low he knew there was no chance of bailing out. 'I'm sorry,' he heard Flight Lieutenant Robert 'Bob' Day say over the intercom, 'we've had it.' Moments later, the Defiant smashed into the ground having ploughed through layers of tree branches, its wings being wrenched from their mounts. The engine was dislodged, as was the Perspex enclosing Day in the cockpit. The turret cupola was also torn away. The aircraft ploughed a furrow towards an oak tree that had survived the 1709 hurricane's force storm with winds of more than 120 miles an hour. Two hundred and thirty-two years later, the twentieth century plane toppled it, with the fuselage coming to rest ten yards beyond the oak's web of branches and cascading golden yellow leaves, that dropped like confetti onto the battered metal tomb and its injured occupants.[82]

The impact had totally freed the Royal Royce Merlin from its mounts and came to rest a few yards ahead. With exposed pipes and wiring, the engine and fuselage ignited, causing flames to pulsate 12 feet into the air. Fortunately, the main petrol tanks were a considerable distant away, lying with remnants of the wings, and the flames subsided.

Although in a dazed state, Townsend hauled himself out of the turret and made his way forward to assist Day who was only just conscious, having sustained serve head injuries. Townsend reached in and released Day's Sutton Harness and with some considerable difficulty tried to move him but found the impact had wedged his feet in the flying boots tightly in the rudder pedals. Townsend managed to extract Day from the wreckage using his RAF issue penknife to cut the sheepskin flying boots enough to haul him out.

Dragging the weighted body away from the smouldering bulkhead, he was given a hand by a local farmer who assisted moving Day to a safe distance. Townsend steadied himself, then retraced his steps to the wreckage. Retrieving the dinghy, he inflated then inverted it to serve as a resting place for the barely-conscious pilot. He then wrapped him in his parachute for warmth. Recovering the first aid kit Townsend administered morphia to Day who was now suffering acutely and applied bandages to his head wounds. He then returned to the wreck and made safe the

.303 machine guns. It was nothing short of a miracle that both had survived. John Townsend was awarded the British Empire Medal and, due to his praiseworthy conduct, the renowned Battle of Britain ace Peter Townsend as his CO took a personal interest in John's investiture which was *Gazetted* on 8 June 1942. Within twenty-one days John had gone from being a SNCO to a pilot officer. Townsend also gave a piece of advice stop using 'John James Stanley,' now you've a thin blue band on your lower sleeves and use the name your parents christened you with.

Trigg and his crew left the Bahamas to collect a newly-built Yagi-equipped Liberator MkV from RCAF Station Dorval, Québec.[83] Sunday 12 July, all had began their journey back to West Africa in one of six aircraft. Unfortunately, they couldn't sweet-talk the Canadians to allow them to fly together. Liberator *D-Dog* with Townsend on board and Trigg co-piloting a B2 Type made the scheduled refuelling stop at RCAF Station Gander, Newfoundland, on the first leg of the long journey home. On 18th, the Liberators began landing at Ras el Ma airfield, Morocco. Here George Goodwin swapped aircraft to fly as co-pilot with Trigg in his B2 Type onto Yundum, it was good to be back over familiar territory. Trigg heard the distorted voice of the controller giving him the all-clear to land, and he acknowledged. The first of four Liberators landed at 15.59 hours. Trigg having shut down the engines scrambled out with Goodwin and the other aircrew.

While Ingle joined the crews for the debriefing, he was deeply concerned about whether the Pierced Steel Planking (PSP)[84] runway would be suitable for the heavier Liberators. His worst fears were realised when torrential rain caused severe challenges for the PSP together with Ingle's conversion and training programme for aircrew on five consecutive days. Ingle paid 100 local men and women two pennies a day to dig shallow drainage ditches for flood water to run away. Problems persisted, so space was found at nearby Rufisque airfield in Senegal for six Liberators, with the assistance of 1st Anti-Submarine Squadron, United States Army Air Corps.[85] On 6 August, Liberators *A*, *B*, *D* and *E* are prepared for flight and flown to Rufisque with additional ground and aircrews arriving two days later as Ingle decided against flying out the previous day, because of continual rain fall and serious flooding. On arrival he was being pushed to complete the crews' training and get the Liberators into the fight off the West African coast.

With Britain heavily dependent on seaborne trade, it was the Commander of Germany's U-boat arm Admiral Karl Dönitz's task to sever those sea lanes. One of these U-boats was *U-468* under the command of Oberleutnant zur See Klemens Schamong.[86] The *U-468* had left La Pallice U-Boat bunker with eight others, escorted by a pair of minesweepers and slowly made its way into the South Atlantic just as the crew had done before when patrolling between Greenland and Iceland.

In April 1937, when he turned twenty, Schamong had decided he wanted to become a Naval Officer entering cadre IV/37 with 416 other potential cadet officers. Starting as a Midshipman, at Naval College it was with immense pride and satisfaction that Schamong learnt that he had been chosen for service in the navy's elite U-Boat Arm. 'At first our training was mostly infantry combat related,' said Schamong, 'Later, we lucky few had to learn every valve and line in a submarine.' When he left on 25 August 1941 it was as a Leutnant with an above average score for Torpedo and Communication at Flensburg-Mürwik, and was soon transferred to *U-333*. He liked the camaraderie particularly with Kapitänleutnant Peter Cremer with whom he became first watch officer with and successfully completed two war patrols.[87]

Early June 1942, Schamong began the intensive U-Boat Commander Training and Commander Torpedo Shooting Course in Memel, on the Baltic Coast and so began the job of taking charge of a Type VIIC U-boat. 11 August 1942 he witnessed the final stages of construction of *U-468* under supervision of 1.KLA, Deutsche Werke in Kiel-Gaarden. Werke No. 299 – *U468* – was signed over to Klemens Schamong and his Chief Engineer Heinz Hamm. Eventually, his crew witnessed action and, on Wednesday 7 July 1943, sailed on their third war patrol. Proud in their successful run all combined with warmth and understanding to produce the kind of team spirit that would be needed to survive the terrifying events to come.

On Wednesday 11 August 1943, forty-nine-year-old Air Vice Marshal John Cole-Hamilton[88] at Air Headquarters West Africa, received the decrypts that several U-boats were operating in the area off Gambia.

In his office Wing Commander William Ingle received the news by telephone, 'dispatch most urgently two Liberator's on patrol'. Ingle called for Squadron Leader Reginald Fowle, flight commander of the Rufisque detachment, and broke the news that an anti-submarine patrol was required. The days training rota had Fowle's wispy signature in dark blue ink at the bottom of the paper, above the typed names included Lloyd Trigg's crew except circumstances had drastically changed that morning from training to an operational sortie.[89]

RAF groundcrew prepared the aircraft with help from their American counterparts. Americans fused[90] and transported the depth charges on trolleys from the dump to the aircraft. Then their armament section handled the loading with a hoist. Fowle stressed the importance of succeeding and ran through the routes. At *D-Dog*, Lloyd Trigg's Liberator, first to board were front gunner and second navigator Townsend, followed by Lawrence Frost and Terrence Soper, the aft gunners. Third to climb the ladder aboard was Bonner the mid-upper; then Marinovich, the navigator; then pilots George Goodwin and Lloyd Trigg. Fowle's crew boarded *B-Betty* there were no frills, and very few comforts. The Americans had designed the Liberator for one purpose; bombing.

Trigg plugged his helmet leads into the intercom and asked each of the crew to call in. They did so. Trigg reminding them no one should be aft of the beam gun position until airborne because of the considerable pitching movements. Rufisque erupted with the roar of Pratt & Whitney engines starting up and then the two began to thunder down the earthen runway and take to the sky. This morning Fowle was airborne at 07.28 hours, with Trigg one minute behind. Both where weighted down by a full bomb bay: Six 250lb. depth charges and two 600lb. Anti-Shipping bombs.

Crews got into position; everything seemed to be in order aboard *D-Dog* when a signal giving new co-ordinates came through at 11.05 hours. Diverting to track a U-boat that had been attacked by Flight Lieutenant Neal Ward. Ward was flying as second pilot to Wing Commander Douglas Baird and happened to have control of the Catalina when the U-boat was spotted roughly three miles away. Its greyness was only just visible to the naked eye in the heavy swell. He began his run immediately reckoning he had dropped four depth charges dead-on. It was not precise enough, however, these depth charges exploded astern, causing the U-boat's bows to lift completely out of the water with the propellers spinning in the air for a short time. With wrecked steering the submarine completed 360 degrees turns as its gun crews exchanged gunfire with the Catalina until it submerged.

En route the American meteorological officer's forecast had been good and Marinovich's navigation brought *D-Dog* ninety miles north of the Catalina's quarry and roughly 240 miles southwest of Dakar. Searching over the cobalt blue sea required intense concentration from everyone because it was important they didn't miss anything. Their tedium was broken when Marinovich called out, 'U-boat on surface'.[91] Both pilots worked side by side to bring the aircraft to bear, Goodwin quickly called Bennett on the intercom to send a sighting report. OK George,' said Arthur.

Roaring low over the water the surfaced U-boat was off to their port quarter, which was barely visible in the heavy seas. One moment they were flying through clear air, the next tracer was squirting around them.

At 6,500 yards lookouts on the conning tower caught sight of a fast moving object. Oberleutnant zur See Klemens Schamong of *U-468* shouted

'*Warnung Ton der feindlichen Flugzeuge.*' Schamong's two gun crews were on stand-by. In quick time they were ready, guns loaded and primed. For the defenders on the upper and lower bandstands the visible target came with a deafening noise of four Pratt & Whitney engines.

Tracer hurtled towards *D-Dog*, some even skimming off the heavy swell. Then, the plane seemed to stand still in the air as cannon shells repeatedly struck.

'We've been hit,' shouted Soper into the intercom then, 'we're alight a stern – its enveloped Arthur's position.'

Lloyd gave the reply: 'Okay, I am attacking.'

As the gap decreased towards the target, Goodwin turned the fusing switches to 'ON'. Lloyd showed incredible leadership and raw courage, keeping the aircraft straight and level, as the Liberator rushed along at 220 miles per hour at forty-nine feet. In the nose, Townsend continued to rattle out .50 calibre rounds towards its prey.

On the conning tower, Schamong stood directing the fire and shouting words of encouragement. Suddenly flames curled out from its exposed bomb bay.

'It's burning! Its burning!' yelled Hans Ritzenhoff.[92]

On board *D-Dog*, Lloyd yanked the toggle causing the depth charges to be released as it tore across aft of the conning tower. Six grey cylindrical objects fell away and splashed into the water, two depth charges exploding six feet from the U-boats hull. As the burning Liberator hurtled over trailing fire and smoke, the U-boat was lifted out of the water by the double explosion sending a cascade of seawater across its upper surfaces. As litres of water plummeted down, Schamong was knocked almost to the floor, momentarily losing sight of his attacker. He stumbled to his feet: 'then I saw it hit the water with a loud explosion,' said Klemens Schamong during his subsequent interrogation.[93]

D-Dog blew up 300 yards from *U-468*, with pieces of aircraft and seawater sprayed across this speck of the Atlantic Ocean. At the West African operations room incoming messages from this sortie ceased and the teleprinter fell silent.

The gunners on the U-boats bandstand were jubilant, their fire had found the weakest spot the Liberators bomb bay. After Lloyd's plane had disappeared, Schamong's men carried out damage control duties. 'Damage was catastrophic, and she began to settle at once with water entering at several points. The engines and motors were torn from their beds, as well as the transformers and the bilge pumps. The fuel tank above the diesels, containing about sixty-five gallons of fuel, crashed down. The battery containers cracked. Nothing remained fixed on the bulkheads, with equipment and instruments strewn all over the floor plates. The wireless room was a shamble, and no distress signal could be made. The aft torpedo tube fractured, and a two-inch stream of water poured onto the floor. Water was also entering the battery compartment; and within a few minutes the U-boat was filled with clouds of chlorine gas. Men immediately began to suffocate and could not get to their life belts. Some panic set in and only about twenty men succeeded in reaching the main deck and jump overboard into the water,' said Schamong. 'The U-boat sank on an even keel within ten minutes.'

Many of the men who spilled into the water were suffering the after-effects of inhaling the chlorine gas and had become disorientated. Swarms of sharks began appearing. 'At any given time, you could look out and see big fins swimming around and around. All of a sudden you heard a blood-curdling scream and you look and you see the shark had taken him under,' wrote Leutnant zur See Alfons Heimannsberg.

At 11.46 hours, seaman Rudolf Gerke discovered one of the Liberator's rubber dinghies intact that had floated away from debris. Gerke inflated it using the oxygen bottle and climbed in with two others. With no oars, the three were at the mercy of the waves, which kept them away from their colleagues floating in the water. About an hour and a half later Schamong, Heimannsberg, Emil Giesbert, and Heinz Hamm, who were helping to support a junior seaman floating on his back, succeeded in reaching the dinghy. Exhausted, the four were hauled in by the other three survivors. Cold wet and uncomfortable, the dinghy drifted on the ocean as day drifted into night ending their first eventful day at sea. The wind increased, and the sea roughened and waves began to break into the dinghy, keeping all seven men baling incessantly. Then during a lull, Schamong told Gerke, Max Friedrich, Erno Mahns, to settle down as best they could. They slept only fitfully, longing for the morning.

Waking they found the wind had dropped to ten or eleven knots but the sea was still rough. Later in the day visibility improved and at 14.50 hours on 12 August, they saw what looked like a flying boat in the distance.

'Fliegendes Stachelschwein,' said Schamong.[94]

'I reckon it's searching for their plane,' said Giesbert as he followed the progress of the flying boat. Its track would take it right to their dinghy. The Sunderland of 204 continued to come ever closer.

Flight Sergeant Charlie Watkinson[95] piloting H-Harry heard over the intercom the words 'Dinghy' spoken, by Flight Sergeant Wilfred Stones, in his South Yorkshire accent, 'five – I count five.'

'Okay starting run, prepare to drop Lindholme gear,' said Watkinson, 'drop now,' he said over the intercom. Flying Officer Patrick Dempsey sent a signal to Bathurst, 'located one dinghy with 5 survivors in position 12.28N/19.18E send immediate relief.' Watkinson continued circling above the dinghy until 18.35 hours, their last act saw Gunter and Gillham release markers and flame floats around the dinghy.

Flight Lieutenant John Pare in the relief Sunderland *F-Freddie* left Bathhurst Bay at 23.23 house, and finally found the yellow dinghy at 04.45 hours, about 240 miles southwest of Dakar.

'Send sighting report,' Pare told Reginald Saffier, then 'Stand by, chaps,' he said, 'I'm going to have a closer look!'

F-Freddie passed at zero feet over the dinghy, then climbed and banked around back. At the right moment Godden lobbed out a cluster of pyrotechnics, a flare, marine markers, and flame floats, 'Markers gone.'

Just behind the pilot's and second pilot's seats on the left-hand side of the flying boat, was Reginald Saffier's navigator's desk, where he was now plotting a course to intercept HMS *Clarkia*, who was also searching for the ditched aircrew. The Sunderland departed.

Meanwhile, Wing Commander Percy Hatfield[96] DFC OC of 95 Squadron had been diverted to search for survivors upon hearing that Trigg had been under fire from a U-boat. He arrived at the scene in Sunderland *S-Sugar*. Hatfield swept in, dropping further supplies while his navigator sent a sighting report back to Bathurst.

F-Freddie found HMS *Clarkia* and Saffier used a lamp to convey the news of the dinghy. The Flower-class Corvette battled through rough seas to reach the dinghy at 06.31 hours, as the sun was rising. Naval ratings threw scramble nets over the side. The rubber dinghy went back and forth in the swell, as each man made his way up the net to scramble aboard. 'German's!' within seconds Naval ratings appeared with rifles at the ready as the bosun searched for concealed weapons. Meanwhile an able seaman retrieved the dinghy. Lined up, at a gesture from the chief petty officer, the seven stood or sat on the edge of number three hatch with their hands behind their back. Schamong stood waiting for the captain, Captain Stanley Darling (RANR). He stepped forward and saluted and stuck out his right hand, 'Oberleutnant zur See Klemens Schamong,' Darling responded and asked, '*Sprechen Sie Englisch?*'[97]

'Yes,' replied Schamong, 'I want to tell you about your courageous flyer'.

The prisoners were placed in the mess, the only survivors from the fifty-three-strong U-boat's crew. Klemens Schamong assisted by Leutnant Emil Giesbert, the Engineer Officer, gave an account of the battle with the Lloyd's Liberator: 'Between 9 and 10 o'clock on August 11, while on the surface we sighted an aircraft and engaged it with all our guns. At first we thought it was a Sunderland, but we now know it we were mistaken. As the aircraft was coming into attack it was hit and set on fire, apparently near the tail. Although the aircraft was well alight, the pilot pressed home his attack, released his bombs from a height of forty-nine feet, attacking from the port quarter and crossing the submarine just aft of the conning tower.'

A momentary pause, then Schamong and Giesbert obliged, by telling Darling of their sincere admiration of the pilot's courage in not allowing the submarine's heavy and accurate fire and the very precarious condition of his aircraft to deter him from pressing home his attack. Schamong continued, 'as the aircraft passed over us we could see our cannon fire entering through its open bomb bay doors. The depth charges exploded near the U-boat and I momentarily lost sight of the aircraft. However, I recovered from the shock in time to see the aircraft dive straight into the sea about 200 yards from the submarine, there being no survivors.' Then Giesbert spoke 'Both myself and my commanding officer were on deck through the engagement and are in entire agreement regarding this account.'

In weeks to come, Air Vice Marshal John Cole-Hamilton sent this account to Lloyd Trigg's squadron, the Commander-in-Chief of Coastal Command Air Marshal Sir John Slessor and the hierarchy of the Air Ministry. A recommendation was made for the New Zealander to be awarded a posthumous Victoria Cross based on information given by Schamong and Giesbert.[98] With endless papers going back and forth finally agreement was reached by both parties and on Tuesday 2 November an announcement in the *London Gazette*, stated that His Majesty King George VI had the honour of being graciously pleased to confer the Victoria Cross was to be posthumously awarded in recognition of most conspicuous bravery to Flying Officer Lloyd Allan Trigg DFC of the Royal New Zealand Air Force. In New Zealand the Defence Minister James Allen spoke the following day in Wellington 'the result of his gallant action his Victoria Cross was the seventh such award to a New Zealander and the second to the Royal New Zealand Air Force.'

One year later, the Victoria Cross was presented to Lloyd's widow Nola Trigg at Park Avenue, Whangarei, Northland; 'It is hard for me today to realise that I am the same woman who kissed him goodbye as he rode off to war and heard him shout "see you soon," said Nola as she was handed the medal case and the citation by Marshal of The Royal Air Force Cyril Newall Governor-General of New Zealand.[99] The final two sentences of Trigg's citation declare that the Liberator captain's exploit stood out in the

Battle of the Atlantic 'epic of grim determination and high courage. His was the path of duty that leads to glory'.

With the ending of the Second World War there had been a hollow feel to the celebrations for many. 'VE or VJ day doesn't mean much to us as my husband died, and we haven't heard how much of a pension allowance I'll receive,' wrote Nola in consecutive years to the RNZAF.[100] Nola never remarried and, sadly, she struggled to bring up their two sons alone eventually selling both VC and DFC medals in the 1960s to buy a house in the Onehunga district of Auckland. In 1998 the posthumous VC group came up for auction and were purchased at Spink Auctioneers on 6 May for the Lord Ashcroft collection.[101] Uniquely amongst the 1,353 VCs gazetted to this day, Trigg's is the only one awarded solely on the evidence given by an enemy combatant.

Chapter 4

Group Captain Gage 'Bill' Sise DSO* DFC*

In a broadcast, Alvar Lidell[102] paid tribute to the 'six, brave and exceedingly skilful men,' that had flown on RAF Coastal Command's latest mission and finished by praising the command's efforts. However, the censor had struck a thick red pencil line through 'the six, brave and exceedingly skilful men,' so listeners heard him praising 'RAF Coastal Command's efforts on their latest mission.' They had been attacking, giving their lives since the first few days of the war but the public perception of their work was minimal.

This was certainly true of the twenty-five-year-old New Zealander pilot, Wing Commander Gage Derwent Sise, more commonly known as 'Bill,' who had flown his first mission on 30 September 1940.[103] He arrived at Dyce to begin his first tour of duty as the Royal Air Force weathered the passing of September, the crisis month of the Battle of Britain. 'As far as the RAF where concerned, this is the critical month of the war: I will be glad when it is past', said Air Commodore John Slessor of the Air Ministry. Since then, Sise had completed a number of missions on the Blenheim fighter. Much of the Command's offensive hopes in 1940 had rested on this twin-engine bomber designed by Frank Barnwell at Bristol Aeroplane Company. The airframe had been adapted to take an aluminium belly pack[104] housing a tubular frame that acted as the platform for four 0.303 machine-guns and their ammunition boxes, machined in Ashford's Railway sheds. The Blenheim IVF powered by two Bristol Mercury XV radial engines, had been developed from the short nose Blenheim IF, little time was lost on the production of this long-range fighter that equipped four RAF Squadrons in Coastal Command which included 254 Squadron.

Harold Hoskins[105] was the commanding officer, an Australian in Royal Air Force wedgewood blue originally from Sydney. In late December 1938, he married Edythe Wilson at St. Johns Church, Stanmore, now twenty-two months later, Hoskins, Edythe and their year-old daughter were entertaining Pilot Officer 'Bill' Sise and the injured Flight Lieutenant William Bain[106] who had just come out of the station sick quarters after receiving lacerations to his derriere, with Sise having misjudged the landing and promptly ripped off the Blenheim's undercarriage on an unseen dry stonewall. With no undercarriage Sise performed a belly landing, he felt the plane scrape along the grass come to a sudden halt. It wasn't the gentlest of landings, unfortunately Bairwell's long-nose design did not hold together and shattered. Shards of Perspex from the shattering nose section caught William Bain's behind when thrown forward face-first on impact.

With William lying literally face-down while medical staff attended to his injuries, Sise was convinced that he would be posted with immediate effect. Fortunately, Sise did not get a red endorsement stamp in his logbook as Hoskins regarded the accident as 'pilot unfamiliar with airfield perimeter layout'.

The following morning, he visited the crumpled Blenheim in Hanger B. 'There was no point in dwelling on my first brush with death or injury the day before. We just had to get on with things, straight away,' he saids.

Sise had joined the squadron in late August. He was a tall, broad-shouldered man, with a clear complexion. His father[107] hailed from Dunedin, New Zealand, where 'Bill's grandfather George at the turn of the century had emigrated from Boston Massachusetts and in due course formed a successful business partnership with fellow American, John Bates. Bates Sise and Company initially served the Otago Gold Rush in 1891, before branching into the import and export business.

Sise rarely talked of his childhood, either to his friends, or younger brother, Royse. Yet he did pick brief moments from his childhood – the officious Victorian up bringing, his nanny, boats leaving the harbour at Dunedin and going away aged nine then 'coming back home to Dunedin in November 1926, to find that I had a younger brother!' Sise attended the prestigious Otago Boy's High School in the city where he swam competitively and achieved exemplary exam results before going into the family business and attending Otago University to gain a commerce degree.

Joining the New Zealand Civil Reserve, he learnt to fly at Otago Aero Club and volunteered for the Air Force. After Elementary Flying Training School at Taieri, Sise was posted to Wigram. Finally leaving New Zealand in early May 1940 a young commissioned officer, thirsting for adventure off to Britain on a seven-week journey, with the final leg through the Atlantic, dodging marauding U-boats and docked in England at the beginning of July. After attending the newly established 1 (Coastal) Operational Training Unit at Silloth, Cumbria – where he carried out a conversion course onto Blenheims and received an 'very above average' assessment – and was among a dozen New Zealanders joining 254 Squadron at Dyce, in Aberdeenshire, in 18 Group, and it was as a member of the squadron he had his disastrous first flight in a Blenheim fighter.

He wasn't impressed by the Blenheim's speed or it's grace. Crewed up at last with Sergeants Leonard Murphy and George Cox, 'Bill' Sise flew his first mission on 30 September – and it was a brief one too, to Invergordon as air cover for the *Ulster Monarch*. His next few sorties followed on a rotational basis against targets on the Norwegian coast.[108]

Sise on Tuesday 12 January 1941 was fortunate to emerge unscathed on a trip to Bergen on Norway's southwestern coast. The target had been an unidentified merchantman, in weather that was far from ideal with persistent rain showers. 'Its white superstructure made it stand out,' wrote Murphy. Pilot Officer Kenneth Illingworth DFC[109] in *B-Beer* was suffering from intermittent R/T failure on the flight that Norman Clarke fixed fifteen miles short of the enemy coast with a pair of scissors and sticking plasters from their planes first aid box. 'Well,' said Illingworth, 'we've made it!' The Blenheims attacked from 250 feet rather than 500 or more. Experiencing no flak, Sise dropped his four-20lb. fragmentation bombs, then followed Illingworth's lead and strafed the vessel's decks. As Sise turned away westwards for home in *J-Johnnie* George Beaton shouted 'One-oh-Nines, at three o'clock, high.'[110]

Sise immediately took whatever evasive action he could to reach the cloud base as the lone attacker attempted to get on *J-Johnnie's* tail. Beaton gave him a short burst of fifty rounds from his single Vickers K machine gun at 150 to 100 yards as the Blenheim surged forward to be enveloped in cloud. Moments earlier, Illingworth's *B-Beer*, was under attack by the second Messerschmitt but he too managed to evade and did not see the German fighter again. At 12.55 hours *B-Beer* and *J-Johnnie* touched down on the grass at Dyce after 'Bill' Sise's first encounter with the Me109E.

Sise's steady rise despite his youth to Flying Officer on 4 May 1941 was achieved by completing a variety of dangerous missions in the squadron's now obsolete Blenheim IVF's. The strain on Sise's CO George Bernard-Smith was immense with his crews horribly over-stretched, as Atlantic escort duty resumed from Aldergrove, Northern Ireland. It was not only the Germans that Sise and his crew had to be wary of when relieving colleagues on a westward route. Climbing to 1,000 feet out of Aldergrove to Lough Erne, Sise passed over a narrow strip of land belonging to Eire between Bundoran and Ballyshannon to Donegal Bay. Any slight deviation from their course over the towns, the Blenheim would receive spasmodic rifle and machine gun fire. It was a fine day, and Sise, after roughly an hour, found the convoy. Murphy signalled the lead British escort using his Aldis lamp, a coded letter that was acknowledged. The Blenheim turned to port and proceeded anti-clockwise around the convoy with Murphy signalling each escort ship in turn. Hours went by it was monotonous sweeping over the ships which where keeping good station each line numbered four or five ships. No stragglers and smoke kept to a minimum, although Cox spotted one with bomb damage to its deck.[111]

It was a tremendous responsibility, with the average age of a crew being just twenty-four, flying to keep the supply of war materials and perishable goods to British ports open. For this reason, Bernard-Smith sent Sise, Murphy and Cox, as he had done with other crews, to the Royal Liver Building in Liverpool, headquarters of the Battle of the Atlantic. Waiting for them was a Wren named Bell who led them down steps to one of the floors to a series of RAF Coastal Command departments. Sise and his crew spent five days from 09.00 hours until 17.00 hours at the headquarters to get a greater insight into the battle than was available at squadron level.

It was then back to Aldergrove, for a maximum effort against a Fw 200 patrol. Covering a large expanse of water George Bernard-Smith led the sortie; it would be one of his last. Flying between detachments on Wednesday 10 December to Dyce in deteriorating weather, he and his crew were flying over clear countryside the next *P-Pip* plunged into high ground. There was an explosion and the aircraft disintegrated with Bernard-Smith and the rest of his crew perishing.[112]

Wing Commander Roderick McConnell DFC[113] took over the squadron. 'I'd done quite well on Beau's,' said McConnell, 'I think that was the reason Philip Joubert chose me to go and lead 254. It was a nice interlude.'

June 1942, saw Beaufighter VICs started to arrive the interlude lasted five months, in which time details of torpedo training[114] were mapped out, while the importance of security was stressed. Both at Dyce, Gosport, and Abbotsinch in the parish of Renfrew, where the new torpedo squadron was now taking shape, security was paramount. No one was to breath a word of their new role. All mail was religiously censored and phone lines tapped. By the end of Sunday, 9 August – it was the unit's first full day as 254 Torpedo Squadron – there were, as prescribed, ten Beaufighters, fifteen crews, and fifty-four ground staff.

Training was rigorous, and, given good serviceability and weather it was anticipated they would complete the flying programme three days behind schedule and by 16 August, McConnell, Bill Sise, with Flight Lieutenant John McMichael and Pilot Officer Frederick Wright were able to carry out a formation attack against HMS *Mistral* under the watchful eye of former Royal Navy Commander Christopher Dalrymple-Hay,[115] now an Air Commodore from the destroyer's bridge. As they approached, Sise dropped low then thundered over water, and as close to 250 feet as he could judge and released his torpedo at 800 yards range. Despite the simulated anti-aircraft fire, Sise had had a perfect run to the 1,825-ton former French Bourrasque-class destroyer.

Dalrymple-Hay and three other senior officers tracked the torpedoes, as the four individual pilots did not observe the progress of their tin-fish as they took evasive action immediately after the drop. 'On our first run in, all four of us attacked simultaneously each scoring a hit. A most encouraging first attempt!'[116] wrote McConnell. Daily low-level training sorties commenced from dawn to dusk, over water for all aircrew, with Sise determined to judge for himself flying with his navigator Harold Bibby whether flying at 120 feet was practicable to release their torpedoes.

Bibby had chosen to be a navigator. After leaving school, aged seventeen, he had got a job then decided to join the RAF instead. His family tried to discourage him, because of the carnage of the last war, but his mind was made up and having got high percentages in geography and mathematics when taking his Ordinary Certificate, he thought that being a navigator would be the best way to utilise the two subjects he excelled at.

Thoroughly enjoying the course, he qualified as a navigator, earning his crown above his third stripe in the second week of November 1942. Having been through OTU he was posted to 254 Squadron and was hand-picked by Sise to fly with him.

Arriving at Dyce to take over command from McConnell was Wing Commander Robert 'Rex' Mack he had the experience required, but such men affiliated to Coastal Command were hard to come by; not many had tours under their belts and were available for immediate transfer from their squadrons. As Bill Sise pointed out, the number of those who finished coastal tours was not high – 'The loss rate was colossal.'

Mack had been born in Chelsea, London, and had grown up in a loving and close family, being educated at Lynchmere, Eastbourne. Aged seventeen in 1930, Mack unexpectedly took a job with P&O Cruises. Disembarking from New York five years later he reported to an RAF Centre applied and was accepted for a short service commission. Then found himself at the Uxbridge Depot was posted to 4 Flying Training School at Sueir in Egypt.

Awarded his wings, he returned by ship to Plymouth and was posted to 48 Squadron at Manston. Here Mack was able to pursue his love of golf at St Augustine's Golf Club when not flying Avro Ansons, managing to get his handicap down to nine. As a flying officer he was hurriedly posted from flying Ansons to the bigger, heavier Vickers Vildebeest, operated by 22 Squadron at Thorney Island, while converting to the Bristol Beaufort. A move to North Coates in April 1940 saw Mack sowing magnetic 'M' mines, in channels German shipping had to pass through, his first being on Monday 15 April. Just a few months later, in December, Mack lived up to the squadron motto 'valiant and brave' as the recipient of the Distinguished Flying Cross. Having four months earlier on the evening of the 17 September, led six Beauforts into Cherbourg Harbour flying so low that Mack watched flak light up the sky above them. Mack got his torpedo away and dodged the ships masts that suddenly loomed towards them. He saw one of their fellow Beauforts hit and burst into flames, then a moment later Sergeant Norman Hearn-Phillips came on the R/T 'Rex I'm hit.'

Every gun and small arm on the ground was firing at them as they turned for home. Hearn-Phillips coaxed his plane home with rudder and hydraulics shot away so the flaps and the undercarriage were inoperable. They made it back to Thorney Island where, jeered on by Mack, Hearn-Phillips safely belly-landed the Beaufort.

Losses were being suffered on most missions, one here two there, but Mack managed to escape station life by driving through the country roads to Marshchapel roughly four miles from North Coates. Here he was able to get some restpite with his wife Joyce. 'I went to bed,' noted Mack in the autumn of 1941, 'troubled by the thought that in four weeks, fourteen aircrew were dead on missions or flying accidents.'[117]

August 1942 the twenty-nine-year-old pilot was given his first command, and with it some ever changing crews and about 500 men. Under his energetic and knowledgeable command, he began to mould 254 Squadron into one of the best in the command and its future role as a leading torpedo squadron in the first of Coastal Command's Strike Wings based at North Coates.

By the time of Robert Mack's arrival, however, far away to the south, events were finely moving fast. After nine months of paper pushing acceptance of the Bristol Beaufighter as a strike aircraft eventually signed off by the Admiralty and Air Ministry during a meeting with the assistance of an expert adviser. For Captain Dudley Peyton-Ward naval liaison officer at Northwood; 'it had been an extremely frustrating experience for Joubert to get them all to agree even on this point, let alone the formation of a shipping strike wing,' he wrote to Hector Bolitho[118] in the first summer after the war. But there was still much to be done.

'Bill' Sise along with Bibby continued tactical exercises in their Beaufighter with fellow aircrews, against targets in The Wash. There were more pilots and navigators arriving to. These included Pilot Officer Raymond Price,[119] from Gloucester, who had enlisted in 1939 and was returning to the fold of 254 after being recommended for a commission by McConnell. He joined the celebrations on Tuesday 29 September in the Officers Mess after the squadron dropped thirteen running torpedoes, twelve of which were successful by Beaufighters in formation. At these festivities was Wing Commander Howard Fraser OBE[120] of 236 Squadron the other unit at North Coates. Fraser had graduated from Cranwell, where he won the converted Royal Air Force's R. M. Groves Memorial Essay Prize, later serving with 25 Squadron at Hawkinge and taking part in the 1934 Hendon Air Display where he was one of three pilots flying Hawker Furies tied together performing aerobatics.[121] After serving aboard, Fraser was posted as adjutant to Oxford University Air Squadron. With roughly three years at the Air Ministry he finally managed to get released after a refresher course at Silloth in September 1942 and posted to command an operational squadron.

Training continued at a pace for 254 Squadron with their Adjutant Flight Lieutenant Arthur Beevor roughly calculating they'd visited over sixteen airfields since June, this having jeopardized a number of healthy marriages across the breath of the unit. Finally, on Wednesday 11 November 1942, they arrived back at North Coates.

Meanwhile, at Coastal Command's Eastbury Park, the results of the trials were viewed very favourably. 'From the Beaufighter trials,' wrote Hector Bolitho, 'it would appear that very little latitude can be allowed in height and speed factors at the time of release, according to Squadron Leader 'Bill' Sise in a recent trial from RAF Whitchurch.'

236 Squadron's missions continued on 17 November, but the weather was unsettled throughout the two following days as 236 and 254 aircrew practiced in driving rain. 'Our task was to attack important convoys transporting raw materials from Norway to the Dutch port of Rotterdam,'[122] wrote 'Bill' Sise, 'Howard's 236 were armed with cannon, machine guns and bombs whilst on 254 we had cannon and torpedoes.' The object of all the exercises and training was for the planes to fly at sea level until target sighted, the leader would fly straight for the target whilst the remainder opened out to starboard and port respectively to beat up the enemy escorts and flak-ships and leave 254 a corridor for our Torbeaus to drop the tin-fish on the button.

The preparation, though, was over on Friday 20 November 1942 the North Coates Strike Wing became operational. Air Commodore

Albert Durston, the Acting Senior Air Staff Officer (SASO) at Coastal Command HQ sent the final Operation Order through, and Mack, his flight commanders David Robertson DFC, and Sise, together with Fraser and his two flight commanders Squadron Leaders Geoffrey Edney and George 'Dusky' Denholm prepared for their first strike wing mission to be mounted.

Two Spitfire VB's of 167 Squadron at RAF Ludham had returned with worthy results from a shipping reconnaissance. Flight Sergeants Albert Featherstone and Walter Yaholnitsky[123] took off at 09.25 hours. It was a perfect day about and twelve miles from the Dutch coast at Texel they sighted a convoy. Tracking it until 10.08 hours, they then made a run for home. Touching down at 10.55 hours, the Intelligence officer wanted to know what they had found. 'Merchantmen,' Yaholnitsky told him. 'Shadowed the convoy from a distance of two miles, twelve to sixteen merchantmen estimated 1000 tons to 5000 tons, no balloons were seen. Largest vessel had two funnels. Smaller vessels could not be defined as escorts. Visibility ten miles, no cloud just sunshine and appeared to be broken cloud over Dutch coast.'

Immediate word had been passed to the Admiralty's Operational Intelligence Centre known as the Citadel, in London. Here the information was studied a conference took place on the scrambler telephone with Durston and Peyton-Ward in the deep underground bunker that was Coastal Command's Headquarters Operation Room only a few hundred yards away from Eastbury Park. Operational orders were issued, notifying 236 and 254 Squadrons. Durston then sent copies to Air Vice Marshal Malcolm Henderson the SASO at Fighter Command HQ. Henderson in turn issued his own orders to the individual fighter squadron that was to act as 'top cover', inadvertently changing the timing of the rendezvous by ten minutes. This major error had not been corrected when details of the operation were issued to 167 Squadron at Ludham.

At North Coates, prior to the mission, crews arrived at their machine for an imminent take-off. Eighteen Bristol Hercules radial engines roared into life, and nine Beaufighters took to the skies heading south to Gosport to get their 'tin fish' hooked up.[124] They began landing again at around 13.10 hours. The activity was then feverish as twenty-six Beaufighters were loaded with 20mm cannon, 0.303 belts and drums of bullets for the gas-operated Vickers K machine-gun. Flight Lieutenant Norman Virgin clambered into his Beaufighter L-London for some pre-flight checks and noticed the wing mounted machine-guns were still exposed, on the starboard side. He quickly found an armourer who hurriedly completed the job.

At 14.00 hours the crews of 236 and 254 Squadron's reported to the Operations Room and noisily took their seats. Silence descended as Wing Commander Robert Mack began the briefing, detailing those who were to attack which target in the convoy: also reminding two of his crews – Pilot Officer Angus Cameron and Flying Officer Robert Sargeant – that it was their business to help silence the flak-ships. Howard Fraser pointed out the last known position of each of the flak-ships using a borrowed billiard cue. Most of these vessels officially named Trawler Type Auxiliaries (TTA) where known as flak-ships to aircrew. All had anti-aircraft guns that were automatic, with a rate of fire of 180-200 rounds per minute, but the four-barrels could continually fire 800 rounds per minute with a quad magazine change every six seconds. There were also 88mm, 40mm and 37mm on board. A single cannon or 88-millimetre shell from any of these anti-aircraft guns had the potential to bring down or obliterate a Beaufighter.

There was a further potential danger from Jagdgeschwader 1 based at Schiphol, close to the planned area of attack. The opposing aircraft were Focke-Wulf 190s which were much faster than Beaufighters and had formidable firepower – 20mm cannons and machine-guns. The men were then briefed by Flying Officer John Gordon acting Meteorological Officer, who declared the weather was due to be fairly clear across East Anglia, but there would be cloud over the target, with light winds. Lastly the Station Commander spoke for a few minutes, winding up with a cheery 'good luck and good hunting'.

Prior to take-off Beevor collected an assortment of material from the twenty-four 254 Squadron men taking part, before they disappeared into the crew room. Coming out, the men were wearing either their varying shades of blue battle dress or Irvin sheep skin flying jacket, clutching parachute packs and Mae Wests. At 14.45 hours the men walked to their respective aircraft, each Beaufighter standing proud, clutching a torpedo under its belly.

At *R-Robert*, Sise grasped the hand rails in the roof of the fuselage and swung quickly into the pilots seat, then strapped himself in, and sat on his parachute pack that was connected to a finely entwined short lanyard that linked a K-type dinghy pack. Behind him, newly-promoted Bibby clambered aboard. Just forward of the main wing spar, was Bibby's small desk attached to two rear tubular uprights that formed part of the support to his chair to enable him to look out of the hood and for him to use the rear machine-gun.

Sise started *R-Robert*'s engines, and then ran up each of them to 1,000 rpm, checking temperatures, pressures, magneto and the vacuum pumps. Everything appeared to be correct. He then asked Bibby on the intercom if all was okay, with a positive response Sise sat and waited to move.

Nearby, in *J-Johnnie*, Arthur Mackenzie[125] was still in a jubilant mood after a double celebration; being promoted to flight sergeant on the very same day as his adorable Norma's twenty second birthday, four days previously. However Mackenzie's mood darkened as the selector switch on the starboard side of the cockpit to release their torpedo was found to be inoperable with the warning light showing on the instrument panel indicating that the torpedo had been released!

This was a major problem. In the rear fuselage, Harold Knight heard Mackenzie tell him the bad news, then heard him add, 'We can't even use the spare aircraft as it will take too long to mount our tin fish onto the plane, so we don't get to go!'

Clambering out, around them the rest were on the move, led by Mack in *E-Edward* and followed by David Robertson in *G-George*. Behind Robertson was meant to be Flying Officer Angus Cameron in *S-Sugar* but instead it was Flight Lieutenant John Stephenson in *A-Apple*, it was 15.05 hours, as this procession rose into the air.

Behind Angus McIntosh, was Frederick Poore, and then came Sargent and Heskel in *P-Pip*, finally after Thomas Carson and Sydney Parsons was 'Bill' Sise, who once he received the green Aldis light, opened up his throttles and gathered speed across the concrete, and climbing into the air to join the armada before it headed for the coast. Sise had taken off for his 109th mission.

Cameron and his navigator Flight Sergeant John Crossley could only watch with mounting impatience as their aircraft's release wiring for the torpedo was fixed. At 15.10 hours, Flight Sergeant John Turton of 236 Squadron lifted off from the ground, with Cameron finally moving off five minutes later. They were at last on their way.

The formation wheeled away southwards towards RAF Ludham twenty-nine miles away. Half an hour later twenty-five Beaufighters were circling anti-clockwise waiting for the Spitfire escort. As Howard Fraser made a turn port in *O-Orange* to arc around for the tenth or eleventh time he became impatient. 'There wasn't any sign of the fighters,' he complained. So, Fraser the Strike Leader, set course for the target.

The Beaufighters scampered after *O-Orange* as Fraser dived for the deck and made off towards the Hook of Holland. However, the anti-flak section on the outer edge of the main formation encountered a patch of low cloud or sea mist at fifty feet and Denholm, Lee, Clarke and Ellis because of radio silence flew on independently, out of sight of each other.

It was impossible to map-read over the sea, which meant relying on the compass and taking regular drift readings, for undetected wind variations. This meant the lead navigator, Flying Officer Reginald Griffin, had to use all the knowledge and skill gained from his recent refresher at Gosport. At 15.35 hours, both the anti-flak and the torpedo aircraft, including Sise's trio, closed toward the Dutch coast. Staying on the planned track of 110 degrees, the estimated point of contact with the southbound convoy was fifteen miles away, giving an estimated time of arrival of 16.02 hours.

At a certain bearing, the remaining six anti-flak Beaufighters climbed to the operational height of 2,000 feet, giving them all a panoramic view of Dutch landmarks; Amsterdam, The Hague, Rotterdam and the mouth of the New Meuse. Fraser spotted, roughly five miles off the coast just north of The Hook, ten enemy vessels. There was one large merchantman with the remainder seemed to be flak-ships. Below, Robert Mack brought his nine TorBeaus up to the dropping height of 175 feet.

Fraser's navigator, Reginald Griffin heard 'Targets sighted'. Griffin had been excited by the entire operation, for it had meant two days off missions and plenty of practice flying in tight formations, low flying and dummy attacks. It had been terrific fun and certainly more exciting than the normal boring reconnaissance patrols and dinghy searches he'd flown in recent weeks with his regular pilot Sergeant Donald Munson.

At around 16.01 hours, in *O-Orange*, Griffin heard, 'Cock cannon. Close doors,' Griffin climbed over the ammunition boxes with the agility of a gymnast and pulled the levers of the four 20mm cannon; these were not usually cocked before take-off for fear of an accidental discharge. He unclipped the metal fasteners holding the two folding armoured doors and slammed the two shut between himself and his pilot. Then went back to his position and pulled back the cocking handle Vickers K gun. Twisting around he could just about see the convoy.

A moment later, Pilot Officer Mark Bateman called[126] out, 'Strike Leader there are fighters about!' then, 'Focke Wulfs! Keep your eyes peeled everybody!'

Fraser acknowledged. 'Griffin watch our tail.'

'Attack, attack attack!' The voice of Fraser came urgently over the R/T into everyone's ears. The enemy vessels were straight ahead. The flak-ships had opened up with their heavy calibre weapons.

'Bit aggressive, aren't they?' commented Griffin.[127]

Fraser was concentrating on one of the flak-ships. As he closed rapidly to within 1,000 yards, the aircraft was met by a flurry of tracer rising up towards him. He pressed his firing button. Cannon hit the ship's superstructure. The vessel loomed towards him. The four cannon continued to chatter, peppering the vessels mast as *O-Orange* hurtled over it and beyond towards the mainland. Suddenly the aircraft stood still.

Close behind Pilot Officer Leonard Lee, in *R-Robert*, saw Fraser's Beaufighter take a direct hit from a heavy calibre 88mm shore battery. In less than a second *O-Orange* exploded. Those still coming in nearby saw it – a mighty explosion. There was no escape for the crew.[128]

'Strike leader's gone!' said Lee into the intercom.

Pilot Officer Alfred Treadwell in the rear of *R-Robert* was stunned and went pale. That was his normal ride![129]

The tragic demise of 236 Squadron's Wing Commander had underlined just how dangerous and difficult a mission this was. Then the flak ceased.

'One nineties at eleven o'clock high!' Flight Sergeant Hugh Haddow exclaimed over the R/T.

The route the convoy was sailing ran pretty close to Schiphol airfield, from where anti-aircraft fire could be heard. The HQ of 1/JG immediately put out an alarm. Unteroffizier Otto Schmid rushed out and sprinted to his Focke Wulf, which was kept at readiness. Right behind him was his wingman. Within a couple of minutes, both were lifting off the runway and retracting the undercarriage in pursuit of the maritime raiders. Pulling back their sticks they gained altitude for maximum surprise and advantage.[130]

'Okay!' Squadron Leader Geoffrey Edney called out response to his navigator's warning. Harrow saw the two machines surge towards them, as he wedged the butt of his machine-gun firmly into his right shoulder.

Moments later, Edney's Beaufighter *C-Charlie*, was under attack. The two Fw 190s of 1/JG careered in towards the anti-flak Beaufighters. Streams of cannon and machine-gun rounds hammered into *C-Charlie*. Edney struggled with irresponsive controls, rounds having shredded cables. He called to Haddow but there was no reply, the intercom was dead. A moment later flames billowed out. *C-Charlie* hurtled into an uncontrollable dive plunging into the sea, raising a furrow of white foam before the blinding flash.[131]

Warrant Officer Alwynn 'Al' Bonnett flying *D-Dog*, registered the red glare but the Canadian now had his own battle to fight. The pair of German fighters banked steeply, with one attacking Bonnett. He instinctively reached across to flick the bomb release switch jettisoning the two 250lb. high explosive bombs from underneath each the wing. Suddenly the Beaufighter lurched upwards as the weight of the bombs left. Bonnett then pushed the nose forward and dived, with the air speed indicator creeping up to 250 mph. He flew low over the water taking evasive action to escape. The second Focke Wulf latched onto Flight Sergeant John Turton, closing in on his starboard quarter whilst his navigator, Flight Sergeant Robert Alexander, waited until the German fighter was within three hundred yards and rattled away defiantly with his single Vickers gun, firing all 500 rounds. Turton was also forced to ditch his bombs whilst under attack. A bullet hit the canopy, and Perspex splinters spat around the confined space, before more cannon shells and machine-gun bullets struck. Turton desperately tried to shake of his pursuer at levels down to thirty feet. Fortunately, *G-George* was spared as the Fw 190 broke off and suddenly their pursuer was gone, ammunition or fuel spent.

As 236 Squadron Beaufighters were being mauled by the German fighters, the remaining nine TorBeaus with their 'tin fish' were wheeling to starboard to start an 'S' manoeuvre to attack the merchant vessel *Schiff 49* from the Dutch coastline on their port quarter. This was to be the start of a bumpy ride.

Robert Mack within four minutes of the initial sighting he instinctively lined up *Schiff 49* dropped his 'tin-fish' made haste and set course for North Coates. In the rear, Flight Sergeant Arthur Jackson[132] noted an orange flash dead amidships with a mushroom cloud of black smoke, although it was not necessarily *E-Eggs* own torpedo. At 16.05 hours, Pilot Officer Ronald Hodge in *B-Baker* was buffeted by heavy flak and small arms being pumped into the sky. It was an uncomfortable ride as bullets and shards of flak clattered against the Beaufighter. Suddenly, the instrument panel lit up as starboard engine warning light flickered. Hodge instinctively jettisoned the torpedo and the Beaufighter was jolted upward with the weight gone.

'Can you see any other damage to *B-Baker*?' he asked Flight Sergeant John Kirkup over the intercom.

'Just starboard engine,' came the reply.

Four minutes later *B-Baker* turned for home, with the starboard engine dead Hodge managed to evade two German fighters by hugging the wave tops on a heading for Norfolk.

One minute behind, Squadron Leader 'Bill' Sise also reached *Schiff 49* through lots of flak. *R-Robert* survived but then had to face the Focke Wulfs.

'Fighter three o'clock,' called Sergeant Harold Bibby into the intercom.

'Corkscrewing – now,' replied Sise.

No sooner had Bibby told the New Zealander than a second Fw 190 roared in, cannons and machine-guns firing, then slid between them and the foreboding sea below. Sise wheeled the Beaufighter hard over when another German fighter attacked, this time daring to get closer. Sise's was one of the most skilled in the squadron, yet he could not shake off the pair. Swerving and yawning the aircraft as much as he dared, he even flew at zero feet with his propellers leaving a wash behind them; but the two fighters trailed *R-Robert*. First the lead aircraft closed until almost point-blank range, and opened fire with cannon and machine-guns, swinging the nose so that it raked the width of the aircraft. Then the pursuing wingman copied. *R-Robert* was been hit in the tailplane, port and starboard wing and outer petrol tank. 'In total the pair made fifteen attacks,' recalled Sise, 'but at least we were still alive.'[133]

With a puff of smoke from their engines, the pair of Luftwaffe pilots broke off and suddenly their two pursuers were gone out of ammunition or fuel almost spent.

At least Sise and Bibby could concentrate on getting home.

It was now 16.15 hours, just four of the ten 254 Squadron Beaufighters remained unscathed after the attack; Wing Commander Robert Mack's *E-Egg*, Robinson's *G-George*, Stephenson's *A-Apple*, and Flying Officer Thomas Carson's *M-Mother*. Before 17.16 hours all four had made it back to North Coates. But while these crews were being de-briefed and then tucking into strawberry jam sandwiches and tea, across this Lincolnshire airfield, the silence of the later afternoon had been stultifying. The minutes ticked by and there was still no distant hum of radial engines to break the silence of the early evening. At 18.00 the duty staff received word to stand down.[134]

It was a long and lonely slog home, as *R-Robert* was coaxed across the North Sea. Sise kept a watchful eye on the instruments, as Bibby carefully plotted a course, he reckoned it was pretty good and soon, Sise saw Felixstowe and the River Orwell that snaked through the town, and which led to Ipswich and north-east, towards Wattisham. So they kept going, low over the rooftops whilst revaluating their situation.

'We've not enough fuel to land at Wattisham, even with the engines throttled right back,' Sise told Bibby over the intercom.

'Lots of flat pastures off to port at Frinton-on-Sea,'[135] came back the reply.

Sise managed to find an open field, and Harold Bibby instinctively adopted his crash position, drawing up his knees, waiting for the impact and what could be his last moments. But then the Beaufighter seemed to glide, just above the stall, and with the ground ahead clear of oak trees, 17.45 hours Sise managed to slide the Beaufighter gently onto its belly. The propellers buckled, and starboard wing was almost wrenched of as it made its way across the field until it came to a halt just short of the London and North Eastern Railway line. Sise and Bibby clambered out of their battle-scared *R-Robert* and, placing their parachutes on the port wing, Sise picked up the F24 camera and took two slightly out of focus photographs of their forlorn steed.

Cameron's *S-Sugar* crash-landed at Wainsfleet, Hodge in *B-Baker* landed at Docking, Flight Sergeant Frederick Poore in *X-Ray* landed successfully at Woodhall Spa, and Parsons nursed *H-Howe* into North Coates with the hydraulics holed. But, *Q-Queenie* had not been lost, but was lost – hopelessly lost. The return leg had, thankfully, been uneventful for Warrant Officer Angus McIntosh except for one thing: not being able to get a fix on their position.[136]

Perhaps, then, the Beaufighter had been flying the wrong course, even though Pilot Office Dilwyn Tilling, the navigator, had already carefully worked out the bearings for quickest route home. McIntosh had begun to lose faith in the gyrocompass and so, decided to use the secondary, magnetic compass. It was reliable enough, but the needle bounced and flickered in any turn or dive.

At any rate, when they finally crossed the coastline, they were pretty certain it didn't look like Denmark. Eventually, at 15.54 hours and with fuel low, McIntosh ordered Tilling, to get a fix.[137]

'Can I use SOS, Mac?' asked Tilling.

'Use whatever you like, but get us to an airfield,' McIntosh replied.

Tilling tapped out the familiar dots and dashes but for what seemed an eternity there was nothing. He tried again, tapping out the signal once more, and then, finally, to his enormous relief, he received a reply and moments later an answer to his request for range and bearing information to the nearest airfield.

Tilling relayed the new course to McIntosh. 'They're sending us to Swanton Morley.'

Studying the map. 'That's just eighteen miles from Norwich and one hundred and nine miles from base,' he told him. 'It means we're over Norfolk.'

At 18.15 hours on the evening of 20 November 1942, *Q-Queenie* joined the circuit of an unfamiliar airfield and in poor visibility touched down at Swanton Morley with only the tail wheel bursting to announce their arrival after some four hours and sixteen minutes in the air; the last of the 254 Squadron Beaufighters had returned; three others did not make it.

Throughout the evening, telegrams travelled along the telegraph wires between North Coates, Plymouth, Northwood and the Admiralty. There was a pronounced silence as Phillip Joubert[138] read the first telegram with Captain Dudley Peyton-Ward, Senior Naval Liaison Officer stood next to him. Joubert studied the second and third telegram too. The reaction to the attack was one of shock. 'The loss of three crews, and others crashed or badly damaged for a claim of one merchantman and two escort vessels hit. The Strike Wings first mission was a tragic failure,' wrote Peyton-Ward.

With the loss of 236 Squadron's Howard Fraser, the Squadron Adjutant was amazed to discover that Arthur Beevor was there at his office with Robert Mack, 'Bill' Sise and George Denholm. Between them they would write and send the telegrams. Notifications of those missing were sent to next of kin: usually parents or wives. Stella Fraser, married for four years, received her 'It is with deep regret …' telegram two days later, Stella had only recently given birth. Whilst in Halstead village Robert Sargent, mother Kathleen managed to buy a garland of red poppies to place around a recent photograph of he son.

Police Constable Charles Witt[139] noted Squadron Leader Neil 'Nebby' Wheeler DFC lay injured, with suspected broken bones. The were marks in the road caused by braking for thirty feet on the nearside of the white line. The marks then veered across the road for a distance of thirty feet to where it crossed several inches over the white line swerving sharply to the left where the collision accrued. This was the latest in a string of motoring offenses with Wheeler stretching back to 1937, but the most fatal for the twenty-six-year-old.[140] Fortunately, he wasn't driving on this occasion. After recovering from serious injuries sustained in the car crash, Wheeler became an instructor at an OTU.

On Monday 30 November, Neil Wheeler newly promoted to Wing Commander arrived straight from Catfoss, to take over command of 236 Squadron. With moral low Wheeler demanded every scrap of information about the mission, the loss of Wing Commander Fraser, the flight commander and files on aircrew. As the North Coates review got underway 'Bill' Sise retained A Flight and Thomas Cameron became B Flight's commander of 254 Squadron. For Sise's gallantry on his first ill-fated mission he was awarded the DFC.

Five months of training ensued, with 'Bill' Sise and Bibby flying twenty practice flights a day, including navigation, battle formations and low-level flying. Sise marvelled at how his flight was coming together. And there was, an upside to all this daylight flying with 326 non-operational flights accrued during April 1943. 'One effective way to keep us off the booze,' Frederick 'Del' Wright, Raymond Price's pilot commented, 'flying in 'Bill' Sise's flight'.

Certainly, as one of North Coates principal squadrons 254 toiled hard and was sacrificing one or two crews a month. April was no different as, on the 5th of the month, the propellers of Leonard Perkins' and Myer

Savage's Beaufighter clipped the seawater and the plane cartwheeled and broke up, killing the crew instantly. Ten days later Arthur Yeates and Sydney 'Syd' Parsons disappeared north of Flamborough Head whilst co-operating with a Royal Navy destroyer.[141] Sise in *W-Whisky* coordinated the initial search for Yeates and Parsons. Taking-off at 15.25 hours, Sise and five other crews scoured the sea but saw no trace of missing aircraft or dinghy. Searches continued until 19.29 hours on 17 April, when 'Bill' Sise touched down after the sixth search between Flamborough and the Tyne.

254 Squadron's new adjutant, Flight Lieutenant Vyse Millard DFC, a former captain in the Essex Regiment and Royal Air Force in the latter stages of the First World War, had the unenviable task of writing to the next of kin. Sydney Parson's wife Elizabeth was heartbroken 'He was the love of my life; I thought he would be safer every few days when I kissed him goodbye. I needed to believe that.'

The following afternoon, Sunday 18 April 1943 Wheeler's North Coates Strike Wing put their intensive training and tactics to the test with the three squadrons attacking together the convoy. Earlier in the morning a north-bound convoy departing the Hook had been tracked by two Mustangs of 613 Squadron, their photographs 'proved it to be a worthy target,' said Wheeler 'except more information was required.' Within the hour Flight Sergeant Alfred Shimmin from 236 Squadron took off.[142] As he drew closer, he sighted the convoy off Ijmuiden. 'Largest roughly four-thousand ton,' he said over the intercom to his navigator. 'Between four and five flakships.'

'Okay got that Alf,' replied the navigator.

Photographs taken, they then cut and ran. Landing back at North Coates only to see Wheeler waiting for him with Flight Lieutenant Archibald Perry of Photography. F24 camera whisked away, photographs were developed the aircrews were briefed to attack. 'We sat and calmly heard the CO say the main target was the 5,000-ton merchantman,' said navigator Robert Irving the son of a Master in Winchester College.

Irving had put down his music baton to join the Auxiliary Fire Service when war was declared then got into the Royal Artillery.[143] Mud and Irving did not make great bedfellows; it was then that the 27-year-old signed up for the Royal Air Force. Irving went into navigational training and was quickly posted to an OTU flying Blenheims, Beauforts and Beaufighters and then onto 236 Squadron. As navigator to Flying Officer Edmund Jeffreys he spotted *Scharnhorst* which earned the pair the DFC. Edmund was transferred whilst Irving stayed and with the arrival of Wheeler agreed to be his boss' navigator.

Wheeler spoke briefly, followed by the Met Officer and then by Denholm, Wheeler's Number Two. The weather was due to change bringing in a deep depression with gusts of wind to about 30-40 mph, but there was enough time to attack the enemy convoy before this weather front closed in.

There were fifty-four men flying on the mission. Nine Beaufighters or TorBeaus, as they had become known, of 254 led by Sise set off, minutes later another dozen Beaufighters joined, slotting into position led by Wing Commander William Bennett – the anti-flak element. After a further eleven minutes there was a total of twenty-one Beaufighters formed up at roughly 13.30 hours. With Wheeler at the helm his navigator Irving gave him a course for Coltishall to pick up their fighter escort.

They flew into a 10mph north-westerly wind with ten-tenths cloud at 20,000 feet towards Texel, an island north of Den Helder. Massed together were the compact formation, flying at 50 feet, with, high above them, thirty-eight Spitfires and Mustangs from 118, 167 and 613 Squadrons, flying as top cover.

At 14.30 hours, with the convoy sighted, Wheeler started a climbing turn to 1,500 feet. Sise in *W-Whisky* led his nine TorBeaus up to 175 feet. Eight merchantmen sailing in two lines of four, protected by six flak-ships with two minesweepers were visible slightly ahead. The TorBeaus consisted of three sections: Red led by 'Bill' Sise, Blue by Sergeant Donald Pengelly, and Green by John 'Johnny' Lown. Radio silence was broken as Wheeler called out: 'Attack, attack, attack!' The formation swung to starboard, the TorBeaus remaining low, as the anti-flak section dived, unleashing cannon, machine-guns and 250lb. bombs at the enemy.

Sise, Pengelly and Lown led their individual pairs, with torpedoes armed. The TorBeaus each picked a merchantman and dropped their tin fish at 800 yards, under intense anti-aircraft fire.

No sooner were the torpedoes dropped then Red section flew over the ships, turned to port and began weaving. Three of the torpedoes struck the 4,500-ton Norwegian merchantman *Hoegh Carrier*. Vast clouds of smoke, metal, and wood spiralled into the sky, the air had become a melee of aircraft strafing, dropping bombs, or torpedoes before the Beaufighters turned for home, taking evasive action whilst the Spitfires and Mustangs dived down and strafed flak-ships and the minesweepers. 'That's enough excitement for today,' wrote Flight Lieutenant Frans Lutz of 167 Squadron, in his log book.[144]

Three hours and fifty-five minutes later, Sise touched *W-Whisky* back down again at North Coates. There had been plenty of flak, and crews following in had seen definite hits. Analysis indicated that the TorBeaus appeared to have done well. Three torpedoes had hit, including Wright's, between amidships and stern. A number of other aircrew reported four escorting minesweepers heavily damaged, one receiving a direct hit from a 250lb. bomb and left burning, others damaged. 'The attack was completed in four minutes and without loss,' recorded an exuberant 'Bill' Sise, who had been temporarily acting CO since the departure of Robert Mack. His new boss Wing Commander Charles Cooper DFC arrived on 27 April.

By the beginning of May, Squadron Leader 'Bill' Sise, having continuously flown with 254 Squadron for two years left the squadron for a brief rest, becoming the chief flying instructor of a torpedo-training unit near Stranraer. Here he met his future navigator Raymond Price. Price had completed a Staff Navigators Course at Cranage, Cheshire, in July 1943, returning to North Coates 'with above average' marks. Price become 254 Squadron's Navigational Officer. He then went to Stranraer. Sise made a point of drinking with Price in the Mess and both got to know one another quite well socially before Sise went on to Coastal Command Headquarters shortly afterwards receiving a DSO. 'We agreed to return to operational flying together at the earliest opportunity,' recalled Raymond Price.[145]

On Saturday, 1 April 1944 – All Fools' Day – Sise flew to North Coates in an Avro Anson from Northolt for the first time in almost a year to collect a bemused Raymond Price. A conversion course at East Fortune saw Sise do a refresher on Beaufighters until a batch of de Havilland Mosquitoes arrived: after five sorties on the type Sise and Price departed for the Cornish Riviera.

He had missed the camaraderie whilst at Northwood of being on a Coastal squadron and, now he was coming back into the fold. Posted to 235 Squadron at Portreath, Squadron Leader 'Bill' Sise and Raymond Price joined on 1 June, as a flight commander and immediately began flying missions near the Brest Peninsula.[146] Sise had reacquainted himself with Canadian Alwynn Bonnett, a former accountant from Vancouver who had flown on the first North Coates mission. Now he was a Flying Officer with a Glaswegian navigator Flying Officer Allan McNicol on 248 Squadron's Special Detachment, flying Tsetse Mosquitoes which packed a 57mm gun.

Their friendship would last a brief nine days. Bonnett's tail plane was sliced off in a mid-air collision over the airfield after a successful sortie.[147] At 18.05 hours Bonnett's and McNicol's Tsetse *I-Ink* passed over the airfield as the port outer aircraft of a vic of five. Wing Commander Anthony Phillips, leading in *Y-Yoke* broke away crossing underneath portside of the formation and turned steeply to port. Bonnett lost sight of the strike leader and also hauled sharply to port. Both Mosquitoes collided at 1,500 feet over the edge of Portreath with *I-Ink* going into a nearby bay, whilst Phillips finally touched down at Portreath at 18.07 hours, using 15 degrees flap with his starboard wing tip broken off. 'Bonnett's Mosquito immediately went into a spinning nosedive just beyond the cliffs, his tailplane dropped onto the grass,' explained Sise. 'Fortunately Alwynn's body was recovered from the sea on 21 June, by a fishing trawler,' and laid to rest.

His next few missions followed in quick succession. On Wednesday 5 July, Sise was promoted with immediate effect to the rank of Wing Commander to command 248 Squadron after Anthony Phillips' Mosquito was hit by flak during a shipping strike on Bénodet harbour the previous day.

'Saw one Mossie diving on the other Minesweeper, on my way in, and seen some smoke, and we went past a burning aircraft in a field, and Flying Officer James 'Jimmy' Orchard my navigator got a photo. I then turned out over the sea, and returned to Cornwall', Wing Commander Robert James scrawled down whilst interviewing Squadron Leader Henry 'Hal' Randall.[148] Sise accompanied Randall in his car to Cliff House in Gunwalloe village to break the sad news to Ann Phillips.[149]

By 12 August, Sise had completed twelve ops. His twelfth trip was to the Gironde the target area having been decided after a reconnaissance flight. A maximum effort: twenty-three Mosquito Mk. VIs, and two Tsetse Mosquitoes were available. At Mount Wise, Plymouth, Air Vice-Marshal Brian Baker's HQ for 18 Group, the news was received, then a telephone was call made to the station commander, Group Captain Duncan Summerville. He received the call in his office. 'John Yonge is on his last day's leave because of his son's christening. His flight commander Squadron Leader Peter Barnes will lead 235 Squadron and Sise the whole formation,' announced Baker.[150]

The airfield was a hive of activity, 235 Squadron was putting up eleven Mosquitoes for the sweep north of Gironde and 248 was to contribute twelve Mk. VIs, and two Tsetse Mosquitoes. Different modes of transport darted to and through between dispersals while groundcrew prepared the aircraft for take-off. Crews arrived at their machine for their air test. Thirty minutes after take-off, and with everything checked, the aircraft began landing again. It was then off to the crews' respective mess for breakfast. Later, at 06.30 hours there was a briefing. The forecast was declared good, but rumours circulated whilst Sise finished up, that it was a dicey job. The operations room had an air of tension. 'We will be sweeping the Gironde from North of Bordeaux to the sea,' explained Sise. 'It means crossing the coast beyond the river and going inland thirty miles. I realise that this is a rather novel experience for seafaring types like ourselves.'[151]

Flight Lieutenant Lancelot Dobson and navigator William 'Dusty' Miller were working well together. Dobson had left Cockington, Devon to live of the Bath Road, Reading, at twenty-nine, was a good pilot having done his elementary training and passed out at Reading Aero Club on 19 March 1939, whilst working as a Miles Aircraft Company clerk in the drawing office. Slipping away to begin his Air Force training at Uxbridge then Cambridge. On Saturday 24 August as air battles raged 37 miles away over Portsmouth, at Odiham Dobson was in the air flying a Harvard before gaining his wings in November. After being appointed to No 2 School of Army Co-operation a couple of months after that he was posted – this time to 53 Squadron at St Eval. It was here that he and his crewmates Kyle, and Hall began flying the Blenheim before converting to Hudsons at Bircham Newton. After his last flight in July 1942, he left for Canada via the United States for further training, and then made the long journey to Scotland as a flight lieutenant. Cranwell OTU followed before Dobson left for a conversion course onto Mosquitoes at Hullavington.[152]

It was a short hop across the Channel. The forecast had been correct en route and around 09.55 hours, the twenty-five Mosquitoes crossed the French coast led by Sise in *S-Sugar*.[153] Immediately a light flak position opened up and Sise gave it a burst, then Squadron Leader Maurice Guedj finished the job. The odd bit of tracer came up on the port side, but the formation was quickly out of its range. It was exhilarating: 'witnessing twenty-five Mossies hedge-hopping over the copse and vines of Bordeaux. The French were waving to us outside their homes, in fields and country lanes,' remembered James 'Jimmy' Rodgers, navigator of David 'Lawrie' Shield in *G-George*, 'I returned the waves and Lawrie now and again waggled his wings as did Maurice on our portside.'

Then at Blaye the formation swung up to the river. *G-George* on the starboard side flew along the north bank slightly in front of Dobson and Millar in *T-Tommie*. 'Flak is virtually non-existent,' noted Peter Barnes. At last, however near Royan, shipping was sighted. At 10.06 hours, 'Bill' Sise, called 'sections as detailed, attack each of the two formations of shipping in sight,' over the R/T then followed this with, 'Attack, attack, attack.'

The approach was ideal, each Mosquito had a good clear run of roughly half a mile or less from the protruding headland, which allowed the attackers plenty of manoeuvrability to pick out their specified target. The problem was not the geography of the landscape but the light and heavy flak. So far as they could tell, there was a *Sperrbrecher* with twelve guns, a minesweeper, one merchantman and three flak-ships.

The flak opened up. 'It's like a carpet,' said Miller on the intercom to his pilot Lancelot Dobson. They managed to dodge the first bursts of heavy flak. Dobson began peppering a flak-ship with his cannon, it quickly replied with what they both realised was something heavier than a 20mm cannon, and within seconds there was a crack as rounds sliced through the laminated wooden structure. It didn't seem to affect the aircraft as Dobson concentrated hard to keep *T-Tommie* level as he raced in at 200mph at 250 feet, bomb doors open. The flak-ship loomed towards them, as its anti-aircraft gunners ensnared their aircraft with flak.

'Bombs gone!' said Dobson.

They hurtled through the vessels funnel smoke and flak as around them Mosquitoes swept in at varying heights from 500, 250 to 50 feet making concentrated attacks, with cannon, machine-guns, 250lb. bombs, depth charges and 57mm cannon.

Sise in *S-Sugar* had lined up a minesweeper, the aircraft was met with a hail of tracer and small arms from the defenders. Sise held steadfast, as bullets and shells pumped out towards him and Raymond Price as the Mosquito raced in at mast height.

He flicked the bomb release switch, jettisoning the two 250lb. high explosive bombs from their hard points underneath each the wing. To his right Raymond Price craned his neck around to witness an explosion that sent up a sheet of flame and smoke into the sky.

'Direct hit,' said Price over the intercom.[154]

On *G-George*, Shield was scoring accurately with the four 20mm cannon, when a cluster of depth charges exploded ahead, forcing him to break off hard to port, and start again. Buffeted by flak, Shields retaliated with short bursts of cannon, but remained steadfast and he released his own depth charges on *Sauerland*. Ahead of Shield a Mosquito was on fire. On board *A-Apple*, Flight Sergeant Frank 'Frankie' Chew and Stephen 'Jock' Couttie called out 'Ditching.' Chew managed to put the burning aircraft down, but its weakened structure broke up on impact. Chew and Couttie clambered out through the canopy escape hatch the port wing and scramble into their rubber dinghy. Despite the intense flak, Sise in *S-Sugar* swopped low over the dinghy, as did Shield, with Rodgers obtaining two good photographs, before clearing off. The time was 11.39 hours. Waving to the passing planes the pair paddled for half an hour only to be captured by a flak-ship.[155]

'Lawrie' Shield made his way home independently. 'Sise had conserved more fuel and sped off towards Cornwall,' said Rodgers, then in the headphones he heard *T-Tommie* – 'aircraft in front, we are going to ditch in thirty-five minutes through lack of fuel.'[156] Rodgers in *G-George* sent out an S.O.S., as Shield reduced speed to come along side Dobson and Miller, Rodgers indicates land by hand signals, but Dobson continues to fly on until they come across a Naval Group near Ushant. Miller fired a red flare out of the cockpit, it was clear the Mosquito was almost out of fuel.

Rodgers manages to speak to Dobson and Miller by VHF, 'Wishing you both the best of luck'. Dobson replied, 'we'll stand you both a pint in the Mess'.

On *T-Tommie* Dobson prepared to ditch as Miller desperately tried to tighten his harness as the aircraft hit the water, he was catapulted forward and knocked unconscious. Dazed Miller came around to find himself in the submerged Mosquito cockpit. Releasing his Sutton harness, he groped around, found the escape hatch, clambered out of the wreck and made for the surface looking around he could see neither dinghy or pilot. Taking a couple of deep breaths, Millar returned to the cockpit. Despite severe pain from both broken ankles he re-entered the cockpit to locate Dobson. The black conditions made it virtually impossible to see however, the Gee Box, and pilots seat had fallen through and Miller returned to the surface lungs aching.[157]

On the bridge of the trawler HMS *Lord Essenden* a shout went out 'Airman in the water!' The vessel pushed closer. Miller climbed aboard it was not a second to soon, because a few moments later the remnants of his plane plunged beneath the water. *G-George* was orbiting above; Lawrie Shield waggled his wings in a farewell gig and headed for Cornwall. Communicating with the controller at Portreath, Shield flew straight in. 'I had the dubious honour,' said Lawrie Shield, 'of being the last one back at 12.08 hours, and with the woeful tail of two ditchings.'

At Portreath the tragic demise of Flight Lieutenant Lancelot Dobson was brought to Sise and Randall attention. Dobson had been wearing an American armour-plated vest,[158] with bottom and crutch plate not wanting to be shot to pieces, on these low-level missions that he had gotten from the USAAF at Dunkeswell.[159] 'Know doubt this contributed to his death,' noted Hector Bolitho in his daily report to Coastal Command HQ. After the debriefings, the crews went to their respective Messes, and then to the bar.

It was more of the same for 'Bill' Sise and Price the following day the Gironde. Flying as a pair with Maurice Guedj they scoured the mouth of the Gironde and chased down enemy shipping to Le Verdon. A few miles away at Pauillac Maurice's Mosquito *C-Charlie* came under attack, a cannon shell hitting the tail fin, causing it to splinter. In *X-X-Ray* Raymond Price reported the sighting and the information was passed onto the crews of 235 and 248 Squadrons at Portreath: 'Sise and Maurice are both on a reconnaissance mission in the Royan and Bordeaux area,' said Randall, 'I'll be leading the whole force numbering twenty-five in total.' The plan seemed sound enough as the crews listened 'we should be able to pick up Sise's and Maurice's sighting reports on the way to the target.' But what was the target?

Most guessed the mission would be a lengthy one, as there had been rumours that afternoon after the Davidstow Moor Beaufighters had sunk two *Sperrbrechers* off Royan at about 09.30 hours the previous day, and that Sise's and Yonge's aircrews would have to finish the job. Fortunately, by midday on 14 August, the *Magdeburg* was already at the bottom of the sea and *Schwanheim* was burning fiercely, with her decks awash.

At five minutes past seven, the last three Mosquitoes pelted down the runway, and had barely formatted when Randall set course at 19.15 hours, with twenty-five Mosquitoes scurrying after their leader. At around 20.49 hours, the Mosquitoes were seconds from crossing the French coast with Randall's aircraft Q-*Queenie*, leading, his navigator James Orchard realised his pilot was evidently south of track, and he made an adjustment as the formation crossed over lake Lac d'Hourtin before reaching their target. As elements of 235 Squadron at the stern in four inverted 'V' formations or 'vics' crossed woodland, two concealed quadruple flak guns pumped out tracer. Flying Officers Noel Russell[160] and Tom Armstrong in Y-*Yoke* together with Lawrie Shield and Rodgers aboard E-*Easy* get caught in the crossfire. Unaware of the commotion behind, Randall turned to port at the next marker at Pauillac and led them down the Gironde. Then at 21.04, Randall saw grey objects in the water six miles out.

'Our targets, a Seetier-class destroyer, a *Sperrbrecher*, and two flak-ships all stopped at Le Verdon,' noted Rodgers, as Orchard called out on the R/T, 'There's the target'.[161]

'Hello all Bordeaux aircraft,' Randall said over the VHF. 'I am going to attack. Come into attack in your order as briefed.' He spoke directly to Squadron Leader Richard 'Dickie' Atkinson of 235 Squadron. 'Hello D-*Dog* you're to take over if I'm hit and have to ditch.'[162]

'Okay, Strike Leader,' Atkinson replied.

Then came 'Attack, attack, attack,' from Randall. In the melee of aircraft E-*Easy* was one of those taking on the *Sperrbrecher*. Through the windscreen Rodger could see tracer hurtling towards them, 'there was a second of panic when Lawrie realised the master switch wasn't on'. Shield managed a long burst of cannon, and dropped his cargo of depth charges, hurtling over the target into clear skies, only to be met by a fury of tracer from the Seetier-class destroyer.

'In seconds Lionel "Taffy" Stoddard and Geoffrey Harker son of a music critic of the *Newcastle Evening Chronicle* in A-*Apple* exploded and span into the water, whilst Goodman in V-*Victor*, and his navigator Reginald

Genno, ditched,' reported Rodgers. The destroyer's light flak claimed two more victims: Warrant Officer Harold Corbin was caught when both main fuel tanks were pierced, 'the fuel just completely drained out,' explained Corbin. Another 20mm round punched a hole through their floor, which disintegrated the IFF and Gee box. Unable to continue Corbin bailed out with navigator Maurice Webb. Squadron Leader Alec Cook saw arcs of light tracer heading towards *U-Uncle*. Instinctively Flight Lieutenant Stanley Pyrah ducked, but the Mosquito was trapped in a hail of cannon and shells. According to the dials and instruments both engines seemed to have survived and Cook was able to adjust the trim while Pyrah navigated a route to Vannes, 193 miles away. Upton heard, '*U-Uncle* heading for Vannes.' But nothing further was heard as they headed on alone.[163]

Roughly 400 miles away, personnel with headsets were taking down notes in the Portreath operations room, while out on the airfield Sise, Guedj, Yonge, and his navigator Harold Hosier of Stepney London watched as groundcrew hurried over to Randall's aircraft. Overhead, others joined the circuit and landed. After half an hour Shield, Rodgers with Russell and Armstrong, who had both joined up off Ushant, also landed safely. Despite Shield's concerns about the damage his aircraft had suffered, the landing was without a hitch and Shield was able to shut his engines off. He clambered down the ladder after Rodgers. 'We had been well plastered with hits on the both spinners, on both starboard and port main planes, also the tail unit on either side and nose,' said Shield, as Sise and Yonge drove out to pick them up with Noel Russell and Tom Armstrong to take them for their debriefing. 'You've had someone looking after you both,' said Sise as he surveyed the damage to *E-Easy*. But as with Randall, Gerald Yeates, Roy Orrock and Philip Kilminster, Lawrie Shield was feeling unquestionably lucky to have made it back considering the punishment his Mosquito had taken.[164]

In the smoke-filled debriefing room notes were being scrawled down: 'Instead of seeing U-Boats we ran straight into shipping which included a destroyer, and *Sperrbrecher*,' said Henry 'Hal' Randall. 'We've lost three warrant officers and their navigators on 248 Squadron.'

Outside the final aircraft touched down. As Squadron Leader Richard Atkinson and Flying Officer Valentine Upton climbed out of their Mosquito, at 23.38 hours, Alec Cook and Stanley Pyrah were dead. The irony was that Cook was within sight of Vannes airfield at Monterblanc when *U-Uncle* entered the sea just off the small island of Île-aux-Moines. The local Maquis leader rowed out with a colleague to the submerged Mosquito and found their lifeless bodies still strapped into their seats. Cook and Pyrah's bodies were carefully lifted out through the roof's escape hatch and gently handed down onto the boat and rowed back to shore. Retrieving French money carried on their person it was handed over to a local priest. A carpenter constructed two coffins, and a draper provided the linen for Cook and Pyrah to rest on. After a full religious service, the pilot and navigator were laid to rest in Île-aux-Moines cemetery.

On Tuesday, 15 August, in the 235 Squadron office, Wing Commander John Yonge up-dated his aircrew dossier, promoting with immediate effect Atkinson to Officer Commanding B Flight in place of Cook then wrote to the former flight commanders mother Florence and Stanley Pyrah's wife Joyce who had a young son Malcolm aged three. Nearby 'Bill' Sise also made an entry: 'Since June 1944, 248 Squadron have lost fifteen pilots and navigators and our sister squadron 235 have lost six in total. No wonder the cry "on, on, to the Gironde" was heard from the men now the invasion of Southern France has begun.'

The war in the Biscay ports was finally drawing to a close, but Sise's fiancée 22 year-old, Section Officer Mary Hollingsworth knew there was still a massive amount of responsibility resting on his shoulders. In the coming days 'Bill' Sise led his aircrew to Banff in northeast Scotland. They reached Banff on the 10 September shortly after 12.30 hours, after a largely uneventful journey. There to greet Sise and Price was Station Commander, The Hon. Max Aitken DSO DFC, who congratulated him on his prompt arrival, just in time for a spot of lunch with himself, Canadian Edward Pierce, Tony Gadd, Norwegian Erling Ulleberg of 333 Squadron's 'B' Flight, and Yonge whose 235 Squadron had arrived six days previously.

Their actions over the next nine months dealt a a devastating blow to German supply lines, Wing Commander 'Bill' Sise was taken off operations in February 1945, after completing 150 missions. Handing over the 248 reins to Roy Orrock DFC, who took a tumble outside Ålesund after being hit by flak and saw out the remainder of the war as a POW. Aitken appointed Wing Commander Norman Jackson-Smith DFC, a combat veteran of Dunkirk and the Battle of Britain flying Blenheim fighters. Flight Lieutenant Eric 'Lofty' Gittins DFC volunteered from 248 Squadron to be his navigator to chalk up his final ops.

'Bill' Sise DSO DFC watched the proceedings from Fraserburgh, marrying his wife, Mary, a year after the war, and together they had a son. 'Bill' Sise remained in the Air Force as a Group Captain until January 1967 returning to Dunedin, New Zealand with his family.[165]

Chapter 5

Flight Lieutenant Dennis Healy DSO NWC – High Arctic Flight

'**D**ear Sir,' Air Vice Marshal Albert Durston, Air Officer Commanding 18 Group wrote. 'Philip Joubert rang me up this morning about the provision of flights to the Arctic.' He told Wing Commander Edward Hutton of his call from Joubert. 'He is as apprehensive about it as I am.' That the Air Officer Commanding-in-Chief Coastal Command appeared to be unaware of the difficulty in flying at altitude in the Arctic was neither here nor there. Nor was the fact that the Catalinas would be only carrying machine-guns and not depth charges. 'He said,' he continued, 'that Command and Admiralty requires it, therefore we need to obtain information on location of the sea ice in the Svalbard archipelago.'

The offices of 210 Squadron were in a cramped Nissen hut. Hutton's was the end room along a corridor a simple square room, with a single metal window on the outward facing wall. A large map encompassing Scotland, Shetland Isles, Iceland, and Greenland, was pinned to the flat wall. Two filing cabinets obscured southern Norway. The utility furniture amounted to a desk, placed at an angle, with two chairs either side, and a single telephone.

Twenty-five-year-old, Hutton had recently got back from his swim at Oban pool. As a former Perth Academy swimming champion in four categories he prided himself in setting an example to his men on keeping healthy. He studied the document from Durston. His flight of Monday 23 March 1942 was still fresh in Hutton's mind now he was being asked to select a crew for a special operation from 210 Squadron.

The squadron operated Catalina flying boats, powered by two Pratt and Whitney engines, developed by Consolidated Aircraft Corporation in San Diego whilst building flying boats for the United States Navy in the 1920s. After a trial with one example in Great Britain at Felixstowe,

Suffolk in July 1939, an initial order of fifty was placed. The production of increasing numbers of the twin-engine amphibian resulted in the squadron being re-equipped to Catalinas in April 1941. Like his predecessor, Wing Commander Gareth Barrett, Hutton believed in the Catalina; 'it's a versatile machine.'

Fortunately for the Commanding-in-Chief, Hutton had a captain and aircrew in mind. 'You will find him absolutely first class,' Hutton told Joubert. 'I'm sure you'll agree to this consummation.' There was no other person who combined, so perfectly, the right attributes for the job. It *had* to be Healy.

Even so, Joubert and Naval Intelligence had to vet Flight Lieutenant Dennis Healy. His files were couriered over to HMS *President* for Commander Ian Fleming's perusal. Healy had been born in Suez, Egypt. His father Henry worked as a manager in the Eastern Telegraph Company, and was one year older than Healy's mother, who had been just twenty-seven when they married and only twenty-nine when her second son, the middle one of three, had been born. Henry Healy was career minded, borne from his father being an officer in the North Staffordshire Regiment who had begun at the bottom rung as a rifleman, therefore Henry strived for his children to reach their full potential. Unlike many of Dennis' contemporaries he had not been sent to boarding school as a six-year-old, but accompanied his parents Henry and Maud, to Cape Town, returning to England in 1924, before a move to Valetta, Malta, where Dennis aged eleven and, his elder brother Brian, became choristers at St Paul's Cathedral.

With a promotion to Assistant Manager it was off to the Greek island of Syra in the Aegean Sea, about eighty miles from Athens where Dennis's parents decided that he and Brian should be sent to boarding school in England. Choosing Abingdon School in Berkshire noted for its all-round education and moderate fees which was appreciated by many parents working for Eastern Telegraph Company. Both boys joined in the Easter Term of 1928, going into Red House. Dennis Healy was hugely competitive whether the fiercely contested Steeplechase run on Abingdon Common beating Basil Quelch, or cycling the twenty-three miles to Henley-on-Thames for the Henley Royal Regatta. Healy coxing the junior fours with Hunt, Engall, Ottiker and Paige, whilst continually making the Under 15 Cricket XI team with average score of twenty-five. Leadership qualities came to the fore in a tight rugby match against Magdalen College School: 'Under Dennis Healy's indefatigable and inspiring leadership the team have improved greatly, especially in the scrums,' wrote the Sports Master. 'Through out the season Healy has drilled the forwards to perfection from his position as scrum half and combines splendidly with Taylor – ought to be very good next season too.'

However, both Healy boys left Abingdon in July 1931 when catastrophe struck Eastern Telegraph Company, which was now part of Cable & Wireless, suddenly, began a rationalisation programme and Henry Healy was pensioned off in June 1931. With a drastic drop in income Henry and Maud were forced to pull both their sons out of Abingdon School. Dennis left to work as a finisher at Debenhams department store, parcel wrapping customers purchases ready for despatch. One year on, he was working for the Gas Light and Coke Company as a staff pupil. There he began the process of learning to be a fitter's mate, attending to gas installations from a cross spectrum of society to the splendour of His Majesty The King's Buckingham Palace. He attended an evening school run by an Abingdonian and obtained first rate passes which enabled him to gain promotion to the company's secretarial and financial departments.[166]

Dennis's leisurely pursuits included being an active member of the Old Abingdonians in London as a committee member and playing for their rugby team.[167] He enjoyed classical music and ballroom dancing, and joined the Gas and Coke Company's amateur dramatic society. Performing plays led him to meet Hazel Madeline Rushworth-Lund. In January 1937, he visited the stage set prior to performing at Stanmore and there spoke with Hazel. After talking to her for some considerable time they realised both had a mutual interest as thespians and of winter sports. Healy asked her out.

'Yes but …' faltered Rushworth-Lund

'Yes, but what?' asked Healy. She explained that she was on strict instructions not to go out with any strange men.

'Bugger that,' said Healy. 'We'll go anyway.'

On a bleak January night after Miss Rushworth-Lund had finished as a dispenser for a local doctor they met for a drink and began an intense courtship. Weekends between September and April saw Madeline chaperoned, to watch Dennis captain the Old Abingdonians Rugby Club. The 1939 season saw them play sixteen matches of which they won seven and lost nine, with the end of season on 1 April, Healy secured another decisive victory against a gifted Chartered Accounts Rugby Club side. On the sideline Misses Rushworth-Lund, Reynolds and Richards calm, collected manner kept thrusts of husbands, boy friends and spectators, quenched with freshly brewed leaf tea.

Five weeks later on Friday 28 April 1939 Dennis wed Hazel Madeline Rushworth-Lund in a quite ceremony at St Johns Parish Church, in Stanmore. The bride wore her travelling costume. His brother Brian Healy was best man. The bridal reception for the youngest daughter of Doctor Jonathon Rushworth-Lund of Everdon Manor was held at Stanmore Hall, the home of the bride's sister, Nelly Blacker.

Both had an emotionally fulfilling life, and by the time war was declared, the family's prospects seemed good. Dennis volunteered for the Royal Air Force. He had already learnt to fly at Fairoaks in 1938 as a Volunteer Reserve with No. 18 Elementary and Reserve Flying Training School – where he had his log book stamped with an 'above average' assessment, Dennis was taking part in the annual camp when war was declared. Flying alternate weekends in nothing more aggressively-modern than Gypsy Moths, and Tiger Moths, with an occasional ride in a Miles Magister, next few months were spent in Cambridge University at Initial Training Wing. 'Receiving our tuition in the lecture rooms and our meals in the dining rooms and we're even allowed to use the university silverware,' he wrote to Madeline.[168]

He returned home for a brief period of leave before being posted to his Flying Training School at Cranbourne in Southern Rhodesia to continue flying training. He finally left Britain in late April 1940 with a mixture of excitement, trepidation and sadness, not least because his wife was pregnant with their first child – Michael – who was born in November 1940. It was a long journey, via Liverpool, across the North Atlantic to Freetown Sierra Leone, then onto Cape Town, South Africa. After school at Cranbourne, where he passed out with an 'above average' assessment, Dennis was posted to the Maritime Reconnaissance Course at No. 61 Air School (SAAF) at George, Cape Province, which was the prelude to a candidate indicating their final destination to be RAF Coastal Command.[169]

Arriving in England in late spring 1941 for a reunion with Madeline and their young son, both of whom he adored, before departing to his OTU at Invergordon. There he began conversion to flying boats and, despite his training on Oxfords, he got the hang of the obsolete Supermarine Stranraer, Saunders - Roe built Lerwick and London flying boats. 'We finally landed,' he wrote in a letter home, 'after being up for seven hours, feeling very tired and weary. We had a small whiskey to ward of the chill, dinner and then to bed.'

By now Healy was ready for an operational squadron. It was 08.00 hours on 1 July that Flying Officer Dennis Healy arrived at Oban.[170] He had been alone among those of his OTU in being posted to 210 Squadron and it was as a member of the squadron that he would fly the Catalina. He had been impressed with his first flight in a Catalina, struck by its speed and agility. Crewed up at last with Flight Lieutenant Percy Hatfield who impressively, on Monday 26 May 1941, together with his co-pilot

Carl Rinehart a US Navy Special Observer, had through twelve hours of accurate calculations and plotting by his navigator Frank Cadman, relocated the German Battleship *Bismarck* after it had eluded the perusing Royal Navy warships.[170] After a brief skirmish with the battleship, Hatfield withdrew and shadowed it until 03.00 hours when he turned his damaged Catalina for Oban, but not before he had a nullified duel with a Blohm and Voss 138 flying boat.

Healy began flying regularly with Hatfield during the next four months, missions were routinely anti-submarine patrols and convoy escort duties, the monotony enabling him to hone his skills. Healy's eighth mission was to Archangel in northern Russia, carrying a group of special passengers. The Catalina put down at Invergordon to top up its main and reserve fuel tanks, then on nearing the Orkneys made a second impromptu stop at Deer Sound to remedy an oil fault. Healy and Hatfield continued having made new calculations of the distance, course, and speed the twenty-hour journey began around the North Cape of Norway to Archangel, as Hatfield touched down in the flat waters on the White Sea. With the Catalina tied to a buoy a launch came out to take them ashore. Here the Soviets transferred the passengers to railway carriages bound for Moscow. Healy, Hatfield and their crew aboard the plane had breakfasted and had taken a ride in the back of a truck through the area then returned. Both reported into the Flight hut with their Russian interpreter, the planes navigator and crew, where the news had arrived from the Met Officer that they could fly after being stuck for nine days. With the weather clear to make the return flight to Oban Hatfield's plane was buffeted on choppy seas as the Catalina landed and edged into the little bay. Operations continued to be carried out by Healy for the next eight months by which time he had been promoted to flight lieutenant. However, the following month brought another change of circumstances. 210 Squadron moved as a complete unit to 18 Group's most northerly flying boat base Sullom Voe on Shetland Isles' mainland, a little under forty miles north of Lerwick. A suggestion by the Air Ministry that the Catalina crews should live under canvas was short lived 'roughly speaking a sixty mile an hour wind in the Shetlands is considered dead calm!' wrote Air Marshal Albert Durston in reply, 'the only local residents are mostly sheep and rabbits'.

So for this next mission Healy, who already had a reputation of a captain to be respected, had to choose his crew. Two key appointments were those of Pilot Officer Ronald Martin, known as 'Ronnie', and Pilot Officer Ernest Schofield. Martin a twenty-four-year-old South Shields man, was imbued with the same kind of 'press on' spirit that Healy liked. He was the son of a self-employed yeast merchant, who worked forty-eight hours a week supplying goods to Matthew Wood & Son Limited and Newcastle Breweries. His father Joseph also furnished dried yeast for baking purposes to local manufacturers, and it was this part of his father's business Ronald Martin entered in 1938. Martin joined the Civil Air Guard Movement at Woolsington[171] when he turned twenty-one. He had hung around all afternoon with two other fellow novice aviators and made frequent trips to the lavatory, Martin was eventually accosted by Howard Mitchell in flying kit.[172]

'Your name Ronald?'

'Yes,' he said.

'Right I'll take you up for your air experience.'

Mitchell led him to a Tiger Moth parked outside the long wooden structure that provided an office and accommodation for the Civil Air Guard Movement and Newcastle upon Tyne Aero Club. Strapped into the front seat the plane taxied out and took off. Conversation was made down a primitive form of apparatus – the speaking tube. Chimneys belching industrial smoke drifted past the starboard wing. In the gloom Martin had no idea where he was or which way the plane was flying. Twenty minutes later the Moth curved in to land on the grass strip and taxied in.

'All right?' enquired Mitchell, 'Don't put your feet through the canvas when getting out.'

Suddenly, carting about the sky in a flimsy plane didn't seem at all dare devil, like W. E. Jones had written in *Biggle's Adventures*. By August 1939, Martin had managed to accumulate seven hours of flying with his instructor Howard Mitchell.

In the June Martin had registered for national service and having obtained high scoring marks for his Cambridge school certificate when aged sixteen had been earmarked for the Royal Air Force. His papers arrived one year later. Armed with a railway warrant, Martin arrived at RAF Padgate in Cheshire having just completed eight dreary hours of stopping and starting from Newcastle and received his first taste of military discipline. Training continued in Torquay. Reporting to 5 Initial Training Wing headquarters at Castle Chambers Hotel as a pilot under training. His ground schooling was exemplary, and Ronald Martin was sent to Sywell, near Northampton, where he went solo after only five and a half hours dual instruction on Tiger Moths. An 'above average' endorsement in his flying log book saw Martin quickly posted to 13 Operational Conversion Unit at Bicester, in Oxfordshire, flying Bristol Blenheims. Here he found himself caught up in a spate of horrific accidents some of which he and his colleagues witnessed. Having been ear-marked for Bomber Command the twenty surviving trainee pilots, including Martin, were immediately sent on a refresher course in Somerset at the seaside town of Weston-super-Mare, followed by further training for months at Cranfield, Bedfordshire, on twin-engine Oxfords.[173]

Arriving at Squires Gate, Liverpool, Martin began the training programme in parachuting, dinghy drills, aircraft layout, fuel systems, low flying, dummy bombing raids, and gunnery practice and was not intimidated when flying the Blackburn Botha. Senior staff leading the course were astonished at his performance and this earned him the highest honour of passing out in first place on his course. Martin returned home for a brief period of leave before being posted to 4 OTU at Invergordon. 'I had barely been on leave for twenty-four hours when a telegram arrived, saying go to Scotland,' wrote Ronald to his cousin.[174]

Oval-faced and dark haired, Martin looked younger than he was, despite the thin wispy moustache that was only retained for five days before being shaved off after his arrival at Oban to join 210 Squadron. Hutton's note was helpful, specifically out lining the key requirement Ronald Martin had to master: 'accurate navigation under moonlight or simulated moonlight conditions and in complete darkness at various heights, which will best afford security against enemy fighter attack'.

The navigation officer advised that the Catalina should fly low-level, mid-level and high-level training flights routed over the area west of the Isle of Mull, extending into the north as far as Stornoway. Finally, he warned Martin's second pilot not to fly anywhere near military ranges. Night simulation was also to be carried out using dark goggles with the 'correct lenses'. These specific routes were flown and Martin soon qualified.

Between training flights, he married fiancée Margaret West, whom he had known since leaving school. Eight months later, at a squadron Christmas Party held at Oban's Great Western Hotel, Margaret was introduced to Dennis Healy and his wife Madeline. She was impressed by his appearance and manner. 'He was tall, slim and debonair. His voice graced the audience with renditions of *Hark! The Herald Angels Sing*, and *Once in Royal David's City* with a glass of beer steadfast in his hand whilst leaning against the grand piano', Margaret wrote in a letter home in the New Year.

These were the two pilots that Pilot Officer Ernest Schofield was fortunate to join on Saturday 14 February 1942.[175] Schofield had been educated at St John's College, Cambridge, he read economics after winning a much-coveted state scholarship during his last year at Derby's Bemrose School. Physical needs were met by joining the University's Light Blue's Rowing Club, whilst studies continued due to the economic depression into a fourth year with Schofield reading history. He was then put forward to take the Civil Service competitive entrance examination, which Schofield passed. His strongest subject being mathematics, he joined the Inland Revenue in January 1939, the position carried 'reservation' from military service but, nineteen months later he easily fulfilled the recruitment brief and, after training around Britain, on 23 May 1941, Schofield was awarded the observers brevet and promotion.

He had also managed to negotiate around the comment 'medically unfit to be and air observer,' on his medical card by seeing Moorfield Eye Specialist Charles Usher, at Adastral House in London.[176] After the examination Usher took out his fountain pen and obliterated the letters 'un', and rubber-stamped and initialled the amendment. Schofield's record then read 'Fit pilot or air observer.' He was then issued with Form 657 stating that Schofield was medically classified fit to serve and, to allay any fears of aircrew that noticed he was wearing spectacles.

Having amassed enough hours at Invergordon, on Tuesday 9 September 1941, the pilot officer arrived at 210 Squadron at Oban. He ambled between aircrews whilst being mentored by Pilot Officer George Buckle who was becoming tour expired and completed his last mission as a trainee on 23 December 1941 under the captaincy of Flight Lieutenant David McKinley DFC, endorsed Schofield's flying log 'qualified for the squadron role'. Three months had disappeared quickly since joining the squadron, on remarkably uneventful flights but these where just dress rehearsals for what was to come.

Contributions towards missions continued as first navigator to Flight Lieutenant Charlie Owen until the whole squadron moved to Sullom Voe fully equipped with Catalinas. This change of circumstances meant Schofield became the full-time navigator to Dennis Healy after the short transit flight from Oban to Sullom Voe on Valentine's Day 14 February 1942 together with Martin. Both addressed each other as 'Tim' and 'Ronnie' and after a brief discussion on the intercom Ernest Schofield became known as 'Scho'. During his time with 210, he had viewed Healy as an ideal role model: someone who would brook no nonsense, but who led from the front and yet was still one of the boys.

Ernest's wife had been expecting their first child and was at home in Derby. He was missing her and feeling on edge now that the birth was so close, yet still unconfirmed. Healy noticed that Schofield didn't know what to do with himself whether to play snooker or have another drink or go back to his digs he shared with Owens, so Healy suggested that they head for a stroll around the base; Ernest agreed.

Sergeant George Kingett was the senior wireless operator/air gunner on Healy's crew. He'd married Irene Crowther in 1937 at Christ Church Barnet, in St Albans Road. Kingett was unable to put a call through to Irene as he had planned to do on 14 February because of their move to Sullom Voe. Telephone calls he knew were only the realistic chance of hearing her voice, as operations were now probably going to be every three days, but even a simple phone call was no easy undertaking. A line had to be booked through the exchange and could involve a lengthy wait anywhere between half-an-hour, to an hour. If and when he did get through, there was no guarantee that she would be there, in which case the entire rigmarole would be for nothing. Instead he had to make do with letter writing and working on a photograph album they had bought together when he had finished his training, filling it with photographs, jottings using a white pencil, and other bits and pieces.

The remainder of the crew were wireless operator/air gunner Sergeant 'Taff' Thomas, flight engineer/air gunners Aircraftsman David Baird and Sergeant Edward Horton, and Sergeant Jonathan Campbell was the rigger/air gunner. Campbell was nominated cook having previously worked in a café prior to joining the Royal Air Force. Their third wireless operator/air gunner was John Maffre, whose pass rate as an air gunner was extraordinarily low but achieved high marks when clay pigeon shooting. At Wireless School he was taught radio and electrical theory, and practical theory on wireless equipment, so he could not only transmit messages but also service a wireless set in the event of a mechanical failure, or damage from flak or enemy fighter. For Maffre, it was not particularly complicated: 'there were about roughly ten valves in the set and you could actually run it on three volts, using all the remaining leads. You had different coils in case it didn't work. On my first trip, the intercom went a bit wrong but Kingett and myself luckily found a loose lead.'

The pace was intermittent at Sullom Voe. After days of heavy rain and wind Healy and the rest of the squadron were now chomping at the bit, when the Royal Navy complained about gaps in air patrols over convoys.[177] Hutton was feeling bullish after receiving a telephone call from Captain Dudley Peyton-Ward RN the Naval liaison officer at Eastbury Park. 'To say we were angry would be an understatement,' wrote Schofield. 'It was rumoured our moral fibre was being questioned.' Broadly speaking Hutton knew his crews were up to scratch, but he had to make sure they were not falling short, so the CO flew on a sortie.

Hutton was to fly aboard Catalina *P-Peter*, on Monday, 23 March 1942, with Dennis Healy and his crew.[178] The objective was to search for any enemy surface craft, but the weather was far from ideal and the single

intelligence officer wrote. 'Unsuccessful.' However, Healy, Ronnie, Schofield and George thought that one objective had been achieved: Wing Commander Edward Hutton had been impressed.

Meanwhile Ernest Schofield's flight log was analysed which was normal practice. It was duly found to be in good order with no errors. Hutton described the navigation as 'unbelievably accurate,' Schofield remarked, 'he certainly used the correct adjective'.

In the weeks to come there was a flourish of activity including the unexpected arrival of Catalina *J-Johnny* from 240 Squadron piloted by Flight Lieutenant Desmond Hawkins on All Fools Day. Back in 1935 it would appear that Hawkins would follow a career in teaching, but instead went to the continent on a walking holiday. While in Berlin learning German, Hawkins witnessed acts of violence. After a short spell working in a mundane job, in March 1938, he joined the Royal Air Force. His Yarmouth, Nova Scotia-born Canadian navigator was Pilot Officer Jerauld Wright commonly known, as 'Jerry'. The second pilot was Roy Semple, with Sergeants Aston, Beverly and Faulkes. On this occasion, the afternoon of 1 April, Hawkins and Wright had appeared in the Mess unannounced – as was often the way with visiting aircrew – looking washed out. A junior pilot officer found Hutton and told him that his visitors looked done in.

Unbeknown, Hawkins had been up since 03.30 hours – as had his crew. None had had more than five hours sleep. They'd been previously detached to Gourock on the Clyde for a week, then upon their return to Castle Archdale their commander, Chris Clayton, told them they would have to fly that day to Voe. This, Hawkins guessed, meant they would be operating the following day. Yes, Clayton had replied, but then had warned him that if he breathed a word, he would be shot.

'We'll catch up with you in Gibraltar or Malta after it's over,' he said to Clayton.

'Yes,' Clayton replied, adding 'Good luck.'

Despite their departure from Lower Lough Erne, that still left three late joiners. One was bespectacled Alexander Glen, who came to Sullom Voe in the afternoon. It was true that he was with Naval Intelligence and had returned from a jaunt in Norway, being recalled to HMS *President* for special duties. Dining at a small illicit restaurant in Charterhouse Chambers with Ian Fleming who requested: 'we want you for a special job. I cannot tell you about it, but it has a diplomatic connotation that the Director of Naval Intelligence thinks important. He wants to see you later but first report to Baker Street this afternoon. Keep in touch. Good luck.'

On Baker Street's third floor he met Frank Stagg and Einar Sverdrup. Stagg in his forthright way, explained, 'as a result of special pleading from the Norwegian government, Spitsbergen is to be reoccupied as early in the spring as possible'. The conditions imposed were pretty tough, as weeks and months passed in a whirl of intensive planning. When asked about personnel Stagg wanted one or two British officers going along with Arctic experience.

'We particularly need a British signals officer.' Said Stagg. 'Do you know of anyone?'

'Yes, 'Brownie' Whatman responsible for our ionosphere work when in the Arctic in nineteen thirty-five.'

Stagg placed a call through to the War Office for Alexander Glen to recruit Major Amherst 'Brownie' Whatman son of Major Amherst Blunt Whatman DSO Somerset Light Infantry (SLI). His father had served in India and the South African campaigns, and sixteen years older than Whatman's mother, who had just been twenty-two when they married in Bengal, India, and twenty-seven when her son was born in Taunton, Somerset. Whatman retired from the SLI in 1910, moving the family to Cambridgeshire and continuing the privileged life of a colonial officer until his sudden death two years later. Myrtle Whatman moved to the New Forest and her son was sent to board at Winchester College where his interest continued with signalling and radio communication and getting a radio call sign licence. Two years after leaving school he was at Woolwich, then he continued his studying as a captain in Mechanical Sciences at St John's College Cambridge. After that he was appointed signaller on Glen's Oxford University Expedition to the Arctic in 1935 to Spitsbergen Island. Now Glen wanted him to participate in his latest venture with Lieutenant Colonel Daniel 'Dan' Godfrey.

Stepping out of Baker Street half an hour later he was at The Ritz for a short period. As he left, he turned down St James's Street and there, standing outside Boodles, was Daniel Godfrey. Glen told him of the jaunt to Spitsbergen and the deal was done.

Glen received the news that the appointments of Whatman and Godfrey had been confirmed by telephone, and then continued helping his planning staff. But the question that remained unsolved what was happening within Spitsbergen?

From the nearest northerly departure point available, it was a long trip 1,200 miles to Spitsbergen and beyond the range of all RAF planes then flying. There was only one that could undertake the return journey or single flight staging on to north Russia – the Catalina flying boat.

It was to RAF Coastal Command Eastbury Park they trooped. Sir Philip Joubert and Air Vice-Marshal Brian Baker: 'they listened intently about our small, peculiar and somewhat unorthodox mission,' wrote

Glen, 'it required the agreement of the Admiralty for a Coastal Command plane to be spared for a special operation.'[179] The Admiralty stone-walled the idea. Joubert suggested an unorthodox move.

'Rear Admiral Eric "Daddy" Brind was an open-minded chap. 'What you require is the release of a plane over many weeks and the Admiralty to agree.'[180]

'Yes,' replied Glen.

'Then it's got to come from the Norwegians.'

Joubert and Brind brought the necessary parties together at a dinner party in early March at The Dorchester for senior staff in the Admiralty, the Air Ministry and Norwegian Ministers and their Ambassador. Everyone quickly grasped the essential purpose and by mid-March a small land-force had been assembled and undertaken weapons and saboteur training in Inverness-shire with the Linge Company. More particularly, Brind convinced the Admiralty to release a Catalina from daily U-boat searches to help two tiny ships and seventy men reach Spitsbergen.

Wednesday 1 April brought Major Einar Sverdrup of the Norwegian Army, and Godfrey to Voe. Classified as special observers along with Glen, they had had a bumpy flight in a Hudson from Hendon to Sumburgh. On arrival they boarded an RAF utility wagon that drove through Lerwick then along the hill road through the countryside to a cluster of huts and a few grey cottages appeared.

'Here was the isolated Coastal Command base, with eight or ten planes riding gentle at anchor on the grey waters,' wrote Glen in his diary. 'Sverdrup, Godfrey and myself introduced ourselves to Hawkins and Wright in the Officer's Mess as their "Special Observers"'.

All four were uncommunicative in the Mess. Healy, Martin and Schofield noticed that Glen wore a white ribbon indicating that he was an Arctic specialist. 'We could do no more than speculate that they were going to Norway,' wrote Schofield. Hutton appeared and introduced himself. In the sudden whirlwind of activity Flight Lieutenant 'Jackie' Holmes secured accommodation for the officers' and non-commissioned crew. The quartet did not break up until 20.00 hours. 'Still no clues about the nature of their mission,' said Schofield to Healy as the pair turned in for the night.

Rising early for the flight, watches were synchronized and everyone had something to eat. At the slipway the men were arriving to board the seaplane tender so they could reach Catalina *J-Johnny*.

'Surprisingly, none of us had flown in a Catalina before, and scrambling through the greenhouse-like blister on the side into the light-green painted interior had a novel thrill about it,' said Glen.

With 1,800 gallons of fuel the maritime plane far exceeded the maximum weight that Consolidated Aircraft Corporation had contemplated. As Hawkins, and Sergeant Roy Semple the second pilot, started the two engines, Hawkins spoke on the intercom.

'Will everyone, I repeat 'everyone' come forward.'

With bodies crammed into the forward compartment, Hawkins spoke: 'I just don't know if we will unstick. It is going to be a hell of a long run on the water and I want all the weight forward. Don't move aft until Roy or I give word after we're airborne. We'll be close to stalling speed even then.'

Thursday 2 April, Hawkins was waterborne at 05.05 hours. The Aldis light flashed green as he opened the throttles and gathered speed, climbing into the air and disappearing northwards. For those watching on the shore, the Catalina looked worryingly slow and cumbersome. Their departure was written up in the stations operational book simply as 'special job'.

At 06.05 hours there was a round of applause. 'We painfully passed with much groaning and creaking 500 feet,' Wright logged. Having encountered nothing but the fine weather that had been forecast, with a flat calm ocean below, no one had spoken on board *J-Johnny*. Radio silence had been demanded and Hawkins, his crew and passengers abided by it, although Hawkins beckoned with hand jesters for Glen to come forward immediately.

At about 72 degrees North, a blanket of icing fog enveloped them. Danger was lurking and instinctively Hawkins began climbing to 4,000 feet. The fog was still dense all the way and only cleared slowly at 8,000 feet. It had been heavy going with only a maximum speed of ninety knots. Throughout, the pulsating-edge de-icers were working manfully but the engine manifolds were beginning to suffer considerably. It was with some relief that *J-Johnny* broke through to clear weather. 'Spitsbergen fifty to sixty miles ahead,' said Wright. As Hawkins turned in, one of the katabatic winds that frequent the area suddenly caught the Catalina – the wind speed exceeding 100 knots i.e. 151 miles an hour. The plane was propelled backwards at a rate of forty or fifty knots. Below the black sea was streaked with long parallels of white, as the fury of the wind drove the sea-ice from the shore. Alexander Glen and Daniel Godfrey began to appreciate the strength and stability of the heavy aircraft as it was tossed around like a leaf.

The fierceness of the wind continued unabated, and Wright gave Hawkins a new course to steer. Changing course to northwest suddenly brought them into calmer air. Isfjord was bathed in sunshine as the Catalina was coaxed back to 8,000 feet for a run over Green harbour, the town a thumb smudge in the florescence light. Sverdrup could see a thin whisper of smoke where the coal mine was still burning as a result of the previous year's demolitions. At Advent Bay the snow lay undisturbed, but Hawkins did not fly as far as Bansö. Had they done so they would have spotted the German meteorologists. As they streaked across the valleys of central Spitsbergen, there was no positive evidence that could be seen of enemy movement on that part of the island.

Semple, in the right seat, continued to zigzag the plane back and forth as their special observers searched and made notes. Now two hours later it was time to go home. Bad weather blighted their return, the Canadian recording outside air temperatures of minus 45 to minus 50 degrees Fahrenheit with heavy icing. It took the combined effort and skill of Hawkins and Semple to avoid disaster. With serious magnetic disturbance, radio communication with base was impossible, and navigation was done entirely on dead reckoning, and a thick layer of cloud prevented Wright getting any star fixes.

Darkness ebbed away as dawn broke seven hours later, Hawkins' course was steady, he could see the water ahead, with waves breaking. It was also the first opportunity for Hawkins to have a look at the accumulation of ice on the leading edges and engine manifolds. He let Semple have control and stepped down from his seat to look through the Perspex. What he saw did little to bolster Hawkins' confidence. At 09.00 hours the recognizable landmark of Muckle Flugga came into view, 'only a few miles from Voe,' said Semple into the intercom.

Already at Sullom Voe was Edward Hutton who, after a mission of twenty-seven hours had returned shortly before 05.51 hours. Desmond Hawkins and Semple put down safely at 06.00 hours and there to greet them after making a short trip from their mooring was Hutton, congratulating them all and with a utility van waiting to take them to the strictly private debriefing. Reporting: 'We've not seen anyone in the settlements they had flown over.' The possibility of a successful landing of an expedition confirmed Operation *Fritham* would go ahead.

The returning crew experienced a range of emotions from the moment they touched down on the water through to debrief. Three of Hawkins sergeants Aston, Beverly and Faulkes had drunk three glasses of rum during debriefing and then gone to bed. A few hours later, the three were woken up and stumbled down to the Sergeants Mess.

The words 'special job completed' where typed into the station log. As the three 'Special Observers' spoke in hushed voices: 'our exhausted eyes were sticking out of our heads like lobsters,' said Glen, 'despite the fatigue, exhilaration was greater. We had had the good fortune of maximum visibility over Spitsbergen which had made the results encouraging.'

'Not everything,' chipped in Godfrey, 'the state if the sea in the North Atlantic and the Barents Seas were much worse than any of we three could have expected. Obviously 1942 is a very bad ice year.'

'It's pointless sending two small ships and seventy men at the moment. We'll have to wait another three or four weeks,' said Einar Sverdrup, 'further more we'll have to find another Catalina, as Hawkins is off to the Far East in a few hours.'

'Bugger,' remarked Glen, 'let's hope we don't have to jump through hoops second time around.'

On Thursday 9 April, in his office at Eastbury Park Philip Joubert was handed a folder of important signals by a WAAF Assistant Section Officer. Reading through them quickly, one caught his eye: 'Admiralty concurred in allocation of one designated Coastal Command Catalina with designated squadron to maintain an unchanged crew throughout the whole series of long range missions.'

At Sullom Voe, Edward Hutton assured his officers that the next long-range Arctic sortie from Voe would be carried out by their squadron. This was confirmed by telex printer on 11 April, with a signal from Eastbury Park, Northwood ordering a long-range flight 'to the limit of endurance' to establish the edge of ice field between Jan Mayen Island and Bear Island and ascertain whether a convoy could pass to the north of the latter.

Healy, Martin and Schofield and the remainder of his crew were not aware of this development, they had gone on leave five days earlier. By the time they'd returned to Voe their Catalina required a test flight. They were about to jump out of the launch when over the Tannoy blared: 'Flight Lieutenant Healy report to your commanding officer immediately.'

Inquisitively they looked at each other. 'Is there something you're not telling us Tim?' inquired Schofield. With a shrug of the shoulders, Healy went off to sign the standard Form 700 and to see Hutton, while Martin and Schofield returned to the room that they shared.

Hutton was waiting for Healy. His squadron commander wasted no time in coming straight to the point. For Joubert, the decision after vetting must have been a straightforward one. Ian Fleming of Naval intelligence had rated Dennis Healy 'highly capable,' and he had, so far as his record was concerned, led his aircrew magnificently and had the respect of his fellow officers, fully justifying the belief he held in him, despite his youth.

Hutton explained what was in store for Healy and his crew: 'The trips will include high latitude flying, demanding the highest technical skill. All those taking part have to volunteer, with no force. Everyone will have to be tough and self-reliant and possess sufficient aptitude to solve any problems encountered without squadron support. You can expect to be away for an unknown length of time with no communication with either families or loved ones. Do you want to do it?'

Healy told him he did.

'Great, first thing, talk to your crew, see if their on board, secondly you'll have to take *N-Nuts* to Gourock I can't tell you any more now.'

Healy then went to found Martin and Schofield, realising that with hazardous missions on the horizon and both being married men, they may not necessarily want to follow their pilot. It would be no easy matter replacing them or the other men for that matter. There were a couple of names that immediately sprang to mind. Predictably, both promptly volunteered. Kingett got Campbell, Horton, Thomas, Maffre, and Baird together to meet their captain down at a secluded part of the shoreline. After an intense discussion, the men whom he had come to know well and trusted, joined him. 'Tim had our respect and if he was prepared to undertake the flights, knowing what was involved, we were happy to go with him,' wrote Schofield.

There was no more mention of it, and for nine days, Healy and his crew kicked their heels around Voe, wondering what was going on. Then eventually on Friday 24 April, orders and a detailed memorandum were sent from Group Captain Charles Dicken, Special Operations Planning Section at Eastbury Park to Durston AOC 18 Group. In the squadron commander's office there was another man – an Air Vice-Marshal. Hutton greeted Healy warmly and introduced Albert Durston, a portly man with an oval fleshy face and baldhead. Pleasantries over, Hutton told him to sit on one of the chairs in front of his desk.

'I asked you a few days ago if you would care to take part in high latitude flying,' Hutton said. 'You said you would, but I have to warn you again that these are no ordinary missions. In fact, the first one will have to be done on 2 May.'

'That's in eight days' time,' Healy replied, 'we've to get our Catalina to Greenock and pick up a replacement.'

'Moreover,' Hutton continued 'the flights that your undertaking are associated with a joint expedition named Operation *Fritham* and your plane are to be ready by 28 April and they have to be strong enough to withstand Arctic conditions. If for any reason you believe it unsuitable, reject it and ask for a better immediate replacement, without disclosing why.'

Initially Dennis Healy was the only one, who knew what was in the official contents of the ice reconnaissance. Later the remaining eight air crew with Healy strutted in to the office. Hutton emphasizing 'no disclosure to anyone what you're doing, especially colleagues at Voe,' he continued. 'All flights are to be typed up on Form 540 and 541 as 'Special Flight – Secret Operation'. Navigational and signal logs are not to be checked by the Operations Room navigational officer unless requested by Northwood.'

From the moment everyone left Hutton's office, they were jointly busy trying to get things in order at Voe, finally with overnight bags stowed away. At 11.00 hours on Sunday 26 April, Catalina *N-Nuts* took off on a three-hour flight to the Clyde. There was a great deal to do once their replacement Catalina *P-Peter* had been towed up the concrete slipway. The logistical headache of conversation was with Scottish Aviation chief engineer and electrical engineer. Trolleys, winching tools, sealed fuel tanks and other essential kit stood waiting.

Despite the accommodation shortage, Martin secured three bunks in one of the many wooden huts nearby. Over the next three days they frequently watched the mechanics and engineers swarm around the aircraft, with the clang of wrenches on metal and the snip of wire cutters and the occasional shouts amplified inside the maintenance building.

Glen, Godfrey and Sverdrup arrived at Greenock around 10.00 hours on Thursday, 30 April. The three had travelled up the previous day to Glasgow by night train, before driving down the following morning. Parking Glen's Humber nearby, they stood bemused as 'coming across the tarmac, were three young officers, a slim Flight Lieutenant with an arresting face who, clearly, was Healy,' wrote Glen, 'He was accompanied by Martin, and Schofield, collectively their skill was to lead to one of the most remarkable pieces of polar flying that had ever been carried out.'

The introduction between them all on the tarmac was like undertaking a masonic ritual, by the secrecy of what each party knew. All six quickly clambered into the Humber for lunch at The Bay Hotel, where chicken, potatoes, carrots, and spinach were devoured, as was a slice of Suet treacle pudding. Glen picking up the tab.[181]

Then back to Scottish Aviation Healy signing the final papers then clambered aboard the seaplane tender out to Catalina *P-Peter*. Healy was given the green light and the flying boat began to move. 'Ronnie' Martin helped steady the Catalina as it lifted off. Healy guided it round for one circuit then brought the flying boat down perfectly, with a clean line of white froth cleaved by the hull. However, the klaxon shrieked loudly – warning of imminent danger. Unseen, a number of rivets in the hull had popped, leaving a gaping hole and distorted pieces of sheet metal, with sea water rushing into amidships bulkhead between six and seven on the aircraft.

The remainder of Healy's crew with Glen, Godfrey and Sverdrup surrounded by all their gear and overnight bags, watched in horror from the main slipway as *P-Peter* began to sit lower in the water.[182] Healy and Martin scrambled in to the waiting tender and were brought ashore. Dennis Healy was furious and strutted out to the senior engineer's office. Startling Hugh Peterson sat behind his desk with his rage, '*P-Peter* is completely useless,' he complained. Peterson said he could not provide a suitable replacement: 'Right, we'll put all the equipment back into our *N-Nuts*', said Healy, who then immediately instructed his crew to begin kitting-out '*Nuts*" Scottish Aviation fitters immediately began to clamber over the Catalina as three additional fuel tanks are installed in the mid-sector of the fuselage. Also fitted were three magnetic compasses, and two specially selected directional gyros. One magnetic was balanced for latitude 47 degrees North and a second, 80 degrees North. Long-range radar was also crammed into the already compact navigator's space

More delays and paperwork: 'Poor Healy, everything was wanted in triplicate twice over,' said Glen, 'I'm sure you could have put a piece of blotting paper in front of him and he'd have signed it'.

By the late afternoon everything was in place. During the wait Healy learnt more at Greenock from Glen about Operation *Fritham* and how it was related to the work they where about to undertake which was more than Hutton knew. At about 16.00 hours, *N-Nuts* flew out over the boundary buoys, with Schofield giving his captain a course for Sullom Voe.

They flew down the west coast, with heather burning on Scarba, to the multi-coloured waters of the Sound of Jura, flowing through the Corryvreckan. Healy went around again, dropping low and then thundered over the whirlpool at 137 mph, and as close to fifty feet as Alexander Glen could judge. They carried out another run with Glen moving down to the starboard greenhouse-like blister to view the torrent of water as they passed over it and then returned to the correct heading flying low level over Cuillins and the clear beaches between Ullapool and Wrath.

Touching down on the water around 18.15 hours, on 2 May. Healy cruised to a vacant mooring point. Stepping out into the seaplane tender, Schofield was followed by the remaining twelve. Pleasant though it was in the early evening, there was work to be done. Healy stopped and talked to 210's 'Chiefy' and within minutes a competent ground crew began swarming over *N-Nuts* to prepare it for the following day.

Breakfast at Voe, was like any other. Daniel Godfrey, awoke with a mug of tea, eaten a full breakfast with everyone before heading over with Glen accompanied by Healy, Martin, Schofield and Kingett to the Operations Room. Everyone present had been issued with special security passes;

security, it had been stressed yet again, was paramount. The briefing was somewhat odd and did not follow the standard pattern. A lengthy telephone conversation between Hutton and Durston culminated in them learning that intercepted signals indicated that there was an enemy party at Spitsbergen. 'Take a look in Kings Bay at the old radio station,' said Hutton. Healy was given the authority to land at his discretion. 'Have a look at Spitsbergen and then return to Akureyri in Iceland, where the Norwegian steamships *Isbjørn* and *Selis* that would be transporting the Norwegian troops to Spitsbergen should be in position,' said Hutton. The Meteorological Officer's charts for the day were already marked up, the forecast was: 'unfavourable conditions, giving only the slimmest chances of Spitsbergen being clear'.

Briefing over, the men clambered onto a truck, clutching their Mae Wests and leather flying helmets they then trundled towards the slipway. It lurched to a stop at the carpenters' workshop, Godfrey jumped over the side disappeared then came out clutching bundles of wood, boxes of screws, a screwdriver, brace and bit. Everyone stared blankly at each other – it wasn't the time to ask questions. With everything ready for take-off, including the extra equipment that had been weighted and stored, a sledge, skies, two-man tent, and 200lbs of food, and Godfrey's collapsible dinghy stowed in the tail compartment. Healy assembled the crew and special observers around the navigator's compartment in *N-Nuts*. Schofield opened the sealed Admiralty chart of the Greenland and Barents Seas, unfolded it then spread it over the table. 'Well chaps,' he began once they were ready, 'you know as well as I do this is going to be special and I think we are more or less set. Firstly, we will undertake an ice reconnaissance from Bear Island to Spitsbergen, then a careful search of Spitsbergen, looking particularly around Icefjord for any tangible signs of any activity, which is assumed to be German. Lastly look for a sheltered place to land sufficiently clear of floating ice so that one member of the crew can disembark with Glen and Godfrey to paddle them ashore. The remaining crew on board will be on high alert and be prepared to take off at the first sign of danger. The crewman in the dinghy will take refuge in Spitsbergen until an attempt can be made to pick them up.'

There was a chance for everyone to say their piece. Kingett spoke on radio silence and about the signals that would be transmitted to them at six-hourly intervals and decoded on the Syko machine. The meeting ended, and Healy and Martin took to their seats. Engines were started at 14.20 hours, but Healy suddenly encountered difficulties a defective autopilot prevented them becoming airborne calmly it was fixed and the plane was airborne at 15.11 hours. Twenty-two minutes later Healy brought the Catalina to Muckle Flugga lighthouse, from where they set course.[183]

Sixty miles north of the Shetland Isles the Catalina entered dense sea-fog. Healy cautiously continued reducing height to 350 feet in the unbroken conditions for the next 1,200 miles. Winds remained light and visibility poor. During this time all the fuel in the internal tanks had been consumed and the greenhouse blisters were opened, and a stream of ice-cold air was blasted through the fuselage, removing all traces of vapour, which meant Jonathan Campbell was able to get the stove lit and give everyone a hot meal and get a cupper on – the thermos flasks were nearly empty. As Healy ate scrambled eggs, Martin adjusted their height to 500 feet with the visibility as low as 100 yards. Schofield moved aft again walking to the bunk section to take a drift-reading finding Godfrey busy drilling holes through two of his skies. The wind was veering and increasing in strength, and the temperature had drastically dropped to minus 2 degrees Centigrade. The blare of the klaxon brought everyone to action stations – unidentified aircraft on the western horizon that disappeared into cloud. 'Unable to recognise whether it was a Catalina, Junkers or Dornier,' Thomas said on the intercom. 'Let's go and have a look,' replied Healy but within three minutes had resumed the correct course. Midnight still minus 2 degrees Centigrade at 700 feet, wind conditions hadn't improved and as the Catalina ploughed on the temperature dropped drastically as they hit snow squalls. The first sighting of brash ice came at 01.40 hours with patches of drift ice. Glen and Godfrey began to record the ice conditions, whilst Schofield handled the F24 camera that had been modified to cope with the fog and Arctic twilight.

Visibility was little more than a few yards as the plane passed over the drift ice, the homing aerials of the radar showed Bear Island on the starboard bow and Martin made a right turn, towards it. Healy recorded that *N-Nuts* and crew had been flying for over ten hours.

Approaching Bear Island and Bear Channel at just a few feet from the sea, Martin could see the water had turned to thickly-packed drift ice. The fog became denser and the icing heavier as the temperature plummeted to minus twelve then minus nineteen as they neared Spitsbergen. At 03.20 hours, Martin glimpsed the towering mountains, looming nearby. Healy immediately turned away on a bearing that took them along the western shoreline for three quarters of an hour, using eyeballs and Schofield's radar. The fog became thicker still until they could not see further than the engine housings on the wings and temperature minus 16 degrees with the cloud base at 500 feet.

'It was very disappointing to find Spitsbergen shrouded,' said Glen, 'sitting in Martin's seat for a while I'd hoped to get a glimpse of the land, but it never materialized.'[184]

Healy altered course away from the land mass for safety. It quickly became clear that they could not continue as Healy flew along the western coastline for three quarters of an hour despite the fog clearing momentarily off Spitsbergen Bay, warmed by the Gulf Air Stream. They flew into fog that became thicker and the engine cowlings disappeared from view and there was no option left but for Schofield to give Healy and Martin the directions for Jan Mayen Island.

By 05.35 hours, drift ice appeared again as did the freezing fog. Healy pushed forward slightly on the stick just a little to descended to 100 feet.

'I made the decision there and then,' said Healy, 'to return to base. We had just enough fuel.' It was bitterly disappointing, but there was no other choice. Healy had made the right call.[185]

Between them they had done astonishingly well, as Jan Mayen Island came into view at 08.50 hours, Mount Beerenberg towering above them, its upper peak shrouded in cloud. Glen and Godfrey were still busy plotting and recording the ice: 'the field of polar pack ice disappeared when close to the island, but the surface was littered with large clusters of broken floes, separated by charcoal black patches of water,' Glen wrote in his note book, 'this was in stark contrast to the heavy polar ice with unbroken fields as vast as fifty miles'.[186]

As the last leg to Iceland commenced, they had been in the air for nineteen hours, the course followed the edge of the unbroken sea ice in a south-westerly direction until it swung away westward. Their ice reconnaissance had finished Healy gently turned to port, for Iceland. However, 'again fog was encountered, persisting all the way to the Icelandic coast where steady rain reduced our visibility to a minimum of 100 yards,' reported Healy. Kingett had received a radio message 'Akureyri Fit' all they had to do was find the entrance to the fjord, which was tricky.[187]

They reached Akureyri shortly before 13.50 hours safely touching down on the water in a patch of brilliant sunshine without any drama. 'We had been in the air for 23 hours,' scrawled Schofield. Dennis Healy switched the engines off, there was a sudden transition to complete silence, broken only by the lapping of water against the hull. Clambering from N-Nuts into a waiting seaplane tender and within half an hour the crew were sat devouring a gigantic meal in the Norwegian Mess of their hosts 330 Squadron based at Akureyri flying Northrop N-3PB floatplanes.[188] From there, preliminary reports were done for Coastal Command and the Admiralty; 'we had to report that we knew nothing more about what was happening in Spitsbergen,' said Glen.[189] Dicken immediately arranged for a further mission to be flown when the weather cleared. Glen and Godfrey went back to *N-Nuts* by tender and collected all the kit they had brought with them. Before departing both wrote letters to Dicken at Coastal Command Headquarters, complimenting the aircrew. 'Healy is especially first class and deserves the fullest recognition for the job in which he did,' wrote Alexander Glen. Congratulating each other for a final time, before Glen and Godfrey walked of in a jaunty mood to join Operation *Fritham*, very quickly the remaining four trooped off to get some rest.

There was more excitement to follow, with Healy and his crew returning on 8 May. Their Catalina had survived the twenty-three-hour flight, but they still needed a better plane to continue the Arctic flights as there would be seventeen more hazardous missions to map the Arctic Ocean. For their service during this period Healy received the DSO, Schofield a DFC and Kingett was awarded a DFM. Despite harrowing experiences 'we just got on with it,' Healy wrote in a letter home to his wife in a blue envelope.[190] He had devised a simple code, a blue envelope meant it did not contain any bad news. June 1942 was busy as Healy and Schofield reported to Eastbury Park, for a personal briefing about the missions that lay ahead supporting Operation *Fritham*. Dicken acknowledged that flights beyond the 80th parallel would be hazardous. Helping to forecast the movements of the ice pack 1,000 miles away. To accomplish this 6,000 gallons of aviation fuel and 250 gallons of oil, spares and equipment would be moved to Spitsbergen as soon as the expedition had established a firm base. Healy would be in charge. SASO George Baker was confident, enthusiastic, and full of assurance, but also cautious.

'You'll be on your own, Good luck!' was Bakers passing message.

The Exploration continued with *Fritham*[191] shut down and replaced by Operation *Gearbox*[192] the Admiralty wanting to know the ice conditions over the sea route to North Russia. There was a pronounced silence. Vice Admiral John Godfrey,[193] former pupil of Bradfield College and now Director of Naval Intelligence, next to him stood Alexander Glen then Healy. 'I've a wider view,' said Glen. 'The completion of a comprehensive survey of the movement of polar ice in the western hemisphere.' First they had to wait for convoy PQ17 that sailed from Iceland to north Russia in July, which was a disaster, fortunately the greater part of PQ18 in September came through successfully to the White Sea. 'So the supply line to north Russia was held open throughout the latter part of 1942,' wrote Glen. 'Many share the credit in Operation *Orator* to protect PQ18.'

Meanwhile, 210 had begun ops from Lakhta, the Russians had been pretty pleased with the way they were going as the Russian CO watched Tim's new Catalina 'P-Peter' being prepaired for another sortie.

On 25 September, Healy flew out from the Kola Inlet, on a due north heading to avoid enemy-occupied Norway. Schofield then gave a heading to turn northwest towards South Cape of Spitsbergen. The weather was as the Russian Met Officer has predicted 'dark, gusty, and rough,' with readings of 40 knot winds the chances of landing at Spitsbergen seemed unachievable.

Their new CO, 29 years-old Wing Commander Howard Johnson from Edenhurst in Caerphilly, favoured an immediate return. It was a long trip seventy miles to the Russian coastline when the plane's Claxton blared. Schofield went to his station as gunnery control officer aft of the two green house blisters. Plugging his intercom lead 'Tim Junker eighty-eight approaching, two miles and closing 500 feet above, at 30 degrees,' he relayed to Healy. Schofields running commentary continued: 'Green attack expected … range now one mile … stand by to turn … range half a mile … get ready to corkscrew … passing on bow …'[194]

The Junkers passed by on the bow. As it did, the Catalinas starboard gunner said 'I'm having a go.' He began peppering the rear part of the fuselage. Then Schofield's vision from the blister was blocked by the mainplane as soon as Junkers went passed. 'Anyone see it?' he enquired.

The Junkers stern gunner quickly replied and moments later there was a sound of bullets hitting the hull as the marauding Junkers headed south. After a second, Ernest Schofield made out the cockpit was dulled with smoke.

A single 7.92mm round had struck Dennis Healy from the machine gun fire. Falling from his seat Healy was caught by Pilot Officer George Adamson and with Schofield's help they got him through the bulkhead doors and laid him on the floorboards. Schofield grabbed the first aid box and then administered a shot of morphia. Adamson cradled his head on his knees and covered him with a goose down sleeping bag in the faintest of hopes that only shock and a bullet wound were the only trouble.

The burst of gunfire had wrecked several dials on the instrument panel as well as the aileron controls that impeded keeping the Catalina straight and level. Johnson, occupying the second pilot's seat, found himself in a difficult situation as the aircraft yawed in the opposite direction to the applied right aileron. Johnson kept the Catalina in flight, steering by reference to wind lanes given to him over the intercom by

The fighting Davenport brothers serving in the RAAF in England, taken together at RAAF Overseas Headquarters, Kodak House. From left to right: 403216 Squadron Leader Phillip Davenport of Sydney, NSW; 403403 Squadron Leader (later Wing Commander) Jack Davenport of Sydney, NSW; 413547 Flying Officer Keith Davenport of Sydney, NSW.

Handley Page Hampden TB Mark I at Thorney Island Hampshire. Built by English Electric Co., Preston, and converted to Hampden T.B.I (Torpedo Bomber).

All photographs have been kindly supplied by the author except those listed. Every effort has been made to trace copyright holders; those overlooked are invited to get in touch with the publishers.

Informal photograph of Ken Dempsey, and William Stanley causally standing next to their Beaufighter Johnnie NT892 taken a few hours prior to flying an op on 9 September 1944.

A unique photograph showing Sam McHardy and Roger Morewood in the foreground with Morewood's Blenheim MKVIF being prepared for the flight to Bircham Newton in May 1940. It is noteworthy because the plane's undersides are completely painted night black as it was still thought that 248 would operate in a night fighter role. Both Blenheim fighters would stay painted in this scheme whilst flying sorties over the Dutch and French coast until they returned to their flights at Montrose and Dyce.

Prince Leopold seen in civilian colours. The vessel participated in the Combined Operation on 27 December 1941 as one of His Majesties Ships. The prompt actions of its captain saved Rhodesian Sergeant Reginald 'Reggie' Smith of 50 Squadron.

Official Portrait of Lloyd Trigg DFC, VC. (*Air Force Museum of New Zealand*)

Official Portrait of Wing Commander 'Bill' Sise DSO* DFC* and Flight Lieutenant Raymond Price DFC. (*John Sise*)

HMS Clarkia, commanded by Stanley Darling HMAS Rushcutter Graduate who had joined RANR as a 14 year old midshipman in 1925. Darling picked up the seven U-boat survivors at 06.37 hours on 13 August 1943. (*Royal Navy Museum Portsmouth*)

Blindfolded and sitting at the stern of a tug are the U-boats officers waiting to be brought ashore in Freetown, Sierra Leone; Right to Left: 26 year-old Oberleutnant zur See Clemens Schamong; 22 year-old, Leutnant zur See Alfons Heimannsberg and 23 year-old, Leutnant (Ing.) Emil Giesbert. (*H. L. Thompson, New Zealand*)

Blindfolded and lying on the rubber dinghy which saved his life, one of the German U-boat survivors, from U-468 suffering from a severe shark bite in his leg, comes alongside the jetty in Freetown where the prisoners were landed. (*H. L. Thompson, New Zealand*)

Dennis Healy's aircrew in February 1942: Flight Lieutenant Dennis Healy, Pilot Officer Ernest Schofield. Standing from left to right: Sergeant 'Taff' Thomas, Sergeant Howard Watson, Aircraftsman David Baird, Sergeant B. Webster, Sergeant G. Kingett, Sergeant Jonathan Campbell, Sergeant K. Jones. Seven of these men would fly sorties in Catalina P – Peter. (*Healy Family*)

Official portrait of Dennis Healy and his wife Madeline taken shortly after their wedding. (*Healy Family*)

Portrait of Pilot Officer Roger Morewood, taken by Walter Bird at his Studios on the Cromwell Road. Bird was commissioned by Tatler magazine to produce portraits of all 56 Squadron pilots for a double page spread. (*Abingdon Boys School Archive*)

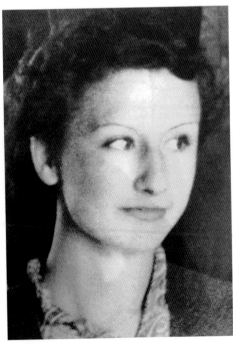

Max Guedj and his fiancée Maria.

Morocco 1940; 'two 'snap's' by Max Guedj showing his colleagues with their 25mm Hotchkiss anti-aircraft gun near Casablanca.

Official Portrait of Wing Commander Howard D Fraser OBE, CO of 236 Squadron. More commonly known as 'Duncan' he tragically lost his life on Friday 20 November, along with his 22 year-old navigator Flying Officer Reginald Griffin of Ilford, Essex. (*John Fraser*)

Squadron Leader John Watson sits for an official portrait after being promoted on 1 July 1944, sole survivor of Sunderland B-Beer. Prior to volunteering for the RAAF, John was a sugar technologist in Richmond, New South Wales, after demobilisation he put himself through business school, worked for Meares and Phillips stockbrokers, becoming President of the Australian Stock Exchange. (*Photograph provided by Virginia, Rowland and Alex Watson on behalf of the Watson Family. (2017)*)

Inscribed Barbara Tribe LONDON 1943 – Barbara Tribe sculpting of Triggs bust was executed swiftly and surely over half a dozen two-hour sittings. Originally cast in plaster, however in 1969 Tribe received a letter commissioning her to cast three bronzes one of which was Flight Lieutenant Allan Triggs, for the Australian War Memorial collection. For these she received £210 per bust. (*Jane Robertson AWM (2016)*)

Official Portrait of 'Ken' Gatward as a pilot officer.

East Dean Grammar School, Cinderford in the Forest of Dean's football team in October 1935. Their captain Gilbert Fern is seated second in from the left – their goalkeeper. He would go onto study a teaching degree, once qualified the war interrupted his ambitions. After being demobbed Fern returned to teach in the Forest of Dean, although he never spoke of his part in Operation Chariot or Squabble. (*Photograph courtesy of Mrs. Judith Fern widow of Gilbert Fern DFM (2017)*)

Adamson from navigational charts, as Johnson was unable to determine the P9 compass' reliability after the dogfight.

Unable to negotiate the sharp contours of the Kola Inlet, he made a controlled force landing in extremely rough waters close to Kildin Island at 15.12 hours, Adamson climbed out and manage to tied the Catalina to a Russian buoy. 'Where was their interpreter, Lieutenant Leo 'George' Trackenburg of the Russian Navy?' enquired Johnson.[195] Eventually a Russian submarine chaser picked up the aircrew, depositing them ashore at Polyarnoe on the Kola Peninsula almost completely north of the Arctic Circle. By 26 September they had reached Grasnaya where the administrative staff at the Allied detachment made immediate arrangements for Dennis Healy to have a military funeral. It took place on Monday 27 September at midday. Adamson, Schofield and members of 210 Squadron still at Grasnaya, collected the coffin, which had been placed, on a small flatbed lorry draped with a freshly starched Union Jack. Six Russian soldiers formed a guard of honour, and eight of 210's men bore the coffin. Mourners were led by Wing Commander Barnard Sandeman, who had taken over from Air Vice Marshal Frank Hopps at the close of Operation *Orator* the defence of PQ18. 210's CO Howard Johnson read the Lord's Prayer; a volley of shots rang out into a cloudless sky.

It was a tragic waste, yet Healy's achievements were Herculean. Now in 2017[196] the ice flow charts are still helping scientists map climate change.

Chapter 6

Lieutenant Colonel Jean Maurice Guedj DSO, DFC*

Squadron Leader Jean Maurice Guedj DSO, DFC was a French Moroccan Jew, he lived with his family in the country's capital Casablanca in the central western part of Morocco. Fortunately, life had been good, as a family, they had not wanted for much during the depression that hit in the 1930s, due to his father Félix Guedj being president of the Barrister of The Bar Association and a senior lawyer business was brisk. Maurice like many French colonial children having been partly schooled in Casablanca returned to France accompanied by his mother to be sent to boarding school in Paris at Lycée Janson de Sailly. Returning to Paris was a happy experience; with occasional excisions to the Right Bank's district of Montmartre. During school holidays, he returned to Morocco or went to relatives in France. Through hard work he received high marks when taking the baccalaureate in 1930 and won a coveted place at the prestigious Paris Law Faculty.

From central Paris the eighteen-year-old began exploring Europe, by different modes of transport. The year 1933 found Maurice, aged twenty, in Germany's capital Berlin witnessing the Reichstag fire early on in the morning of Sunday 28 February, before arranging a ticket back to Paris. His prospects were remarkably good as a lawyer, impressing senior administrators, judges and lawyers within the Palais de Justice mahogany-stained panelled courts with his mastery and oratorical skills, 'he will keep the ear of the judges,' lawyer Vincent de Moro-Giafferi noted.

Maurice journeyed back to Casablanca and began practicing law with his father. Business was brisk and rewarding but he still looked for new experiences. It was agreed that Maurice would join the Army Reserves, and subsequently during his service volunteered for flying training, which was undertaken in Morocco using First World War vintage Nieuport biplanes and other types, gaining his French Aeronautical Certificate in

1938. Despite his passion for aviation Maurice continued his army training with his colleagues.[197]

Maurice Guedj found love in their law office.[198] The girl who was occupying so much of his thoughts was a beautiful trainee lawyer from Spain with a sparkling personality. Although Maria was in her twenties, the morals of the day made it very difficult for young girls, but they did get to see something of each other, meeting for a meal, in a friend's apartment or at parties, which occasionally French artist Jacques Majorelle frequented spontaneously conversing about his Majorelle Blue construction. Maurice occupied much of Maria's time over the next few months and they hoped to soon be man and wife. Maria had by now agreed to marry him, although she was understandably worried about her Spanish parents, reaction. They had after all not met Maurice.

In the Guedj's house they listened to Chamberlain announce, on Sunday 3 September 1939 that Britain was at war with Germany. Both Maurice's parent's families had experienced first-hand, just over a generation before, the Kaiser's invasion and the country being devastated by war. Later that afternoon the family troublingly listened to the radio, as French Prime Minister Édouard Daladier announced that the deadline for German troops to be withdrawn from Poland had passed. 'I heard this voice saying we were now at war with Germany,' Maurice said, 'there was just stony silence.' Despite the mobilisation of his unit, the 2nd Regiment of Light Infantry, Maurice, as a practicing barrister was officially excluded from joining the fight against Germany, although he believed it was his duty to play a part.[199] Maria was very supportive, and there were no great emotional upheavals as they snatched brief moments between his military training. In spring 1940, his fiancée gave birth to a healthy baby girl to help them start a new life together. However, Maurice said farewell before arrangements to marry could be finalized: urgently called back to his unit wearing his 1914-vintage uniform and an oval helmet to match. How the war was changing everyone's lives.

All he could do was to listen or read about the story unfolding about his mother country, as the Battle of France was fought. One month later, Maurice who, bearing a third stripe commanded a dozen conscripts manning a twin-25mm Hotchkiss anti-aircraft gun, was disheartened as he listened to Marshal of France Philippe Pétain, deliver a radio address to the French people announcing his intention to ask for an armistice with Germany.

The repercussions of the armistice, signed on Saturday 22 June 1940, soon reached Casablanca. Maurice learnt under Articles 5, 6, and 7 of the armistice terms France had to hand over to Germany 'all arms, planes and fortifications.' Article 9 called on the French Government 'to prevent members of the armed forces from leaving the country or fighting against Germany.' Demobilisation was swift, the French Moroccan authorities quickly brought in strict measures to prevent individuals from trying to join de Gaulle's forces in Britain after his broadcast on the BBC, announcing that 'the flame of French resistance must not be extinguished and will not be extinguished.' It was extremely difficult for Maurice to leave being in a position of authority in the legal profession, however this also had advantages.

Maurice aided by his father Félix Guedj in a subterfuge fictionalized documentation for a court case in Tangier in which Maurice was acting as lawyer at Tribunal de commerce de Tanger for the convicted party. The twenty-seven-year-old said goodbye to Maria, his daughter and parents, then left by car with a trusted chauffeur who drove him to Tangier carefully negotiating Vichy police who were suspicious and at times obstructive at checkpoints on route eventually reaching the city centre. Stepping out he saw some Spanish soldiers near a slogan 'Tánger español' being painted out and walked to the bustling quayside. With a permitted travel visa,[200] he managed to get through the French and Spanish officials and onto a ship that was leaving port. Maurice had thought the boat would take him to Gibraltar, or Lisbon, but instead it sailed to Plymouth in England.[201] Thursday 26 September 1940, on arrival the young Frenchman left the Devonshire port making his way to London and, after being screened by British Intelligence stepped through the charred debris from a night of violence 'I was immediately struck by a strong smell of smoke. It wasn't the musty smell of long-closed houses. It was a mixture of the acrid stench of burnt timber,' said Guedj.[202] Arriving at Charlton Gardens the headquarters of the newly established Free French armed forces, Captain Emile Bouderie of the Free French Air Force welcomed Guedj and asked about his escape. 'You must prepare yourself patiently for a long struggle,' Bouderie said, then with a firm handshake and words of encouragement he let Jean Maurice Guedj go, to Hampshire.[203]

South of the small market town of Odiham, Hampshire, was where he found himself sent; here he would begin training to be an aviator. Four weeks earlier Air Vice Marshal David Donald, Director of Organisation had designated RAF Odiham airfield as the Flight Training School for the Free French Air Force and it was here that Maurice gained experience on de Havilland Tiger Moths and Miles Magisters, although stipulated to fly French types. The Magister was more modern looking than its contemporary the Tiger Moth. Besides the obvious difference in being a monoplane, the Frenchman was surprised to find it had brakes, flaps and a tail wheel – it also handled better than the Tiger Moth.[204] With his language skills it helped that English was the main tongue spoken during training. After completion of the course Maurice moved on to Advance and Operational Conversion Units. Pilot training continued at Sywell, under the tutoring of Commandant Edouard Pinot.[205] Pinot had originally been an air mechanic in the First World War before transferring to retrain and qualify as pilot; May 1940 saw him commanding 23 Elementary Flying School at Le Mans and Vannes before heading across the Channel with 115 men aboard *La Trébouliste* a lobster boat to England.

Unusually, he was then posted to Shawbury were he carried on with his conversion to British twin-engine types, at any rate they were a vast improvement on the Potez 630 he'd flown at Odiham. Here he gained his wings and a commission as a Lieutenant in the Free French Air Force in the summer of 1941. A brief break, then Maurice transferred to No. 2 (Coastal) Operational Training Unit in Catfoss, in Yorkshire.[206] He and his compatriot Gérard Weil found flying the robust Bristol Beaufighter with its solid gun platform 'a piece of cake.' With 'above average' marks Maurice and Weil were advised that they'd been posted to 248 Squadron at Bircham Newton, near King's Lynn, in 16 Group.

On 19 February 1942, the Frenchmen arrived as 2nd Lieutenant at the station. It had been the intention of Wing Commander Stewart Wise DFC to crew them up straight away, however, as CO, he was now at Dyce, so Squadron Leader Roger Morewood stepped in. Maurice Guedj would stay crewed with Sergeant Charles Corder as at Catfoss.[207]

Corder had joined the Royal Air Force back in May 1940. He was of medium height, quiet and thoughtful, but his face occasionally raised a smile. His father Charles hailed from Reading. Shortly before 1911 he became a sales ledger clerk in West Thurrock and married Corder's mother.[208] West Thurrock village was a pretty remote spot, although it had two pubs, a post office, bakery and a general store. Corder had a round trip to Palmer's Grammar School in Grays of nearly five miles. Starting in September 1929 he joined Priestley House, and continually gained distinctions in mathematics. Becoming one of the House Captains in 1935 he also sat the Higher School Certificate and passed in two subjects.[209] With the right qualifications, he joined Lloyds Bank and by the time war broke out he was working as a senior clerk.

By May 1940, when he had turned twenty-one, Charles had already decided that he wanted to be a pilot. Unfortunately, during the medical, the eye test revealed his vision in his left eye borderline. He was told he could do ground duties. 'But I had my heart set on being a pilot,' he said. Showing the same forthright determination that would come forth later, he 'scraped a pass of 88 per cent,' when taking a wireless operator's course at Yatesbury, and was then finally recommended a place on a navigation course at Torquays Initial Training Wing. Fatigues, inspections, physical training, lectures, flying training and assessments continued to form part of the daily routine, until Charles successfully passed out being posted to 248 Squadron. Over the following days Bircham Newton became a like a child's spinning top, as detachments went to Portreath, Sumburgh, Dyce, and Leuchars.

Morewood was busy trying to keep the aircrew and ground staff on the same page, as pilots and navigators were posted on detachments or transferred to the Middle East. It was a logistical headache, with new crews hastily brought in.

Within days, Maurice had taken off on his first familiarization trip, doing one wide circuit with Morewood. Corder and Maurice were working well together. He was a good pilot and Corder trusted him, which for obvious reasons was essential for the harmony and success of any crew. However, the partnership was broken on 18 March, when Corder was paired with Sergeant Alan Welch who together with Pilot Officer Adam Wills and Sergeant Ronald 'Alf' Voce left Bircham Newton for Leuchars on a seven-day detachment.[210]

Between training flights the softly-spoken Maurice wrote letters to the bureaucratic Air Ministry requesting to adopt an assumed name, as he'd shortly be operating over enemy territory.

On Friday 27 March 1942 the Commissariat National à l' Air in Queensberry Place, London, confirmed Jean Maurice Guedj could adopt the nom de guerre Lieutenant Maurice on receipt of a letter from Flight Lieutenant André Ribo: 'I had received reports that my father had recently been sentenced to imprisonment in Morocco on account of his pro-British sympathies and propaganda, and wanted to safeguard the 'Guedj Family,' Maurice wrote.[211]

Reunited with Corder Maurice's first flight was a navigational exercise. The cloud base was low, and the visibility was so bad Maurice had to fly under the clouds, at about 300 feet. They missed one of their landmarks but managed to return to base without trouble, and then on Wednesday 1 April they found themselves at Dyce being briefed to fly a convoy escort. The ships were being shadowed by Heinkels and U-boats the sortie would be led by Pilot Officer Frank Bates in *X-X-Ray*, with Maurice Guedj in *C-Charlie*.

It was 13.50 hours when they got airborne after four and a half hours of resolute concentration looking for the enemy in appalling conditions with visibility less than a mile Bates made the decision to return to base,

Maurice landing away at Leuchars. 'Made extensive search for enemy, but sighted nothing,' wrote Corder in a letter.

Both Maurice and Corder over the next twelve months gained experience on maritime missions over European and Mediterranean waters. On the morning of Wednesday 10 March 1943, they were airborne at 07.15 hours with three other Beaufighters, led by Squadron Leader Frederick Burton DFC who, until seven days previously, was with 132 Operational Training Unit as an instructor having completed an operational tour. The chosen four flew on, leaving Predannack airfield and England behind, dropping low over the Channel. Their line patrol had begun, on a course of 194 degrees. It was soon after that they were approaching the vast open expanse of the Bay of Biscay. *U-Uncle* was on the port side of the formation, her pilot Flight Lieutenant Aubrey Inniss, suddenly spotted a moving shape, 300 degrees at 4,000 feet.[212]

'Eight-eight!' he exclaimed over the R/T.

Inniss, Reginald Stinger in *T-Tommy* and Maurice in *W-William*, all climbed to get round onto the Junkers tail to come out of the sun in line astern. Moments later Inniss closed to within 1,000 yards. 'I could see it clearly. Some sort of coloured markings,' said Inniss. Within seconds the Junkers had roared upwards towards the clouds leaving puffs of exhaust fumes, Inniss closed to a range of 700 yards: 'I pressed the gun button on the stick. But I hadn't fired! Not a single cannon round,' Inniss continued, 'frustrated I yanked the stick and broke away to starboard for "Reggie" to have a go.'

Stringer heard 'misfire,' on the R/T and saw *U-Uncle* break right. He accelerated and pursued the Junkers, firing short bursts of 20mm from *T-Tommy*, rounds were seen hitting the port tailplane. Feldwebel Joahnn Kurth keeping their rear covered, and got off a burst at *T-Tommy*, a bullet severing the hydraulic pipeline. In response to Stringer's breaking away, Maurice was then the lone attacker. From 300 yards dead astern he opened fire with a two-second burst of 20mm cannon, which penetrated the port engine, and disintegrated the canopy. Instinctively Maurice edged ever closer to within 170 yards.[213] Within moments a second burst of 20mm cannon had struck. Flames leaped out from the port engine, spreading to the fuel tanks and enveloping the Junkers in an orange glow. Oberleutnant Ernst Stickel pulled the plane steeply to starboard, allowing Kurth to return an accurate burst as it slowly dropped, flame and smoke trailing behind before it broke up plunging into the sea. It then exploded into a million pieces.

On board, Maurice had miraculously survived the hail of bullets, the plane's cockpit having caught the full force of Kurth's rounds the Frenchman was now desperately trying to keep it airborne. The instrument panel had been punctured, the cable to the port fuel cock had been severed, the port pitch control lever had been broken and splinters from the cockpit's Perspex canopy had showered Maurice slashing his head and both legs. The Beaufighter was practically uncontrollable.

With no reply from Corder over the intercom he tried to attract his navigator's attention to the unfolding drama. With the intercom dead Charles Corder crawled forward pushing the doors aside to assist his pilot, desperately struggling to keep the stricken aircraft airborne.[214] Corder came up behind Maurice in the cramped cockpit and assisted yanking the stick, and it suddenly responded. Corder returned to the rear, picked up the Aldis lamp in an attempt to signal Burton, Inniss and Stringer, but a stray bullet had pierced the casing. Returning to his seat, Corder began taking bearings and went forward to give Guedj a course to steer for their Cornish base, 180 miles away.

He stood behind Maurice who was still battling to keep the plane in the air, while in trying to assist Corder pulled back the jammed port airscrew pitch control lever; it came away in palm of his hand. Annoyed, he went back to his radio and sent a message to 19 Group Headquarters in Plymouth that they were returning to base and that Maurice was injured. Then, Corder repaired the intercom using his folding pocketknife but then realised their port engine had seized.

The Beaufighter momentarily seemed to hesitate, but it was too late. The nose dropped. Swooping down directly towards the sea Guedj, with the stick virtually in the pit of his stomach, regained control at about thirty-five feet. Then fifteen minutes before reaching the English coast, the starboard engine caught fire, with smoke and flames spreading to the cockpit. Grabbing the port side handheld extinguisher Corder doused the flames until extinguished. He then transmitted an SOS and fired distress cartridges to attract the attention of those ashore. As they approached Cornwall, it was clear that the aircraft had either to ditch in the heavy seas or clear the cliffs.

As Corder guided Maurice to the cliffs' lowest point, observers on the ground were convinced that the plane would crash. He instinctively pulled up, climbing a fraction to clear the hills beyond Kynance Cove and Charles reassured him over the intercom 'only one point four-zero miles to go!' The airfield was straight ahead. As he approached, to make an emergency landing the starboard engine seized, with the control tower ordering Maurice to 'come straight in.' At 09.32 hours, *W-William* careered across the Predannack grass after three hours and forty-five minutes in the air, it ground to a halt. The forward section of the plane then burst into flames, belching thick acrid smoke. In the aircraft, Corder was able to open his blister and clamber out then jumped through the flames, and scrambled to the nose. Maurice, despite his wounds, released the pilot's hatch, and hauled himself out, as Corder ran round to see if his pilot was out of harm's way, which, fortunately, Maurice Guedj was.[215]

They congratulated each other, feeling pretty cheerful notwithstanding their ordeal, with medical staff making them clamber into the ambulance so they could be attended too. Afterwards both filed their reports. 'With muscle I undoubtedly hadn't used since my youth, after that kind of sortie I rapidly scrambled clear,' said Maurice to his commanding officer, Arthur Montagu-Smith, known as 'Monty,' a pre-war officer who had joined up in 1935 and 'been there and done that,' before commanding 264 Squadron in the autumn of 1940, and was now in his third year with Coastal Command.

They would both live to fight another day, although how they avoided plunging into a watery grave was something of a miracle. Maurice and his English navigator had had a very, very lucky escape.

Guedj told one reporter: 'It would have been impossible without my navigator; he was really the key man on board the most hair-raising adventure we have lived through.' For their actions in recovering the aircraft, Maurice Guedj and Charles Corder were put forward for decorations, which were confirmed thirty-five days later. There was a Conspicuous Gallantry Medal for Corder, the first of Coastal Command's GCMs and for Guedj a Distinguished Service Order, the first French airman to receive the DSO.

General de Brigade Martial Valin, Commissare National à l' Air, had been having breakfast when notification arrived. It read: 'I Air Chief Marshal Sir Philip Joubert de la Ferté, Air Officer Commanding-in-Chief Coastal Command, have the honour to bring you notice that the Air Ministry has informed me that The King has been pleased to approve the immediate award of the Distinguished Service Order to Lieutenant J. Maurice (Guedj) of the Fighting French Air Force in recognition of his distinguished service in air operations.'[216]

The citation was worded: 'while patrolling over the Bay of Biscay on 10 March 1943, this pilot attacked and destroyed a Junkers 88. Although his own aircraft was severely damaged, and he had sustained wounds to his head and both legs, he returned to base.'

Back at Predannack in Cornwall, Montagu-Smith, knew that both men had completed 300 hours flying and their seventy-fifth mission together and were due a rest, but he wrote an immediate request to Valin and Joubert that they allow him to retain Maurice and Corder.[217] Montagu-Smith was unable to influence his seniors and on 23 March, it was confirmed that both must be rested at a non-operational unit.

For their farewell Air Vice-Marshal Geoffrey Bromet officially visited on 21 April, shortly after half past four, against the backdrop of a 248 Squadron parade. Lieutenant Maurice Guedj was presented with his DSO and a Distinguished Flying Cross for the excellent work he had carried out during the past year with the squadron. Bromet, also congratulated the squadron as a whole for flying 141 operational missions.

Maurice, and newly commissioned Pilot Officer Charles Corder, were posted to Catfoss, as ordered. Almost immediately, Maurice found living and working at a non-operational base a torturous experience, writing *'Je me sens cerné'* – 'I feel hemmed in'. Three weeks after arriving Maurice was in charge of the pilots' gunnery skills course and the results on marksmanship began to rise, as did his spirits.

After a period as an instructor, a second tour beckoned. Unfortunately for Maurice, in March 1944, when he learned that he would be posted, he found there had been changes in command. He took himself off to Seaford House in Belgrave Square, home of the Allied Air Co-operation and Foreign Liaison office, and pleaded to Flight Lieutenant William Herrera, to be allowed back onto 248 Squadron.[218] Compatriots were getting killed or, in 'Reggie' Stinger's case, learning to swim.

Fortunately for him it was brought to Coastal's new Commanding-in-Chief, Sholto Douglas', attention. He urged Air Vice-Marshal Sir Brian Baker, then AOC 19 Group, to take him on. 'You'll find him absolutely first rate, according to Arthur Montagu-Smith,' Douglas told Baker, 'and this is a one-year-old promise now in fulfilment.' Herrera in Belgrave Square was notified by the Air Ministry that Maurice Guedj's move had been approved and with it a promotion to Commandant equivalent to a Squadron Leader. Wing Commander Anthony Phillips received a cablegram that Maurice would be transferring from 132 OTU to 248 Squadron. Which was now based at Portreath, in North Cornwall, and with it came a change of navigator. Flying Officer Ronald 'Alf' Voce, who had received a commission and completed one tour of operations with 248, arrived in his Austin 7 from 3 School of General Reconnaissance in Blackpool. He was pleased to be crewed-up with a pilot who already had operational experience and whose previous navigator he'd known as a sergeant. He flew his first mission with Maurice on 25 May – a five-hour patrol over naval vessels.

His next few missions followed in quick succession. '6 June 1944 – D-Day the liberation of France has begun,' Voce jotted down. Maurice and Voce took off from Portreath leading a quartet of Mosquitoes, with no enemy ships or aircraft sighted they turned about when Voce sighted a Naval Motor Torpedo Boat low in the water. He hastily looked to his left out across the wing, seeing Voce was right, 'see if they want an escort,' said Maurice on the intercom.[219] *N-Nuts* accompanied the vessel to within a mile of Falmouth then re-joined the formation to touch down. A second wave of ten Mosquitoes led by Randall droned out towards their rendezvous with seventeen Beaufighters, before Maurice and Voce had reached a vacant dispersal.

Flying Officer John Green DFC in *G-George* and Flight Sergeant's Lionel 'Taffy' Stoddard and navigator Charles Watson in *F-Freddie* on the outer edge of this formation became separated and, at roughly 21.30 hours, stumbled across a lone Junkers 188 storking British destroyers north of Ushant. In this one-sided engagement Green fired, but his cannon missed. The Pontypridd-born Stoddard took advantage and pounced, firing at extremely close range and the Junkers fell out of the sky into the sea.[220]

Luck played a huge part in whether or not crews survived, particularly now they were penetrating the Biscay ports and rivers. A chance burst of flak struck the de Havilland Mosquito *Y-Yoke* of Wing Commander Anthony Phillips DSO DFC on Tuesday 4 July, when blasting two merchantman and a coaster with high explosive cannon shells in the River Odet at Bénodet with his two flight commanders Maurice and 'Hal' Randall. 'Phillips was hit badly, and crashed in flames into a field, exploding on impact,' wrote John Yonge. New Zealander 'Bill' Sise moved straight across from 235 Squadron to become 248's CO, although looking through the files in the commander's office, Sise's navigator Raymond Price was horrified to find the loss rate stood at nearly 17 percent.

Maurice and Voce continued their partnership on anti-shipping missions until 24 July; he then had a succession of ten navigators until Flying Officer James 'Jimmy' Orchard flew with him on Thursday 17 August. 'He wasn't a mixer on the ground, as far as some SNCOs were concerned. Even though he had flown with Corder earlier in the war,' said William 'Bill' Parfitt. Dennis 'Benny' Goodman, Reginald Genno's navigator, rather agreed.[221] 'Maurice seemed to have great difficulty in getting down to talk to people below his rank, he was the leader.' There seemed to some at Portreath that there was a bit of discrimination on his part, this was understandable, but in fairness to Maurice Guedj, such were the pressures on his time, as a flight commander assessing the potential of a new partnership during a single mission and with two different messes for officers and NCOs, it is hard to see how he could possibly get to know his navigator – there simply wasn't the time or the opportunity.

On the rare occasion Maurice was actually around in the Officers' Mess, having a drink with the chaps on 27 August, New Zealander Hector Bolitho tried to seize the opportunity to get an interview with the Frenchman. 'Inducing pilots to talk is an art and I am learning it slowly. However, getting a story out of this French pilot is like opening fresh oysters with your bare hands.[222] But I am also arrogant,' wrote Bolitho in his *Letts* notebook. On the Saturday 2 September, Commanding-in-Chief Sholto Douglas, by then nine months in office, was satisfied that the reallocation of squadrons to Scotland was completely sorted out. Senior staff notified 'Bill' Sise at Portreath that 248 Squadron would relocate on 10 September to Banff in northeast Scotland, after 235 Squadron's departure. On the same day Bolitho, from 224 Squadron's officers' mess the Watergate Bay Hotel, jotted down: 'our task in the Bay ended in early September. The last of the U-boats had withdrawn and were making their way north, underwater all the way.' Both headed north, Bolitho in a 244 Squadron Liberator to Stornoway, and Sise leading his flight commander Maurice Guedj to Scotland, 'to fight another fight,' said Maurice.

The Norwegian coast had become the focal point for anti-shipping missions. Their first successful mission had seen the combination of 144 and 404 Beaufighters and 235 and 248 Mosquitoes damaging a 3,000-ton merchant ship, a second of 2,500 tons and two flak-ships. On 24 September, four Mosquitoes from 248 Squadron led by Maurice with Orchard as lead navigator undertook another sortie. Making landfall at Utvær Lighthouse, seven minutes later, they struck vessels in Hjelte Fjord. Caught by surprise a Tsetse Mosquito fired a brace of six-pounder rounds at the merchantman, two seconds after the anti-flak Mosquitoes raced in firing cannon and machine guns at the single flak-ship. Both were damaged, and the flak-ship left ablaze.

Friday 13 October saw twenty-two Mosquitoes and sixteen Beaufighters with Maurice at the helm cross the North Sea on course for Southern Norway's Kristiansand to form up at first light around flares and flame floats dropped by an air sea rescue Vickers Warwick. Deteriorating conditions in the area meant most aircraft missed the illumination, and, consequently, the merchant ships. Individual aircraft flew searches along the rugged coast, however, tumultuous clouds were encountered and strong winds which flipped the Mosquito of Flying Officer Patrick 'Pat' Ross DFC, 'like a pancake on Shrove Tuesday,' he would later write.[223] These tempestuous conditions caught out a second Mosquito that failed to return. Flight Lieutenant George Nicholls and Flying Officer Antony Hanson being the first 248 crew lost since August: it was a bitter blow to this tight-knit coastal community.[224]

On the afternoon of Saturday, 21 October, Maurice led a small force of Mosquitoes in *A-Apple*. The four planes pounded anchored merchantmen in the harbour at Haugesund. Two merchantmen were set on fire, and rockets fired by a trio of Canadian Beaufighters did further damage. The force encountered fierce flak causing damage to Tsetse *I-Ink*.[225] Maurice and Orchard saw the plane five minutes after they took on the targets, then Maurice spotted green florescence and wreckage on the water roughly three miles from shore. Norwegian fishing boats were sailing towards the debris. Flying Officers Robert Driscoll and Tony Hannant managed to struggle out of the wreckage but were not so fortunate when they surfaced. Despite them being in good physical condition they drowned.[226]

C-in-C Coastal Command Sholto Douglas, and Air Vice Marshal Sturley Simpson who headed up 18 Group summoned all the squadron COs and their flight commanders and said they'd decided to fly the Mosquito and Beaufighters Wing separately.[227] Maurice his CO 'Bill' Sise and Stanley Nunn flight commander of 'B' Flight agreed with the decision to take advantage of the Mosquitoes superior range and speed. Douglas had also sanctioned the expansion of the Banff Wing with Wing Commander 'Sam' McHardy DSO DFC flying in with his intrepid 143 Squadron from North Coates. Aircew began converting from Beaufighters to Mosquitoes using a pair of training versions of the plane. McHardy's first official flight with Maurice Guedj had not been a disappointment – never before had he felt so much power in a twin-engine aircraft.

Poor weather hampered missions off the Norwegian coast in November, and Maurice had to be content with being deputy strike leader to 'Bill' Sise on 21 November as fifty-five Mosquitoes were marshalled into the air over the Banffshire countryside. Maurice paired up with Ronald Voce, joined the circling formation in *A-Apple* and watched *D-Dog* form up on their starboard side. In *L-Leather*, Flying Officer Kenneth Wing and his navigator had been rather taken aback by the number of aircraft in the air – eighty-seven with fifty-five Beaufighter's from Dallachy and twelve single-engine Mustangs flying top cover. At Ålesund harbour targets failed to materialise so Sise wheeled the large force around and headed back to base. At around 17.30 hours Maurice touched back down at Banff only to see the Station Commander waiting for him. He immediately wondered whether it was about refusing Bolitho another interview, but all Aitken wanted to know was whether he wanted to take over as CO of 143 Squadron the first week of December when McHardy became tour-expired.

6 December 1944. Maurice Guedj became CO of 143 Squadron the Frenchman already easily surpassed what should have been required

of him, as had a fellow ship-buster Australian Wing Commander Richard 'Dickie' Atkinson DFC, who had already fought in the Pacific on Catalinas, before arriving in Great Britain and doing a stint on Tsetse Mosquitoes with his English navigator Valentine 'Val' Upton.[228] Now CO of 235 Squadron, on the 13 December Atkinson had been the vanguard of a mission to Eidsfjord. Precision was key, with tracer arcing towards them in their dive, the plane jolted as cannon shells struck, then an 88mm shell ripped of *R-Roberts* starboard wing and the aircraft plummeted into a watery grave. It was now 17.00 hours. Just after Atkinson's plane slammed into the water, Angus McIntosh and his navigator in *F-Freddie* encountered difficulties with a startled duck – tragedy was avoided by a whisker. Angus was led home by their Norwegian guide, Lieutenant Thor Stensrud.

Tuesday 9 January 1945 saw 18 Group issue a brisk priority target in the form of a raid against Leirvik.[229] This particular anchorage had already been hit fifteen days previously on Boxing Day, resulting in the loss of Flight Lieutenant Ernest Fletcher and his navigator Flying Officer Alfred Watson in *G-George*. 'Increased activity has been spotted in Leirvik harbour, four large merchantman and three trawlers, one is a large merchantman of about 5,165 tons is anchored within. This is your primary target,' said Maurice Guedj during the briefing, using information brought back by their Norwegian guides.

Maurice, and his London-born navigator, Flight Lieutenant John Langley, took off from Banff at 09.05 hours, leading sixteen RP armed Mosquitoes in *T-Tommy*. Crossing the Norwegian island of Utsira, he saw the forests, and land spreading out beneath them covered in a silky white blanket of snow. As they droned on, altering course northwards, Maurice heared 'Target is in Leirvik!' from their Norwegian guide before arcing around Stord to sweep in over Leirvik, partly shielded by a thick gauze of snow. 'We attacked from the starboard side hurtling over pine trees, and laden roof tops of brightly coloured houses which sent flurries of snow into the air,' wrote Langley. They ran into single and four-barrelled light anti-aircraft guns. Maurice fired back for all he was worth as eight rocket projectiles (RPs) left the rails. Four of them scored hits on the main target, the merchantman *Claus Rickmers*, lying alongside the quay. In total, roughly forty RPs struck the forward section, the aft being afforded protection by buildings. *Claus Rickmers* begins to burn, but the vessel did nor sink, as it was already resting on the bottom of the harbour. Despite the odd piece of flak damage, they all successfully crossed the North Sea, and, with a round trip of nearly four-and-a-half-hours, touched back down at Banff. They had made it.

Later that day, Group Captain Max Aitken, as Station Commander, received confirmation from 18 Group that intelligence had learnt, 'One ship sunk at moorings, four others severely damaged.' Aitken let Maurice know, who was working in his squadron office. Maurice was busy with paperwork: reports to write, letters of commiseration, plus an insubordination hearing in the station headquarters. There was just enough time to go for a test flight for twenty-five minutes with Langley in *T-Tommy*.

The pair then flew a cross-country point-to-point as around them the rest of the Banff strike wing continued to fly operations over Norwegian coastal waters, firing RPs at a submerging submarine. On the 11th, the pair watched fifteen Mosquitoes leave and disappear for a combined sortie with Beaufighters of the Dallachy Wing to a target sighted in Flekkefjord. The two observers then walked back to 143 Squadron office then later appeared at the base's operation centre.

Flight Lieutenant Robert McCall from Koorawatha, New South Wales, led the Beaufighters and Mosquitoes in *M-Monkey* at the front of the formation, and made landfall at 14.35 hours spotting the glint from Perspex ahead.[230]

'One-oh-nines!' McCall exclaimed over the R/T. 'At twelve o'clock.' McCall then immediately peeled off to the right. Calling 'Being attacked by bandits!'

This was followed by, 'Wing keep tight' and 'Take evasive action when fired upon.' Moments later, Beaufighter, *R-Roger*, on the right edge of the formation, was under attack, bullets smacked into the tail as its pilot, Flight Lieutenant Kenneth Sawyer, executed an evasive manoeuvre, managing to exchange fifty rounds of 20mm at the Focke-Wulf in a short duel with the lone attacker before Sawyer headed for the deck.

In Mosquito *R-Robert* Flight Lieutenant Noel Russell turned to follow McCall and was bearing down on one of three Messerschmitts.[231] Russell didn't know it, but this was Uffz Klemens Köhler of 14./JG 5 himself, a good pilot who was being attacked, and in moments Russell's 20mm cannon shells had struck the stern.[232] Adjusting the angle to rake the width of the plane. Flame lashed out from the Daimler-Benz engine, spreading to the fuel tank that caught alight and enveloping the fuselage engulfed by fire the Messerschmitt exploded into millions of pieces. As the machine surged away from the debris Pilot Officer Henry Hosier, his navigator, spoke calmly into the intercom, 'One-oh-nine off to starboard.' Russell swerved and yawed his Mosquito, as he got astern of the speckled grey Messerschmitt.

Flying Officer Donald Hamar watched the battle as the Me 109 tried to shake off *R-Robert*.[233] The German fighter dropped even lower, flying at zero height. Uffz Werner Nieft was unable to hold it steady. A moment later, it ploughed into the water, cartwheeled and exploded into a fireball.

'That was a close shave,' said Hamar to his navigator as Beaufighter *L-Leather* joined a trio of 489 Squadron planes withdrawing, cresting the wave tops as dogfights ensued.

Aboard Mosquito *M-Mother*, navigator Waverley Harris sighted four Beaufighters streaking for home, while craning his neck to make sure no fighter was on their tail, he and Belgium Pierre Smoolenaers, piloting *M-Mother*, then heard shouts and expletives through their headphones.[234] As Smoolenaers weaved through the aerial battle, someone shouted 'Pierre fighter on your tail.' Smoolenaers reacted instantly, yet he could not shake of the Me 109. Swerving and yawing the aircraft as much as he dared, he then dropped rapidly, flying just above the water. Fähnrich Hans Vollet closed until he was almost at point blank range, then he opened fire with both cannons and machine-guns, gently moving the nose so that the rounds did the maximum amount of damage.

With controls impaired the Mosquito became unstable. Pierre managed to hold it in the air long enough for Harris to transmit in a faint voice 'urgent assistant required.' Minutes later, *M-Mother* ploughed into the sea.

At 14.47 hours, a rescue bid by Flight Lieutenant John Moreton of New Herrington ended in tragedy as a Messerschmitt's combined 20mm cannon and machine-guns caused the Fraserburgh-based 279 Squadron Warwick *B-Baker* to break up, killing all seven crew instantly, roughly twenty miles from the Norwegian coast.

Flying Officer John Savard in Beaufighter *O-Orange* arrived to discover a bright yellow dinghy at the location, although both pilot and navigator were unable to tell if the type came from the disintegrated Warwick or Mosquito. Savard then headed for home to Dallachy. He was back, just over five and a half hours after they had taken off. Joining thirty-two colleagues for a quick debrief, some thing to eat, a rest then training or another mission.

Thirty-three minutes away at Banff, all the remaining Mosquitoes had landed safely back, except for *M-Mother*.

As far as The Hon. Group Captain Max Aitken DSO DFC the base commander was concerned, it had been a successful day – all had safely returned; except one. For those returning from 143, the aftermath was slightly bewildering. Crews were handed mugs of coffee then went for their debrief, watched over by Maurice Guedj and their old boss 'Sam' McHardy DSO DFC now residing in the 'ops' room.

'To see both together was strange but reassuring in an odd way,' wrote Flying Officer Donald Clause, 'it also threw our exhausted American 1st Lieutenant Frederick Alexandre, when he saw 'Sam' and Maury.'[235]

The following day there were telegrams that needed writing and to be sent that Friday 12 January. The task of sending the telegrams to the families of Flight Sergeant's Pierre Smoolenaers and Waverley Harris was left to the Squadron Adjutant, Flight Lieutenant Sebastian Marvs. Two letters were typed up for Maurice to sign too.[236] Harris' father, William, received his, 'It is with deep regret' telegram at home in the quite suburb of Annerley in Brisbane, Australia, via the Royal Australian Air Force. Waverly Harris had only been with 143 Squadron since 18 October 1944 and taken further navigational exams in the station's gymnasium on Sunday 31 December attaining satisfactory results for immediate promotion. Maurice just had to sign Form P/P75.[237]

While Banff Mosquitoes concentrated on operations, a high–altitude Mosquito at Dyce took off to photograph the Leirvik area. Flight Lieutenant Donald French had been briefed to be over Leirvik by 08.00 hours.[238] It was a far from ideal day for taking photographs, patches of snow showers mingled amongst the grey skies. 'I was flying at 30,000 feet,' he wrote, 'as I made my two runs over the harbour there seemed to be a lot activity.' There was no difficulty in seeing the almost ear-shaped harbour. The islands adjacent to Leirvik were completely laden with pine trees and even from his position high above, he could see movement in the water from propeller washes.

At about 11.00 hours, he touched down at Dyce. Airmen clicked open the camera compartments on the fuselage and underside of the pale blue Mosquito releasing the bulky cameras and the sped off to the photographic block. The developed images were quickly sent to Pitreavie where the intelligence section confirmed 'damaged but not completely destroyed.' Another mission was required.

Jack Davenport, 18 Group Operational Planner, began organising with Flight Lieutenant Owen Burns, a former combatant who was a few days away from being posted to 19 Group.[239] Owen had temporarily been assigned to Pitreavie having helped re-write gunnery instructions for aircrew in Edinburgh. Davenport studied the priority target he turned to Owen for the allocation of aircraft. It looked as though there would be twenty-four available, of which four or so would be Tsetse Mosquitoes the remaining MkVIs.

Focke-Wulf fighters had been spotted at Herdla and estimated to be between ten and twelve minutes from Leirvik. 'Do we have fighter escort?' inquired Davenport.

Burns found the folder, quickly read through the notes. 'The Poles of 315 Squadron are moving from Peterhead back to 11 Group and 133 Wing, at St. Andrew's Field in Braintree Essex to act as fighter escort for Bomber Command,' said Burns. 'Their replacements 65 Squadron are not arriving until the fifteenth I'm afraid.'[240]

No fighter escort! The Focke-Wulfs awesome firepower of machine guns and 20mm cannons could destroy a Mosquito with a carefully aimed shot. Cannon shells came in different forms. Some were armour piercing indicated by a coloured multi-layered metal head, while others were high explosive. They would shatter a Merlin engine or blast huge holes through the Mosquito's skin. If they hit the bomb bay or rocket rails before they had been used, the effect was even more devastating.

The bald facts were rather chilling with both 235 and 248 Squadrons having a loss statistic of 18 percent Davenport was keenly aware that the odds were against them. The sortie had to go ahead. 'Blast this bloody ship to smithereens!' Sturley Simpson replied. 'Put Banff on immediate alert.'

Aitken received a signal at about 16.00 hours, and with the weather charts looking fairly promising for the entire night and into the morning of Monday 15 January, Simpson gave the final authorization at 16.30 hours. By the time this cypher message came through, the crews knew they would be operating the following day. In his office Wing Commander Maurice Guedj received the news by telephone he would be strike leader, and Langley lead navigator, then called his two flight commanders and broke the news; it would be Leirvik.

At the station HQ, Corporal Joyce Trovey typed out the anxiously awaited take-off and estimated return times.[241] These had been given to her by her boss Max Aitken. Take-off was to begin at 09.30 hours with Maurice departing with 143 Squadron before 235's and 248's contingent. Return time was given as around 13.15 in the afternoon. Armed with these timings the new Station Adjutant, Squadron Leader Tony Mottram DFC, worked out buses, meal times and flying rations and be on hand to accept wills, cash, letters to next of kin, and any items that the aircrew might want him to keep for them in the head quarters safe.

Meanwhile, the 143 Squadron mechanics working on Maurice's usual Mosquito had to admit defeat.[242] His aircraft would not be ready. Fortunately, there was a spare aircraft K-King. It was one which Joseph Selka had flown a mission on the 12th, and prior to that 'Archie' Kaufman on 6 January. The plane, though, was in perfect working order. It would do.

At 08.00 hours, thirty-six freshly groomed airmen ploughed their way through their traditional pre-flight meal of bacon, eggs, sausages, and fried bread with, in some cases, a dollop of American ketchup on the side.[243] Irrespective of rank 'we all ate in the aircrew canteen,' Donald Clause wrote, 'Maurice sat opposite me, during our pre-briefing meal.' Arthur Simmonds said to Maurice, 'Can I have your meal if you don't come back?' He meant the post-flight meal a touch of black humour to ease the tension. Maurice swore in French. From there the crews made their way to the Operations Room, with the scrape of chairs 'the crowd was pretty raucous,' until Aitken and Squadron Leader George Bellows walked in, then there was a nervous silence.

Many of the thirty-six assembled were smoking, pipes, cigarettes or cigars, the smoke forming a layer of smog in the fetid air. On the wall was the normal outline of Northeast Scotland, with the expanse of water then Norway with the coast, leads and fjords. A white tape pinned to it marked two routes – the route in and route out. 'The briefing began at 9 o'clock of course headed up by Maurice,' wrote Clause, 'as he announced the target there was a large in-take of breath.' Maurice then ran through the running order, he also briefed them on enemy defences, warning them of known flak positions, and fighter units and airfields. 'It was enough to make any man gulp. He said that any enemy fighter would come from the south, therefore after the attack we must turn north – break left to port,' said Clause. Maurice spoke for about fifteen minutes. He'd been up since 05.30 hours, and barely stopped, going into the squadron office to make sure General Conduct Forms for Flight Sergeant's Pierre Smoolenaers and Waverley Harris had been signed by his Adjutant, Marvs the Frenchman then counter-signed adding 15 January 1945 and, unusually, the time, which was 06.00 hours.[244] Within a couple of hours, he would be leading members of the Banff Strike Wing on what was unquestionably an extremely difficult and arduous shipping strike into one of the most heavily defended harbours in occupied Europe.

The Met officer followed him. The weather was due to be about as good as they could hope for. The sky would be frequent snow showers over the North Sea and right up to the Norwegian coast – there would be strong winds over the sea, particularly at lower levels, gently rising as they pushed in land. Over the target there might be 20 – 26 mph north westerly's but by that time they would have enough visual information to easily correct any effects of wind when launching their rocket projectiles.

Each navigator had his own Navigation Log, in which the various points and courses they would be taking, distance, and speed, were all noted. Arthur Simmonds' trusty navigator Leonard Murphy wrote 'two-zero and three-zero' in pencil. This was far from ideal as it meant consistently checking for any drifting, as navigating over the sea was the hardest task as there was usually no visual markers. Snow would make their job even harder.

It was by then around 09.15 hours. Watches were synchronized. Tony Mottram had the buses ready, flying rations, escape money, were there, waiting to be collected, flasks of coffee or tea were available.

With a final: 'Good Luck, prang the bloody ship,' from Max Aitken, the men grappled with their flying gear and parachutes as they left the briefing room.[245] Many were already wearing their sheepskin Irvin's as the outside temperature was about two degrees with slight drizzle. Outside at various dispersal points, around the perimeter their Mosquitoes waited. They clambered aboard clutching Mae Wests, parachute packs and leather flying helmets. As they reached the aircraft, the buses stopped, and two men stepped down and walked over to the waiting Mosquito, each with its rocket rails laden with eight dart-shaped objects. First to take off would be Maurice Guedj's *K-King*. Groundcrew fussed around their aircraft. At *X-X-Ray*, Donald Clause's Mossie, the starboard entrance door was already open, a small five rung telescopic ladder fixed into place. First Donald, then navigator Flying Officer James Diggory, climbed aboard.

A little further along, at *K-King*, everything seemed to be in order. Maurice and John had carried out a brief flying test the previous evening, a quick take off and a circuit, then completed and signed the Form 700. Maurice plugged his helmet leads into the intercom, then flicked the twin electric engine starter switches. The engines slowly coughed into life, first the starboard, then the port, Maurice ran up both engines.

Around the airfield, other Merlin engines spluttered into motion for the run-up prior to take-off. Then the first section began to move, led by Maurice and followed by Robert Fitch in *U-Uncle*. Behind Fitch came George Morton-Moncrieff in *D-Dog* and Frederick Alexandre in *V-Victor* closely followed by *X-X-Ray* with Donald Clause, then *F-Fox* with Pilot Officer John 'Tony' Hawkey and navigator Warrant Officer Charles Milloy. Simmonds led 235's contingent of four. In *A-Apple* were Flight Sergeants Frank Chew and Stephen 'Jock' Couttie, both of whom had only recently resumed operational flying after being captured and then released after their escapade in the Gironde. Leading 248 was Angus McLeod.

At 09.30 hours, a green Aldis lamp flashed through the drizzle. *K-King* was first to become airborne. With throttles pushed forward, and the port slightly ahead to counter the slight tendency to swing to port, the laden Mosquito began to hare down the runway, engines developing more power, both pushed back into their seats. The speed quickening until the tail raised from the ground, and the Mosquito rose into the air. Maurice moved the undercarriage selector swiftly to 'up', the red indicator lights go out.

The Operation had begun.

Eight minutes later the last green Aldis light was flashed and Flying Officers William Woodcock with his navigator Conroy Vacher sitting to the right of him, watches Woodcock open the throttles and sped along and climbed into the air to be the final plane to latch onto the formation in their 248 Squadron Tsetse Mosquito *S1-Sugar* before disappearing into the raw grey sky.

Maurice's trio crossed the Scottish coast over Sandhaven, having encountered nothing but drizzle. In *K-King*, both remained silent, although the strike leader was busy in his own thoughts. He had only recently been officially informed by Flight Lieutenant William Herrera from Seaford House, of the tragic loss of his father Félix Guedj who had died in prison.

Crossing the North Sea was monotonous and required intense concentration, because it was imperative that they crossed the Norwegian coast precisely where they planned to do so. 'Ploughed out through pretty dismal and fairly rough weather,' wrote Clause afterwards, 'had flown low the whole way across in snow showers, my windscreen wiper blade worked amiably.'

The force made landfall at Geitungen lighthouse at 11.10 hours, and within seconds they were over the small island. 'Up to this point nothing had been sighted, fly north waiting to receive word from the pair of Norwegian guides,' said Clause. While the Norwegians searched along the inner waterways, Lieutenant Thore Stensrud in *G-George* of 333 Squadron, with navigator Erik Friis, heard the unwelcome sound of the German radar defence system. The Mosquitoes have been heard and spotted.[246]

The air raid warning sounded at 11.18 hours in Leirvik at about the same time the order '*Alarmstart*' was received at Herdla.[247] Immediately the pilots of Focke-Wulf 190s of the 9 Staffel of Jagdgeschwader 5 *Eismeerjäger* rushed out to their machines. Commanding the Staffel was Oberleutnant Werner Gayko, an experienced combat veteran and, within a couple of minutes, nine Focke-Wulfs are hurtling down the runway and into the air heading south for Leirvik harbour, only four minutes before the pair of outriders reach the primary target.

As the Mosquitoes headed in they came under anti-aircraft fire for the first time. 'Target in Leirvik,' Thor said over the R/T, just as the Mosquito of Norwegians Kåre Sjølie and Sjt. Ingvar Gausland exploded, killing both men instantly. Thor quickly breaks away to avoid being hit by any debris from *R-Robert*. Leaving the burning mass and enemy flak behind he then heads to pick up the Mosquitoes: 'we had been on the coast twenty-five minutes, flying northwards, the second outrider took us over Bømlo. Then we made our approach to the target from the northwest in our sections. There was lots of snow covering the land and houses making everything look bleak,' said Clause. Thor identified two merchantmen and a flak-ship.[248]

11.29 hours, at Leirvik harbour, Maurice Guedj issued, 'Attack, attack, attack, then break to port,' over the R/T. He carried out his run in on the primary target *Claus Rickmers*, through heavy flak opening up with his cannon and machine-guns, before releasing a salvo of rockets and then peeling away. Alexandre kept his section well to the left, leaving Clause with a clear run in on a flak-ship. 'The primary target had been fixed fairly well by the leading sections. I saw Tony's rockets go and there was a considerable explosion on the flak-ship as the boiler room or ammunition store blew up,' wrote Clause. 'I shamefully released my rockets too early and they arced down into the water so would have only been classified as underwater hits. Then I turned my attention fully onto a flak-ship, which was pumping out all sorts of light flak at X-X-Ray. Big plump explosions bursting yards above and in front of us, there was no way out except to go between an island and the shore, both of which were omitting muzzle flashes in our direction. As a result, the Mosquito passed over the flak-ship at mast height, and I had just kept steadily pressing the firing button the whole time. From our ringside seats we could see my fire knocking pieces off the bridge and superstructure, at least it made them keep their heads down!'

Clear of the obstruction, Clause turned to port at 45 degrees and quickly lost height down to fifty feet and began weaving back and forth. 'I'd done exactly as requested 'break to port' and found myself all alone flying up a fjord in a northerly direction, with high sided mountains on either side,' said Clause. X-X-Ray hurtled down Langenuen Strait, in minutes the Mosquito has covered twenty-six miles. Negotiating mountain terrains by climbing and diving, Clause and Diggory exited south of Marstein Lighthouse then flew straight into a huge snow cloud. His navigator Diggory hearing the distinctive voice of Couttie in *A-Apple* called out 'we've only one motor,' a reply came from Frederick Alexandre, 'All right I will keep with you,' as his navigator John McMullin gave a thumbs up to Couttie.[249]

In *U-Uncle*, Fitch and Parker had been rather taken aback by the ferocity of the flak, which came from every direction. They now circled, picking out individuals with *K-King* then, after about two minutes, the pair got out in the direction the Banff Strike Wing had flown in. The planned route out from the small harbour was unravelling; the force was scatted over a wide area.

Picking out landmarks they entered Bjørnafjorden and turned west, but at the same time the Focke-Wulf 190s of 9 Staffel entered the fjord from the north. Almost immediately Werner Gayko put a warning out over the radio: '*Achtung, achtung – mehrere Tommies vor Stord!*' The German formation divided into three flights, of three aircraft apiece. Suddenly the Focke-Wulfs were bearing down on the widely scattered Mosquitoes. Flying Officer 'Gracie' Fields, navigator of Tsetse *Z1-Zebra*, observes three single-engine fighters at 11.32 off the Northern tip of Stord and instantly shouts over the R/T 'Bandits, Look Out, Bandits.' Alexandre also calls out 'Bandits' in response to Field's warning.

'Roger, all aircraft keep together, wing men keep tight!' The 32-year-old, Maurice calmly spoke in response to both warnings. A confused dogfight begins with machine-guns and cannon streaking across the sky over a wide area, as *K-King* and *U-Uncle* both weaved across the sky. Maurice opened his throttles and followed Fitch down to 450 feet. Beside him, John Langley was turning around, frequently peering out through the Perspex looking for enemy fighters within seconds Langley shouts 'One-ninetys on our tail.' Three Focke-Wulfs had latched onto *K-King* and *U-Uncle*. Maurice's spoke on the R/T: 'His voice came over very cool, calm and deep,' remembered Donald Clause, 'calling help! help! I am being heavily attacked'.

In moments a Luftwaffe pilot's cannon shells had struck *U-Uncle* tail plane, with large holes torn in the balsawood and birch structure, other rounds had caught the left-hand side outer petrol tank, wing tip, and aileron. On board *U-Uncle*, Fitch struggled to keep his aircraft in the air as Parker watched with mounting horror as the water rushed towards them. But instinct took over and Leslie helped John grapple with the stick to regain control and stability – just long enough for John to heroically get *U-Uncle* behind one of the two 190s on *K-King's* tail and fire a burst of cannon.

For the attacking German fighters, it was all too obvious that *K-King* was weakening. Flames pulsated from the port engine and with control surfaces damaged and an engine out, even Maurice was unable to hold the Mosquito airborne. A second later, one of the two German fighters attacked. This time the Mosquito seemed to glide down, just above the stall, and with the water surface ahead, Maurice managed to slide the crippled *K-King* onto the water. The six tons of spruce and plywood finally came to a halt in the fjord at 11.36 hours. It may never be known what really happened after the ditching, as Maurice Guedj and John Langley both perished.

Just eleven to twelve minutes, the aerial combat lasted. Stensrud navigator Friis makes a note of the time 11.47 as Stensrud began shepherding the crippled *U-Uncle*, with Claus in *X-X-Ray*. The surviving planes fly back out over the North Sea, heading for home through heavy snow showers. At 12.53 hours, the first Mosquitoes from 235 Squadron arrived safely back at Banff, then the remaining survivors of 143 Squadron. Despite the damage Robert Fitch and Leslie Parker touched down at 13.10 hours, in rain showers, along with Donald Clause and John 'Tony' Hawkey. There to greet them as they clambered out was Wing Commander Christopher Foxley-Norris who shepherded the crews towards debriefing. While Aitken, Bellows and Mottram joined the crews for debriefing, the last three clawed their way back. In *S-Sugar* Warrant Officer Robert 'Bob' Ellis landed at Fraserburgh, whilst *Z1-Zebra* touched down at Dallachy. Seven minutes later, at Dallachy Flight Lieutenant James Ellis in *E1-Egg* safely landed. He was exhausted and had even handed the controls to his navigator Flight Lieutenant Gaston Palombi for part of the journey across the sea.[250] It was only once they had taxied and come to a halt that they discovered the thud they had felt in the confused dog fight had been a cannon shell that had gone straight through the fuselage on the starboard side, then on through the port wing, without hitting anything vital. Such was the randomness with which aircraft could be hit. At 13.13 hours, on the afternoon of 15 January 1945, *S1-Sugar* safely landed back at Banff after some five hours in the air, the last to return.

The Leirvik Raid was finally over.

And yet the cost had been high. On any anti-shipping strike, one or may be two might not make it back, but to lose five out of sixteen was a massive loss. The task of sending telegrams to the families of those dead and missing was left to the Squadron Adjutants. There were ten men missing in all. Notifications that they were missing were sent to the next of kin: parents or wives usually. Luckily Stephen Couttie had survived the aerial dual that had seen Alexandre and McMullin in *V-Victor* perish.[251] Forced to ditch *A-Apple*, Couttie was the sole survivor and clambered into the aircraft's dinghy. The message that the Scotsman was miraculously, still alive and in hospital for the remaining months of the war would arrive later.[252] From the five Mosquitoes shot down he was the only crewman living, after one of the biggest air battles over Norway.

The telegram arrived at Maurice Guedj wife's home. 'He was the sun of my life, we were so happy together,' said Maria. There would be no dream Parisian or Moroccan apartment where Maurice Guedj, Maria or his daughter could live out long and happy lives together.[253]

Chapter 7

Wing Commander Roger Morewood MID

Roger Morewood was born in Worthing, East Sussex.[254] His father was a Royal Naval officer advising Hussein Kamel of Egypt, having begun his seafaring career aged fifteen in the Merchant Navy, and was four years older than Morewood's mother, who had been thirty-two when they married and only a year older when she died. Proud and remote, Owen Morewood was emotionally distant after his previous wife had died during childbirth in Egypt. His second wife Alice Percy had attended Cheltenham Ladies College, taking her public examinations, continuing her study at St Hilda's College, Oxford before qualifying as a nurse.[255] After a brief courtship, Morewood married Percy when she too became pregnant. But determined not to risk her life giving birth in Egypt, Morewood sent his wife home to England. The pregnancy was not a happy experience for Alice Morewood and after giving birth to her son, on Tuesday 7 March 1916, Alice encounter complications six weeks following Roger's birth suffering a postpartum haemorrhage and died.

Owen Morewood briefly returned to England for his wife's funeral and met Alice's former Head of Boarding House Mistress Annie Wilderspin, 'he had a privileged lifestyle in a colonial office and was aloof and remote,' Wilderspin noted in the college diary.[256] Thereafter, Morewood had little more to do with his father, when passed to a relative Caroline Morewood his father's eldest sister.[257]

Living at 80 Hamlet Gardens, Ravenscourt Park, with Caroline, Roger was also provided with the emotional stability of his maternal grandparents Edward and Ellen Morewood who resided there too. Edward worked in senior management as a highly successful shipping broker, whilst his daughter Caroline toiled as an independent historical researcher, her clientele included the aristocracy.

Roger knew Caroline as Aunty Lena. She raised him more or less on her own as Morewood grew up in splendid surroundings. After some home tutoring Morewood attended Grange Preparatory School aged six and eventually went to board at Abingdon School in Oxfordshire. His competitiveness came to the fore in the 1931 Easter holiday photographic competition winning with a piece entitled *Basingstoke Canal* in his respective professional class, with Dennis Healy coming first in the amateur class with *On Guard* however, the overall special holiday award went to Morewood. He excelled in school activities in the sphere of rowing and sport in general.

Morewood rowed in the School Regatta on Thursday 16 June 1932 a brilliantly fine day, which helped considerably as Barr, Morewood and cox Pfordten of Red House beat a strong Green House team by almost a length at Wilsham Reach.[258] Another local regatta at Culham saw Morewood in a four that passed the finishing post five lengths ahead of their rivals. Morewood rowed his final regatta in 1933 through rumbles of thunder, fortunately the rain held off until his senior four had won. Despite not doing well academically in his School Certificate exams, Morewood obtained a coveted place as an art student at Edinburgh. A place he had come to know during school holidays with Aunty Lena.[259]

Here Morewood was able to indulge in making and using his own materials – oil paints from natural pigments, glazes, waxes, learning colour theory and other techniques, gaining a thorough practical understanding of the disciplines developed by renaissance painters to abstract impressionism.[260] When not at tutorials or working on commissions, Morewood discovered the joy of motoring and riding pillion, Morewood acquired a Royal Enfield after persuading Aunty Lena, who then telegraphed his father in Egypt to pay for the motorcycle.[261] Transactions complete, the bohemian artist with a beard, moustache and slightly longish hair made haste through the city's back roads and sped along the quiet country lanes, and occasionally went further afield to the Lake District, Yorkshire Dales through the industrial haze of Birmingham, Banbury then occasionally on through the Chiltens to Kensington, London and Eastbourne in Sussex.

He never lacked commissions, for addition to his painting there was decorative and photography projects in hand. When Abingdon old boy Edward Rice had his veterinary practice entrance hall and staircase repainted in Godalming, Morewood prescribed the exact mixture of powder colours – ultramarine, raw umber, a touch of ochre necessary to obtain a French grey.[262] Morewood brewed the distemper, whitening and size over a gas ring in the small kitchen. Decorations appeared on the door panels and around the fireplaces in the form of black and white photographs in simple wooden frames. They inspired his friend, Pfordten, to commission a piece of photography for his Shanghai office, which kept Morewood busy during the latter part of 1934.[263]

Around the same time the Defence Deliberation Committee with Douglas Hogg, Viscount Hailsham, who was serving as Secretary of State for War, were meeting on a regular basis, there was a great deal of urgency with Germany rearming, Hogg told Neville Chamberlain that it was essential to accelerate the Air Force programme despite the financial constrains to provide 22 Squadrons for Home Defence and three for the Fleet Air Arm in two-year's time. The scheme was modified and strengthened in certain aspects since its conception.

'I am gravely perturbed by the situation, this country cannot accept the position of continuing inferiority in the air,' Hogg berated Charles Vane-Tempest-Stewart, 7th Marquess of Londonderry, Secretary of State for Air prior to him leaving in June 1935.[264] Vane-Tempest-Stewart had encouraged the planning of the new low-wing monoplanes Hawker Hurricane and Supermarine Spitfire. Compulsory powers for the acquisition of land for aerodromes, and construction of buildings, and procurement of men for training began. It was essential to get the squadrons and crack on with interesting the right sort of men for flying training. The advertising worked, and Roger Morewood joined as a direct entry untrained pilot on 30 September 1935.

Introduced to service life at 4 Elementary and Reserve Flying Training School, a former civilian flying school at Brough in East Riding Yorkshire were two months elementary training began. There was a wonderful assortment of fellow pupils like Morewood who thought they could fly a bit already, the instructor Wilfred Smith had a double job to do – first showing pupils that they could not fly and then teaching them the right, official Air Force way. He was among those of his training school posted to Desford, one of the airfields in the Air Force expansion scheme.

'The machines we flew were de Havilland Tiger Moths, open cockpit biplanes of great stability and little speed. They were such very forgiving planes,' noted Morewood. Suddenly, flying did not seem at all daredevil, *Boys' Own Paper* affair it was cracked up to be. Crooked loops, bad slide slips, flat turns, bumpy landings, and gradually Roger Morewood's flying improved: 'I felt like giving her a lump of sugar or an extra ration of oil, or something in return for past favours.'[265]

The groundwork for Morewood was at least for him pretty hard, especially the Morse. The 'da' and 'dit' was confusing, he managed to learn the code and get up to about six or seven words a minute, sending and receiving on the buzzer. But, receiving signals on the Aldis lamp foxed him completely, and in the examination, Morewood failed on the lamp, the only one to do so on his course. The examination on air ground subjects was quite a stiff one. Navigation, airmanship, rigging, engines and armament – Morewood just scraped through.

After passing out with an 'above average' assessment as a pilot on RAF Form 1416 he was posted to Uxbridge, becoming an Acting Pilot Officer with a short service commission. After further training at Grantham, he finally left to join 56 Squadron at North Weald on Saturday 24 April 1937. Roger arrived registered and stepped straight into the Officers Mess and made himself known to those of his new squadron who were present. One of the first men Roger met was his Commanding Officer, Charles Lea-Cox, a first-class pilot on the Gloster Gauntlet.[266] Flight Lieutenant Ian Soden suggest to the men that they retire to a public house down the road to get 'a little pissy', Ian's term for a party. Morewood was pleased and a little flattered by the congratulants he received on having done so well at EFS. Roger had not been aware that he had, but Morewood was assured that only people who had distinguished themselves in their initial training get into a crack squadron like 56. 'It was like joining the Grenadier Guards,' said Morewood. In the coming months and years as the squadron's Gloster Gladiator replaced Gauntlet's, Roger himself welcomed newcomers with this harmless but morale boosting deception giving them confidence in themselves and a pride in their squadron.

The squadron acquired a Miles Magister, an open cockpit, two-seater monoplane trainer and the pilots began receiving training in March 1938. Morewood's instructor was Lea-Cox. Morewood had got to grips with the Gladiator, but his new machine, the Hawker Hurricane, required some entirely new skills – and a level of airmanship that had taken most of the others who were equipped with the type some six weeks to perfect. Despite the ticking clock, the timetable was, it appeared on track for 56 Squadron in terms of delivery of Hurricanes.

On 3 June, Harry Hawker visited the squadron and gave a two-hour lecture on the Hurricane Mk 1, 'it was really enthralling lecture given in the cinema,' noted Morewood in a letter to Dennis Healy. Flights continued in the Magister. It stalled viciously when the air speed dropped, in which case it would go straight into a spin pointing towards the ground. Fortunately, Squadron Leader Albert Pratt managed to get them out of the predicament with less than 700 feet to spare. Pratt and Morewood stumbled back to North Weald over hedges to arrive unscathed just in time for tea being served in the anteroom at 16.00 hours.[267]

It was in the late summer of 1938, at the height of the Munich crisis when fourteen new Hurricanes arrived, as did a new commanding officer,

Squadron Leader Edward 'Teddy' Knowles. Rough details of training were mapped out, while the importance of security was also stressed. 'My Hurricane L1998 had a constant speed Rotol propeller with wooden blades, it was like a new motorcycle or car with the intriguing smell of fresh paint, oil and grease,' recalled Morewood, 'we flew our Hurricanes roughly once a day from the outset.'

On 27 October Morewood was posted to 248 Squadron, Hendon, as a Flight Lieutenant and his black Cocker Spaniel Andrew went with him.[268] This transfer had called for a brisk drive to Gieves Tailors in London to get another band of ribbon put on the sleeve of his uniform jackets. This accomplished, it was off to North London.

Morewood arrived at Hendon around teatime on Tuesday, 31 October. He had not taken leave or seen his wife of five months, Clare, after they had married in Staines. Parking in the allocated bay outside the Mess, he walked inside with Andrew at his heels. The Mess at Hendon was a large red-brick building with the outside painted green and black.[269] There was a large reception room, bar, games room and large dining room along the front, and with two wings of officers' rooms extending behind. It was a design and layout similar to many around the country built by The Ministry of Works in the previous ten years during the expansion of the Air Force.

Hendon was an enormous station. The Mess was to the south, as were other utility buildings including Claude Grahame-Whites' watchtower which had been purchased with the airfield by the Royal Air Force in 1925. Now it to was painted with large curves of camouflage blending in with Grahame-Whites former factory that had gone through a similar process. There were accommodation blocks for the non-commissioned crews and ground personnel of the same rank. Other station offices included the parachute store, briefing room and Sergeants' Mess and Airmen's and Women's Mess. Cement or tarmac roads linked this bustling self-contained Air Force village; there was plenty of open expanses of grass too.

Beyond the brick buildings to the north were six First World War hangers, numbered one to six with apron and perimeter track to the side then the longer of the two cement runways. The hangers were completely empty except for a lone Airspeed Oxford being serviced by mechanics in overalls buzzing around the plane. There was a clang of tool's hitting the ground as Morewood and his Spaniel Andrew ventured inside.

'Whereabouts is two-four-eight?' enquired Morewood.

'Hanger Two sir,' replied Chiefy Wainwright.

The squadron's offices were inside of No. 2 Hangar, a single-skinned, brick construction, with a row of rooms linked by a corridor and a flat roof. The 'A' and 'B' Flight room was shared, a square cream and green affair with a single metal window on the outward wall and with two desks facing each other.[270] Entering he found Flight Lieutenant Alan Pennington-Legh, recently arrived from 43 Squadron at Tangmere near Chichester, to become 248's 'A' Flight Commander.

'Morewood?' queried Pennington-Legh.

'Yes, Roger Morewood,' he replied.

'Your, 'B' Flight's Flight Commander.'

There was the desk, a wooden editor's-type chair and two telephones.

Pennington-Legh had recently been caught up in a road collision on the by-pass road at Titchfield earlier. He had been driving towards Fareham when he collided with the rear of Brian Gorman's motorcar travelling in the opposite direction, whereby Gorman's car overturned twice or more until it righted itself and was facing towards Fareham. Been completely dazzled by Gorman's headlights being set on full beam. Pennington-Legh had not reduced his speed: 'inadvertently careering across the road into the other vehicle,' declared Judge Barnard Lailey KC. Allan Pennington-Legh was asked to pay £90 to Gorman.

Putting this incident behind him Pennington-Legh got on with the job in hand and 248 Squadron's Wing Commander George 'Hutch' Hutchinson, with his two flight commanders, began pulling the squadron together. The aircrews were just one part of a frontline squadron with an estimated 500 men and women in total making up the unit. Groundcrew and administration staff were far more numerous than the air crew themselves; each Bristol Blenheim required a team of roughly two dozen to get it airborne, of which just three were the crew.

Securing ten to twelve aircraft was the immediate problem, as Fighter Command 11 Group had initially signalled that 248 Squadron was going to receive Hawker Hurricanes, but this was then rescinded 'the squadron is to be formed as a Bristol Blenheim Night Fighter Unit,' signed Keith Park, RAF Uxbridge. The only Blenheim at Hendon was a short-nosed version, lying in a heap of ashes and twisted metal behind No. 3 Hanger. In the meantime, Morewood was a flight commander of a single Mile Magister.[271] Morewood obtained through his old Adjutant, Edward Holden, a supply of tools. Beds, blankets, pillows, typewriters, furniture, vehicles, parachutes, flying suites with boots, and stationary were just some of the items that needed to be acquired. It was a herculean task.

Nonetheless, progress was being made as men arrived from Sealand and other Flying Training Schools, and by 6 November, Morewood had nine pilots; Richard Haviland, Archibald 'Eddie' Hill, Frank Elger, Joffre Fripp, Holmes, Gordon 'Barry' Atkinson, Arthur and Maurice Baird. At

Hendon these men began to master daytime arrivals with their Magister at North Weald, Biggin Hill, Tangmere, and Manston in time for luncheon, but found when training for night flying they could also make an entrance at dawn for breakfast too.[272] Their antics were curtailed on 17 December, when Atkinson and Holmes returned from Tangmere. When it was found the Magister had reached its maximum number of hours and an inspection and major maintenance was due. The plane was also regularly returning with scrapes and dents and bit of foliage from trees or hedges, all of which had to be repaired and logged. 'Fortunately, it didn't have to be flown over to Woodley,' said Morewood in his squadron diary.

Pilots kicked their heels in the Mess, the rumours were that the squadron would disband as there were all sorts of issues to be resolved first and foremost they needed Bristol Blenheims, if not the fighter type, then enough ordinary Type 142s with which to start training. Morewood and Alfred 'Alfie' Fowler, an electrician from Foxton, New Zealand, collected two of the three waiting at Kemble. That was a start.

Groundcrews fitted the gun packs, and armourers harmonized the four 0.303 machine-guns, training was required to be carried out, although Hutchinson was massively hampered by how little he knew himself. Then, however, on Tuesday 16 January, sixty-six days after forming the squadron, Hutchinson was given the greenlight to allow Morewood and John Holderness – a scholar from Rhodesia – to take 'B' Flights two Blenheims up to Sutton Bridge with 'Sam' McHardy of 'A' Flight in one of that flight's aircraft. Morewood found, when trying out the aircraft's ring sight, he could not keep the devise from moving fractionally. There was the vibration and movement of the sight, therefore he used a grease pencil to make a mark on the Perspex itself. 'This worked just as well,' he declared.

Morewood's, Holderness' and McHardy's air and ground firing was cut short, and within twenty-four hours they returned, with each of the New Zealanders' Perspex bearing a grease pencil mark. There were still arrivals of new crewmembers, but departures too. A couple of weeks later, the whole squadron departed for North Coates. 'It was a bit precarious,' remembered Baird. 'Roger had a folded map taped to his left thigh with a red pencil line indicating our route with the bearing's taped to his instrument panel'. By this stage, Morewood and Pennington-Legh only had a total of eight Blenheim fighters. More Blenheims arrived: one on 3 March, from 25 Squadron, North Weald, and then a second on 9 March. Those fighter types that had already seen service required major overhauls as squadrons palmed off those planes with time-expired engines, or other dysfunctional kit. 'Wainwright and his men were certainly kept busy,' wrote the 'B' Flight commander.

Hutchinson departed as commanding officer; replaced by Victor Streatfield. Then within a space of twenty-two days, on Saturday 30 March, two more pilots arrived: Arthur Tatar and Douglas Peterkin, together with six navigators, pilot officers John Morris, Ernest Leathem, Edward Schollar, Malcolm Wells, Douglas Warren and Maurice Green.

Another officer at North Coates was Pilot Officer Herbert Sharman, a Londoner, and at thirty-two years old considered too old to be trained as a fighter pilot, and instead was selected to be a navigator.[273] Sharman had grown up in Wood Green in Eldon Road, finishing his education at Trinity County Grammar School. Through hard work as a clerk at Lloyds he then qualified as an accountant raising his prospects. Marrying Elsie Burgess in 1932, both travelled extensively in South America for business and pleasure before returning to Southgate. One year later, in 1938, anxious at the continued rise of fascism, which Sharman had first witnessed on the streets of Marseille as a twenty-year-old clerk ten years' previously as Italians arrived fleeing Benito Mussolini's persecution. Acutely aware of the realities of the rapidly deteriorating world situation Herbert and his colleagues sought official endorsement with Lloyds to join the Territorials or Auxiliaries.

Herbert volunteered for the Air Force in February 1939 and had a narrow escape when Irish Republican Army bombs exploded at Lloyds in The Strand on 24 June. He left his position in September to become an airman-untrained navigator. After Bombing and Gunnery School at Jurby on the Isle of Man, Sharman was among four navigators being posted to 248 Squadron with an above average assessment. It was as a member of the squadron that he converted to Blenheim fighters. He had been impressed with the configuration of the glazed-nose layout as a navigator and the exhilaration of flying at only fifty-feet off the ground at 285 mph, as fast as Canadian Patrick Woodruff would take him over The Wash, as pilots and aircrew were hurriedly scrambled into the air for training flights.

'There has been a general improvement in the weather which has enabled the squadron to increase its monthly hours,' wrote Streatfield. This continue into April for five days, when Streatfield heard rumours that something might soon be afoot and then on Monday 8 April, he learned that Coastal Command Headquarters wanted 248 Squadron at Thorney Island.[274]

Hurrying into 'B' Flight's office, the flight commander asked Streatfield what was going on?

'Pack your bucket and spade Morewood, we're off to the Seaside – Thorney Island in Hampshire,' replied Streatfield.[275] Just before midday the phone rang at 'B' Flight dispersal with orders for them to depart. They headed off in two flights, Baird with 'B' Flight led by Morewood and McHardy, following Pennington-Legh's 'A' Flight. Having taken off they each formed up into two sections of three and followed a designated route to the airfield.

Streatfield landed at 14.00 hours, fifteen minutes after Pennington-Legh, Morewood roughly ten minutes later. All had made it safely through the industrial haze after one-hour-thirty-minutes to the base. The remainder of 11 April was spent sorting out accommodation. A meeting in Group Captain Henry Scroggs' office was postponed, so it was not until 17.30 hours, that it finally got underway with Squadron Leader Roy Faville of 42 Squadron, Streatfield, Morewood, Pennington-Legh and a beleaguered supply officer.

One of Morewood's men, Arthur Tatar, was an eighteen-year-old Canadian from Lethbridge, in the Rock Mountains of British Columbia.[276] It certainly was not as remote as a sheep station in Foxton, New Zealand, where Arthur Bourgeois had been brought up. It had been a good place to be nurtured, being the economic centre of southern Alberta with nature on its doorstep and plenty of fishing, hiking, camping and freedom. His father George moved his family to Courtenay on the east coast of Vancouver Island where Arthur continued with his schooling. Courtenay held limited opportunities for him and conditions at home were cramped, so Arthur considered enlisting in the Army. Although he had always been interested in planes and flying, having watched floatplanes take off and land on the lakes, the RCAF was not recruiting and he was unable to get in; however, the Royal Air Force was. His father signed the paperwork and in due process Arthur was given a short service commission. In the spring of 1939 Arthur crossed into the USA to sail to England to begin training in the Air Force. A trip across the Atlantic saw him arrive at Plymouth in Hampshire. After his initial training, and then onto his OTU, he joined 248 Squadron.

On 15 April, Tatar was finally given a room of his own on the station, however, before he could finally unpack his clothes, he and his fellow pilots were discovering just how quickly situations changed with a second signal in nine days to relocate to Gosport in Hampshire, a Fleet Air Arm station. Chiefy Wainwright's maintenance party had only just finished unloading the lorries!

Both Morewood and Tartar were quite impressed by what they found at Gosport. In any case, there was plenty to do. There was the opportunity to do gunnery practice at Ford in West Sussex another Naval station. Morewood made the trip repeatedly between 1 and 7 May firing at marine markers in the sea and air-to-air at silk drogues at the end of a wire being towed by an unfortunate Hawker Hart. 'Continually used four 0.303 machine guns in the belly pack, with the armourers adjusting them so to narrow the spread and concentrate the bullets,' wrote Morewood, 'and Aircraftsman Eric Ringwood blasted away from his turret.' Back on the ground again after training flights on 10 May, Morewood, and McHardy were ordered to move, to Bircham Newton to bolster 235 Squadron. Morewood mustered Ernest Leathem, with Ringwood as his air gunner, whilst McHardy chose John Morris and Corporal Peter Neale.

April had turned to May and thrust RAF Coastal Command into the fray. Around 04.10 hours on May 11, one of the 235 Squadron Blenheim fighters flown by Flight Lieutenant George 'Wiggs' Manwaring, had the first aerial clash that morning when ordered to provide cover for the Royal Navy. As Manwaring expanded his circumference into Dutch air space south of The Hague his air gunner, twenty-one-year-old Sergeant Francis MacPhail, suddenly spotted the silhouette of a Heinkel 111 bomber.

Moments later, Manwaring's Blenheim *P-Pip*, attacked. With no return fire, the Heinkel exploded, out of which Obergefreiter Siegmund Klug baled-out, slowly dropping into a field. The remains of the aircraft ploughed into the sand at Resnesse, north of Haamstede at 06.30 hours. Arriving back at Bircham Newton to claim his first victory, Manwaring would survive another eight days.

At 05.35 hours on 12 May, Morewood and McHardy scrambled into the air, and made tracks for Manston in Kent, given the task of covering a single minesweeper to the Hook of Holland. While the pair were in the air No. 16 Group orders were sent, recalling them back to Bircham Newton. Grim news arrived hours after landing. Pilot Officer Norman Smith, his navigator Sergeant John Robertson, who had been one of the first senior non-commissioned navigators in the squadron, and eighteen-years-old Leading Aircraftsman Thomas Lowry the air gunner in one Blenheim, and Pilot Officer Alfred Savill, Sergeant Henry Sunderland and air gunner Roy Tyler in another, had failed to return; Smith had survived a crash-landing, but died in hospital and Savill had managed to escape a bullet-riddled aircraft by parachute.[277]

The only one to get back was Flying Officer Reginald 'Pissy' Peacock. Tall, good looking, with combed back dark hair, Peacock had first become fascinated by flying when his father Thomas, a valet, had an occasion to be with him at Croydon airfield in May 1930, and there Reginald had watched the pioneering female aviator Amy Johnson take-off in *Jason*, her De Havilland Gipsy Moth.[278] Six years later he would gain his aero certificate on the same type of plane at Cambridge Aero Club. Then, he joined the Air Force after training at Leuchars. Having gained his wings, he was posted to Gosport and, five months after the outbreak of war, had joined 235 Squadron.

All three Blenheims had been patrolling with Blue Section Hurricanes of 151 Squadron, which departed back to England after roughly thirty minutes, as fuel was getting low. Peacock, Smith and Savill were told however, to continue the patrol out over The Hook at 4,500 feet. They did as they were ordered and Peacock, Smith and Savill were bounced by at least five Me 110s which dived on them from 1,000 feet above. As the three Blenheims were getting the better of the twin-engine Messerschmitts, the odds worsened when four Me 109s joined the air battle. Peacock shouted, 'Messerschmitt One-oh-nines' on the R/T, keenly aware that instead of continuing with the odds against them they needed to get themselves out of there quickly, again shouting 'One-oh-nines.' Turning sharply to the left, he disengaged for a few seconds, made sure his aircrew were all right, and re-entered the fray. He spotted an Me 109 off to starboard and opened fire, to his amazement bits broke off, and there was a puff of black smoke, then suddenly the Messerschmitt plummeted from the sky down towards The Hague. His navigator, Sergeant Clifford Thorley, had watched helplessly, despite his warning, two Me 109s simultaneously open fire and Clifford saw cannon shells and machine-gun tracer slam into Smith's Blenheim. Fortunately, Peacock, Thorley and Wilson managed to escape unscathed – but he had not seen what happened to Savill.

It had been hard air fighting, during the ensuing two days. The Dutch resistance was crumbling, German troops reaching the shores of the Zuider Zee: the German military machine was unstoppable. Struggling against the mounting tide of refugees and the incessant Luftwaffe attacks, the Royal Navy requested assistance. Morewood, McHardy, and their aircrews were on stand-by. 'You're to protect ships in Den Helder, take-off immediately', 235 Squadron's Canadian commanding officer, Ralph MacDougall ordered.

Doing as he was ordered, Morewood with McHardy, duly took off, to fly protection cover over HMS *Valentine* and a Dutch destroyer which were firing shells along the Zuider Zee shore line. From their vantage point in the air Morewood witnessed huge clouds of smoke rise above The Hague. After only ten minutes flying over the vessels, Morewood heard a series of loud bangs. Frantically glancing around, he saw five Messerschmitt 110s, three of which within seconds made frontal attacks, at varying distances together. Initially, he panicked, and although he managed to fire off two short bursts, his four machine-guns had no effect against the more powerful German cannon and machine-gun combinations. Although hit, Morewood managed to evade his attackers, all accept one, which came round to the rear and followed *S-Sugar* down to the deck. Ringwood called out the range, whilst returning fire using the single Vickers K mounted drum-fed machine-gun. A single drum of sixty rounds was gone in seconds – he continually replenished until there was none left.

Weaving from side to side Morewood climbed to fifty feet off the sea, as fast as the Blenheim would take him, making for the safety of HMS *Valentine's* anti-aircraft guns. Morewood scribbled in his diary, 'I was praying that the Naval gunners would recognise the Blenheim and not shoot us out of the sky.' *S-Sugar* sped by, exposing the Me 110 to anti-aircraft and small arms fire, and its pilot broke off his pursuit.[279]

He could feel no pain – only a sense of relief that he was still alive, mingled with the apprehension that Leathem, and Ringwood may have been killed or wounded. As it transpired, Ringwood had survived the attack in the turret but found the intercom dead. So, he scrawled a note saying 'Okay', attached it to a jubilee clip on a bicycle chain mechanism and launched it at Morewood. Leathem had also been lucky and Morewood returned to Bircham Newton without difficulty until within sight of the airfield when the port engine began misfiring, but he landed without difficulty.

Switching off Morewood, Leathem and Ringwood clambered wearily down, then stood by the port wing and surveyed their battered Blenheim. Walking round the plane it was a wreck; and Ringwood's Perspex turret was pierced in one panel. As the plane was patched up an engine mechanic found the port engine fuel pipe had a single bullet hole, but the offending object acted as a stopper, even though fuel had been trickling out for roughly 182 miles, and only badly misfired the last two.

'Flight Lieutenant Morewood on loan to 235 Squadron in an aerial battle over the Zuider Zee area met in combat five Messerschmitt 110s and returned with forty-seven bullets holes in his aircraft,' the duty officer wrote in the 248 Squadron diary 'this is the first squadron engagement.'[280]

Morewood left the beer drinking to Leathem, McHardy, and Morris and went and had a hot bath. It was only then that he realised how lucky everyone had been. For the rest of 235 Squadron it had also been a busy day. After his first air victory, Cross had flown continually but not managed to increase his tally, despite being called at 03.00 hours, and told to fly cover off the Dutch coast with pilot officer's Michael Ryan, and Norman Jackson Smith. It was not before 05.00 hours, that they finally got going on 18 May. Watching minesweepers and a destroyer speed along the Dutch coast, by 09.00 hours they had flown back to Bircham Newton. 'No enemy action encountered what so ever!' wrote Cross, before departing on ten days leave.

Pennington-Legh from 248 Squadron temporarily replaced Richard Cross, and brought with him Alfred Fowler. On their arrival they were immediately considered operational. Pennington-Legh was called at 14.00 hours, and told to fly cover for minesweepers with Sergeant John Bessey and Pilot Officer Dudley Relton. They were vectored to the position by Morris and eventually got a visual sighting. Despite repeated attempts by Morris using an Aldis Lamp to communicate, the Navy did not respond. Nevertheless, they carried out a continuous oval pattern over the vessels in line astern, which required intense concentration because it was important that they did not cross the Dutch coast. After roughly five hours, the three Blenheims landed. Morewood was pleased that Pennington-Legh had found the ship, as his early morning mission had negative results, Morewood, along with pilot officers Curran Robinson and Dudley Warde could barely see the water below so returned after an hour.

Two days afterwards at 13.40 hours, Pennington-Legh, McHardy and Fowler were sent off on a mission covering a vessel sailing from Ostend. The tedious patrol was broken by the sighting of three Me 110s and saw to their destruction. The three pilots and their aircrew returned exhilarated by the scrap. Pennington-Legh, and McHardy had each claimed a Me 110, Morewood was desperate to emulate Alan and Sam's success.

Before he went back on sorties, Morewood heard that Curran was shot down one mile off Nieuport, by a Bloch 152 of GC II/8. He and his navigator, Sergeant Donald Mosley, and LAC Albert Waddington had no chance to abandon their aircraft. Roger, was one of the lucky ones, after a four-hour mission on the 19 May to provide protection for a minesweeper and the troops being despatched back to British ports from France, on landing Morewood received orders that he was re-joining 248 Squadron. On 20 May, ten days after Morewood, Leathem and Ringwood had been issued with the operational order to proceed to Bircham Newton, Air Vice-Marshal John Tyssen, AOC of No. 16 Group, had issued his own operational order for 248 Squadron's detachment which included Pennington-Legh, McHardy and Fowler, were to rotate out of the fray.

The Commander-in-Chief of RAF Fighter Command, Air Chief Marshal Sir Hugh Dowding, was deeply concerned about the shortage of aircraft. Dowding could still only call on forty-seven squadrons, of which roughly twenty-two were equipped with Spitfires and Hurricanes. The continued wastage of each aircraft over the Continent and English Channel meant that he simply did not have enough for an adequate home defence. Inevitably Dowding recalled from the Commander-in-Chief of RAF Coastal Command Air Chief Marshal Sir Frederick Bowhill, the four Blenheim fighter squadrons 'as they're only used for shipping protection' wrote Air Vice-Marshal Keith Park, AOC No. 11 Group. They had been busy shooting down German planes but there was nothing like enough of them to cope with the fast and more manoeuvrable Messerschmitts as Blenheim fighters were scythed from the skies in the coming weeks operating over Dunkirk and Channel ports.

'It took some time to obtain a clear picture of what was happening to the rest of 248,' wrote Morewood in his diary. The Blenheims of 248 Squadron or what remained of the twelve after Bourgeois and Tatar became the squadron's first casualties in the war when their plane hit the sea whilst making dummy fighter attacks against a Beaufort of 42 Squadron just a few miles offshore from Thorney Island, left Gosport for No. 13 Group. As the Blenheims flew out, bundles of kit lay on the ground as groundcrew frantically packed up.

Morewood with 'B' Flight, was ordered up to Dyce in Aberdeenshire, whilst Pennington-Legh, McHardy, and Fowler went to Montrose, thirty-eight miles north of Dundee to join 'A' Flight. After a two-hour trip from Bircham Newton, Morewood landed at Dyce.

It was good to be back amongst his old friends once more, although there were a number of faces missing. Roger learnt from Streatfield that Dowding had been keen to ditch their navigators and air gunners. It had been a sobering day for the squadron, to become a dedicated home-based Fighter Command unit. What was already self-evident was that not enough thought had been put into their move to No. 13 Group. There could be no benefit to losing their aircrew which were integral part of operating Blenheim fighters. All had gone to Silloth in Cumbria; Dowding reversed his decision thirty-two days later when 248 reverted back to being a Coastal Command squadron. 'The squadron received with some surprise the news that it had once again been transferred to Coastal Command. Since the formation of the squadron it has twice been in Fighter Command and twice in Coastal Command and has been to five different airfields, three of which were experienced in one week,' wrote the squadron diarist.

Still considered operational in less than a day, Morewood was called at 14.00 hours, to be sent off on a sector recce for which nineteen-year-old, LAC Norman Martin volunteered to be his air gunner. *R-Roger*, climbed away towards the hamlet of Blackdog to cross the coast out into the vast expanse of the North Sea. Morewood's air gunner saw nothing but sea and sky. In fact, Martin was rather enjoying himself. He had been excited when the Gunnery Officer Pilot Officer, Alfred 'Al' Smitz, had called for volunteers, after all it meant extra wages and he had been practicing firing the Vickers machine-gun at Thorney Island and Gosport. After one and a half hours, *R-Roger* had safely made it back to Dyce. De-briefed Martin went straight back to his main job as an air mechanic.

With no flying scheduled for the remainder of the day, Morewood got the opportunity to go into Aberdeen. With its wide streets and grey granite buildings, it was a lovely city although this was largely lost on the majority of late-teens and twenty-somethings of the RAF who visited, of which Dyce airfield was just one, coming from as far as the north-east bases at Kinloss and Lossiemouth, to meet the local girls. A favourite haunt was The Aberdeen Hotel near the main railway terminus, it was more up-market and considered officers only; while a private bar down King Street catered for the more adventurous clientele.

On Sunday 26 May, Morewood, flying *S-Sugar*, became the target for 602 Squadron Spitfire Mk1s, in an operational exercise. Another exercise saw 'B' Flight take off at 11.55 hours, and form up into two sections of three, maintaining tight 'V' formations as three Spitfire pilots made fighter attacks on the Blenheims to give the air gunners practice in giving their pilots evasive action instructions and in the use of their single Vickers machine-gun defensively, though for this demonstration they were fitted with a camera, so that the results on could be analysed on the ground then shown in the station cinema. Morewood was able to report to Streatfield and Air Vice-Marshal Richard Saul, AOC of No. 13 Group, that all crews on 'B' Flight were progressing well, with formation flying, formation air drill, and mastering low-level flying over water. Most crews had now amassed between ten and fifteen hours of daylight flying on the Blenheim and a minimal amount of hours night flying. Although Morewood had managed over thirty-two – with zero night flying, he also managed to fly cross-country to Kinloss which gave pilot Richard Haviland the opportunity to demonstrate that his map reading skills had not been forgotten whilst Leading Aircraftsman Reed got use to using the receiver transmitter which, despite the short range, could be enhanced by opening a hole in the fuselage floor and dropping an aerial out. Communication was by Morse code, and Reed's hand-tuning was therefore somewhat critical, so not surprisingly, the results were patchy.

June gave way to July and the Luftwaffe had begun stalking and attacking shipping. In the North Sea, skirmishes against Heinkel 115s from Luftflotte 5 began over convoys plying back and forth along the eastern coast of Scotland and England. Occasionally a He 115 got lucky as Morewood found out: 'The first bomb missed, the other four hit, with large mushroom columns blossoming in the air. From the air we could see fires breaking out on the ship as her cargo began burn. Lifeboats were hurriedly launched with at least a dozen men being tipped out into the sea on the starboard side. We flashed an emergency signal to a corvette who went scurrying back to round up its flock,' recalled Morewood. As 248 met the threat of Luftwaffe attacks on Allied shipping Victor Streatfield realised that one area that had been neglected was air-sea rescue. Little provision had been made by the Admiralty or Air Ministry, and he wrote to Fighter and Coastal Command on the attrition of his crews over the sea on standing convoy patrols 'there should be some means of rescuing ditched aircrew,' he wrote in one letter to Bowhill at Eastbury Park, Northwood.[281]

'B' Flight continued flying reconnaissance patrols and acting as air cover over convoys, in between which Streatfield sandwiched a training programme. Morewood was the only individual pilot on the flight at Montrose who had any experience of fighting the enemy, and Streatfield need him to lick his younger aircrews into shape. Morewood had them training and operating as a full flight, divided into the standard 'vics' of three. He taught them to all constantly look around, repeatedly shift their position and when the sun appeared in the northeast of Scotland keep up-sun as far as possible. Each pilot was rotated to fly with different navigators and air gunners. Roger had teamed up with the new squadron gunnery officer Robert Kenworthy from Caterham, who had attended the local Caterham School as a dayboy, before he joined Lloyds Bank.[282] By 1929 he had enlisted in the Royal Air Force as an aircraft hand trainee Wireless Operator. He was discharged in 1935 but re-mustered in 1939 and was accepted for aircrew training. When he left on 6 September 1940 to begin his Bombing and Gunnery Course at Loughborough, he reacquainted himself with Norman Smith whom he knew on 41 Squadron, then finally, with his Air Gunners wings on his tunic and the thin ring of a pilot officer on his cuff, he was posted to 248 Squadron and began the job of getting to know the Bristol Blenheim. Kenworthy's first flight with Morewood had exhilarating, and that same afternoon of 3 June, he flew his first mission a reconnaissance, two more followed in quick succession, then air tests, formation flying and air attack training.

By early July, they were on the move again, this time to the Shetland Islands. 'It was a bleak period for the squadron and 'B' Flight. A place of tents that had been cunningly devised to collect all available rain water into icy streams for precipitation upon the beds of honest aviators,' wrote Morewood. August arrived and between the first day and the end of the month, Morewood flew five times, only once on an operational sortie. 'We would be up before dawn, down at our office for first light and on standby, crews would leave to go on reconnaissance to Bergen, Haugesund or Trondheim and I'd be schooling the youngsters,' Morewood explained.[283]

He found the endless training and waiting the hardest thing to bear, and he badly missed the excitement of his days at Bircham Newton.

Wildly exaggerated reports had reached Sumburgh that on Sunday, 18 August, 235 Squadron had virtually been wiped out at Thorney Island by dive-bombers. Streatfield enquired if 248 Squadron was required to join the fray. 'Bowhill is conducting Coastal Commands battle with the information he is given, and the situation in the air is far rosier then you may perceive,' was the reply he received.

The Blenheims continued with their daily missions but, as they were discovering to their great cost, whilst it was far easier to find the Norwegian coast it was far harder to find anything to report about in the inlets and fjords. On 11 September, Morewood flew a reconnaissance and wrote 'Nothing of Value – Generally Bad'. There was no change in the remaining months of 1940. Debate about tactics raged endlessly in the Officers Mess, 'whether a Blenheim climbing from 50 feet to 250 feet at a relatively low speed would stand an earthly chance against flak defences on ship or shore,' jotted Morewood, 'and in the grand scheme of things, what were we achieving?' The consensus was that it was time for a change to the Bristol Beaufighter. The debate continued and was only curtailed with an importune move to Wick to support the Royal Navy in convoy protection and the Highlands from German hit-and-run raiders.

On Friday 13 December 1940, it had been decided that 248 Squadron should be utilised by Bowhill. At Donibristle, Air Vice-Marshal Charles Breese's HQ at 18 Group, this information was received and passed down to Victor Streatfield. In his office near the operations room, the Wing Commander received the news by telephone, then called his flight commanders and broke the news – seven Blenheims were required at Wick by 18.00 hours.

Crews flew out for their air tests, checking everything from guns to bomb-release gear, before landing and heading off to the Sergeants or Officers Mess for lunch. Pilot Officer John Dodd, and Alexander Pettet rushed to find a place knocking Frank 'The Lucky One' Thompson over onto his backside.[284]

'Steady on boys what's the rush?' enquired Morewood.

'Fish Friday,' replied Pettet. The twenty-eight-year-old had been ordained as a Deacon in Derbyshire but upon seeing the plight of the Kindertransport children and the tyranny unfolding in Germany, Pettet volunteered for the Royal Air Force in September 1939.[285] Born in Wigan Lancashire, he was raised in Hassocks, West Sussex a remote place with a railway station called Hassocks Gate after a tollgate on the main road to Brighton. It held limited opportunities for him, and with his Christian upbringing the church seemed a good idea. After studying at Leeds University and the College of Resurrection at Mirfield gaining a B.Sc., Pettet was ordained by the Bishop of Durham, Doctor Hensley Henderson, at the chapel within Auckland Castle. He was in the transitional period, preparing for the Anglican priesthood when he changed his cloth for Wedgewood Blue. Pettet began his initial training to become a navigator at 11 Air Observer Navigational School, joining the new entries on No. 2 Observer Course which started on March 18 and by the end of June 1940 had completed with a 'very above average.' After Bombing and Gunnery School he was posted to his OTU, at Silloth and arrived on 248 Squadron with John Dodd his pilot. Dodd was a member of The Institute of Chartered Accountants having qualified in London 'an astute young man with a promising career in chartered accounting ahead of him,' wrote the business editor of The Surrey Advertiser.[286] With his colleagues going in to the Army he joined the RAF Auxiliaries in roughly March 1939 but was not called up until the September, completing his training he was commissioned on 24 August and posted to Silloth to complete his airmanship.

The mealtime heralded a lot of noise as they sat down to freshly-caught fish with potatoes, once devoured Dodd and Pettet went back and picked up their wash bags and enough clothes and a spare pair of shoes for their stay in the Highlands. Finding their air gunner Sergeant Archie Hook they joined the others and listened to Streatfield who was followed by the Met Officer. Around 15.30 hours, the men began arriving at their Blenheims, as well as aircrew men from ground trades to keep the aircraft serviced would travel as passengers.

Aboard B-Baker, John Dodd was running up each of his engines. The airframe was rattling as each radial was run up. Sat on the fuselage floor between Archie and the centreplane was nineteen-year-old, Willesden-born, Laurence Bright and Arthur Moore from Paddington. Everything appeared to be in order, Dodd and Pettet sat and waited. Next to him in S-Sugar were Sergeants James Hamilton and Harold Walmsley, his navigator in the nose compartment, Hamilton now heard that Stanley Julian and Graham Monks were in position from Sergeant James 'Jim' May his air gunner. May had joined the squadron at Dyce. He was fairly tall, with an athletic build borne from playing cricket for Finchampstead in Berkshire.[287] There he went to the small village school, which was a short walk away. Later at fourteen-years-old, he joined H. E. Hall & Co, Auctioneers, House and Estate Agents in Wokingham and began collecting rent for their Lettings department and used to see aeroplanes fly over fairly regularly on his rounds from nearby Woodley aerodrome. By 1939 he had volunteered for aircrew, and it was to Hamble in Hampshire May was then sent, followed by postings to Upper Heyford then finally Penrhos in Wales.

All May could see from his position was a line of waiting Blenheims with their motors running 'any more hanging about and they'll overheat,' he heard Morewood say in his headphones. At seven minutes past one, the first of the seven thundered down the runway. Circling out over the sea the seven were formatting nicely at 2,000 feet when a plane on McHardy's portside flew up and over onto his starboard side and struck the right wing of Dodd's Blenheim. Already in the No. 3 position, McHardy watched the spectacle unfold as the two loaded twin-engine fighters went into a vertical spin plunging into a watery grave. Breaking formation McHardy went down to sea level, to searched for survivors with his navigator Sims and air gunner Wilcock frantically looking for signs of life amongst the debris in the raging sea. 'I turned about and landed back at Sumburgh to report what had happened. With the accident details recorded on paper I flew out towards Wick landing at 15.25,' said McHardy, 'the whole thing was tragic for all concerned and a nasty muddle for the Court of Inquiry to unravel.'

At 14.40 hours, the three remaining Blenheims reached Wick as scheduled. Morewood had no idea that Dodd and Hamilton and their crews were dead until McHardy touched down. There were ten men missing. Three days of continuous rain and strong winds curtailed all missions from Wick and the five returned to Sumburgh on the 19 December.

With the arrival at Sumburgh of a new CO, James Coats, it was left up to the squadron adjutant, McHardy and Morewood to send the telegrams to the families of those who had died. Notifications that they were missing were sent to the next of kin: Gertrude May, parent of James received her 'It is with deep regret …' telegram little over two days later at her home in the quiet Berkshire village of Finchampstead. She had also sadly lost her mother and husband earlier in the year.

They were in party spirit leading up to Christmas Eve as large amounts of beer and spirits had been hidden away and by the time they reached Christmas Day all aircrew were decidedly worse for wear by the time they were meant to serve the Airmen their Christmas Dinner. Despite crashing hangovers No 18 Group ordered that a single Blenheim should carry out a reconnaissance to Trondheim in the morning. With Morewood dispensing his culinary skills in the kitchen, McHardy, Sims and Wilcock scrambled into the air. Reaching Stadlandet, Sims received a coded message at 09.25 hours to abort the mission 'as no planes should fly over enemy territory on Xmas Day'.

At the end of December, Air Chief Marshal Sir Frederick Bowhill was preparing for change in the New Year. There were glimpses of what lay ahead with the Air Ministry approving the issuing of Bristol Beaufighters to Coastal Command and a new Air Officer Commanding was appointed on 14 June 1941, when Air Marshal Sir Philip Joubert de la Ferté returned to the post he had previously held before the war, replacing Bowhill. The previous day Bowhill had his last success before he left, when 42 Squadron Beauforts, torpedoed the German cruiser *Lutzow* off the Norwegian coast.

Meanwhile, Morewood and 248 Squadron continued their missions along the Norwegian coast.[288] Danger now came from marauding Messerschmitts, and they began to notice an increase in the number of flak-ships. These were normally requisitioned fishing trawlers fitted out with vast numbers of anti-aircraft guns: two 88mm and light 20mm guns, either Flak 30s or Flak 38s. These were either single or four barreled with a rapid rate of fire. Whether 20mm or 38mm calibre, all had the means to bring down a Blenheim.

Despite the plane being obsolete Joubert had little choice but to continue to commit them into the fray. But in doing so many valuable pilots and aircrew went to early deaths, as Beaufighter deliveries were very slow, with just a sufficiency to allow 248 Squadron to start gradually replacing its Blenheim fighters in July, although missions were run jointly with both types until full complement had been achieved. There was also a flurry of comings and goings of aircrew, and 248 Squadron were certainly spawning some heroes.

By the start of 1942, there were still only three squadrons in Coastal Command, 235, 236 and 248 Squadrons equipped with Beaufighters. Bircham Newton on Sunday 8 February, saw Morewood team up with navigator Sergeant Robert 'Bob' James, a Welshman from Newport, Monmouthshire, to do a triple air test on *W-Whisky*. At 10.00 hours, *W-Whisky* edged round until it reached the end of the runway. Cleared to go, they took to the air with James sat in the nose at his small collapsible table, with his flying helmet unstrapped and the leads plugged into the intercom. He had rechecked the domed blister to make sure it was firmly sealed and clipped into place, so it would not fly open, as had been the case with so many recently. Morewood crossed over the Norfolk Riviera out into the North Sea, dropping down to fifty feet on a route towards Rotterdam across the blue grey sea that swirled below.

Morewood began the repetitive search for the convoy of merchantman and its escorts. Flying at almost zero feet, James peered out of the domed blister to see the odd fishing boat. After roughly fifty-five minutes he received a recall notice and Morewood decided to head back the same way they came finally touching down at 11.45 hours. Both clambered from their Beaufighter then headed off to be debriefed. Afterwards Morewood and James were told, 'you're both off to Coltishall on the 15th and Dyce on 19 February,' by their commanding officer Wing Commander Ernest 'Johnny' Hyde DFC, who had recently filled the space after the death of Leslie King, had died within a month like his predecessor James Coats.

Morewood then flew with their Maurice Guedj on the 3 March to carry out a weather reconnaissance in *A-Apple* but after twenty minutes they returned to base.[289] He was then reacquainted with Norman Martin, then a flight sergeant, who had shown aptitude and gone on to qualify as an observer. Both spent four days repeatedly doing air tests with *S-Sugar*. Then followed the usual air test drills until the 20th when Morewood flew *R-Roger* on fighter escort: 'We had a long trip over the North Sea at zero feet and we were freezing to death, the route seemed to get progressively closer to the Norwegian coast,' recalled Morewood, who landed away at Lossiemouth. Making the thirty-minute flight back he recommended air tests at Dyce.[290] Hyde's Beaufighter *X-X-Ray* tail wheel had broken off after a normal landing by him. It was attributed to being severely weakened by a previous heavy landing when a novice pilot was at the controls. The Category E damage was fixed on the 26 March. After repair, Morewood with Corporal George 'Erkraft Fixer' Smith, carried out the trial, touching down the tail wheel functioned normally, and *X-X-Ray* was signed off 'Okay'. Afterwards Morewood managed to borrow a De Havilland Hornet Moth and flew over to Leuchars. Returning, at 12.30 hours and then, having had something to eat, Hyde wanted Morewood to fly *C-Charlie* with him as an observer. A circuit around the local countryside and with fifteen minutes the Beaufighter touched down after a successful air test. Hyde signed the chit and walked off 'he was like a dog without a ball, without Paget,' wrote Ricketts.[291] Jack Paget his navigator had left to quickly attend his grandfather's funeral in Hornsea, Yorkshire.

Now by the evening of 28 April, Paget had returned to Dyce 'to every one's relief,' and at around 19.30 hours, Hyde and Paget, with Squadron Leader David Cartridge and Sergeant Morris Osborne, were ordered to carry out a mission near Trondheim. At twenty-five minutes past eight, Hyde left the runway, and swung the planes towards Norway dropping down below the enemy radar. Watching from the hangar was Morewood. He was worried about *X-X-Ray*, 'Hyde should have gone in *S-Sugar*'[292] as Roger had done a ten-minute air test for weather night flying in that particular aircraft, ready for their mission flown in conjunction with Bomber Command against the German battleship *Tirpitz*.

Crossing the sea, they had excellent visibility all the way and made landfall precisely where planned. Danger was never far away in Trondheim, which was particularly well defended with a mixture of anti-aircraft guns protecting the harbour facilities. There were also the Messerschmitts of 9. Staffel of JG 5 based at nearby Lade, it's twelve or so aircraft being mostly Me109Fs, which were much faster than Beaufighters and had 20mm cannons and machine-guns. There was also an effective radar system. The German pilots had achieved considerable success in the preceding weeks, with 9. Staffel shooting down five Photographic Reconnaissance planes – three Spitfires and two Mosquitoes – as the RAF surveyed the German battleship *Tirpitz* in Fættenfjord roughly forty miles northeast of Trondheim.

Hyde and Cartridge weaved their aircraft through the islands, past Stadsbygd, to begin their 'S'-shaped run-in.[293] They swung into the main fjord, and as they thundered over the water both came under extremely heavy anti-aircraft fire from both sides of the fjord. On *T-Tommy* Cartridge and Osborne were shocked by the ferocity of the flak.

As they curved in towards Trondheim and Lade airfield, they caught the full force of Munkholmen Island's multiple Flak 38 emplacements just outside the town's harbour area. Managing to dodge this and other coloured tracer hosing up from the town, Cartridge made sure his gun button was set to 'fire' and, upon clearing the last house roof, began strafing the airfield, as did Hyde.

Both came under intense anti-aircraft fire and small arms fire. Cannon shells hurtled past them, then, a moment later, there was a thud as shell hit *T-Tommy* 'but it did not seem to have done any harm,' said Cartridge. Despite the flak and damage, *T-Tommy* went in again for a second attack, before setting course for home.

As Hyde turned *X-X-Ray* tightly round and made a second run. With tracer arcing towards them, he replied with cannon as he swept into the fjord. But then the plane jolted as cannon shells struck. The gun crew commander directing the fire from the Ladehammeren battery saw the flow of tracer pounding into the twin-engine aircraft and a moment later it dropped towards the water.

On board, Hyde battled to control the aircraft. Jack Paget released the escape mechanism, ejecting the rear dome as Beaufighter X-X-*Ray* hit the water. Hyde and Paget, although badly injured, managed to get out and clambered into the already inflated dinghy, pushing away from the submerged wreckage. They floated around for some considerable time until rescued by a party of German soldiers who had commandeered a Canadian-type canoe and paddled out in search of the fliers. Brought ashore, both Hyde and Paget were placed on stretchers with critical injures and died at an unspecified time on the morning of Wednesday 29 April.

David Cartridge and Osborne in *T-Tommy* touched down at Sumburgh at 02.44 hours. 'I had the dubious honour of being the second one back at Sumburgh,' said Cartridge, 'Alec Cook of 235 Squadron had beaten me by twenty minutes!' Meanwhile groundcrew had hurried over to Cartridge's badly holed aircraft.

There was a ten-minute wait for the last of the Beaufighters. The crew of *J-Johnnie*, unlike Cartridge, had a comparatively easy flight. Pilot Officer Anthony Englefield and Flight Sergeant John Phillips had passed unscathed into their area. Seeing a fire already alight near their target, they then lost visual contact 'so we set course for home,' reported Englefield to their Intelligence officer. With no word on Hyde or Paget both were posted as missing. It had been a long night for the crews, and they headed off to get some rest, this was soon interrupted, however.

Halifax *C-Charlie* reached Sumburgh shortly after ten minutes past four, Canadian Warrant Officer Herbert 'Pete' Peterson and his crew from 10 Squadron safely landed at 04.16 hours with a large hole in the tailplane. The flak that caused the hole had shot away the leads to the fuel cocks, which led to the inner starboard engine failing over the target area. 'With prudent engine management Peterson got to Sumburgh', wrote Reginald 'Taffy' Manning, 'and was awarded the immediate DFC'. A second visitor arrived at 05.45 hours – Pilot Officer John Whyte with his crew in *X-X-Ray* having only been able to fly the home leg at a reduced 110 mph due to the flaps sustaining damage, which fell into the down position causing considerable drag.

With 248 Squadron receiving another new commanding officer James Pike, Morewood found the month of May another soul-destroying month to say the least with a little instruction work, then air tests, and ferrying aircrews around. 'Morewood you seriously need to increase the rate of missions your flying,' said Pike. The cluster of missions began 5 June. 'Fighter interceptions' with Sergeant Terence Keech. He was in the air again on the 7th, though the sortie was uneventful. But, two days later, while 100 miles out *F-Freddie* was vectored towards a 'bogey'. After a further twenty miles a Blohm & Voss BV 138 was spotted. The trimotor flying boat turned for home and its pilot began taking what evasive action he could while the Beaufighters cannon shells flew across the sky, striking the hull then suddenly one of the trimotor Junkers Jumo engines was aflame.

'My blasted guns have jammed! Looks in poor shape though,' said Morewood on the intercom to Keech, 'better send out a SOS.'[294]

'Okay Roger,' replied Keech.

Immediately turning away on a heading back to Dyce. 'It's been a good day for Morewood who claimed a probable,' wrote Ricketts in the squadron diary. Morewood continued the fighter interception patrols with Keech, interspersed with six other navigators, before he was tour-expired and posted, on 4 July, as an instructor to 9 (Coastal) OTU at Crosby-on-Eden near Carlisle.[295]

The instructing stint was by no means a holiday. As an instructor he remained a squadron leader, and his days were full of instruction and training flights. As he tutored the next generation of Coastal Command pilots, 248 Squadron was deployed to Malta to battle with Italian and German aircraft. After a successful tour, the squadron deployed back to Great Britain on 23 August, minus their Beaufighters. Re-equipped with aircraft James Pike and his aircrews settled into long-range fighter patrols from Chivenor in Devon.

Morewood began agitating for a more active post in early 1943. He missed the camaraderie, unfortunately Roger learnt he would soon be posted to Aldergrove, to continue as an instructor, with further moves to Castle Combe, Hullavington, Crosby-on-Eden and Haverfordwest in Pembrokeshire. His patience and diligence had not gone unnoticed and in 1944, five months after Air Chief Marshal Sholto Douglas had taken over as C-in-C of Coastal Command, Morewood was given notice of his new command. Morewood, still only twenty-eight at the time, was given command as Wing Commander Flying at Langham. Roughly twenty-seven miles northwest of Norwich, its location was ideally suited for Coastal Command missions, being only three miles from the North Sea.[296]

Douglas notified Air Vice-Marshal Frank Hopps, AOC 16 Group, that Morewood should go straight to North Coates and meet the out-going Wing Commander Flying. When Roger arrived, Tony Gadd, who was in the throes of packing kit, told him, 'strictly speaking you're not compelled to fly sorties, but any opportunity to have a crack at the blighters I'm there'.[297] Gadd, was moving to become commanding officer 144 Squadron that August, releasing Wing Commander David 'Buster' Lumsden DFC. He left Roger Morewood with 'bags of advice,' before making haste to Langham in a Moth Minor.

Stepping inside the station headquarters, the first to greet him was the station commander New-Zealand born Group Captain Arthur Clouston DFC AFC who had commanded 224 Squadron flying anti-U-boat sorties over the Bay of Biscay before taking the Langham job. Also in the room was Wing Commander Jack Davenport CO of 455 Squadron, and the commander of 489 Squadron who was thirty-year-old John 'Johnny'

Dinsdale from Te Kuiti New Zealand. Commissioned as a pilot officer at twenty-five in 1938, Dinsdale spent seven years in the Royal Air Force being awarded a DFC whilst flying with 42 Squadron. Later, after his marriage to Agnes Tullis, he transferred to the Royal New Zealand Air Force.

Clouston told Morewood that he was committed to establishing good relations with those in his squadrons and wanted Roger to be 'on the same page' as he was respected by those whom he commanded and did not want a loose cannon as he set the tone for the high morale which Davenport and Dinsdale fostered. Morewood had barely finished settling in to his new surroundings when orders arrived for 'an attack on enemy shipping.' Clouston called them together for a briefing and promptly introduced them to their new Wing Commander Flying, and explaining to Roger Morewood that the Australians and New Zealanders were patriotically known as the Anzac Wing but in official circles Langham Wing. He advised the aircrew that there would still be occasions to combine with Stubby and North Coates strike wings and assured them they would be kept busy with missions and Morewood's training. Between missions off the Dutch and Norwegian coast, on training exercises both Beaufighter squadrons were averaging about twenty hours per week. 'It was tiring work but the practice was paying off,' noted Davenport. 'That was down to Roger's perseverance tutoring individual pilots, and aircrews.'

Roger Morewood had teamed up with another Englishman, twenty-year-old Harry Alderman.[298] Originally from Windsor in Berkshire, the Kiwis on 489 Squadron immediately christened him 'The Duke.' With Alderman as navigator, Morewood flew shipping strikes off the Dutch coast.

On 9 September at 05.16 hours, the sound of radial engines interrupted the still calm air around the Norfolk base. Flying Officer Allan Lynch was first up one of nine Beaufighters whom he would led formed up then once over the English coast dived down to fifty feet and at roughly 200 mph, headed off in the direction of Terschelling one of the Frisian Islands. Except Q-Queenie piloted by Morewood became separated from the formation when carrying out a change of course: 'I made the decision there and then,' said Roger, 'to return to base.' It was bitterly disappointing but there was no other choice, 'wing reconnaissance did not go!' wrote Morewood in his flying logbook.[299] For Coulson 'Roger made absolutely the right call, couldn't have him gallivanting off on his own. Far to a valuable fellow!' Within four hours Morewood and Alderman were airborne for a second time after an urgent call by 16 Group for a search west of the Frisian Islands, which proved negative, as did one flown by Flying Officer

Charles Tapper to Den Helder, and a third sortie by Flight Lieutenant Peter Branton covering the eastern end of the Frisian Islands. 'Despite the negative reports valuable information was gathered,' claimed Clouston.

Morewood had little success on the 18 September when the North Coates and Langham Wing combined in a third operation for September, to Heligoland Blight. Another followed on Monday 25 September, led by Cartridge's 254 Squadron towards Schiermonnikoog, one of the West Frisian Islands. This time it bore fruit. Roger Morewood heard Cartridge say 'attack, attack, attack!' Morewood, assigned as anti-flak, begun his run, tracer hurtling towards *M-Mother*. This was a terrible moment as the enemy pumped the air full of lead, and still they had not been hit. A few hundred yards from their target he hosed the flak-ship with 20mm cannon and men fell off the raised flak tower as they hurtled over the vessel and beyond. There was suddenly a huge explosion, one of the TorBeaus torpedoes had struck and sunk the flak-ship. Morewood safely landed *M-Mother* back at Langham. In the usual understated way, he jotted down 'some damage was done to minesweeper and merchant ships.'

After the ops debriefing, Arthur Clouston met with Roger and told him he would be leaving the Langham Wing, at the end of September.[300] Posted out of Coastal Command after roughly five and a half years to Castel Benito in Libya with Transport Command, then a spell in Italy's Naples. His time as a Coastal Boy was lengthy, he hadn't won any gongs but had earned but two Mentions in Despatches. Roger Morewood had had a profound effect on many in Air Force blue thus rounding of his wartime service. With the return of peace he left in 1947 only to re-muster in 1951 to serve in the Far East then came a pleasant interlude commanding Edinburgh University Air Squadron at home Roger finally retiring in 1957.

Chapter 8

Flying Officer Allan Triggs MBE, DFC and Flying Officer John Watson

Not everyone had mastered taking-off in a modified Vickers Wellington, which was why there was a gradual process of training flights at RAF Chivenor, in north Devon under the direction of Squadron Leader Jeaffreson Greswell. A former scholar at Repton, Derbyshire 'Greswell, had a fascination with aeronautical mechanics,' wrote his Housemaster. With the right school certificate examinations, he entered the Royal Air Force in 1935, on a short service commission. Gaining his wings Greswell was posted to 217 Squadron at Boscombe Down. After scurrying around the British Isles flying Avro Ansons evading Messerschmitts during the Battle of Britain, roughly four months later he was seconded to the Coastal Command Development Unit, where he came into contact with Wing Commander Humphrey de Vere Leigh, who had hunted U-boats in the First World War.

Leigh developed a two-million-candlepower searchlight – the Leigh Light – which Vickers Wellington twin-engine bombers were adapted to carry. In the New Year of 1942, Greswell was selected to command No. 1471 Flight based at Chivenor, to introduce the light operationally.[301] Coastal Command's special flight had been given a number, but was immediately absorbed into 172 Squadron. Presiding over them was Wing Commander John Russell, who had flown missions over the Bay of Biscay with 502 Squadron as a flight commander on Armstrong Whitworth Whitleys, Russell now became a flight commander.

By the end of Saturday, 4 April – the unit's first full day as 172 Squadron – there were fourteen pilots and more-or-less complete crews. Pilot Officer Allan Triggs, a former banking official with the National Bank in the

Prahran, a suburb of Melbourne, was one of those. Despite the depression in the 1930s, he had relocated from Malvern and his prospects with the bank seemed good with incentives to take up a managerial role. Allan volunteered for the Air Force transferring from the Artillery. Twenty-seven, single and anxious to explore beyond the boundaries of Australia, in 1939 Britain gave him that opportunity declaring war on Germany.

Initial training started when he arrived on Sydney's North Shore in civilian clothes, as uniforms were still being hemmed and stitched. He worked hard on the month-long course and achieved a respectable score and heard he was going to 5 Elementary Flying Training in Narromine. With the vast open country and clear air space Triggs loved the freedom, and thoroughly enjoyed the course too, and he became a qualified pilot. His only offense was at Narromine: 'Triggs continues to neglect to obey standing orders and engages in dangerous low flying,' wrote Squadron Leader Ernest Redman on Form P8a. Completing his Air Force training Triggs finally left Australia, sailing for Canada. He spent a year flying Ansons and was commissioned as a pilot officer on Tuesday 10 June 1941.

Arriving on his passage to Britain in Iceland, Triggs briefly joined Ferry Command after taking their special course bringing a twin-engine Lockheed Hudson into Britain in January 1942 with William Hewitt a Liverpulian. Having been through OTU Triggs was posted to 172 Squadron in the April. Tragedy struck the fledgling unit when one of the four operationally-equipped Wellingtons went missing on a transit flight to St Eval. Allan Triggs would stumble upon the wreckage.

Its captain, Pilot Officer Hamar Russ, had voluntarily enlisted in Edmonton Canada in July 1940 but it was not until May 1941 that he received his commission. Crossing the Atlantic, he piloted one of the Hudsons that came across with Triggs, with navigator Colin Badham from Bankstown, New South Wales. After a further course Russ was posted to 172 Squadron. Five days after his arrival he took off at 14.00 hours, in heavy drizzle, on Monday, 13 April with Flying Officer Edward Blair as co-pilot on a transit flight to St Eval, crewed up with Le Bon, Noble and Daniel.

In the early hours of the morning news was received that wreckage had been sighted seven days after the aircraft had been posted missing. John Russell organised a search party to walk the cliffs between Clovelly and Hartland Point. Triggs found the crumpled wreckage scattered over the remote Beckland Bay. Medical Officer William Noble, Russell and Triggs descended the cliff and retrieved the five bodies.[302] 'Bodies had sustained substantial impact blows and burns,' Noble jotted later in his medical report. The Analysis Officer, Group Captain Charles Carey of Coastal

Command's Accident Department, wrote in his monthly report for Air Chief Marshal Sir Philip Joubert de la Ferté and 19 Group: 'Conditions were not good, the pilot flew at a reduced altitude and collided with the cliff face, he had also not completed a familiarization trip and was therefore NOT familiar with surroundings.'

As 172 Squadron buried their dead, a replacement aircrew arrived on 23 April in the form of Pilot Officer Justin Devonshire from 3 OTU and Harry Grace from 254 Squadron. In the evening both attended Allan Triggs' birthday celebrations in the Officers Mess, which then moved onto Barnstaple until the local constabulary dropped eight inebriated men back at the main entrance to RAF Chivenor. 'In a matter of only a few minutes we found ourselves cooling of rather rapidly,' said Grace as 'Russell and Greswell were waiting to stand us a pint in the Mess!'

As 172 Squadron's five aircraft and crews trained, Coastal Command continued to fly over the waters surrounding the British Isles. On the night of 3 June, operational missions finally got the green light from the Commander-in-Chief to hunt for U-Boats. At Chivenor, the activity on four dispersal points was feverish, belts of bullets were loaded, and a cluster of depth charges hauled into the Wellingtons' bomb bays. At 18.30 hours, the briefings began with Russell introducing Air Vice-Marshal Geoffrey Bromet who commanded 19 Group, and ended after the briefing from the Met Officer.

It was now roughly 19.00 hours. Watches had been synchronized to BBC time, but until take-off crews dispersed to either the Sergeants or Officers Mess, Half-an-hour later the men arrived in the Crew Room, with many in shirt sleeves, or just battle dress. There were twenty-four men flying on this anti-U-Boat mission. The men walked to their planes. At *F-Freddie*, Jeaffreson Greswell's Wimpy, the hatch was already open, and a small telescopic ladder was held in place. First the navigator Pooley, climbed up, followed by Sergeants Edward Walker, Evan Roberts, and Denzil Archibald the rear gunner. Then came Allan Triggs and Greswell.

With everyone aboard, the engines were run up and the pre-flight checks religiously done. This completed, the Form 700 was signed by the captain and passed to one of the groundcrew on the ground. Then gradually the four Leigh Light Wellingtons were on the move around the perimeter track, to reach the end of the specified runway.

At 20.54 hours, Greswell saw the green Aldis Lamp flash. *F-Freddie* was the last to speed down the runway. Tail up. Speed gradually increased with throttles pushed forward the Wellington, rose into the air.

172 Squadrons first mission had begun.

Their search area was a sequence of squares in the Bay of Biscay. Greswell's Wellington flew over the now familiar landmarks that included Pooley's nearby hometown, Launceston. Crossing the English coast just west of Bishop's Rock and turn on a track towards the northern coast of Spain, maintaining radio silence.

At a certain point Greswell began the repetitive flying back and forth whilst Pooley scanned the radar screen for any blimps. Triggs kept an eye on the altimeter; so long as *F-Freddie* stayed below 500 feet the aircraft was unlikely to be picked up by radar. This didn't mean the crew was safe. Enemy *Nachtjagdgeschwader* night fighter units based in Brittany had Junker 88 which was considerably faster than the Wellington and had an array of 20mm and 30mm cannons.

A potentially far bigger danger was from a U-Boat on the surface equipped with light flak guns. Coastal Command aircrews had been made aware that seven months previously, on Wednesday 17 December 1942, a Royal Naval Martlet aircraft flown by George Fletcher, was brought down by U-131's anti-aircraft fire – the first aircraft to be shot down by a U-Boat in the war.

As Greswell made his port turn at around 01.43 hours in *F-Freddie*, Greswell's navigator, Pooley, suddenly saw a blip on the radar screen – a U-Boat he suspected.

'Contact,' Pooley said into the intercom, 'six and a half miles to starboard.'

Another sweep on the radar produced a second contact.

'Good – stand by gunners,' Greswell replied. 'We're going in.'

At roughly one mile from the contact, co-pilot Triggs flicked the switch for the Leigh Light. The intense illumination showed a U-Boat on the surface three-and-a-quarter miles dead ahead. Flying at 200 mph, and at 450 feet, they were admittedly in a too-steep dive, which caused a momentary eclipse of the target. With a few expletives Greswell reset the altimeter and hauled the aircraft ninety degrees to port, and lost height.

'They're firing recognition signals,' Triggs announced on the intercom, as he trained the beam of light squarely on the submarine. At fifty feet Greswell made sure the bomb doors were open, and four depth charges were dropped as the Wellington roared over the U-Boat. 'Three explosions, Skipper' Archibald called into the intercom.

Weighting 296lb, the depth charges had straddled the target with a spacing of thirty-five feet. Three exploded, one on the starboard quarter about five yards from the hull, and the other two on the portside.

A second U-Boat – the Italian-built *Morosini* – was in the area, approximately twelve miles away, which fired a burst of recognition star shells. Greswell flew towards the submarine and at a height of 150 feet passed over the submarine from starboard to port. Triggs had positioned their Leigh Light so that rear gunner Denzil Archibald had a clear view of the enemy vessel, and he managed to get off 200 rounds, most of which ricocheted along conning tower and hull.

F-Freddie was still intact; there had been no defensive fire. Greswell resumed the square search before heading for base. They reached Chivenor, landing safely at 05.57 hours. There to greet them as they clambered down was Wing Commander John Russell congratulating them all. Russell had had a miserable patrol in *C-Charlie* and had touched down thirty-seven minutes earlier. They immediately headed for their debriefing.

F-Freddie had opened the scoring for 172 Squadron. Greswell had proved that the procedure worked, going to Northwood to meet Joubert the next day, 'our success gave him the ammunition to boost the production of Leigh Light Wellingtons,' claimed Greswell.

The U-Boat attacked was in fact an Italian submarine, *Luigi Torelli* commanded by the flamboyant Tenente di vascello Augusto Migliorini on a passage from Bordeaux to the West Indies. Fearing a total loss, Migliorini grounded his boat near Cape Penas. The *Luigi Torelli* survived further attacks on 7 June, from both Tom Egerton and Edwin Yeoman in Sunderlands of 10 (RAAF) Squadron.

Allan Triggs continued to fly as co-pilot with Greswell until the July. He then started flying with his own crew, their first sortie being on Tuesday 11 August. Triggs, Walker, Cartwright, Badham, McLean, and Devonshire were roistered to fly again on a night anti-submarine patrol. For this mission Triggs had been allocated an Wellington, *D-Dog*, his normal charge *F-Freddie* was being given a major overhaul. He expressed his concerns about the Wellington that had not been flown since 28 July, but, doing as he had been ordered, Triggs duly took off at 20.30 hours, with two other aircraft flown by Fraser and Bramwell. His first mission with 172 Squadron had been on 3 June and now he was about to take part in his eleventh.

For Triggs and his co-pilot, Sergeant Neville Walker, it was a peaceful night patrol in the Bay of Biscay. The last hour was always the longest, like the last few miles home. At 03.35 hours, bright flashes lit up the cold interior of the tail turret. Pilot Officer Justin Devonshire methodically rotated his turret thirty-five degrees. After a few expletives Devonshire's voice came through Triggs' headphones: 'There's excessive sparks, from the starboard engine, Skipper.'

'Sparks? What do they look like?'[303]

'Clusters of stars,' replied Devonshire.

'Are you sure? Have another look.'

'Okay, they've tripled there's more than ever now. I can still see them trailing behind us when they're a hundred and fifty to two hundred yards back.'

Triggs glanced at the oil pressure gauge. The needle was steady for a fraction of a second, and then he watched with silent alarm as the pressure dropped rapidly to zero. He instinctively moved his right-hand to close the throttles slowly whilst his feet adjusted the rudder. The note of the engine changed to a rough and laboured cough and then the engine and propeller seized. Triggs automatically cut the fuel supply to the non-responsive engine to lessen the risk of a blaze, and increased the revs on the remaining radial engine.

Flying at 1,200 feet, Triggs had little manoeuvrability, and in the prevailing weather conditions it made the aircraft very difficult to fly on the one remaining engine. Flight Sergeant Arthur Cartwright heard Triggs' voice: 'Send an immediate S.O.S, telling them we're on one motor,' then he was onto Pilot Officer Charles 'Col' Badham, 'Give Cartwright our co-ordinates.'

Badham gave Cartwright their position before Cartwright transmitted the S.O.S on the emergency frequency. He then wound out his trailing aerial so to repeat it on the long-wave distress frequency. Suddenly the Wellington lurched earthwards and lost 200 feet. Triggs gave the port engine some more boost and 2,450 revolutions per minute, and tried to keep the air speed needle at a constant 120 mph.

'Engine temperature rising,' Walker said on the intercom.

In spite of the increase in power *D-Dog* was steadily losing height. 'Jettison everything you can,' Triggs demanded, 'parachutes, flame floats, all loose equipment.' The Australian opened the bomb bay doors, armed the depth charges and jettisoned them into sea. Despite doing this he simply could not get the Wellington to climb.

At any moment it looked as if they would plunge straight into the water. 'Prepare for ditching, chaps!' said Triggs. The wind strength was roughly thirty miles an hour, and Badham calculated the waves were breaking two to three feet high, running downwind of the swell. They were roughly 110 miles from land. In the cockpit, Walker helped Triggs tighten his safety harness, and release the escape hatch before getting into his ditching position. Laying down feet first in the fuselage bracing himself against a ledge on the floor next to Badham. He had also untightened the astrodome bolts and made ready the floatation gear. Cartwright was still sending distress signals to 19 Group.

Triggs turned into the wind, but with a load of radar equipment aft, *D-Dog* was becoming tail heavy and extremely difficult to handle. He immediately closed the port throttle, put the port propeller into course pitch and turned off the fuel. It wasn't the gentlest of ditchings. The tail hit first, and the water cascaded over the plane, but fortunately Barnes Wallis' geodetic design held the aircraft together. Triggs felt the Wellington come to a halt. Four of the six men sustained minor injuries on impact, with Cartwright, who was flung forward, suffering a deep gash above his right eye.

Badham made it to the astrodome hatch and undid the four bolts, this was moved out of the way and Cartwright and McLean lifted themselves out onto the mainplane. Badham looked down the fuselage for Devonshire, as by this time the water was three feet deep. But the Canadian rear gunner appeared, and both clambered out the hatch to escape.

Triggs managed to undo his quick harness as waves swamped the cockpit. Within seconds the cockpit was submerged, the Australian realizing that there was no movement from his co-pilot Walker, who'd been thrown forward on impact, his forehead slamming into the instrument panel knocking him out cold. Now underwater and unconscious Triggs undid Walkers harness, partially inflated his Mae West, and kicked him to see if he would come around. There was no response, so he manhandled Walker out of his seat. With the Mae West giving buoyancy to the unconscious co-pilot Triggs found a foothold on his padded seat and armrest to extract himself. Disregarding his own safety, and the elements, he lay down, put his upper torso back into the cockpit, and heaved Walker out. Then slid down onto the port wing cradling his co-pilot, who was at last slowly regaining consciousness, joining the rest of the crew who were standing on the wing up to their knees in water.

'Where's the dinghy, has it floated away?' he enquired.

Triggs found that the automatic dinghy release had failed but he managed to prise open the fabric with his bare hands. The dinghy then began to inflate, but then Badham realised that the supplies were still in *D-Dog*! Scrambling out of the dinghy he wadded across with Triggs.

'Give me a lift up, I'm lighter than you!'

'What was that you said?' asked Triggs.

'Best just get on with things.'

Clasping both hands together, a drenched flying boot was placed in the hold, then Badham was hoisted upwards, and, managing to grip with a hand in a foothold opening, heaved himself up on to the top of the fuselage and disappeared through the astrodome. Badham plunged into darkness it was cold, smelly and with the water above waist height, he was momentarily disorientated. Badham fumbled around for the supplies and the distress pistol. 'Coming out now,' shouted the navigator and two packs of supplies were slid down the fuselage.

'Where's the bloody Verey pistol?'

'Let's get in the dinghy,' said his fellow Australian.

Triggs was just about to clamber in when he saw an emergency pack floating away; he swam out and retrieved it, before being manhandled into the dinghy by the tall Canadian, Devonshire.

Shivering, Badham lifted the left corner of Triggs' flying helmet, cupped his hands to captain's ear, 'The butterfly nuts securing it were too tight to be undone,' Badham said. 'We've got the flares that are packed in the dinghy?'

'Yes,' Triggs nodded his agreement.

'Check the box?'

'O.K.'

Before Badham could check, the dinghy was lifted in the rough seas to almost near vertical on a huge wave and their stomachs churned. All were overcome by the nausea of seasickness until sunrise. When they woke from their fragmented sleep Badham prized open the box which should have four smoke flare, but instead only contained two distress flares. Despite this all began to scan the empty horizon.

Meanwhile, Robert Bramwell and his crew landed at 06.21 hours, with Donald Frazer in *N-Nuts* having touched down twelve minutes earlier on Wednesday 12 August. At Chivenor their Squadron Intelligence Officer James Dingwall, of Newcastle-upon-Tyne and formerly of 19 Group Headquarters, heard no positive news on Triggs nor his crew's whereabouts. Dingwall and Russell caught the last signal transmitted at roughly 03.35 hours, they could not understand however why the Wellington had ditched.

21-year-old WAAF Eira Buckland-Jones was asked by Dingwall to type up an accident report form. 'To my knowledge, everything aboard the aircraft was serviceable before it took off, and the aircraft was completely airworthy,' wrote the Chief Engineering officer. They would have to wait eight and a half hours before the first reports of a dinghy in the water began to emerge. After a careful analysis, a fix was obtained and the search ordered.

Sergeant Jonathan Orr and his crew took off at 11.16 hours in Whitley *H-Harry* except for his co-pilot Leslie Stocks, whose seat was occupied by Wing Commander George 'Hutch' Hutchinson, commanding officer of 235 Squadron. Reaching the co-ordinates Orr methodically commenced a square search, sighting the dinghy at 14.40 hours and sending a signal: 'Am over a dinghy believed to contain five aircrew.'

Beaufighters *E-Edward* and *S-Sugar* stood off whilst Orr instigated a number of passes occasionally waggling his wings as his navigator calculated wind speed and drift in readiness to drop a smoke float, spare dinghy and an emergency Thornaby Bag containing food, cigarettes and drink.

'Whitley circled dinghy, containing aircrew all of which waved frantically and signalled V sign. Spare dinghy not retrievable, Thornaby Bag dropped 100 yards downwind and should be easily reached,' Flying Officer Jack Foss of 235 Squadron later wrote in his weekly diary.

The Wellington crew recovered the supplies, but despite repeated attempts in the choppy sea, the second dinghy blew to far up wind and was not retrievable, although later it was to play a significant role.

Half-an-hour later a second Whitley appeared. Allan Triggs fired the Verey Pistol and within seconds a reply came from the aircraft; 'Sunderland … Coming'

'Chaps, It look's like we may be rescued!' said Triggs.

Everyone broke into broad grins and their elation was heightened in the early evening when they heard the unmistakable throb of Bristol Pegasus engines. Allan Triggs pulled out one of the distress signals from the dry interior of the Thornaby Bag and fired one off at 19.15 hours.

The aircraft they could hear was piloted by thirty-year-old, Wing Commander Neville Halliday, of 461 Squadron, who had taken off on an anti-shipping patrol at 15.40 hours. Halliday and his crew in Short Sunderland *B-Beer* began patrolling a segment of Biscay when a single Focke Wulf 200 dived upon them. There was an exchange of fire before Halliday took whatever evasive action he could. After this obstacle the wireless operator, received new co-ordinates to start searching for a dinghy.

'We begun cutting up this square into smaller squares,' said Flying Officer John Watson, the twenty-six-years-old navigator from Sydney New South Wales had been working for Colonial Sugar Refinery Limited when war was declared.[304]

The flying boat had just turned off the first leg of a square search when tail gunner Sergeant William Ramsey, spoke on the intercom:

'Orange blossom star burst approximately two miles on the starboard side,' Skipper.

'You're sure?'

'Yes.'

'Right let's go and take a look,' replied Halliday.

Halliday turned and found the dinghy containing the men almost enveloped by high waves, also spotting a second empty yellow K-Type dinghy nearby. Before he could consider landing on the water in a 26-knot

175

wind and a heavy swell, Halliday had to jettison his load of depth charges. This was accomplished, all bar one which stubbornly refused to budge. Halliday also dumped 500 gallons of fuel.

A smoke float was then discharged to determine the wind conditions. When he judged his positioning was correct, Halliday said over the intercom, 'stand by, places everyone.'

In the cockpit co-pilot, Flying Officer Roger Barker, transmitted a signal, which reached Chivenor Flying Control at 19.53 hours: 'Sunderland over dinghy and alighting to pick up the crew.'

Halliday reduced the Sunderland's speed to roughly 144 mph and trimmed the flaps to two-thirds out, as John Watson, moved to the vantage point of the astrodome, and looked out: 'I saw waves of ten to twelve feet in height coming up, I instinctively undid two clips out of the four of the astrodome, and we made what appeared a good gliding landing, but we hit the top of the first wave, this impact appeared to break the step, the aircraft then bounced.'

Halliday pushed open the throttles to give the Sunderland flying boat an extra four to five hundred yards distance. The nose and front turret touched the water first at an extreme angle, the forward keel hit heavily, breaking through the step and perched lightly onto the third wave top, just keeping enough momentum not to stall. The airframe creaked and groaned as 58,500 pounds of weight sprung free, in just a matter of seconds a large wave slammed into *B-Beer* carrying the portside float away. The impact slewed the aircraft to starboard, knocking everyone off balance.

Watson was knocked heavily into the portside of the plane on the upper deck. He then made a dash for the astrodome and hurriedly undid the two remaining bolts with the assistance of the two engineers. Warped by the heavy impact, through dogged persistence they managed to release it, and the two engineers clambered out onto the mainplane. Watson turned around to retrieve the dinghy, Verey pistol and cartridges and anything else that he could physically carry. Wadeing through two or three feet of water on the bridge, to exit through the astrodome suddenly the outward pressure of the water slammed it shut on the observer.

From within the confine of their yellow dinghy, buffeted by huge waves, the Wellington crew watched the flying-boat touch down on the first wave and then execute a long bounce over three waves and stalled momentarily into the sea. Becoming waterborne the tip of the starboard wing was ripped off, together with one propeller, by a huge avalanche of water. There was a raging scream as the nine-cylinder air-cooled radial engine, continued to revolve minus its propeller and caught fire. Triggs strained his neck to see the catastrophe unfold as his dinghy itself reached the crest of a wave.

Allan Triggs could not see any survivors.

'Poor Buggers,' Triggs said out loud.

'Rotten luck,' replied Devonshire.

Though unseen by the men in the dingy, Halliday and Barker, managed to climb out of the cockpit onto the still-floating mainplane. As the airframe made creaking and gurgling noises, the Sunderland started to go under. Flight Sergeant Alfred Betts who'd escaped through the astrodome realised Watson wasn't behind him.

'Whereabouts is Watson?' Betts shouted.

Laurenti waded back along the mainplane. Unsure how long the weakened structure would remain intact. Betts, Fletcher, Wright and Laurenti manage to rip the astrodome free.

'I see him,' said Wright, 'he's unconscious.'

Glamorgan-born Ronald Fletcher lay down and gradually lifted the seemingly lifeless Watson out, so that Laurenti could support his body weight. Regaining consciousness Watson's torso was still inside the flying boat but his head was protruding through the escape hatch, clenched between Laurenti's thighs. David Laurenti was sitting in the hatch with his legs and feet hanging down supporting the shivering body. Watson was then lifted out and saw the remainder of the crew on the mainplane preparing a J-Type dinghy, which had been retrieved from aft. Laurenti and Watson made their way to the remaining main float. Neville Halliday and four others had clambered into the dinghy, Halliday waved them over.

The driving torrent of water had toppled some aircrew into the sea and swept them away. Roger Barker was bravely treading water approximately 100 yards south of the flying boat with his Mae West on fully inflated and swimming east from there. William Ramsey and Thomas Betts were approximately sixty yards away due west of the wreck and treading water, their yellow Mae Wests bobbed up and down, amongst the twelve-foot waves.

John Watson clambered into the dinghy and sat down, but he passed out again. When the flying Officer recovered from his ordeal he asked, 'Anybody hurt?'

'Not that I know of,' replied Halliday.

Watson surveyed the tight cluster of men in the dinghy: Halliday, Wright, and Turner both of whom had scratched faces, Sergeant Charles Bentley of Hoddle Street, Richmond, Victoria, was keeping every one's spirits up by cracking jokes which put a smile their faces. Watson and Laurenti had their right hands clutching the leading edge of the wing and the left on the dinghy. Ronald Fletcher and Charles Unsworth were hanging onto the dinghy rope and riding the waves using the buoyancy of their Mae Wests and dinghy.

Within five minutes of the dinghy being launched, a bulging blister appeared that continued to expand, and grew on the nose of the J-Type dinghy to a foot square and then burst. Startled, everyone grabbed the single rope that skirted the perimeter edge of the dinghy; it still floated so they hung on.

'Chaps, I'm awfully sorry about this,' said Halliday, 'our only hope is for someone to go for the empty dinghy, can anybody swim for it?'

No body answered for a few minutes or deep in their own thoughts, and then a voice broke the silence.

'I can swim alright,' replied Watson.[305]

Getting up, he tried to steady himself against the buffeting waves hitting the fragile dinghy, when a hand clasped his right hand, the grip tightened. Watson looked down to see whom it belonged to; the beaming face of Bentley stared back.

'Wait a minute more until you're over the concussion a bit.'

But, time was of the essence, so Halliday crawled to the nose of the dinghy and gave Watson a pat of reassurance on his left leg.

'Hang onto the side to get your breath and then paddle towards the dinghy which is downwind from us.'

'Okay, let's do this!' said Watson.

With a firm handshake from Halliday, he placed a leg precariously over the side. The force of the water nearly toppled him backwards, but, steadying himself, Watson plunged over the side, momentarily disappearing beneath the black water, only to surface seconds later through the buoyancy of his Mae West.

With muted shouts of encouragement, Watson gulped air into his lungs, wiped the saltwater out of his eyes and kicked out, using the front crawl before changing two thirds of the way to swim sidestroke. After three-quarters-of-an-hour Watson reach the J-Type dinghy. Physically exhausted and weak having swallowed quantities of seawater, he was repeatedly sick, he clung onto the dingy, hoping to act as an anchor and keep the dinghy from getting further away before his colleagues arrived. His hands began to go numb and his grip on the ladder loosened, so Watson decided to clamber into the dinghy. He flopped into the dingy, exhausted: 'My lungs ached with every breath, it was as if my chest was on fire,' wrote former beach lifeguard Watson.

He then crawled around the dinghy wall searching for the wooden paddle but could not find one. Watson stood up and caught sight of the full Wellington dinghy, but there was no sign of the flying boat's remaining float, Halliday or the others.

Approximately 400 miles away at Plymouth coordinated searches had got underway. Squadron Leader Paul Fairbairn of 19 Group had received a 'reported overdue' from Mount Batton of *B-Beer*, one of fifty-five in Coastal Command that day. 'Effective and prompt action to locate this genuinely overdue aircraft started,' wrote Fairbairn. Several hours' searching yielded no sign of the missing men in the Bay of Biscay, until forty-five minutes after midnight.

Watson woke, to hear the unmistakable drone of Rolls Royce Merlins throbbing away in the darkness.

'Engines!' Said Watson, Engines!' The delay until the pitched roar reached him was agony.

Roaring over the water, Sergeant Charles Newham made sure he flew low and straight at an altitude of 1,000 feet. But as he sped over the water, two orange pyrotechnics illuminated the darkness roughly eight miles west of his track. This came as some relief after eight hours of searching, for all aboard Whitley *E-Egg*.

'Stand-by we're going to take a look,' said Newman. It was then 21.55 hours. Co-pilot Bruce Threfall got a better view at 200 feet. Large dark patches of oil were seen on the surface and Pilot Officer Daniel Wilson tried to get a fix. Stuck in the tail turret Flight Sergeant Reginald Smith voice broke the silence 'There is a large dark object down there, which may be a dinghy.'

'48N07W,' Wilson noted the position.

'We're going around again. Here we go,' said Newman.

But as they manoeuvred round they lost sight of the object 'owing to our fuel state I'm returning to base', Newman said on the intercom. They reached Chivenor shortly before 23.10 hours, with the airfield in complete darkness. Charles Newman and his crew safely landed four minutes later. After a largely uneventful night, Derbyshire born Sergeant George Goodwin, piloting Whitley *D-Dog*, was still in the debriefing room being grilled by Wing Commander John Embling for 'accidently releasing his six depth charges and four 250lb. bombs,' when Newman, Threfall, Wilson, Albert and Ralph Smith arrived.

For John Watson, with just stars for company, he took stock of the provisions aboard the dinghy and found a sea anchor, a valise container, and some tinned water. The floor of the dinghy was still full of discoloured water, and Watson was still too weak to bale the water out and tried to settle down for the remainder of the night to get some sleep. In the cold he suffered from cramps, shivers and sickness. Fear that the dinghy might topple over because of the height of the waves, prevented him from sleeping fully just for short periods, but even three hours sleep was immensely refreshing.

Finally, dawn arrived on Thursday 13 August. The wind dropped to twelve or fifteen knots, but the water was still rough, and the dinghy moved precariously around on the whim of the seas. Watson restarted his search for emergency aids within the dinghy, finding a graduated mica beaker with which he began bailing. Next, he untangled the mast and erected and rigged the small red sail. As the light improved, at approximately 08.00 hours, Watson sighted the Wellington dinghy roughly six miles to the northwest. Getting to his feet, Watson waved, but did not get any reply.

The situation aboard Allan Triggs dinghy was precarious, with two of his crew repeatedly vomiting and the third's ankles suffering from salt-water sores, having used his shoes for baling out on their first day at sea. Throughout the day various aircraft skirted around their dinghy, but none spotted the bright yellow dinghy.

It was on the ninth rescue mission that afternoon, at 16.05 hours, when Lieutenant René Casparius, piloting Beaufighter N-Nut, sighted two bobbing objects. Reducing height, the Frenchman could see that the first contained one man who waved profusely, and that the other, roughly half-a-mile downwind, held seven or eight men, four of whom waved in recognition.

'Send a cyphered message telling them we've found them,' Casparius said to his navigator.

'Right,' replied Sergeant Alfred Davis, 'better give them our position.'

Davis transmitted on the frequency 6666, and then wound out the trailing aerial so as to repeat it on the long-wave frequency. Unfortunately, both systems malfunctioned, and messages could not be sent back to Chivenor because of static interference.

Watson was baling out water that slopped in and doing exercises despite the conditions to maintain some warmth and circulation. 'A sleek twin-engine Beaufighter appeared on the scene flying extremely low. It was early or late afternoon and it couldn't have been more than two hundred and fifty feet,' Watson later wrote. 'I reckon it was searching for both plane and crew. They've seen me! It then continually circled my position, the small RAF roundels showed up clearly on the underside of the wings.'

Casparius completed his final 360 degrees and moved off. Triggs impatiently fired the Verey pistol as N-Nut flew over the second dinghy and took another long orbit to fly over the men, then set course for base. Casparius touched N-Nut back down again at Chivenor.

There had been heavy rain showers over both dinghies, and had it not been for René Casparius seeing Triggs and Watson straight away, the search would have almost certainly have been a failure. His navigator had got fixes on both positions and his message had got through despite difficult atmospheric conditions.

At around 15.30 hours, thirty-five minutes earlier than Casparius' sighting, the first of two Whitleys took off, after Joubert had issued his search order. Station commander, Group Captain Peter Cracroft AFC, had issued his own to 77 Squadron on the base. Flight Lieutenant Ian Ralston of Wirral Cheshire, in aircraft *V-Victor*, leading a second Whitley, descended one mile off the Isles of Scilly to 150 feet. Ralston's co-pilot, the twenty-three-year-old, Sergeant Charles Smith changed course southwards, with James Hawkes' navigation bringing the planes to roughly eighty miles off the Spanish coast with Sergeant Freddie Boyd astern in the second aircraft. Boyd and his crew were among those drawn-in to take part in Coastal Command missions from 10 OTU at Abingdon, detached to St Eval. Crews at OTU were not yet with operational squadrons, as they had not finished their training, but by using them Joubert had given his Command a tremendous boost but had done little to convince Naval and Air Ministry sceptics that Coastal Command could pose a serious threat to Germany's U-Boats and shipping.

However, Boyd and his crew were proving their worth. Having successfully reached the position, Boyd started the first loop over Triggs' dinghy, and Ralston orbited Watson. After five minutes Boyd made his last wide circuit before altering direction for a straight slow approach just above stalling speed to release a bag of supplies. But the bag disintegrated upon impact with the sea and its whole contents became completely saturated.

Sergeant William Wishart the co-pilot's, voice broke into Boyd's headphones from beside him. 'Oil pressure on port engine has risen slightly, Skipper. Do you think it's alright?'

Boyd tapped the oil pressure gauge on the instrument panel with his right hand. It remained constant for a moment, and then watched with alarm as it spiralled down. He began to close the throttle a fraction, correcting with the rudder.

He called Parker his navigator. 'Give me the quickest route to base, urgently.'

The engine sounded rough and was labouring when it shuddered and completely seized the propeller rotated to a halt and hung like a piece of sculpture. Boyd quickly cut the fuel supply to the dead motor to lessen the risk of fire, and increased the revolutions on the remaining engine.

'Send an S.O.S, William, tell them we're on one fan.'

'O.K. Skipper.'

'Parker, give William our D/R position.'

'Right away.'

William transmitted the S.O.S on the controlled frequency and repeated it on the long-wave distress frequency using the trailing aerial. There was sudden drop in height, as Wishart repeated his S.O.S message on the control frequency and then automatically changed to the distress frequency and waited for a reply. Boyd watched the starboard engine temperature rising, its only complaint under the increased strain at 2450 revs per minute. In spite of the increase in power, the remaining engine was unable to maintain sufficient height, and straight and level flight could not be obtained.

'Ditch everything you can,' he said into the intercom, 'Quick as you can we've not much time,' was his last line. As he spoke he pressed the depth charge red-tipped bakerlite jettison button. Boyd eyed the altitude needle still moving slowly anticlockwise, whilst the starboard engine temperature needle now resided in the red. William sent out a final desperate S.O.S on the controlled frequency at 16.08 hours.

'Prepare for ditching, everyone. What's the wind direction?'

'Two hundred and seventy-nine degrees true,' said Parker.

'Strength about twenty-five miles an hour, rough calculation waves are about nine to ten feet high.'

'Great, Parker well done.'

Boyd kept the aircraft heading for base and tried to work out his ditching problems. Unfortunately, the remaining engine hadn't read the script and suddenly the skipper called into the intercom: 'Sorry, having to ditch now chaps, can't stay airborne.'

'Height less than thirty-five feet, speed seventy-one knots. Turning into wind now.'

Boyd judged he was about thirty degrees across the swell. He closed the starboard throttle fully and put the propeller into coarse pitch and turned off the petrol.

'Hold tight, brace yourselves, we're going in!'

The aircraft hit the water at 16.16 hours. Boyd, Wishart, Parker, Raymond Crouch, and Alfred Hendry survived the ditching and managed to get out of the plane before it sank in two minutes. Despite the shortage in dinghy training Crouch and Hendry paddled away from the scene but wind and currents soon swept them away. Boyd and his crew were forced to bob about in their dinghy in the Atlantic swell for roughly seventy hours before finally being picked up by a British destroyer. They arrived in Falmouth badly shaken. 'The trip took us rather longer than it should have,' noted William Wishart. 'The captain called us up on a megaphone and said that he would take us on board.' A short while later Freddie Boyd discovered their Whitley was the first to be lost whilst on detachment at St Eval when the base commander Group Captain Walter Dawson said, 'See to it that you don't loose an aircraft again.' It was hardly a major reprimand, but the tone had been sufficient to ensure Boyd and his crew returned after each sortie.

German radar had, however, picked up the RAF search missions and three Arado 196 floatplanes of 5./BFGr.196, took off to intercept the Whitleys.

Five minutes after Boyd's aircraft had left the scene, Ian Ralston widened the circumference of his circle to do a lengthy slow approach to drop a bag of supplies.

'The White Whitley went into a wide circuit southeast of my position,' recalled Watson. 'He was just turning in for the approach when three single-engine floatplanes appeared from the north diving out of the cloud about one miles away and gaining level flight at approximately 150 to 200 feet. The Whitley crew apparently must have sighted them as its pilot hauled the aircraft's nose up and at the same time turned away to the east.'[306]

The Whitley was at roughly 4,000 feet and one mile from nearest cloud layer with the Arado's in steep pursuit in a high-speed climb, momentarily catching the bomber. 'Three Arados are almost upon us, one astern, one slightly to port, third has gone underneath us, watch out,' said the Tooting-born Sergeant Sydney 'Uncle' White in the rear. Depressing the four machine-guns, he tracked the one coming astern, holding off the temptation to open fire early. Bright flashes erupted from the Arado's nose and wings; White braced himself as rounds burst around the tail. It was a game of patience, when the floatplane closed to within 400 yards he opened fire and made every shot count.

Instinctively Ralston turned *V-Victor* to port then starboard, swerving to get out of the enemy pilot's line of sight. Behind him, Flight Sergeant Raymond 'Ray' Martin sent the following message at 16.10 hours: 'Am being attacked by enemy aircraft'. Two minutes later a second signal was sent and received: 'Enemy aircraft – 3 Arado 196 floatplanes.'

Ralston and Smith were still desperately trying to fly. John Watson watched the battle unfold: 'I heard a lot of gunfire erupt, and almost immediately the Arado attacking from the rear did a steep turn and was in a vertical dive towards the water. Visually, I lost him over the horizon and the floatplane did not reappear and I believe he had been shot down. By this time the Whitley had made cloud cover which apparently was fairly thin. Gunfire continued and seemed to increase. Then there was complete silence and I heard a large explosion and saw a column of smoke about 500 feet high-rise from the water. I concluded that the Whitley had been shot down, they hadn't had an earthly chance.'

The Australian returned to his exercise whilst being buffeted by choppy waters. Gradually, however, the weather improved, and his clothing became almost dry. Much later, in the falling light, he sighted a small fishing boat coming towards him and for a split second he thought it might possibly be a rescue boat, only to be disappointed once again.

The weather deteriorated, and the wind blew hard from the south. In this boisterous sea the hours passed interminably, whilst Watson dozed. Waking next morning he was surrounded by low dense fog, 'it was practically on the deck,' the wind was blowing from the south-west and with visibility almost at zero he lost sight of the other dinghy. 'The condition for any sort of rescue today was zero,' Watson later wrote.

For two consecutive days, on 14 and 15 August, searches were curtailed from airfields in southern England. Out at sea, Watson sighted a gunmetal grey Junkers 88, flying at 1,500 feet travelling north-west. Nothing else was noticed except a fin in the water. Watson recognized the fin quickly enough. It was a basking shark. He had nothing to scare it off with, but the shark disappeared.

The basking shark reappeared near the Wellington crew's dinghy. McLean, who was keeping a lookout for the other dinghy, saw something sticking out of the water. Alerting Triggs, the Australian loaded the Verey pistol and held it at arms-length tracking the shark's movements. 'If the fin or tail rubbed against the thin rubber material it would have sliced through it,' wrote Triggs. After cruising around the dinghy for two minutes the shark made off.

The six aircrew were becoming increasingly despondent and ill-tempered, with the realisation that their chances of being located were dwindling. The sole survivor from the Sunderland was faring better by following an established routine and keeping active and attentive. Sighting a cluster of a dozen French fishing boats on the horizon, Watson quickly took down the windsock and sat tight. If they saw him it would mean being captured. Nothing else was seen except an occasional shark and Watson continued to do moderate exercise between bailing water out of the dinghy. As dusk began to settle in, he drank another half tin of water to keep in good working order and made himself comfortable and went to sleep.

'Next morning the weather was worse still. I had to continually move around the dinghy walls to protect myself from the wind. At some point

I rigged up the valise on the mast to increase my speed northwards towards the Scilly Isles, and put out the sea anchor which helped to stop the dinghy from slewing round,' wrote Watson.

On this day, too, the second dinghy tried to make some slight progress towards home, with an improvised sail, made by breaking the telescopic mast into two and taking the odd corners of their sail, tying them to the two pieces of mast with fishing wire. Cartwright then secured the new mast onto the external rings, thus creating a weather apron.

'This worked a treat,' said Triggs

'How much faster do you think we're going Col?'

'I'll work it out for you.'

Still a Coastal Command navigator to his fingertips, despite the stubble, sore lips and discomfort, Badham calculated it had increased their speed by a half to three-quarters of a knot.

Watson was skimming along too. But, his thoughts were of food; he'd eaten nothing for four days. A small fish came up from underneath the dinghy and plopped out of the water, he tried to catch it between his hands but could not. 'Started doing my routine to take my mind of my hunger until Sunday night, when I drank some more water and chewed my leather wrist watch strap,' recalled the Australian observer.

Just after midnight torrential rain drenched and revived him, but the rain persisted until daybreak. The empty water tin had preserved some rainwater so at least he had some fresh drinking water.

Next morning it was clear; the whole of the western sky was blue. Watson took advantage of the sun's heat and undressed. Battle dress, jacket, trousers, then shirt, socks, vest and pants dried on the mast in the wind which was now blowing directly from the north. Using a small amount of rainwater, he cleared his eyes, ears and mouth of salt.

The Met Officer had scuppered any planned rescue missions Hutchinson, Cracroft, and Russell could not convince the decision makers at Northwood to put anything into action from Chivenor either. 'Our weather is occasional rain clouds, visibility 10 miles. Air Sea Rescue still the prominent feature of squadron ops as we endeavour to bring in ditched aircrews as their situation is becoming desperate,' noted George Hutchinson in an unofficial diary. The major concern was time.

A chance of rescuing the aircrew came four days after the first ditching. At midday Sergeant's 'Steady' Smith and Duncan Marrow located two dinghies. 'One large yellow dinghy containing about 4 to 6 men the other with mast and triangular flag containing one man,' jotted down Marrow onto his small pad. A message was sent back to base giving position and visual state of airmen.

'It was the first aircraft seen for two and a half days,' noted Devonshire, 'the aircraft then moved off towards the second dinghy.'

Engines! A grey-green Beaufighter appeared and circled above. The warmth from doing the exercises increased as he vigorously signalled 'FOOD' with his handkerchief tide to a stick. A beaming face signalled back from the observation blister 'S5' which Watson couldn't understand. Marrow had tried to signal 'SS' meaning 'Sending Supplies.' Within minutes a second Beaufighter arrived. One flew straight overhead and disappeared, however Verey lights lit up the skyline and I saw the Beaufighter doing circuits. Squadron Leader Anthony Binks of Shepperton saw a man on his own laying down spread-eagled in the dinghy looking malnourished.

'Wallis, prepare to drop supplies,'

'Thornaby Bag ready,' replied Sergeant Wallis Walters. Binks began the count down, '500, 400, 300, 200, 100, 50 yards Go drop bag!'

'Bag gone,' announced Walters.

It tumbled 300 yards away from Watson and sank immediately in the swell. Binks prepare to run in again. Throttling back just short of stalling speed, in the rear Walters released the second Thornaby Bag, falling 100 yards away upwind of the dinghy together with a pair of fluorescent smoke floats. The bag burst and remained afloat around one of the red smoke floats, but without a paddle it was impossible to reach. 'I dare not try and swim for the bag, for fear of losing my dinghy,' recalled Watson.

Marrow had begun signalling to the Wellington crew, 'contact other dinghy'. Below Triggs repeated 'contact other crew,' he said it as though they'd been asked to row the whole length of the famous Henley Royal Regatta Course. Badham replied using a piece of reflective material indicating, 'Beyond us.'

Smith completed its last 360 degree circuit and climbed to 1,000 feet and, being low on fuel, set course for home. Binks opened the throttles, and made for the second dinghy, and circled whilst Walter's signalled: 'contact other dinghy – injured man aboard.'

'Devonshire, haul in the sea anchor,' said Triggs.

'I'll navigate,' replied Badham.

'Do we need a cox?' Walker laughed at Cartwright's suggestion. They began to paddle, Triggs dividing the crew into three shifts of two. The physical exhaustion was thirsty work, the small tins of water diminished during their row, whilst above Binks darted back and forth between the two dinghies, guiding the men paddling hard forward. The true course was kept, but it took five hours to cover 1,000 yards separating them from Watson.

Binks was relieved to see the arrival of two Lockheed Hudsons of 279 Squadron and a pair of Beaufighters before departing and putting down at Land's End airfield with roughly fifteen gallons left in the fuel tanks. 'A good trip and largely successful,' Binks jotted down in his diary after a six hours and ten minutes long search with Wallis Walter.

The air around the dinghies erupted with the roar of radial engines, as they begun thundering overhead. 'There was suddenly a lot of activity. Two Hudsons appeared with a Beaufighter escort. One Hudson came over me and released a smoke float, then did a wide orbit, and then came directly towards me, the bomb doors juddered open and dropped some packages downwind which unfurled tired together. These splashed into the water 100 yards away, and I did not get to these as I lost sight of them amongst the waves. The Hudson circled again then reduced height and flashed, 'Have dropped food' they flew around me once and made off. In the meantime the second Hudson had been doing circuits over the Wellington crew and joined up with the other and left!' stated Watson.

'Unfortunately, Hudsons of 279 Squadron did not remain with the dinghies as requested, but scurried home after one dropped Lindholme gear,' Flight Sergeant George Woodcock noted. The Canadian Devonshire was open-mouthed as he watched John Faux in *Y-Yorker* make a slow approach and release a large object, which fell within 100 yards of their dinghy. All six clasped their hands on top of their heads and waited anxiously for an eruption. But when the water subsided they saw what appeared to be an up-turned hull. They changed direction to paddled, reaching it within a few minutes. One by one they removed their garments to take turns to right the upside-down object, and after a tremendous struggle they succeeded with words of encouragement from the three recovering aboard the dinghy. In relays they emptied all the contents into their own dinghy, and then continued to paddle towards the former Whitley dinghy. Shortly afterwards the pair of Beaufighters dipped their wings in salute. In the rear twenty-seven-year-old navigator, Flight Sergeant William Ginger from Northampton, flashed with the Aldis lamp: 'Won't be long now' as they travelled northwards. On the return track the pair sighted two High Speed Launches from Falmouth with Beaufighter escort heading towards the two ditched crews.

Watson was in urgent needed something to eat: 'I began to search for the dropped packs of food and caught sight of the other dinghy about a mile away and so I rigged up the small sail again and made towards them. After half an hour I'd only made slight progress, so I removed a section of the mast, took an empty water tin, put holes in it with my pen knife, and pushed it onto this section of the mast, then squeezed it flat to make a paddle. This helped the steering considerably.'

After two more hours of paddling hard Watson was near enough to the other dinghy for them to see him and wave. 'I could see that they wore RAF blue battledresses,' and between 17.00 hours, and 18.00 hours, he hailed them:

'I am all for the open life, how about you?"

'You wouldn't be Australian, would you?' they replied.

'Yes, of the Sunderland flying boat, did you see any of the others?'

'No - Being on your own we thought you were a German,' an airman with a Canadian accent said. Though deep-down they suspected that the rest of the Sunderland crew had perished, no one dare ask this Australian how many the crew of a Sunderland might be.

While Cartwright and McLean steadied the two dinghies, Triggs and Badham took hold of Watson and hauled the lone Sunderland survivor aboard.

He joined them in the large dinghy which was dry, they undressed him and gave him a thorough rub down to stimulate the circulation with the sleeping suit packing material, painted his cuts and abrasions with antiseptic, then encased him inside the one-piece waterproof sleeping suit from the kit salvaged from the Lindholme. He gave him a meal consisting of a Horlicks malted milk tablet, two biscuits, some sweet dark chocolate and half a tin of tomato juice. After exchanging experiences of life on the open sea, for half an hour, the remaining minutes before another hour had ticked by was spent sucking a second malted milk tablet, eating a biscuit, two squares of chocolate and, to finish of this gourmet meal, a cigarette. Watson held the cigarette between his chaffed lips; Triggs shielded it with both of his hands from the wind and spray whilst Badham lit the tip, and Watson inhaled then exhaled. Then took a deep breath and composed himself. He took one final draw on his cigarette and flicked it into a nearby empty tomato tin. He then got some rest but awoke a quarter of an hour later to the sound of radial engines! 'Fw190s' Cartwright yelled, whilst continuing to scan the sky. 'Four'. Approaching low and fast, the German aircraft completed a circuit above the stranded airmen in their finger of four formation before peeling off. The methodical growl was deafening as one by one they flew over the dinghy at thirty feet and waggled their wings. They did another circuit during which one pilot 'waved' and all departed due east.

Fifteen to twenty minutes later a Beaufighter approached from the north-west flying at low level and turned north-east, apparently searching for the dinghy. In view of the proximity of the enemy fighters they decided not to fire the Verey pistol in case it should attract their attention. Then as the Beaufighter became a speck to the naked eye two more Fw190s came out of the clouds with their throttles fully open. They did not appear to see the yellow dinghy being buffeted by the sea and went in the direction of the previous four due east. As the light diminished a Short Sunderland from 461 Squadron appeared.

'Sunderland' shouted Watson.

The word threw a heavy silence across the drifting dinghy, as everyone drew a short breath as the flying boat flew directly overhead from the northwest at 800 to 1,000 feet, seemingly unhurried, carrying out a methodical search, but again they decided not to signal it.

'He was looking much better after his second meal, there was more colour in his cheeks, stopped shivering and his teeth chattering,' Triggs noted of John Watson, 'with all the events that had happened throughout the day it certainly convinced us that with God's good will this would be our last night adrift off Brest.' The sea was moderately calm, and for the first time since their ditching, everyone had a good night's sleep with their bodies huddled together against the walls of the dinghy in their waterproof sleeping suites.

Shortly after daybreak on 17 August, a pair of Fw190s went streaking across the dinghy before disappearing into the clouds at 3,000 feet above. Twenty minutes afterwards two Beaufighters escorting two Hudson's appeared. Triggs and Watson removed the upper part of their individual sleeping suite and retrieved the underwater torch from the Lindholme survival aids. They leaned over the side of the dinghy and whilst Triggs held the torch Watson signalled them 'To go away as there were Focke Wulf's about' he repeated the message once more. However, the Hudson crews did not take any notice or even acknowledge the signal. A third Hudson arrived, and both Australians repeated the signal but to no avail.

'Do they want to get shot down?'

'Stupid,'

'Serve them right if they do, we've told them to bugger off.'

'We're so close to being rescued and these chaps may scupper it, replied Watson, 'Keep your fingers crossed they don't' interjected Devonshire. A message was flashed to them 'It won't be long now,' the jubilant airmen chanted it together in unison 'It won't be long now!'

As if to remind them that their elation may be somewhat premature, three Arado floatplanes circled some distance off. After five minutes the trio of Hudson's departed north at 500 feet only to begin circling an object after approximately five minutes, because of the moderate sea conditions the airmen could see a grey object approaching.

'Destroyer'

All eyes turned and followed Allan Triggs' pointing finger.

The dinghy rocked in motion widely as they strained their necks to see.

'Bloody Hell mate, you're a bit out on your ship recognition,' drawled Badham, 'but it's a British boat all right. A small motor launch, I reckon.'

'Looks like they've sent a whole flotilla,' shouted Watson.

During this prelude everyone made preparations to be taken off the dinghy. Shortly afterwards, H.M. Launch Q180, commanded by Lieutenant Kenneth Gennell, throttled back their speed to reduce the wash. As the distance decreased, Triggs stood up whilst Badham and McLean steadied the rubber dinghy so that he could shout to the captain. Cupping his hands to his mouth he bellowed, 'Can you signal our chaps that there are enemy fighters about?'

'Certainly.'

John Newman flashed the signal in the direction of the RAF aircraft, but the two Beaufighters from 235 Squadron stayed. Sergeant John Warburton in Beaufighter A-Apple sighted a fourth vessel and went to investigate and found a German launch with the three Arados as escort. Suddenly heavy flak burst around the Beaufighter. Sergeant Edwin Sillitoe then observed the Arados manoeuvering to form a wedge between the Beaufighter's and Q180.

'Look Arado's coming in low and fast!'

Suddenly, Triggs Watson, Badham, McLean, Devonshire, Walker and Cartwright realised that the Germans were actually after them – the ditched airmen!

Warburton turned 180 degrees and, in the process, gained height, tracking the floatplanes. He then put the nose down: 'Hang on Ed were going fishing.' The Arados responded by breaking formation, as the Beaufighter dived towards its pray with Warburton levelling off at fifty feet.

'Focke Wulfs' shouted a Naval Rating.

'The last thing any of us want was to end up back in the drink,' recalled Badham.

German fighters made two attempts to attack the vessel, they dived in turn only to be pursued by Beaufighters as the waters and sky exploded in an angry flame of smoke and cannon shells. Both sides left the fray roughly ten miles from Scilly Isles.

'They all slept until they berthed alongside the other motor launches at Newlyn,' wrote Air Vice Marshal Peter Cracroft in his debriefing report.[307] 'Crew eventually rescued having been at sea 124 hours.' All were ferried to West Penzance Hospital five minutes away. 'They looked completely done in.' said Nurse Bolter. She and nurse Allen were charged with looking after Arthur Cartwright.[308]

'Cartwright's teeth were chattering, he stumbled when walking, and was mildly confused. Physically his hands were puffy whilst ankles, and soles of his feet were in bad shape. Fortunately, none of his toes had stuck together during the lad's exposure after his shoes were used for bailing out the dinghy during the first hours.'

Someone took his sodden clothing, wrapped in the naval blanket, away to be cleaned or incinerated, as his rehabilitation got underway. Wrapped in fresh blankets Cartwright sipped a mug of sweet tea and was then taken to have a warm blanket bath. Bolter assisted by Allen helped the twenty-on-year-old into a pair of clean pyjamas, and his ankles and soles were completely covered with antiseptic and wrapped in light bandages.

Despite Watson's ordeal he 'suffered only mild hypothermia,' and 'the hours spent inside the sleeping suit, helped him considerably.' Going onto the Ward all were given a sedative to make them sleep for at least twenty-four hours. A telegram was hastily dispatched to Chivenor and Mount Batten and Cracroft and Henderson from Chivenor left for Cornwall immediately in his staff car. His WAAF chauffeur routed through Launceston and small hamlets, to West Penzance Hospital about 121 miles away, so that at 18.00 hours, both officers arrived to get statements and bring the Wellington crew back.[309]

At Mount Batten, the reaction was mooted. 'Colin' Lovelock who had taken charge after Neville Halliday had been posted missing was making preparations for a move to Hamworthy. Lovelock wrote, 'Flying Officer John Watson rescued by motor launch, now at Penzance,' then on Tuesday 18 August he added, 'Watson arrived back at unit after being rescued.'[310] John Watson had been discharged from hospital and caught buses back to his base where he would recount his experiences to the unit's intelligence and air sea rescue officers. After two weeks of survivor's leave John Watson was promoted to flight lieutenant and became 461's Navigation Officer. For some inexplicable reason Watson was not put forward for a decoration. Allan Triggs and his crew amazingly went straight back on missions again after a couple of days leave..

For the families of the RAAF and RAF men lost there was some confusion. They were notified on the 25 August and again on 12 September 'that everyone was safe' only to be told thirteen day afterwards that it was now confirmed that Halliday, Barker, Bentley, Laurenti, Unsworth, Betts, Fletcher, Turner, and Wright had perished between the 12 and 17 August. From John Watson's debriefing statement came positive confirmation that Ian Ralston and his crew were shot down and the families were duly notified in early September. Allan Triggs' courage and leadership during this ordeal led to the award of the MBE, and months later, after a propeller and reduction gear came a drift causing an engine to fall from his aircraft into the sea, he and his navigator, Colin Badham, received the DFC for bringing back the aircraft and touching down safely.

Afterwards their lives took a different course. Triggs posed for Barbara Tribe, an Australian aged twenty-two had sailed to England to pursue her career as a sculptor, having won a three-year scholarship at Royal Academy School, she also began studying at the City & Guilds School of Art in Kennington under Edgar Frith, then at the Regent Street Polytechnic School of Art with Harold Brownsword. Her command of the human form as expressed in a pair of bronzes, 'Lovers I' and 'Lovers II', brought admiration from the Bloomsbury painter, teacher and RAF officer, Flight Lieutenant Duncan 'Bunny' Grant.

Barbara spent most of the war years in Kensington, at her Stratford Studio and supplemented her income working in a clerical job at the Ministry of Supply, then the Office of Works employed in the Inspectorate of Ancient Monuments.[311] In 1943 her team was tasked with recording the interiors of 10 Downing Street in case of further damage or destruction. When cataloguing in the Prime Minister's office, Winston Churchill returned unexpectedly, and furious at their presence, 'rudely ejected' the inspection team.[312] During this period High Commissioner Stanley Bruce at Australia House requested the Rayner Hoff student to be commissioned to sculpt portrait busts of Australian servicemen. Allan Trigg was one of seven airmen whose busts were created under difficult conditions and the sculpting had to be squeezed into the evening hours, with the assistance of Air Vice Marshal Henry Wrigley, who arranged for the Australian airmen to sit for her.

The portrait busts were executed over half a dozen two-hour sittings and reveal the lively individualism of the sitters. 'It was certainly different working with Barbara,' say's Triggs who, after completing thirty missions, returned to Australia where he flew Liberators with 23 Squadron RAAF in the Pacific War.

Colin Badham of 172 Squadron joined Triggs. Wednesday 6 June 1945, saw the pair move to Darwin with 'Judy the Crash Crew's dog and family of 6 pups,'[313] from there for the next few months the Liberators attacked targets in Northern Borneo and other Pacific islands. 'Beer bottles full of urine and sundry bombs hurled at Limboeing and Boeloedowang airfield, on Celebe Island,' remembered Triggs, with obligatory propaganda leaflets distributed down the flare chute.

Fifteen days later, led by Wing Commander Richard 'Arch' Dunne, Flight Lieutenant Reginald 'Reg' Hocking and Triggs whose, call sign was 'Duty Three', set off with the aim of 'neutralising Limboeing as a Japanese's flying base,' wrote Dunne. The Liberators kept low over the jungle canopy and stuck religiously to the planned route. Fortunately, they experienced no small arms fire on their route in. Reaching the target area, Dunne 'Duty One,' and Hocking 'Duty Two,' made a turn to port for their first target, 'Strip Duty 2.'

With a vibrating whirr, the bomb bay doors opened, and in unison they confirmed 'Bombs gone!' over the R/T. Then Triggs announced the sighting of target number two: 'Strip Duty 1'. Guided by their bomb aimer, they headed towards a clearing beneath the forested hills. 'Steady' the bomb aimer told his pilot, then said, 'Bombs away!' The Liberator shot upwards like an elevator as the bomb load left its bay, suddenly the rear gunner 'Click' Staples saw a single-engine fighter.

'Oskar!' he yelled over the R/T. 'At Five o'clock high!'

Within seconds the Japanese Nakajima Ki-43 Hayabusa fighter, known to the Allies as 'Oskar' was bearing down on Triggs' plane. 'Honorable Japanese pilot endeavoured to singe moustache of 'Trigger' Triggs,' said Dunne.[314] The Oskar made two passes, then a further two as Triggs re-joined Dunne and Hocking, all the while Norman 'Norm' Williams, their mid-upper air gunner from New South Wales, was on the intercom 'let's see what you've got,' and 'come on then,' Williams was licking his lips. He had flown with RAF Bomber Command over Europe, earning the Conspicuous Gallantry Medal and a DFM & Bar and credited with shooting down eight German fighters and damaging another dozen, making him the RAAF's only 'ace' who was not a fighter pilot.

Out on a sortie in August with Squadron Leader John Finlayson's plane, Triggs' crewman Beckmann sighted a large barge. This was robustly fired upon, caught fire, and when engulfed in flames keeled over and settle upside down in shallow water. The aircraft then dropped leaflets over Flores Island.

Flight Lieutenant Allan Triggs Air Force career had virtually come full circle. Time was called on his operational career on Wednesday 16 January 1946. Then, like countless other servicemen Triggs and John Watson resumed their pre-war occupations and went into obscurity, survivors of a remarkable encounter.[315]

Chapter 9

Flight Lieutenant 'Ken' Gatward DSO, DFC* and Sergeant Gilbert 'George' Fern

The tall and unassuming 'Ken' Gatward walked into the gallery and took off his cap, sat down, and took out his notebook and pencils, then lit another of his cigarettes. Next to him sat the pot-marked face with a wisp of a moustache of Neville Smith, reporter for *The Essex Chronicle*, as well as another from the *Chelmsford Gazette*. Seated nearby were Alexander 'Sachie' McCorquodale and his wife, better known as novelist Barbara Cartland.

'Whose up next?' Gatward asked.

'Bradley,' replied Smith, 'Justice Alexander Roche chairing this case.'

Ongar Magistrates Court consisted of two upper rooms in the Town Hall with Edwardian charm and considerable functionality, which was approached by separate staircases. Stepping out, Roche passed the stairs for 'No.1' labelled in gold leaf and went straight to 'No.2'. Waiting for him was his personal assistant who looked as formidable as her boss. Handed a folder with a collection of tabs protruding, he continued towards the bench.

'All rise,' came a voice obscured from view by bewigged men in black. There was a pronounced hush as he entered the room for these afternoon hearings of the Essex Summer Assize on Wednesday 15 June 1932. A central chair and three trestles tables had been placed in the room, around which stood the Judge's Advocate, High Sheriff of Essex Harold McCorquodale, the Sheriff's Chaplin The Reverent George Nesbitt rector of High Ongar, Henry Gepp the Deputy Sheriff, and Frederick Smith, 2nd Earl of Birkenhead.

The Grand Jury was sworn in, which included two captains, three majors and four lieutenant colonels. Roche studied the list of all twenty-one names, then, after conferring, with the Earl of Birkenhead, he announced to Edward Robey – who was appearing for the Director of Public Prosecutions – that he was ready. Cecil Bradley ruddy-faced and broad shouldered, stood before the judge. 'Roche gave the twenty-one-year-old a stony glare, enough to show his displeasure,' Gatward noted down. 'Bradley, a farm labourer of Fennel Farm, had been involved in a motorcycle accident in spring last year on the Epping Road. The accused struck an approaching car after his machine skidded on a quantity of motor oil on the road surface. Bradley summersaulted over the car and landed in the road. As he lay there another on-coming car also ran over him adding further serious injuries to his already battered body. He was admitted to hospital having been concussed and when he came out he noticed his sister was keeping house,' Robey told the court.

'I understand. Just get to the offense in question Mister Robey,' said Roche, 'we've twelve more cases to hear today.'

'Indeed, I will sir,' said Robey. 'Bradley committed an offense against his sister who was aged fifteen-and-a-half-years-old last year. I can confirm the young girl gave birth to a female child on the 4 May 1932. And, therefore it has been suggested that the act took place roughly during the ninth month of 1931.'

Mrs. Bradley formally a resident of Hornsey, London, was called to give a statement: 'When the child was born I asked if my son knew anything about it.' And what was the accused reply enquired Robey. 'Cecil said the child was his.'

'Thank you, Mrs Bradley,' said Roche.

Police Constable Harry Sly stepped forward to give a statement: 'When at Fennel Farm interviewing Bradley he admitted to the offence,' said Sly, 'however, he declared that he did not know he was doing anything wrong.'

In the dock Bradley had his head bowed looking petulantly at his feet as Roche summed up: The offence committed by the defendant, Cecil Bradley, who had been discharged from hospital following the accident that took place on 12 May 1931, sustaining serious concussion which caused a distressing head injury. Three months afterward he commits an act on his young sister.' Turning to Wythe the foreman: 'how do you find the defendant?'

'Guilty of unacceptable behaviour,' replied Ernest Wythe.

After deliberating with Birkenhead, Alexander Roche sentenced Bradley to six months imprisonment. As the accused was led away, Harold McCorquodale turned to Roche and beckoned to Robey. This particular conversation concerned the young girl's child, as McCorquodale's wife, Grace, was involved in a charity for babies and young mothers.

Almost a year as a journalist and yet Gatward could still see the wrongs in society. It was all very frustrating and, largely due to factors beyond his control, all he could do was continue to cover the stories and make sure they were published. William Gatward, his father, had seen the hardships of an impoverished society all too frequently as a young Police Constable in London's Metropolitan Police since roughly 1890. Gatward had been born on 28 August 1914. His father was a Detective Inspector in the police station on Tottenham Lane, Hornsey, and had been married seventeen years. Gatward's mother, had just turned twenty-three when they married and aged forty years old when their latest child, the youngest of nine, had been born. Gatward joined five brothers and three sisters in the shadow of war. Roughly one week later, at Camberwell Christ Church, he was christened Alfred Kitchener Gatward in a short ceremony with relatives from Shepherds Bush and Stoke Newington attending

This proved to be a hectic few weeks, for DI Gatward that included a murder nearby. Ken's mother Ayton tried to shield her son from the people in the cells as the Gatwards lived on the upper floors of Hornsey Police station. Ken learnt from an early age that some people in the community were weighed down by significant personal issues.

At six, Ken had, like so many police officer's children before him been sent to Palmers Green Boys School in the parish of Edmonton. School was a happy experience, and during the school holidays, the younger ones were often cared for by their older sister Ayton, or brother William. This loving and close family relationship continued as they moved to Wood Green in 1929. With an interest in writing, Gatward enrolled onto a journalism course, 'where the object of the curriculum was to supply people with an advance insight into the social aspects of their profession,' the London School of Journalism booklet stated.

After passing his exams his energetic and youthful looks, along with his personality, continued to get him assignments after qualifying, as well as at the age of twenty-four he broadened his horizons by joining the RAF Volunteer Reserves in 1937. Recruited for a minimum of five years, Gatward received flying training at Hatfield and Old Sarum. There his 'weekend flier,' colleagues christened him 'Alf' which Gatward took great offence to, so they stuck with Ken which he had been known by since an early age.

He had been mobilised at the outbreak of war, yet it would be another five months before Gatward reported to 53 Squadron at Odiham airfield to the south of the small market village. As a sergeant pilot, Gatward became part of 'the other ranks,' as Flying Officer Anthony Brown the Adjutant frequently typed on Form 540, until breaking this austere custom on 28

September 1939 when mentioning Sergeant Wilfred Whetton a navigator on the squadron by using his rank and surname name. Gatward had seen the squadron's first two Bristol Blenheims land at 53's pre-war Hampshire base on 19 January. Three months later aging Hawker Hector Biplanes that had been 'superb fun to fly,' departed. Their Blenheim twin-engine bombers had been greeted with some euphoria by all. With its two powerful Bristol Mercury radial engines and glazed nose, curving lines, the Blenheim was the ultimate cavalry reconnaissance machine for Army Co-Operation.

As things gathered pace in anticipation of the beginning of hostilities, Ken Gatward was sent to finish his training with four other auxiliary pupil pilots except they were left kicking their heels in the Sergeants Mess at Odiham for a month and a half before being sent to complete their flying training. Gatward finished his flying training on Airspeed Oxfords and was commissioned in August 1940, but then found himself caught up in further courses, finally ending up on No 2 School of Army Cooperation near Salisbury. Individual and specialist training completed, Gatward, Eric Plumtree, Harry Faulkner and Ernest Tedder returned to Odiham for operational training though there were mere bystanders as the Battle of Britain unfolded until 22 September 1940, when the five drove up to RAF Detling.

Meeting their new CO, William Murray, who was in a boisterous mood having been promoted to Wing Commander along with 'Archie' Brown and Wynne 'Dick' Maydwell, who had become squadron leaders, Wynne, always known as Dick, was one of the pre-war founders of 53 Squadron, having been commissioned in the Somerset Light Infantry after Sandhurst in 1933. He learnt to fly at Brooklands before voyaging to join the 2nd Battalion at Poona, India. Volunteering for a four-year secondment to the RAF, Maydwell returned to Britain joining the fledgling squadron at Farnborough. He miraculously survived the German *Blitzkrieg* and, unable to get back to his unit, Maydwell served as the adjutant of a Hurricane re-arming and refuelling unit at Rouen, before escaping from St Malo to Jersey.

Re-joining in July, three months later, Dick and 53 Squadron, now part of RAF Coastal Command and frustrating German invasion plans in 'Battle of the Barges,' along with Bomber Command. There were roughly 2,000 invasion barges moored all along the Channel ports, as Ken Gatward had seen with his own eyes. The Germans had ingenuously requisitioned barges from the Rhine, rivers and harbours throughout Germany and the newly-occupied countries. Amassed in large numbers some river barges were quickly converted to landing craft ready for the invasion of Britain.

Gatward had crewed up with navigator Sergeant George Hammond and air gunner Sergeant Phillip Gibb, flying their first mission on Tuesday 24 September aboard *Y-Yorker* over a southbound, Route A, convoy in the North Sea. 'Hundred percent clear effective visibility in the northern area reducing to twenty-five percent on our southern boundary, sea calm,' said Gatward after touching down at 11.15 hours, 'no enemy aircraft seen.' The trio were airborne again on 25th: 'Good heavens!' Remarked Hammond on the intercom; 'we should be able to see Rotterdam and The Hague, from this height.' Leaving his seat in the nose Hammond came and stood next to Gatward. Visibility was excellent – roughly ten miles – and using the binoculars he could see the ruined landscape and the remains of St. Lawrence Church from their vantage point, before Gatward dropped down to 500 feet. 'Invasion barges strung together like paper chains,' remembered Gatward. It was not until 5 October, however, before Gatward was able to attack the massed enemy vessels. Five Blenheims were loaded with bombs and small incendiaries and at 19.00 hours, led by Ian Jameson, they pounced on the assembled craft at Rotterdam.

'Rotterdam Harbour was littered with barges and boats,' said Gatward. The noise of the approaching planes alerted the defences and they encountered intense flak from heavy batteries, of which, as far as they could tell, six were land-based guns, with another twelve or more aboard the ships.

Despite the flak, *T-Tommie* made it in to the harbour, and 'attacked from the seaward side and encountered small arms fire and accurate flak'. Gatward released three 250lb. bombs and sixty-one 4lb. incendiaries. Hammond wrote that the time of release 19.45 hours in his navigator's log. Passing over the vessel safely, Gatward climbed away. For some reason, as the bomb doors closed, two red flares were released but it was clear the aircraft was all right as, at 21.42 hours, Ken Gatward and his crew touched down with Jameson landing fourteen minutes later. Another of the attackers, Pilot Officer John Mallon from Bell Block, Taranaki, New Zealand, in *O-Orange*, landed moments afterwards. He had managed to release his bombs and incendiaries across the target area and 'met fairly accurate anti-aircraft fire,' Mallon explained at the debriefing, 'holed in a few places, nothing serious.'

The popular New Zealander had arrived in London from Auckland on Saturday 29 July 1939, on board the passenger liner RMS *Rotorua*, with fellow Kiwis John Bethell, Charles Bush, and Bruce Cleary. It had been a long journey from New Zealand, and just two days after their arrival they were posted to an OTU in Wiltshire flying Tiger Moths, and Hawker Harts. Gaining their wings and a commission in the Royal Air Force

Volunteer Reserve, Mallon was posted straight to 53 Squadron. The pilot officer survived unscathed until 31 July 1940. In abysmal weather, after a fruitless reconnaissance, Mallon's visibility disappeared on his approach to Detling as the ground drew ever closer, and his Blenheim slammed into it. There was a cloud of spray, earth and smoke, but Mallon, Sergeants Charles Wilcox and Arthur Shackleford managed to slither out along the crumpled fuselage and jump free. Mallon was mentioned as wounded in an 11 Group Fighter Command Summary that was then struck through with thick red crayon. 'I do hope the damage isn't too bad,' wrote Jameson.

Gatward was on a two-day rotation and wasn't scheduled to fly until Tuesday, 8 October, so Jameson made the daily foray out over a southbound, Route A; convoy out at sea. After three and-a-half hours he landed back at Detling, rolling the Blenheim across the grass to a vacant dispersal. Having shut down the engines and unplugged his leads, he extracted himself and walked to the flight office. Ian found that his aircrew, sergeant Robert McDouall and John Miller were required to fly with Murray too.

'Reports and information indicate a build up at Gravelines,' ran the wording of the signal addressed to Flying Officer Harold Aspen. But, Aspen had been caught when the Luftwaffe smashed the airfield on Tuesday, 13 August – *Adlertag* – causing massive damage to hangers, buildings and the operations block where the forty-five-year-old died.

Murray had flown that morning in Blenheim *O-Orange* on an air test. Detling was still scared with roughly-patched craters on the grass, and blackened buildings. He had wandered back from dispersal, signed the Form 700, and spent the rest of the day catching up on paperwork. He then tried to catch half-an-hour's worth of sleep before the mission but did not succeed. The waiting around was difficult for those on the mission as take-off was not until approximately 18.30 hours. There was a lot of tension in sitting around in the cramped dispersal. Those waiting were Canadian William 'Bill' Wigmore, Murray, Mottram, Mallon, Patrick Ritchie, Ian Thow, and Gatward with their aircrews. All had already flown an air test that morning. Hammond had spent time talking to the fitters, riggers and engine mechanics, but the afternoon wore on.

After eating their evening meal, a short briefing followed. Then everyone collected their flying helmets and parachutes before heading towards their individual aircraft. Gatward, Hammond and Gibbs boarded *T-Tommie*, which would be the last to take-off. Hammond, sat steadfast, as their aircraft began it take-off down the shortened 600 yard runway at 18.45 hours, reassured by the sight of the Blenheim *S-Sugar* flown by Thow in front climbing into the air, laden with three 25lb. bombs and between sixty and sixty-five incendiaries. Gatward took off without any hindrance and joined Ritchie and Thow whilst ahead of them were the other four Blenheims. The weather continued to deteriorate as they neared the Continent running into heavy rainstorms and a cloud base that had diminished to 1,500 feet over Gravelines. This would clearly hamper the mission, although Blenheims going in alone was hardly going to cause mass destruction.

By 19.20 hours, only Ritchie and Thow had found the target area, dropping their loads from 3,000 and 5,000 feet blind 'with no results observed owing to almost complete cloud cover,' reported Ritchie, 'few searchlights and no flak over target either.' With no visual markers the other five stayed in the area from 19.15 to 19.30 hours, 'all planes stooged around the target for twenty minutes,' wrote Murray in his diary. Abandoning their mission, they headed back over the Channel. Gatward finally touched down at 20.52 hours. 'Full bomb load brought back,' scrawled Samuel Thompson the adjutant, who then enquired, 'Did any of you see Mallon?'

'No,' was the universal reply, except for Murray who said that he had seen another aircraft in the target area with its downward recce light on but couldn't identify the type. Mallon had approached in *K-King* from the north-east but getting bombs onto the target was proving difficult. Shackleford had got them from base to target but visibility on the Aa River, one of the key markers, was non-existent with heavy cloud. Calais, therefore, looked a suitable alternative, and Shackleford plotted a course for Mallon to steer.

As the Blenheim approached Calais, a mixture of coloured tracer burst through the cloud and knocked and shook the aircraft. Despite evasive action, this furious tracer fire still zipped up towards them as they attempted to get away from the flak and the accompanying searchlights. Mallon could not shake them off swerving and yawing the aircraft for three and a half miles as much as he dare. The concentration of fire continued towards *K-King* and a moment later, the Blenheim crashed in a field at Fréthun ploughing through the soil, its fuselage ripped in two. Villagers rushed to the scene. John Mallon had miraculously, survived, although badly injured he was dragged out of the wreckage by four Frenchmen. In the darkness Wilfred Whetton and Arthur Shackleford lay dead. Whetton with an Air Force career spanning thirteen years, had won the DFM in July for 'gallantry and devotion to duty,' and had just completed a few days leave with his wife May.

When the Fréthun Mayor arrived at 21.46 hours, minutes after the crash the twenty-four-year-old Mallon was being carefully lifted onto a lorry and driven to a nearby hospital, where surgeons and two nurses under German supervision eased the pain. Despite their efforts to stabilise the New Zealander, John died of his injures on Friday, 11 October on a ward containing English soldiers badly injured at Dunkirk.

Throughout the remaining twenty days in October, Ken Gatward flew on ten of the missions, despite the weather. There had still been a steady loss of pilots and crew. On 24 October, Gatward and his Blenheim crew bombed Caen airfield; one day later it was Antwerp. On 30 October, it was Ostend again, and this time the bomb-release switch malfunctioned during the first attack. On the second attempt, north Londoner Sergeant Alfred Hutson, saw their bombs straddle the harbour mouth and fires raging from where Anthony Dottridge, Maydwell and Payne had already struck. On the return flight, fifteen miles off the Belgium coast, an unseen flak-ship caught the plane, a 88mm shell blast flung *V-Victor* 200 feet in the air knocking out their wireless and intercom. Hutson was now going to earn his money since dead reckoning was the main navigational tool. He repeatedly took drift readings and adjusted the course accordingly as they droned over the sea. Clearly, a plotted course could go wrong, but Alfred was delighted when they landed safely at 20.27 hours, 'it was a relief to complete my second op since bailing out of Jack's aeroplane on the twenty-first,' remarked Hutson as he began to recount their narrow escape.

The plane Hutson had jumped from was skippered by Pilot Officer John 'Jack' Meakin. They'd been caught by friendly anti-aircraft fire near Maidstone returning from a sortie. George Hutson had fired off the colours of the day but 'this just seem to incense the gunners even more,' he recalled. Meakin was still trying to control the aircraft, while holes appeared in the fuselage cutting the cables to control surfaces. Meakin called out 'bail out,' to Hutson and Hadnam as the summersaulting Blenheim did one last aeronautical flip. In his manic attempt to get out Meakin escaped through the top hatch, he fell out of the plane, the port propeller tips amputating his fingers. Grimacing in pain he tugged the D-ring with his bleeding stumps to utilise his parachute.

Meakin soon discovered that his parachute had not fully blossomed as he floated down landing in a copse of oak trees near Tinley Lodge, Shipbourne. The tree canopy and branches broke his fall but left him dangling precariously. Captain Bernard Johnson of the Royal Army Medical Corps had seen his plight from a nearby country lane and had his driver at the wheel rush to the scene to assist. His driver scaled the tree, slithering out onto a sturdy branch to cut the cords and manhandle Meakin down gently using the parachute cords. Johnson treated his injuries and stepped toward the vehicle with Meakin. With both aboard the driver accelerated away from the copse and onto the road until coming to a halt outside Pembury Hospital in Tumbridge Wells. Jack had been lucky. He would eventually fly again, as would his aircrew.

Poor weather continued to hamper missions as 53 Squadron switched bases to Thorney Island in Hampshire most of which had been directed at Dutch barges, and the ports of Brest, Dieppe, Dunkirk, as well as Eindhoven, Lorient and French airfields, as they and 59 Squadron maintained Coastal's anti-invasion coverage. John Maguire was killed, having returned to 53 Squadron on 28 November. Newly promoted from wireless operator/air gunner to navigator, he had been called on to join seven other aircraft on a raid to Lorient in north-western France. With his pilot, Flight Lieutenant James Steuart-Richardson and Sergeant Vincent Vowles wireless operator/air gunner, they climbed into their aircraft that had received an engine change, and under gone a ten-minute air test flown by Gatward. Steuart-Richardson duly did his pre-flight checks and left the dispersal, trailed by Pilot Officer George Newton in *F-Freddie*, then twenty-four-year-old Peter Cundy in *B-Beer*, Ralph Mottram in *E-Edward* and Robert 'Bob' Marriott in *A-Apple*. At 06.00 hours, Steuart-Richardson duly took off, but despite having the throttles wide open, simply couldn't get the Blenheim to climb more than 300 feet. *F-Freddie* sailed by the faltering machine which appeared to hang in the air.

Within seconds the replacement radial engine had lost all power. The Blenheim stalled and then plummeted to the ground. In moments the aircraft was on fire, the crew unable to scramble clear before their bombs exploded. The following three aircraft continued down the runway, veering away from the crash site, as the fire wagons raced to the scene. There was then a short delay of six minutes before Richard Muspratt and Brian Bannister climbed away.

Cundy led them all to Lorient, now being utilised by U-boats for their passage into the Atlantic. The weather report was inaccurate as on their arrival a blanket of cloud obscured the target. With no visual fixes, three of them dropped blind, only Bannister dipped below the cloud to 2,000 feet, from where Sergeant William Densham released the bombs and saw them explode on the southern docks on the west side of the harbour. In *L-Leather*, Bannister was surprised by the ferocity of the flak: 'Immense difficulty in evading back into cloud,' he reported, after landing back at 10.30 hours. His aircraft was so badly knocked about that it had to be taken away for repair.

The cost had been high during 1940. On any sortie, one or maybe two did not make it back. Five in four weeks during July in particular, equated to six crew slightly injured; two crew captured by the enemy and ten killed in action. By the end of the year the adjutant had roughly calculated seventy aircrew had been lost.

'British and Commonwealth resolve, with not a little German indecision, has won the day,' said Air Vice-Marshal John Tyssen commander of No 16 Group, in a letter to Arthur Harris the Deputy Chief of the Air Staff. Germany had not won air superiority, but as the German U-boat force continued to grow they had begun to tighten the noose on the sea-lanes in the Atlantic. Every week the Chiefs of Staff and Cabinet were presented with a list of shipping that had been lost. For Bowhill of Coastal Command, Admiral Forbes, the C-in-C of the Home Fleet, and Admiral Dudley Pound, the First Sea Lord, it made sombre reading. The U-boat crews called this the 'Happy Time,' and the ill-equipped squadrons of in Bowhill's command could do little about the havoc being wreaked out on the convoys.

Between Wednesday 1 January 1941 leading up to Wednesday 5 March, seventy-nine ships had been lost to enemy U-boats. Winston Churchill was informed by Pound and Bowhill, which resulted in him giving the Battle of the Atlantic directive: 'We must take the offensive against the U-boat and the Focke-Wulf … the prime minister declared. 'The U-boat must be hunted.'

What was clear to Naval Liaison Officer Dudley Peyton-Ward at Coastal Command HQ, was that the existing system was not working. This meant a radical change in policy: 'Coastal Command had to attempt to checkmate their opponent,' said Peyton-Ward. It was however, still short of aircraft and occasionally the Air Ministry interfered, deciding what and where to bomb, while Bowhill was left to provide the means, when really Bowhill and Peyton-Ward should have been left to do their jobs without any interference. Despite their frustrations Coastal aircrews in the frontline continued operations none the wiser.

Gatward had officially replaced Hammond, who had left to be commissioned with Alfred Hutson, while 53 Squadron began operating from St Eval in northern Cornwall with frequent trips to French harbours on the West coast, under the leadership of Wing Commander George 'Tubby' Grant former Deputy Director of Intelligence at Kingsway in London. One month later he oversaw their move to Bircham Newton. By lunchtime most if not all of the aircrews had reached the Norfolk base, and Grant realised some kind of briefing was in order. Assembling them together in the station cinema, Grant gave a speech that was short and to the point. 'Aircrew, you're here to begin conversion to the Lockheed Hudson, you'll stay in your trios and please don't crash any as they're seventeen thousand pounds each!'

Bircham Newton became a whirlwind of activity as the transformation took place. Saying farewell was Ken Gatward, newly promoted to flying officer, who on Monday 21 July was given notice to join 236 Squadron at Carew Cheriton in Pembrokeshire, southwest Wales.

It was only by the end of August 1941, that the whole of 236 Squadron was fully reformed. 'A' Flight with, its eight Blenheim fighters, had been based in Aldergrove to patrol the eastern Atlantic for U-boats and the Focke Wulf 200 Condor, a four-engine long-range convoy spotter and bomber. With a directive to start missions within an hour of their arrival – having ferried ground crew across by air – they quickly found the refuelling system was unsatisfactory and obsolete. 'There were no bulk storage facilities for fuel and the Crossley re-fuellers had to be filled from four-gallon tins by hand that was time consuming,' recalled Flying Officer Stanley 'Baby' Nunn, 'A' Flight's Commander. With neutral shipping also being targeted, any ship steaming in the direction of the British Isles was liable to be attacked and sunk by the Condors which were now operating from the French Atlantic coast.

Allied ship losses continued at an alarming rate, as Rear Admiral Ernest King observed as a passenger on Flight Lieutenant Richard Dennison's *V-Vic* when a Focke Wulf 200 was reported attacking a convoy, four miles off Larne on the east coast of County Antrim. 'With the needle stuck at 280 mph, we reached the convoy to find the enemy had made off,' Dennison later remarked. 'All that remained was wreckage on the surface and lifeboats crammed full of survivors.' With sergeants Norman Barron and Van Waeyenberghe in the other two Blenheims, King signalled the corvette shepherding the laden merchantmen: 'will escort you into the North Channel.' As they hurried as fast as they could towards the strait between north-eastern Ireland and south-western Scotland, Barron spotted one little dot, which developed into a twin-engine plane. 'Oxford,' Norman called into the R/T. They dually returned to Aldergrove with an impressed Rear Admiral who obligingly sent half a case of Navy Rum for the Officers Mess.

236 Squadron had suffered a succession of commanding officers almost as much as their frequent moves to new bases. 'Bircham Newton, St Eval, Aldergrove detachment, Carew Cheriton, St Eval detachment, Portreath, Bircham Newton and Sumburgh,' noted Squadron Leader Frank Harrison who became CO of 236 Squadron after George Montagu failed to return from a Brest-Ushant patrol, known as 'Bust Patrols'. On Thursday 12 December 1940, Harrison departed after five months to be replaced by Squadron Leader Alfred Glover. He had gained his wings and was commissioned in about 1921 taking a place at the Welsh airfield Shortwick, then soon after found himself in Egypt.

Returning to Britain in 1926 he served under Air Vice-Marshal Amyas Borton at the Air Ministry and began travelling extensively to the USA and Canada from 1929, returning every year up to 1932. Glover then sort another means of employment gaining a Class A certificate as a Flying Officer, he became an instructor at Southend, and Heston airfields. Later Alfred married Gwendoline 'Wendy' Pearson to live in Ladbroke House, a Georgian red-brick house with an extensive garden in Kenilworth owned by his father, whilst Glover purchased the marital country residence in Castle Bromwich.

Aged thirty-eight he assumed the role of CO at a time when aircrew were on rotating convoy escorts. Almost immediately, Glover found living and working at an operational station without actually flying, torturous, and after just a couple of weeks Stanley Nunn had given him half-an-hour's respite in Blenheim *C-Char*lie. Later, he began flying unofficially a Beaufighter borrowed from 248 Squadron.

The Beaufighter, developed from the Blenheim, was the miracle aircraft to take on the command's offensive role. On Sunday 24 August 1941, the first of 236 Squadron's Bristol Beaufighter MkIC's joined the circuit at Carew Cheriton. It was classified as a 'Priority One Wait' aircraft and was flown in by the Air Transport Auxiliary. Approaching too slowly, the machine stalled, hit the runway and ripped off the tail wheel. The second plane arrived two days later, and by Tuesday 21 October their eighth Beaufighter had flown in – enough for the aircrew to start training with.

That same day, Glover, also received a detailed training notification from 19 Group signed by AOC Air Commodore Geoffrey Bromet, and Stanley Nunn's replacement, Flight Lieutenant Anthony Cairns, arrived to command 'A' Flight. Glover then conferred with his flight commanders, Cairns and Squadron Leader Harold Woods, outlining the training brief for the Bristol Beaufighter that was to start straight away. A local circuit was agreed on to hurl the twin-engine long-range fighters around Pembrokeshire. Woods used the newly arrived eighth Beaufighter as a theatrical prop for ground instruction before allowing local flying in the other seven Beaufighters.

All around Gatward there was a new confidence. The Bristol Blenheim phase was about to come to an end, but sorties continued in the aircraft for Gatward and his crew. They took off from Carew Cheriton at 09.40 hours on 26 October to escort one of the civilian Douglas DC-3 airliners that re-fuelled at Chivenor before journeying on to Lisbon. Gatward picked up the straggler a quarter of a mile from the Devonshire base, and set course. It was a perfect day over the Channel as Gatward, sergeant's Edward Leaver and Robert 'Bob' Langhorne in *M-Monkey* kept station on the portside until near the Strait of Gibraltar. After leaving Gibraltar, Gatward touched back down at Carew Cheriton and completed a couple of ten-minute air tests. He was woken the next day at 05.00 hours by his batman to hear Cairns had him and Bertram Cooper down to fly. Having finally roused himself he went over to the Flight Office and heard Norton would replace Leaver as he was scheduled to fly with Pilot Officer Ronald Baseby. The men clambered into *M-Monkey* and *X-Ray* the latter being Gatward's and they flew out as a pair, landing at Chivenor to await the appearance of the DC-3 from Whitchurch, Bristol.

Half-an-hour later and cleared for take-off, there was a crackle and Cooper's headphones went dead. It was quickly clear the intercom and VHF were not working. With the noise of the Bristol Mercury engines, and with their leather helmets on, the only way they could hear each other was by Crowhurst being inches from Cooper and lifting his helmet clear from his right ear to yell. Sergeant James, wireless operator/air gunner, seeing the commotion, scrambled over towards his pilot and navigator. They had to be able to talk to one another and if they ran into the enemy they would be seriously compromised. It was disappointing, but there was no other choice but to abort their part in the mission.

Gatward continued alone with the operation, shepherding the DC-3 into the air. But as the two planes approached the Channel Islands they ran into trouble - heavy rain. 'Visibility was down to less than fifty yards,' Gatward noted. It became extremely difficult to judge height and Garward decided to turn back, the DC3, however, sped on.

As 1941 drew to close, 236 Squadron continued to provide adequate air protection using both Blenheim and Beaufighters. There was, though, a decline in the manufacture of new Beaufighters. The Bristol Aeroplane Company relied on the Austin Motor Company to fabricate a number of components, including both wing sections and main spar. The trade unions demanded an additional allowance for aircraft workers in the latter's Austin East Works. The union's stranglehold saw a decline in output, but by 20 January 1942, thirteen had reached Carew Cheriton. At this point Glover was told that all operational flying by Blenheims would cease and that all aircrew had to be fully conversant with the Beaufighter enabling them to be operational on the type in preparation for posting overseas.

Four days later, Gatward committed himself to staying with 236 Squadron together with Squadron Leaders Harold Woods and James Pike, who had arrived wearing the purple and white ribbon of his recently-won DFC with 203 Squadron. Glover was able to report to Coastal Command HQ that all crews had progressed well and had amassed roughly ten hours of daylight flying.

Eight of the nineteen Beaufighters in their possession were then flown to Catfoss. Within a few days Glover was notified the unit was then to become a Cadre Squadron, which would complete the training of aircrew from Operational Training Units that were being posted overseas to the Middle East.

Wattisham in Suffolk beckoned. Ken Gatward led the ground party from Pembroke Dock to Ipswich and after arriving he followed Pike into a camouflaged office block where a rather exhausted Wing Commander Alfred Glover, was waiting. It had been a frustrating few days of shuffling paperwork. Having decided on a Training Rota for the 12th Course from 2 OTU Catfoss the weather intervened, so Glover, Gatward, Pike and Wood tutored the aircrew in Hangers 1 and 2.

Daylight flying began on Sunday 1 March. Most pupils accumulated approximately ten hours, with a further six hours night flying. With thirteen days of training gone, Glover received notice that 236 Squadron was to become operational, with three aircraft to be dispatched to Thorney Island in Hampshire. One aircraft was to proceed direct from Wattisham to patrol convoy routes near Le Harve.

At 09.30 hours on Sunday, 15 March 1942, Pike and Woods were shown a list of aircrew from the 12th Course that would join the squadron and take part in ops that afternoon. Gatward could not fly; Pike and Sergeant Iain Pinkerton would fly *G-George*, Flight Sergeant Edward Ford with Sergeant Eric Anderson would be in *H-Harry*, and the twenty-six-year-old from Narrabbi, New South Wales Sergeant Jack Hannaford and his navigator Arthur Robinson from Bombay, India, would be in *U-Uniform*.

The outward journey began at 12.02 hours. They reached their target, where the pair found three laden tankers and one merchantman. At 14.16 hours, six Messerschmitt Bf 109s based near Le Havre, dived upon them. Rather than engage in a protracted fight, Pike opened the throttles to increase speed, 'and we left them behind,' Pike later told the Intelligence Officer at Thorney Island. Roughly forty-five minutes later, near Le Havre, twenty-six-year-old Jack Hannaford had seen nothing of their fellow Beaufighters but was in no way concerned as he was rather enjoying his first mission. But with little time to practice air fighting and learn essential tricks and skills before going on a mission, Jack now found himself up against some of the best in the Luftwaffe when Robinson shouted into the intercom, 'Fighters, eight o'clock.'

Seconds later, Hannaford's *U-Uniform*, had a pair of Messerschmitts bearing down upon him and in moments cannon shells had struck the Beaufighter. Flames erupted from one of the engines, the plane slowly dropped height, flames and smoke trailing behind, before plunging into the sea. Feldwebel Helmut Baudach from Jagdgeschwader 2, the 'Richthofen Wing' based at Katwijk in Holland, had claimed his second victim that afternoon.

In the early evening, with *U-Uniform* long overdue, the news was received that the pair were presumed dead as a result of air operations. A good friend of Hannaford's had been twenty-four-year-old navigator Sergeant Gilbert 'George' Fern a quiet, unassuming young man. Fern had been to East Dean Grammar School, Cinderford, and Loughborough College in Leicestershire and after qualifying took his first teaching post at Stourbridge School in September 1939, when war broke out. Volunteering for the Royal Air Force, Fern had gone to Yatesbury where he qualified as a wireless operator. He then went onto Staverton, excelling in navigation and meteorology, obtaining the seventh highest score on his course. Here he was christened with the nickname 'George' by his mates as one lecturer always exclaiming 'by George,' when Fern received top marks. After gaining his observer brevet and having already been singled out as a good mathematician, by the autumn of 1941, he was on the 12th Course at 2 OTU Catfoss, which transferred to Wattisham. Fern missed being sent to the Mediterranean theatre, as there was a short fall of aircrew on 236 Squadron and instead received notice that he was to be posted as a sergeant navigator to the squadron.

Flying Officer Albert Lees had arrived with Fern after his refresher at Catfoss, and they were crewed up for a sortie on 16 March. Their briefings for the operation had been given at 08.00 hours that morning at Thorney Island. Shipping, they were told, was moving out of the St Malo area, which was approximately forty-five minutes flying time away.

Soon afterwards they found themselves staring down at the sea below. 'A good trip fairly successful sighted four; a tanker, trawler and two merchantman,' Fern subsequently reported. Fortunately for him, flying was temporarily curtailed after the loss of Ford and Anderson on the 19th, following which Glover gave permission for men to go into Emsworth roughly two miles away from Thorney Island.

Fern and Pinkerton did not go far, just to the Sussex Arms. The pub was very much an airman's haunt. Before last orders Fern slipped away to telephone his wife Mary, whom he had married thirteen months ago and was staying with her parents in West Dean. She was a secretary in a textile firm, with Fern smitten and it seemed the feelings were mutual their love flourished and the couple tied the knot.

Pinkerton's second trip was to Brest by the River Penfeld where his pilot James Pike sighted a lone flak-ship. As Pinkerton cocked the 20mm cannon the, plane's nose dropped. Pike could see arcs of tracer rising up towards them in reply to his 20mm. It was quickly realised that the flak-ship was firing something heavier than the Beaufighter, and Pike aborted his attack.

By 23 March, Pike, Pinkerton, Lees and Fern had been recalled to Wattisham, Glover had returned from Eastbury Park Coastal Command HQ where he was briefed personally by Group Captain Alfred 'Fred' Willetts along with Air Vice-Marshal George Barker Joubert's Senior Air Staff Officer (SASO), who explained the purpose of his squadron's next mission. This had been in response to Admiral Sir Charles Forbes request on 19 March for a squadron of Beaufighters to be made available for a Combined Operation raid to destroy Normandie Dock at Saint Nazaire which boasted the only dry dock on the Atlantic that could accommodate the one remaining German warship that caused concern to those on the British Isles: The *Tirpitz*. Anything that might remove the threat posed by the *Tirpitz* was considered. Combined Operations had received a new CO in November 1941 in the form of Lord Louis Mountbatten, who had managed to link the location for the a raid with a convincing and unanswerable case to the Admiralty for going ahead with the plans drawn up by Captain John Hughes-Hallett and his two staff officers.

Tuesday 24 March 1942. At Predannack south Cornwall one of 19 Group's bases, the station commander received news that eight Beaufighters would be arriving to escort a naval force. This information was then passed it down to the various sections: maintenance, officers and sergeants messes, cook houses and the watch office. In his office at Wattisham, Wing Commander Alfred Glover received the operational order, called his two flight commanders and broke the news about Operation *Chariot*.

An assortment of vehicles flowed to the dispersals, taking aircrew to their machines for their air test, while ground trades prepared the Beaufighters for imminent take off. Soon after, the Suffolk airfield emitted the noise of Bristol Hercules engines as the Beaufighters thundered down the runway and lifted off into the cobalt-blue sky.

Twenty to Twenty-five minutes after take-off, everything had been tested and the aircraft began joining the circuit to land, except Glover and Fern who remained aloft for thirty-five minutes. They taxied around the perimeter to be marshalled into an empty dispersal and were soon onto the back of a van without its usual canvas roof to take them back to the sergeants' and officers' messes for lunch.

Within half-an-hour there was the briefing. At around 13.30 hours, the briefings began in Wattisham's operation's room. Glover ran through the flight order to Predannack and stressed they needed to be on the station by

18.30 hours. He was followed by the intelligence officer, then Met Officer. The weather was good but was set to worsen later in the afternoon. It was then around 14.30 hours. Watches were synchronized to BBC time, but until take-off, which was in thirty minutes, the crews collected a change of clothes, shoe polish and their wash kit. Gilbert Fern wrote a short letter to his wife Mary and said another would follow as he was short of time and a job to do. He signed and sealed it and left it at the collection point in the Sergeants Mess and made his way back down to the flight and crew room. Parachute, helmets, goggles, flying jacket, boots and gloves all collected, Fern then trundled over to Glover's aircraft *J-Johnny*. Fern climbed the small retractable metal ladder, into the narrow confines of the fuselage and the smell of fresh paint, rubber and oil. He now waited for the CO.

Aboard *Z-Zebra*, Harold Wood was ready to move, followed by Pilot Officer Ronald 'Ron' Rankin from Majors Creek, New South Wales – a gifted Wallabie rugby full back wearing the deep sky-blue of the Royal Australian Air Force – with Pinkerton as navigator.

In *H-Harry* twenty-eight-year-old Percy Schaefer and Sergeant Denny Lawton, edged forward with Sergeant's Geoffrey Avern, and Philip Crossan to the rear. At 15.00 hours, the signal to take-off was flashed Woods, and Rankin gathered pace, and climbed away. Schaefer opened the throttles, pushing back in his seat as the speed quickened and the machine rose into the air. It should have been a straightforward enough but not everyone had mastered taking off in a Beaufighter, which was why all the new aircrews were still training. His plane unexpectedly swung to starboard crashing to the ground. In seconds the Beaufighter was ablaze, a dazed Schaefer and Lawton scrambled clear, then stumbled to a safe distance before collapsing. The plane became a ball of fire that eventually burnt itself out, as the first deviation from the plan took place.

At 17.30 hours, the control caravan finally flashed its green Aldis light and Avern opened the throttles and his aircraft gathered speed and climbed into the air. The former Australian school teacher encountered bad weather en route to Predannack and, as the wind became stronger, Avern, concerned with the worsening conditions, returned to Wattisham where he landed *O-Orange* safely.

Fortunately, Avern's warning of turbulent weather had caused Glover and Pike to abort their flights out now all they could do was wait. Muttering and cursing, and conscious of the clock ticking a replacement crew was sort. The Adjutant had hurried off to find Pilot Officer Walter 'Tommie' Smith and his navigator Sergeant Alfred 'Bob' Treadwell. Smith had completed roughly twenty-five hours of local flying, and had accumulated a minimal amount of air-to-air firing at a drogue using various Beaufighters on 236 since 15 March, and was thought to be the most competent after loosing Schaefer and Lawton.

11.10 hours the following day Glover in *J-Johnny* followed by Pike in *G-George* await the signal to get airborne. Cleared for take-off Gilbert Fern sat behind the bulkhead armoured doors facing forward on a swivel seat, flying helmet on and leads plugged firmly into both the intercom and the radio and wireless set.

Throttles pushed forward, the Beaufighter's two 14-cylinder radial engines developing maximum power pushed it down the runway. Sixty-miles and hour, seventy, eighty, ninety, the plane bounced over every section of the runway with a tar cavity then a jolt the tail lifted and with in seconds *J-Johnny* rose into the air.

Pike formatted on the left-hand side both made tracks for Predannack stopping one hour into their journey at Roborough north of Plymouth. Here Glover attends a private briefing with Willetts, Forbes, and Bonnett during a lengthy discussion they gave him general instructions including orders for communications when the mission commences. By 16.25 hours both Beaufighters were airborne and roughly thirty-minutes later they'd touched down at Predannack airfield.

Replacements Smith and Treadwell had flown a test flight in *M-Mother* earlier that morning then had its compass swung and adjusted before the plane had been loaded with fuel and ammunition. At 14.30 hours Smith took off for the cross-country flight to Cornwall.

Avern, who had served in Sydney University Regiment for two years, had to wait still longer for his Beaufighter to be made ready, and he finally moved off on 27th, at 17.30 hours. Watching the last of the airborne detachment take to the air Gatward now had to get the seven sets of groundcrew to Cornwall by rail in time for the mission.

At Predannack the signals office was busy. Pilot Officer Thomas Gray, a signals officer from Pembroke Dock, had arrived two days previously to assist 236 Squadron. Gray was there with Glover when he received confirmation that 'first sortie to commence on 28 March, aircraft to be in position by six-thirty,' from 19 Group. He had rearranged the battle order. Harold Wood and Allan McNicol were pulled from being first off, replaced with Ronald Rankin and Iain Pinkerton. Wood's and McNicol would be second off, it was recognised by the two Carew Charlton operations staff that Glover needed experienced pilots spread throughout their twelve hours of air cover over Operation *Chariot*. It was probably just as well, for Archie Taylor, Hilary Parfitt with Smith, and Avern were still far from ready for combat operations. Therefore, Glover and Fern would fly with Pike, to cover the latter stages of their mission.

The morning of Saturday, 28 March 1942 was grey and cloudy. Met men and women were scurrying around taking readings and the weather charts of the day were being marked up, ready for interpretation with those issued by Middle Wallop of 10 Group.

The first foursome had been up since 03.00 hours and thirty minutes later Glover appeared too. Breakfast in the Predannack messes was porridge then sausage, potatoes or a kipper, followed by bread, marmalade or jam, and there was plenty of tea. For Glover, there would be barely a moment's rest, with Bonnett's final Operational Order being received at 04.30 hours which included up-dates on the routes and timings, and of the signals procedure for all participating aircraft. Gray and the two other operational staff could share his burden and got to work.

At approximately 05.30 the briefings began with Glover briefing all the pilots and navigators and at 05.50 Wood in *Z-Zebra* led Rankin's *K-King* into the air. They flew on the exact course and track at low level to Ushant before turning southeast and due west of Belle-Ile Rankin sighted five torpedo boats, which the novice pilot thought were part of the operation. 'Better give the recognition signal,' Rankin spoke into the intercom, 'don't particularly want to go for an early morning swim courtesy of the Navy.'

Pinkerton picked up the Aldis lamp and flashed a series of Morse code messages to the vessels below. Receiving no reply, he pushed out flares indicating the aircraft was friendly and not hostile, however within seconds tracer was arcing up towards the Beaufighter. 'Had to take avoiding action,' said Rankin, 'we were therefore unable to identify them.' He had a more pending problem, however, in that the revolutions on the starboard engine were fluctuating, and the oil pressure gauge was dropping. Despite this, Rankin resumed the creeping line search, then started back to search ten miles either side of the triangulation point. During this processes Pinkerton spotted an unidentified aircraft 'Beaufighter,' he exclaimed excitedly on the intercom, 'it's Eddie.'

Wood came alongside his navigator Allan McNicol exchanging jovial hand jesters from his blister with Pinkerton. Together they scoured the tranquil waters for the *Chariot* vessels but without success. In heavy cloud at 2,000 feet, Rankin lost station with *Z-Zebra* and decided it was time to return to base 'due to engine failing badly,' Rankin wrote in his log. It was terribly disappointing, but there was no other choice. Rankin had been sensible. With the starboard engine throttled right back, they crawled towards base. Pinkerton requesting a QDM magnetic heading to guide them in, as by his calculation they were nine minutes overdue. The undercarriage locked down a hundred yards before reaching the beginning of the runway and Rankin adjusted the flaps and touched down. The time was 10.25 hours.

The other crews, those of Taylor, Smith and Avern, had taken off and were patrolling their particular square of water. An hour-and-a-half into the search for the *Chariot* vessels, Archie Taylor found them. 'Shortly before 9.00 a.m., a British Beaufighter began escorting us,' wrote Commander Guy Sayer, commanding officer of HMS *Cleveland*. They'd sighted *Cleveland* and HMS *Brocklesby* on the westward leg of their track as well as two Motor Launches *270* and *446* and Motor Torpedo Boat *314*. From the signals received Sayer knew that HMS *Atherstone* and HMS *Tynedale* had been engaged by the enemy torpedo boats, 'this was flashed to our guardian in the sky,' wrote Sayer in his report.

For a while Taylor and Rolfe flew around, taking *Y-York* over the passing the vessels, circling round at 200 miles per hour at just 100 feet above the sea. Hilary Rolfe deciphered 'need to get to a port as soon as possible,' as his pilot circled in a wide anti clockwise turn. At approximately 09.36 hours Rolfe spotted the silhouette of a twin-engine aircraft. 'Eight-eight,' he exclaimed over the intercom. 'At three o'clock high!'

Oberleutnant Raymund Schoelke and the men of K.Gr.106 had discovered that morning they had been ordered to attack British destroyers off the coast of Saint Nazaire. Thick cloud had been the first obstacle since taking off from Dinard in north-western France, but then offshore, below 2,000 feet, he and his crew saw the tiny specks below. Then Raymund heard someone shout, 'English fighter!'

Taylor had flipped over his reflector sight, locking it into position adjusted for range and wingspan of the enemy aircraft. Switched the gun button to 'fire', excitement mounting. Behind him Rolfe cocked the cannons and closed the two blast doors as his pilot continued to manoeuvre astern of the Junkers, which had increased its own speed. Now aft of the plane, Taylor closed the distance, and opened fire – they were his first shots in action. The melee continued for eight minutes as he pumped rounds into the enemy machine. To his amazement, bits of aircraft begun flying off, followed by smoke and then a great lick of flame. The Junkers exploded but just as suddenly, the Beaufighter plummeted from the sky caught in a mass of debris.

Guy Sayer watched *Y-York* tumble down until it eventually hit the sea with a great burst of white foam. Immediately HMS *Tynedale* was ordered to search for survivors but the two crew had obviously been killed; 'An appreciation of the general situation at this time,' wrote Sayer, 'seemed to indicate that a heavy air attack was imminent, in addition to which an attack by surface craft known to be in this vicinity was considered a strong possibility.' Smith and his navigator Treadwell had taken *M-Mother* to the southeast search area at 10.03 hours 'without sighting anything,' wrote Smith. He eventually was forced to set course for base at 12.03 hours.

Avern and Crossan flew down their track and started a creeping line. Avern saw a Heinkel dive through the layer of cloud to 200 feet, he immediately swung the Beaufighter in its direction to intercept. However, the Heinkel took evasive action and concealed itself within the cloud. Stalking him through the cloud, had a negative result and contact was lost. He emerged out of the cloud and resumed his search for the Royal Navy, which proved fruitless. Back at Predannack there was still no word of what had happened to Taylor and Rolfe, with Gray forced to write in his initial report 'cause remains obscure'.

The fifth sortie of the day was conducted by Glover and Fern. It was Glover's first recorded operation on RAF Form 541 since taking over as CO with Gilbert Fern as his guide. By 10.50 they'd flown out with James Pike but lost contact when Glover spotted a Heinkel 115 at roughly 200 feet. Speed was of the essence as *J-Johnny* gave chase but they, too were unsuccessful in their attempts to shoot it down. But Pike became aware of another aircraft flying parallel to him. Sergeant Harold Kent, recorded taking a fix, followed by 'enemy floatplane.' Pike sped towards the enemy aircraft, which began taking evasive action. Closing from the starboard side at 200 yards he pressed the gun button and fired 20mm cannon at the machine as its pilot zig-zagged towards the clouds. Before gaining cover its navigator responded, firing off two star shells, indicating to his compatriots in a second He 115 that they had sighted the 'English Ships.'

As Pike engaged the Heinkel near the *Chariot* flotilla, a strong head wind reduced the speed of the ships from sixteen knots to ten knots. 'It was eventually clear that even this could not be maintained,' wrote Sayer, 'in MGB *314* commanded by Lieutenant Dunstan Curtis, the water was gaining slowly, in spite of the efforts of her crew and finally one of her engines broke down.' With the impending threat of air attack, the decision was made to take the crews off the motor launches and motor gun boats, the vessels being sunk by gunfire from the destroyers.

Pike and Kent did as they were ordered by a ground controller and immediately resumed scanning the waters of the Bay of Biscay. As the cloud base lifted, James Pike caught sight of the *Chariot* vessels. Now *G-George* was out of 20mm cannon shells and with the Heinkel seemingly having disappeared, Pike began flying air cover. 'Someone's copped it below,' remarked Sergeant Harold Kent on seeing the thick acrid smoke billowing from the three naval vessels.

Pike instructed his navigator to load up more ammunition, and Kent lifted the floor panels, plucked out a fresh drum of 20mm to replenish the first of the two starboard Hispano-Suiza cannons, and repeated the process for the portside cannons. No sooner than he had notified Pike that the cannons were loaded and cocked, he heard the pilot shout 'Heinkel!' Pike pushed *G-George* within 200 yards of the enemy aircraft and opened fire. Suddenly, a responsive flash from the floatplane and seconds later, Pike's Beaufighter had bullets hitting the nose. On the portside of the cockpit a bullet severed the hydraulic pipe and oil caught alight. It burned for several minutes before extinguishing itself as he climbed through the clouds to try and spot the Heinkel but it had vanished. Minutes later Pike picked out a third floatplane in the sky but was in no fit state for a fight.

With fuel low, Pike headed for home, repeatedly calling Glover over the R/T, but with no response. As they swept over the sea back towards Cornwall with no hydraulic pressure to lower the main undercarriage and tail wheel Harold calculated a course to an alternative airfield – St Eval.

Pike made a wheels-up landing on the grass that caused little damage to his Beaufighter. When he finally unbuckled his leads and harness and jumped down onto the grass, he discovered a blaspheming Station Commander, Group Captain Arthur Revington – the grass had just been mown. Flight Lieutenant Kenneth Illingworth, and Pilot Officer John 'Johnny' Lown of 254 Squadron helped defuse the situation and led the bemused Pike and Kent off to be debriefed. '12.15 p.m., encounter with first He 115 – Chariot Escort,' reported Kent, 'a few feet either way and it would have been curtains.' The day had been one of ferocious fighting in which the aircrews at Predannack and St Eval had lost colleagues. Pike helped 254 Squadron aircrew Illingworth, Lown, Pilot Officer Robert Pole and Flight Lieutenant 'Bill' Sise raise a glass to the deeply respected Anthony Parnell and Herbert Mullineaux known as 'Pop' having been born in October 1913 'and then he went to bed,' Pike wrote in a letter home. The following day he and Kent bade farewell and headed to Wattisham in Suffolk with their parachutes and flying gear on a train.

At Predannack, Fern went to the room he shared with Archie Taylor, Hilary Rolfe and Harold Kent. Everything looked exactly as it had been left in the early hours of the morning. Archie's razor, shaving brush, comb were on the bedside wash stand and his towel still hung on a wooden towel rail where he had hurriedly left them nearly five hours ago.

A new phase was starting on their arrival back at Wattisham. The head of Coastal Command had made the decision to renew the anti-shipping offensive after Roundell Palmer's staff at the Ministry of Economic

Warfare presented a good case for increasing the effort in north-west Europe. To fulfil this task Ken Gatward had been instructing new aircrew at Wattisham to learn and change on their own initiative. Some did others did not. He began to instil in them the importance of working as a team whether they were searching for shipping, enemy aircraft or a ditched plane. Men of 236 were quick to realise that Gatward was a pilot worth listening to and precisely what the new squadron members required.

One was Sergeant Maxwell Addess, a young Jew from London's East End, who four weeks after Chamberlains speech walked into the RAF recruitment office in Kingsway. He was rebuffed initially, but it had always been the Royal Air Force that he'd really wanted to join, so he waited. With the onset of war and the defeat at Dunkirk with his qualifications Addess accepted for pilot training. So he went for his initial training, put in some flying hours and then to OTU at Catfoss.

By March 1942, he was attached to Coastal Command but without a navigator. At Wattisham he teamed up with Sergeant Bryan Lane. The pair carried out their first cross-country flight in a 236 Squadron Beaufighter on Saturday 4 April and flew their first anti-shipping reconnaissance off the Dutch coast the next day between The Hook and Terschelling Island. 'Did my first operational trip. It was not extremely exciting, but not every one is, you can well imagine,' Max wrote to his sister Hettie.

Coastal Command had established that enemy convoys travelling northbound along the Dutch coast left the Hook of Holland at 10.00 hours and had calculated a point along the Dutch where such convoys were likely to appear. At the Government Code and Cipher School at Bletchley Park in Buckinghamshire, in the wooden huts in the grounds, there was still limited ability to decrypt the relevant signals. Fortunately, a tanker named *Eurosee* struck a mine near the Dutch islands when part of a convoy of six merchantmen, a decoding room full of women got to work, providing 236 Squadron with their next couple of ops.

By the time Harold Woods had walked into the operations room at Wattisham the signal – in the form of a cyphered cablegram – had arrived requesting a search the length of the Dutch islands. On the morning of 12 April, Lee and Hope were due to fly, and were airborne at 07.30 hours to search for the tanker. The forecast had not been good and en route lived up to expectations. On reaching the Frisian Islands they hit 'heavy sea fog north of Ameland with nil visibility,' as Hope reported roughly an hour and a half later, with 'no enemy movements'. Again, he signalled 'persistent fog with nil visibility'. Lee was then instructed by a WAAF ground controller to make landfall at Cromer and land at Bircham

Newton. Hope worked out the bearings for the route home, and at 10.30 hours, *C-Charlie* safely touched down on the tarmac.

Addess and Lane had relocated to North Coates for their mission and received a briefing. There were aerial photographs of the coastline and a large map with convoy routes carefully prepared for them and red flag marking the position of the tanker *Eurosee*. Bryan Lane studied the information and drew tracks and worked out the flight plan and marked up his map accordingly covering The Hook and the Frisian Islands. They would over lap *C-Charlie* search area and fly a search six miles off the southern Norwegian coast. Addess and his navigator took off from North Coates at 08.15 hours and ran straight into sea fog over the North Sea. This presented Addess with a difficult conundrum. Return to base or continue on course and grope their way through the fog and hope that it cleared.

The downturn in the weather meant the Kriegstagebuch 1.Sicherungdivison had cancelled all convoy sailings and *Eurosee* was being slowly moved by tugs. However, owing to heavy fog, they had to drop anchor, reported the Kaptain of *Sperrbrecher 145*. The tanker was still taking on water in the engine room, and a request was made for a pumping steamer. All around them was a blanket of heavy sea fog.

Shielded by the thick gauze of fog and with the commotion and noise aboard *Eurosee* above, Beaufighter *Z-Zebra* sliped by the flak-ships, the *Sperrbrecher* and the cluster of support vessels, its aircrew unaware of the commotion. Hopelessly lost in heavy sea fog, *Z-Zebra* disappeared without trace. One of those culpable for the loss of Addess and Lane was the ineptness of the North Coates base commander to recall *Z-Zebra*. Glover, the squadron commander, had been demanding this but he would only scrub Desourdy's sortie.

The following day, Desourdy and Lee got airborne to seek out the tanker *Eurosee*. In *C-Charlie*, Desourdy arrived to discover nothing in the specified grid square – *Eurosee* had been moved and was safely beached near Borkham and Buoy 53, guarded by a cluster of flak-ships.

Satisfied that they had completed the search, Desourdy headed for Norfolk. Concerned about his fuel state WAAF controllers diverted the plane to West Raynham. Desourdy came into land, but it was a poor one. His inexperience and over-excitement, had led to him keeping the throttles open as he headed back causing both engines to overheat 'the cylinders were virtually glowing,' wrote the Chief Engineering Officer. 'Certainly a red endorsement offense for his log-book.' Like his fellow aircrew, over the next six days he was learning on the job.

Ken Gatward having been on instructional duties, required a navigator to go back on ops. And so Gilbert Fern had been summoned. On Saturday

18 April Gatward and Fern in *C-Charlie*, carried out a long low-level search between Borkum and Texel islands north of Den Helder in which they sighted two flak-ships and three merchantmen. The Beaufighter was welcomed by a mass of light and heavy flak pumping high above the aircraft with Gatward was flying at just thirty-five feet. Fern in the rear yelled that if they flew any lower they'd soon be touching the wave tops and he could go for a paddle.

The next day, Gatward and Fern were part of a relay, following a convoy off Ijmuiden. On 21 April, a Heinkel 59 bi-plane intercepted Gatward when searching for an inflated dinghy thought to be from a Vickers Wellington of 156 Squadron lost the previous evening. In the ensuing scrap, with the Heinkel now just ahead of him he shot away the starboard float, but to his surprise seemed to fly straight through his cannon and bullets during its violent curve to starboard as four star shells blossomed above the floatplane. Somewhat bemused Gatward broke away for Fern to replenish the four Hispano-Suiza cannons but had forgotten the mantra 'Beware the Hun in the Sun' and was horrified to see an Me 110 as he glanced in the mirror. Ken immediately saw cannon shells and machine-gun tracer whizz by over his head. Turning violently to the left, he began to zigzag *B-Baker* as the Messerschmitt closed the distance firing four shot bursts in quick succession. One caught the blast tubes of the inner cannon just forward of the breech and magazine drum. Ignoring the holes being punched through the floor just aft of his seat, George continued to talk calmly into the microphone in his oxygen mask giving commands of which way to turn as they continued to be pursued. A second Me 110 briefly joined his colleague but his rounds did nothing more than churn up sea spray as Gatward increased speed to 310 mph and, after thirty-minutes, both were shaken off. Landing at North Coates at 17.38 hours, *B-Baker* was hastily repaired, refuelled and re-armed then flown low over the North Sea to complete the sortie 'but we failed to sight dinghy,' said Gatward. Returning to Wattisham, there were further sorties flown in April, searching for ditched aircraft and an encounter with a Junkers 88, but having latched onto it, after Gatward's first burst his reflector sight malfunctioned.

Despite Glover's concerns his aircrews completed fifty missions and 111 hours operational flying however, the Air Ministry sent a brisk cable to him. All but four of his aircrews were to leave Wattisham with their planes for the Middle East, by way of the bases of St Mawgan and Portreath to Gibraltar. 'Just when the nucleus of this squadron was being moulded into a fighting unit, it seemed to have had its heart ripped out,' wrote Squadron Leader Harold Woods, when he assumed command from

Alfred Glover. By the end of his first day in charge he learnt that Geoffrey Avern and Philip Crossan lay dead a short distance from Gibraltar. 236 Squadron colleagues saw Beaufighter *G-George* shot down by ground fire from Gibraleón in neutral Spain.

James Pike also left with a promotion to take command of 248 Squadron. Replacing Pike was Squadron Leader Harry Daish. The son of a medical practitioner from Victoria in South Eastern Australia, Daish became a Jackaroo working on a mixed sheep and cattle farm not far from Booligal, and from there he used to see commercial aeroplanes fly over on a regular basis. By July 1935, when he turned twenty-two, Harry decided to join the Australian Air Force and it was at Point Cook Flying Training School he was commissioned as a pilot officer. He was selected as one of the six top graduating officers to earn a five-year short commission in the Royal Air Force. Departing from Fiji he crossed the oceans to London on the *Strathnaver* in mid-August 1936, leaving behind his girlfriend.

Daish had met Irene Ireland from Sydney and been instantly besotted. 'She was gorgeous,' said Harry. Irene had only been twenty-three when they became engaged, not surprisingly her father was sceptical at the prospect of her marrying a young aviator. However, being over the age of twenty-one, she told her father that she could do as she pleased and in 1937 sailed to Britain and married Harry Daish who had managed to get permission from the station commander, as he was unusually young amongst pilots to marry. After completing Flying Training School, Daish was transferred to 218 Squadron and in August 1939 received a telegram saying he had been promoted to flight lieutenant, which elevated his pay to twenty shillings and two pence. This increase in income made all the difference when living outside Boscombe Down.

Daish had flown his first operational sortie on 17 September 1939 in a Fairey Battle. Since then he had completed a number of operational sorties on Battles, and Wellingtons and, after thirty ops, an instructors job beckoned, or a second tour of twenty missions. Fortunately for him, after the posting a year on, Daish arrived as 'B' Flight's Flight Commander. With his reputation for thoroughness and professionalism he and 'A' Flight's Squadron Leader William 'Bill' Jay with Woods, McNicol, Gatward and Fern helped to mould 236 Squadron's new personnel from the 14th Course at 2 OTU Catfoss into an efficient unit.

With the last navigational exercise on 12 May, the squadron became fully operational, and just a few days later Flight Sergeants Joseph Bourasse and Wilfred Williams, together with Jules Delatte and Thomas Pearson, scrambled into the air, the latter seeing twelve laden merchantmen with a brace of escorts off the Dutch coast. Bourasse returned exhilarated but disappointed as the weather closed in and no attack could be carried out. That evening both were consoled by Fern, who stood them a round in the Sergeants Mess and yet somehow, somewhere along the line, it should have been Bourasse and Williams buying Gilbert Fern a pint as his next mission with Ken Gatward was exactly one month away.

Nearly five months before Gatward and Fern's next op was given the green light, the original idea had begun to be formulated in Paris the capital of France. Just existing in Paris had become a challenge for 33-year-old Benjamin 'Ben' Cowburn, an agent in the field for Special Operations Executive (SOE). Living anonymously in a small studio apartment in the suburb of Neuilly-sue-Seine.

Outside German troops and officers were putting the Parisian café owners at ease ordering coffee, others had pretty Parisian women seated with them, a cluster of people had gathered around one table as an officer or may be more, Cowburn couldn't see with no French vocabulary had sent their ladies into peals laughter with their enthusiastic but bumbling efforts to woo them using their German-French phrase books. Maxim's and Larue's on the Rue Royale were full too.

Cowburn continued walking turning into the Avenue des Champs-Elyséss, passing two Seine fishermen trying to get goujons to nibble on their lines. There was a muffled sound of a brass band in the distance. The sound was approaching from the bottom of the vista and soon Cowburn was able to distinguish German bandsmen, headed by an officer on horseback with a drawn sword, glinting in the morning sun. A few mothers with young children stopped but many Parisians walked on with sidelong glances of distrust. Cowburn too carried on walking.

It was just after midday. The German Military Band's musicians were blasting out with reed instruments, then brass, percussion and more brass, were now at arms length. 'It was blaring out *Wenn Wir Marschieren*,' said Cowburn. 'One soldier had a decorated frame with a set of bells on which he was ringing the tune with a small hammer.'

They continued marching up the Champs-Elyséss towards the Arc de Triomphe. Cowburn passed Germans in uniform walking on the pavement who formally salute the troops on the march advancing towards that unique monument to Napoleon's Grande Armee who had conquered most of Europe in 1805. Their French Emperor commented: 'You will return home through arches of triumph' now this victorious occupying force passed under the Arc de Triomphe with a show of pride and domination as it had done two years previously. However, the rosy-cheeked Bavarians, and Rheinhessen boys had moved on to fight on other fronts and had been replaced by older greyer faced troops.

Walking back to the Place de la Concorde, Cowburn believed in the need for a unifying symbol against this oppression. He moved along by the Seine towards the Louvre. In the absence of river traffic the usually turbid Seine was silky smooth and tranquil. The Louvre, a labyrinth of abandoned galleries, its art treasures absconded to chateaux's and isolated villages. Outside the once flourishing ornamental gardens have been transformed into a vegetable garden. The remaining hours are spent in streets and avenues of the city walking past his old family residence in the suburb Boulogne 'as I try to get used to the idea of being a Parisian again,' said Cowburn.

He was able to move around freely and had successful trips away from the city reconnoitring potential targets for RAF Bomber Command and transmitting the details to London by radio operator André Bloch first from the Paris suburbs then from Le Mans. A couple of months later, with more men and material arriving, he felt imbued with a sense of great confidence for the future; the only dark point had been the arrests and loss of Bloch much to his annoyance.

Cowburn stepped out of his apartment and later mingled with the unsuspecting Parisians waiting for the German Military Band strutting up the Champs-Elyséss. It was noted that they always followed the same pattern, he made a firm decision – it had to be a worthy target.

The agent was then called back to Britain. His initial extraction by *MGB 314* from Moulin-de-la-Rive on Thursday 12 February 1942, in a melee against German soldiers which saw Dunstan Curtis's Australian officer, First Lieutenant Ivan Black, captured along with agents Geoffrey Abbott and Gustave Redding.

Cowburn had got over this potential stumbling block. Precariously making his way to Marseille. The mountains beckoned. Crossing the Pyrenees with the help of the escape line to the Spanish frontier he was repatriated through Gibraltar. Then it was back to London to be cross-examined starting on 30 March about morale, strength, and habits of the German Army in France and Paris.

'It was,' Cowburn noted in his journal, 'quite clear that sending an Air Force plane had caught Colin Gubbins imagination he obviously thought it could be a success.'

So at the beginning of April 1942, Gubbins had written a memo, which was circulated around the Air Ministry. His agent's idea received more enthusiasm within Air Ministry circles and eventually wound up on C-in-C Fighter Command Air Marshal Sholto Douglas desk, whilst a second arrived at Philip Joubert's Eastbury Park HQ. Separately the pair headed to the Air Ministry building. A long and business-like meeting in the building began, Douglas shouted down Gubbins suggestion: 'it's lunacy to risk a Beaufighter night-fighter being caught in broad daylight,' said Douglas. But Joubert calmly replied: 'I've got a day Beaufighter which might do it.' Operation *Squabble* was born.

Planning continued for the operation although the precise form it would take had still to be agreed to minimize civilian casualties. Certainly, there was all number of hurdles to overcome, from the continued issue of suitable long distance weather forecast to the far thornier matter of choosing an aircrew to fly the mission. While such considerations were being weighed up and agonized over, amongst those personnel files George Baker looked through were Ken Gatward and Gilbert Fern, two of just seven officers and seven SNCO aircrew potentially earmarked for the mission. Having sent out copies of a questionnaire to a dozen Beaufighter squadron and station commanders, the response was as he had expected: all had one or may be two crews they could recommend.

By the 30 April, Baker and Joubert had reviewed the folder on the matter, choosing Gatward and Fern. Events moved swiftly after that. A letter was drafted for Joubert to be dispatched to Wing Commander Edward Woods to release Ken and Gilbert from ops. A few days later, on 5 May, Gatward and Fern had been ordered to Coastal Command HQ by way of RAF Northolt.

The pair had no idea of what the C-in-C of Coastal Command wanted to discuss. The cable from Eastbury Park was, for the most part just as vague, although their CO Woods knew it was due to his recommendation their names hadn't been added to the Mayfly for Thursday, Gatward and Fern arrived at Northolt where an Air Force driver then made much haste, at a furious pace. Twenty-four minutes after leaving the airfield their chauffeur turned into the main gate of RAF Coastal Command's Eastbury Park at Northwood. Passes were checked and rechecked then, Gatward and Fern had to hand over a brightly coloured security pass before making their way up a long driveway that led up to the gothic entrance of Eastbury Park. Stepping out, Gatward and Fern passed the entrance and were shown straight into Joubert's office, which was on the ground floor, along with those of his other senior staff.

Waiting for them was Baker and his boss Joubert. He quickly put the two airmen at ease, took off his cap, sat down and waved a hand for them to sit, while next to him stood the fair skinned Barker.

Their interview began. 'Gatward and Fern, there's a special mission coming along, I wondered if you'd be interested,' asked Joubert, 'I'm afraid it's not very safe!'

'What's it all about?' replied Gatward.

'It's a difficult situation. I can't divulge anything to you, unless I know you're interested.'

Within seconds came a positive response from Gatward. 'What about your navigator,' Joubert asked Gatward.

'Sir, I do not think Fern will be interested because he is married.'

'Oh, yes I am,' he replied.

Joubert spoke about the Paris parade on the Champs-Elyséss, whilst Baker laid out a map of the French capital, and recent photographic reconnaissance snaps.

'But, what is the actual mission?' Gatward asked Baker.

'Fly low level down the Champs-Elyséss, strafe the musicians and soldiers, and if that fails attack the Gestapo Headquarters in the Ministère de la Marine.'

The meeting at Eastbury Park ended and it was back to Wattisham. Then on Wednesday, 6 May, Baker rang up Woods and told him that Gatward and Fern had to be at Thorney Island and report to Wing Commander Oliver 'Giles' Gilson the base commander. The training started with the pair flying *C-Charlie* from Thorney Island on repeated feint attacks against a wrecked hulk in the English Channel. Accompanying this training was a vast array of written and photograph material which the two men pored for many hours, including maps of northern France and photographs of Paris. SOE had expressed a willingness to co-operate and gave a couple of covertly taken photographs of the Ministère de la Marine too. However, in Eastbury Park, a change of tack had taken place with planners adding a symbolic twist to the mission.

At 09.00 hours on 8 May, Ken Gatward and Gilbert Fern arrived at Portsmouth Naval Dockyard. Their passes were checked twice then both were given directions to the Naval Quartermasters Store. A civilian in a buff coloured coat greeted them.

'We've come to collect the largest Tricolour you stock for the Navy,' said Gatward. The storekeeper duly complied and, after both airmen had signed several forms, they left with a suitably large French flag. 'When you make the run, we want you to drop the flag out over the Arc de Triomphe,' Barker had told Gatward on the telephone. They began experimenting this firstly on the ground with Fern pushing the flag down the planes flare chute. It was a large and cumbersome piece of material, which got jammed even when the propellers were run up. Stuck for ideas, Gilson introduced them to Cynthia the WAAF Section Officer in charge of the Parachute Packing Section: 'We cut the Tricolour in half, then got the girls to sew into the corners iron bars of roughly 4lb. in weight,' remembered Ken. In the evenings they would carry out drop trials by using maintenance trestles in Hanger 1 throwing them as high as they could up to the corrugated roof to see how they would unfurl when dropped and discovered the best way to fold them to get the correct unfurling.

One week after their arrival the Met Officer gave them the green light. At 11.30 hours, *C-Charlie* roared off, the Beaufighter disappearing across the Channel. But they had no sooner crossed the French coast than the cloud cover evaporated. Gatward turned about as instructed at the briefing for the mission given at 1100 hours that morning. Two days later, they aborted again and headed back to base. 'We tried it twice in the last two weeks of May, it didn't really look as though it was going to happen, because we'd be lucky to get cloud cover all the way to Paris,' wrote Gatward. In the Officers Mess he was surprised to see Pilot Officer's Alfred Sherwood and Richard Freshwater of 236 Squadron who had arrived that afternoon. Both greeted Gatward and gave him moral support 'as Gatward's patience was by then nearly exhausted,' say's Sherwood. They had brought *V-Victor* over with groundcrew from 8236 Service Echelon to provide maintenance on *C-Charlie*. Within an hour and a half of their arrival mechanics had began working on Gatward's aircraft. *V-Victor* would act as back up. As it was the Beaufighter would not be needed, but it was readied for use if called upon.

Despite whatever shortcomings there might have been, these dress rehearsals stood them in good stead. The afternoon and evening session on the 11th with the Senior Met Forecaster at Eastbury Park indicated to Joubert and his SASO the weather conditions were right. A brisk cipher was sent to Thorney Island that Operation *Squabble* was to be executed on 12 June.

It was another dismal day the Met weather forecast was plentiful and informative at Thorney Island it was raining, in France ten tenths cloud at 2,000 feet with heavy precipitation was about as good as they could possibly hope for, the Station Met Officer told them. Their briefing had been thorough now the operation was just an hour away. With satisfaction Gilson had seen the youthful Gilbert Fern plan his route meticulously, and also saw that Gatward and Fern had decided to ignore the stipulated safety height of 4,000 feet given by Baker, opting to fly at zero feet.

11.00 hours Fern had clambered into the back, and Gatward had strapped himself in. With everyone aboard the engines were run up and the pre-flight checks begun. Everything appeared to be in order aboard *C-Charlie*, just as he had expected as they had carried out a brief ten-minute take off and circuit taking in Chichester Cathedral and had already completed and signed the Form 700. With his helmet leads plugged into the intercom Gatward asked Fern if he was okay. The Beaufighter was ready to fly.

Fifteen minutes later *C-Charlie* thundered down the runway through a squall of rain and spray to climb into the air disappearing into the grey. Gatward dropped the plane to hug the waves and began the tedious flight across the Channel in the back Fern looked out through the Perspex blister canopy searching skies for enemy fighters before going back to check the co-ordinates twenty-eight minutes after take-off they were about to make landfall.

'French coast in one minute,' Fern declared.

Instantly Gatward eased the nose up slightly to get over the dunes. The rain easing off as they sped over France just eastwards of Fécamp at around thirty to fifty feet off the ground. Rouen came into view and then, in bright sunshine, they traced the line of the River Seine. From that low height Gatward could see masses of horses in fields and occasionally people stopped and looked in wonder at this low flying British plane. Twenty miles past Giverny, they caught sight of the Eiffel Tower and George took a bearing from the structure and guided Gatward straight into the Paris suburbs. Cruising at 220 mph, Gatward looped round the Eiffel Tower at 12.27 hours, then made off towards the Arc de Triomphe.

'Are you ready with the first flag?' asked Gatward.

'Yes, I'm ready all right, but the slip stream is nearly breaking my arm,' came the reply.

Fern was pushing the furled flag down the flare chute so that it caught the slipstream from the propellers. At the right moment, Fern loosened his grip and the Tricolour was gone. *C-Charlie* banked to port and roared down the Champs-Elyséss but there was no band or parade and the Parisians hadn't noticed their aircraft 'we didn't go far before we turned for our second circuit at 300 feet as low as we dared in case they had light flak emplacements on the roof tops,' explained Gatward, as he kept a wary eye out for obstacles.

'Flak,' shouted Fern into the intercom.

Fortunately, the tracer missed, and the plane was never in any danger as it began its second circuit, turning south towards the Opera House and the Seine. Gatward was on the right course to come square upon the Ministère de la Marine. Roaring along at below rooftop height, Fern could now see this time the Parisians running into the boulevard and one or two faces pinned to windows of apartments peering down on them. Figures in uniforms were scattered or hidden behind vehicles as their propeller wash ruffled chestnut trees, sent newspapers flying and German officers' caps cart-wheeling along the cobbles as *C-Charlie* raced along at 220mph. An eyewitness on the ground, Monsieur Luc, heard the engine noise but couldn't see anything at first and then he saw the aircraft. It was so low it seemed lower than third story apartment widows. Around him Frenchmen and women stood bewildered and dumfounded in the street and boulevard, while German officers and soldiers brushed down their uniforms and retrieved their caps. And got on with business as if nothing had happened.

As Luc watched from the ground, Fern was snapping away with a handheld F24 camera hoping that they'd be in focus, before Gatward altered course by turning 270 degrees. With a 'turning now,' over the intercom, Gatward brought the aircraft squarely onto the target. Then, making sure there were no Parisians in the line of fire, at a range of around 500 yards Gatward pressed the gun button letting fly with the 20mm cannon, swinging the nose so that it raked from the second floor to the apex. Gatward flinched as he guided the Beaufighter over the roof with less than five feet to spare. He heard Fern on the intercom; 'Second flag gone, it went out like a harpoon.'

'Lets hope it landed squarely across their front door,' replied Gatward.

He wheeled the Beaufighter round and at 12.30 hours, shoved off home, closely followed by 20mm tracer from a flak emplacement as Stab/ Flak-Regiment 59 responded to the wailing sirens.

Clear of the French capital they dropped to thirty feet and hugged the ground. 'It was somewhere in the countryside when Ken first went smack into a swarm of flies,' remembered Gilbert Fern. Flies hit the windscreen and using the wiper blade just made it worse! They then dodged a French barge being pulled by a horse and, as the Beaufighter lurched upwards, a startled crow flew into the starboard radiator, which caused the oil temperature gauge to fluctuate, as swarms of small flies continued to pester *C-Charlie* all the way to the French coast. Eventually the bird started to disintegrate, and the radiator begun to cool down, much to the relief of Gatward. Luckily, crossing the Channel they flew into rain and this helped wash all the flies off. Nothing else troubled them. The open sea now lay before them as Gatward followed Ferns route home.

13.00 hours Baker and his WAAF driver left Eastbury Park and drove to Northolt, reaching the base within half an hour. Ken Gatward and Gilbert Fern landed there safely at 13.53 hours. There to greet them was the Station Commander, John Hallings-Pott, congratulating them with Baker who whisked them away to Eastbury Park, Northwood. On arrival, Air Chief Marshal Joubert hurried over to personally greet the arrival of Gatward and Fern. Gilbert handed over the heavy F24 camera and it was swiftly taken away for the film to be processed to give confirmation of their flight – roughly sixty-one photographs were developed. 'Some good low-level ones, including a superb shot of a large notice outside the Grande Palais that read *"La Vie Nouvelle"* – The New Life,' said Gatward, 'which was something of an understatement given the amount of repression.' Finishing their report both returned to Northolt, there the mechanics had removed what remained of the French crow and laid it to rest on the airfield.

Beaufighter *C-Charlie* flew into Thorney Island and Gatward was immediately impressed by the reception from Sherwood, Freshwater, Woods, Kent and Gilson all congratulated them. When Ken and Gilbert returned to their base at Wattisham two days later in driving rain, the Parisians knew about the gallant aviators, and the dropping of the Tricolour in Paris as leaflets descended on the capital proclaiming the success of Operation *Squabble*. Then on 17 June, at 12.15 hours, after the familiar notes of Beethoven's Fifth Symphony, the broadcast from the BBC began with the words; 'Last Friday before mid-day, Parisians had an unexpected visitor ...'

The message stiffened the resolve of the people throughout France and that of the Resistance. Their Paris visit also came at the same time General Erwin Rommel, out in the North African desert, launched an attack near the Gazala Line. Allied troops were driven back to Tobruk, and by the evening of 20 June, Tobruk had been scythed in two and with no hope of breaking through the German lines, the white flag was raised. Tobruk surrendered with the loss of 32,000 men. 'As these men were struggling desperately against powerful enemy forces the RAF Coastal Command Beaufighter tourist excursion to Paris was a balm for hurt pride,' wrote the editor of *Tatler* magazine.

The investiture of medals for Operation *Squabble* took place in London, Sergeant Gilbert 'George' Fern received both his Distinguished Flying Medal and a raise in rank and pay with an immediate commission. Gatward was present with a Distinguished Flying Cross. There was an immediate clammier for every scrap of information about their extraordinary wartime achievement. Soon after other engagements, both would return to flying coastal missions against enemy shipping – a new chapter was dawning.

Glossary

AA	Anti-Aircraft
AASF	Advanced Air Striking Force
AOC	Air Officer Commanding
ASDIC	Anti-Submarine Detection Equipment (Sonar)
ASR	Air Sea Rescue
BDST	British Double Summer Time
BEF	British Expeditionary Force 1939 – 1940
BST	British Summer Time
CdeG	Commander of the Legion of Honor
CGM	Conspicuous Gallantry Medal
C-in-C	Commander-in-Chief
CIU	Central [Photographic] Intelligence Unit, Medmenham
CO	Commanding Officer
COTU	Coastal Operational Training Unit
DFC	Distinguished Flying Cross
DI	Detective Inspector
DSC	Distinguished Service Cross (an officers-only award)
DSO	Distinguished Service Medal (an officers-only medal)
Do	Dornier
FFAF	Free French Air Force
FAF	French Air Force
Feldwebel	German non-commissioned officer equivalent to a sergeant
Flak	Anti-Aircraft Air Defence
Flak-ship	see Vorpostenboot
Fw	Focke-Wulf
Geschwader	Luftwaffe group of squadrons (staffeln)
He	Heinkel
HF/DF	High Frequency Direction Finding

Hispano-Suiza	Spanish-Swiss automotive/engineering/aviation company. French subsidiary of Hispano-Suiza purchased by French Government 1938. Developed 20mm auto cannon, one being the HS 404. It was licensed for production in Britain in the Second World War and equipped the Bristol Beaufighter and de Havilland Mosquito
HQ	Headquarters
IFF	Identification Friend and Foe
JG	Jagdgeschwader – fighter group
Ju	Junkers
KG	Kampfgeschwader – bomber group
Kriegsmarine	German Navy
Luftwaffe	German Air Force
Mae West	Inflatable life jacket
Me	Messerschmitt
MGB	Motor Gun Boat (MGB 314 – Fairmile 'C'- Class boat)
ML	Motor Launch (Fairmile 'B' – Class boat)
MO	Medical Officer
MP	Member of Parliament
MTB	Motor Torpedo Boat
MT	Motor Transport
NAFFI	Navy, Army and Air Force Institutes (British Armed Forces 'shop')
NCO	Non-Commissioned Officer
NWC	Norwegian War Cross
OKM	Oberkommando der Marine – Supreme Naval Command
OTU	Operational Training Unit
PC	Police Constable
POW	Prisoner of War
PRU	Photographic Reconnaissance Unit
RAAF	Royal Australian Air Force
RAF	Royal Air Force
RAFVR	Royal Air Force Volunteer Reserve
RCAF	Royal Canadian Air Force
réseau	Resistance or Escape and Evader Network
RMS	Royal Mail Ship or Royal Mail Steamer
RN	Royal Navy
RNVR	Royal Navy Volunteer Reserve
RNZAF	Royal New Zealand Air Force

Rt. Hon.	The Right Honourable
SNCO	Senior Non-Commissioned Officer
SOE	Special Operations Executive
Sortie	An individual operational flight by a pilot or aircrew, so a squadron or flight could fly up to twelve sorties at one time
Staffel	German squadron
TA	Territorial Army
U-boat	abbreviation of Unterseeboot (undersea boat) German submarine
VR	Volunteer Reserve
Vorpostenboot	Requisitioned fishing trawler strengthened to carry one or two medium-calibre guns (e.g. 88mm), many light automatic anti-air artillery pieces (20-40mm), and a varying number of machine guns
WAAF	Women's Auxiliary Air Force
Wehrmacht	German armed forces
Y Service	British signals intelligence
Zerstörer	Destroyer – Luftwaffe name for the Messerschmitt 110

Notes

Abbreviations used in notes

AC   Authors Correspondence
AI   Authors Interview
NAA   National Australian Archive
PR   Personal Relative
RAFM   Royal Air Force Museum
TNA   The National Archives

Chapter 1: Wing Commander 'Jack' Davenport DSO, DFC* GM

1. Kristen Alexander, *Jack Davenport*, p. 4
2. Philip Davenport cited Norwegian NRK interview 2005
3. ibid
4. NAA B4747, Davenport/Jack Napier; NAA B883, Nugent/Anthony Arthur Banks
5. Papers History & Heritage, Air Force Canberra
6. Philip Davenport unpublished memoir
7. Ian Gordon, *Strike and Strike Again*, p. 7
8. Harry Moyle, *Hampden File*, p. 9
9. NAA A11271, 20/AIR
10. Philip Davenport author's interview BBC Studios VE-Day Special 2005
11. Philip Davenport cited Shelia met Jack on 13 November 1942 at base dance so was familiar with surroundings when the couple return from honeymoon
12. NAA A11271, 1/1/AIR
13. NAA A11271, 107/P1

14. Accident and Inquiry Report; Baird Adj; Davenport Sqn OC; Coulson base CO RAF Museum and Papers History & Heritage, Air Force Canberra
15. RAF Form 540/541 455 Squadron ORB and Inquiry Report RAF Museum and Papers History & Heritage, Air Force Canberra
16. Papers History & Heritage, Air Force Canberra; NAA A705, 166/38/682; British Journal of Plastic Surgery Sept 1971, pp. 419-20
17. Honours & Awards Form via History & Heritage, Air Force Canberra and NAA A9300, Davenport J N

Chapter 2: Wing Commander Edric 'Sam' McHardy DSO, DFC* CdeG

18. Unpublished memoir, *Some One on My Shoulder* (Eric 'Sam' McHardy 1991)
19. PR Sally Goldsworthy, Sam's School Diary
20. Cited in *Some One on My Shoulder* (Eric 'Sam' McHardy 1991)
21. *New Zealand Herald* 1 May to 31st May 1938 advertisement insert
22. RAF Accident Report Card RAFM
23. Cited in *Some One on My Shoulder* (Eric 'Sam' McHardy 1991)
24. MS-2003-107, Box 22 AWM Museum, New Zealand
25. Cited in *Some One on My Shoulder* (Eric 'Sam' McHardy 1991)
26. No. 118/40 Transfer of Fighter Squadrons to Coastal Command Signed D. G. D. Donaldson, Air Vice Marshal, Director of Organisation 14 Feb 40
27. Cited in *Some One on My Shoulder* (Eric 'Sam' McHardy 1991)
28. PR via Ancestry website
29. Cited in *Some One on My Shoulder* (Eric 'Sam' McHardy 1991)
30. Cited in *Some One on My Shoulder* (Eric 'Sam' McHardy 1991)
31. Andrew D. Bird, *Coastal Dawn*, p. 55
32. Cited in *Some One on My Shoulder* (Eric 'Sam' McHardy 1991)
33. Cited in unofficial 235 Squadron War Diary for 1940
34. Cited in *Some One on My Shoulder* (Eric 'Sam' McHardy 1991)
35. TNA AIR27/2074
36. Ancestry website & Canadian Armed Force Archive Ottawa, Canada
37. Crump/Raymond RCAF Papers
38. TNA AIR27/1807
39. The National Museum of Royal Navy Portsmouth – HMS *Prince Leopold* Damage Control Notes & Papers Operation *Archery*
40. TNA DEFE 2/80

41. AHB Medical Report – amputate leg; with prostatic leg Day took a staff role . . . going back to fly missions over Europe.
42. Cited in Reginald Neville Smith letter to Headmaster January 1942
43. TNA AIR27/487; Reginald Neville Smith letter to Headmaster January 1942
44. Cited in *Some One on My Shoulder* (Eric 'Sam' McHardy 1991)
45. The National Museum of Royal Navy Portsmouth – HMS *Prince Leopold* Papers Operation *Archery*
46. ibid
47. Cited in Reginald Neville Smith letter to Headmaster January 1942
48. Cited in *Some One on My Shoulder* (Eric 'Sam' McHardy 1991)
49. University of London Queen Mary's College – Remembering The Fallen
50. Cravens Part in the Great War www.cpgw.org.uk
51. PR Illingworth Family Scrap Album; Lot 141 C. W. Harrison & Son Collectors Items - Wednesday 3rd December 2014 - J. Mosby Auctioneer
52. AIR27/1515
53. McConnell Diary entry December 1941 (Authors copy)
54. Cited in *Some One on My Shoulder* (Eric 'Sam' McHardy 1991)
55. AIR27/1786
56. MS-2003-107, Box 22 AWM Museum, New Zealand
57. Cited in *Some One on My Shoulder* (Eric 'Sam' McHardy 1991)

Chapter 3: Flying Officer Lloyd Trigg VC, DFC

58. TNA AIR27/1173
59. C.B. 04051 (85) U-468 Interrogation of Survivors – October 1943 Royal Navy Intelligence Division, uboatarchive.net
60. Cited in Watkinson Log Book 13/08/1943
61. Cited in newspaper clipping undated Air Force Museum of New Zealand Collections & Research – Lloyd Trigg VC DFC Archive Box
62. ibid
63. Papers Royal Australian Navy Captain Stanley Darling, DSC**, VRD, RANR
64. TNA AIR28/71
65. NAA A12372, R/327/H
66. TNA AIR28/71
67. ibid
68. Air Force Museum of New Zealand Collections & Research – Lloyd Trigg VC DFC Archive

69. Maeve Waggott, Whangarei Boys' High School, Whangarei, New Zealand; Air Force Museum of New Zealand Collections & Research – Lloyd Trigg VC DFC Archive
70. Ancestry website
71. Air Force Museum of New Zealand Collections & Research – Lloyd Trigg VC DFC Archive
72. ibid
73. ibid Trigg Logbook 4/5/43 – Ref: 2015/342
74. ibid Trigg Logbook 5/4/43 – Ref: 2015/342 gives initials Earl L – US Air Force Historical Research Agency Maxwell, AFB, USA supplied logs giving pilots surname
75. Ancestry website & Canadian Armed Force Archive Ottawa, Canada
76. USA Entry & Immigration Card
77. TNA AIR27/1173
78. Goodwin/George Nicholas, J/14450 Canadian Armed Force Archive Ottawa, Canada
79. National Probate Calendar 15Mar1945 & British Newspaper Archive
80. 1939 Census
81. TNA AIR27/1802
82. RAF Accident Report Card and Award Citation RAFM
83. Air Force Museum of New Zealand Collections & Research – Lloyd Trigg VC DFC Archive Box
84. TNA AIR27/1173
85. ORB US Air Force Historical Research Agency Maxwell, AFB, USA
86. U-468 War Diary Summary German U-boat-Museum Cuxhaven, Germany; C.B. 04051 (85) U-468 Interrogation of Survivors – October 1943 Royal Navy Intelligence Division, uboatarchive.net
87. Peter Cremer, *U-Boat Commander*, p. 146
88. Leonard Turner, *War in the Southern Ocean*, p. 152
89. Air Force Museum of New Zealand Collections & Research – Lloyd Trigg VC DFC Archive
90. ORB US Air Force Historical Research Agency Maxwell, AFB, USA
91. Day Ops Secret Form Orange 11Aug43 faded negative of dialogue *D-Dog* SANDFA
92. Air Force Museum of New Zealand Collections & Research – Lloyd Trigg VC DFC Archive
93. C.B. 04051 (85) U-468 Interrogation of Survivors – October 1943 Royal Navy Intelligence Division, uboatarchive.net
94. 'Fliegendes Stachelschwein' = Flying Porcupine
95. TNA AIR27/1173
96. TNA AIR27/761

97. C.B. 04051 (85) U-468 Interrogation of Survivors – October 1943 Royal Navy Intelligence Division, uboatarchive.net
98. TNA WO98/8/792 Victoria Cross details of Trigg, Lloyd Allan
99. Air Force Museum of New Zealand Collections & Research – Lloyd Trigg VC DFC Archive
100. ibid
101. www.victoriacross.org.uk

Chapter 4: Group Captain Gage 'Bill' Sise DSO*, DFC*

102. BBC Archive Caversham, Berkshire broadcast script dated 22 November 1942
103. TNA AIR27/1514
104. Andrew D. Bird, *Coastal Dawn*, p. 216
105. NAA B883, VX43668
106. RAF Accident Report Card RAFM
107. PR John Sise, son of the late Group Captain
108. AC 1995
109. PR Illingworth Family Scrap Album; Lot 141 C. W. Harrison & Son Collectors Items - Wednesday 3rd December 2014 - J. Mosby Auctioneer
110. NA AIR27/1514; PR John Sise, 'Bill' Sise Logbook 12/1/1941
111. RAF Coastal Command Quarterly Review 1941 RAFM; TNA AIR27/1517
112. ibid
113. McConnell Diary (author's copy)
114. TNA AIR27/1517
115. uboat.net
116. McConnell Diary (Authors copy)
117. AC Joyce Winifred Mack, Poole, Dorset 1993
118. Cited in Papers addressed to Mompesson House, The Close, Salisbury. Courtesy of H. H. Bolitho Estate, Brighton, East Sussex 2011
119. AI Marlow, Buckinghamshire 2012
120. PR John Fraser, son of the late Squadron Leader cited in press cuttings
121. 1932 RAF Hendon Display Programme and typed biography of individual display pilots of 25 Squadron taking part RAFM
122. Cited in AC 1996
123. TNA AIR27/1092 and Canadian Armed Force Archive Ottawa, Canada
124. PR John Sise, 'Bill' Sise Logbook 20/11/1942

125. NA AIR27/1517 and Analysis of Faults All Coastal Command Station Aircraft Prior to Operations for 1943 via NAA
126. AC with Angus McIntosh 1990
127. ibid
128. TNA AIR27/1517
129. PR Mrs. Treadwell cited family letter about Fraser. 1994
130. Dutch Air War Study Group. 5./JG 1 claimed a Beaufort at 16.08hrs 75km West of Zandvoort.
131. TNA AIR27/1517 and PR Ann Maris Edney – Geoffrey Edney did not see his baby daughter born 2 February 1943. Ann herself died in 2006.
132. AC memories of North Coates, Portreath and Banff 1994
133. PR John Sise
134. AC with Angus McIntosh 1990
135. PR John Sise 'Bill' Sise Logbook 20/1l/1942 and RAF Accident Report Card RAFM
136. TNA AIR27/1517
137. AC with Angus McIntosh 1990
138. From handwritten notes by Dudley Peyton-Ward for MRAF Sholto Douglas on history of RAF Coastal Command 1946
139. GB 0099 KCLMA Wheeler, N
140. *Hampshire Telegraph* 31 Mar 1939, *Sevenoaks Chronicle and Kentish Advertiser, Kentish Courier* 16 Jun 1939 and *Western Morning News* 22 Sep 1937
141. Cited in letter Elizabeth Vivienne Esnie Parsons memories. Died January 2007 a widower Norwich, Norfolk.
142. TNA AIR27/1448
143. 1939 England and Wales Register
144. Papers Canadian Armed Force Archive Ottawa, Canada
145. PR Felicity Cuttle cited in interview with her father the late Group Captain Raymond Price Marlow, Buckinghamshire 2015
146. AIR27/1444
147. Court of Enquiry RAF Form 412 dated 9 Jun 44 via Canadian Armed Force Archive, Ottawa, Canada
148. PR Anthony Phillips son of the late Wing Commander and Frederic Henhoff
149. Cited in Squadron Leader Henry 'Hal' Randall's interview by Frederic Henhoff
150. Cited in unpublished diary for 1944 of Wing Commander John Yonge
151. Cited in unpublished *A War Time Diary* 1944 of James 'Jimmy' Rodgers

152. 1939 England and Wales Register; PR Robert Letcher cited in letter 24 Aug 1940
153. Cited in unpublished *A War Time Diary* 1944 of James 'Jimmy' Rodgers
154. PR Felicity Cuttle cited in interview with her late father Group Captain Raymond Price Marlow, Buckinghamshire 2016
155. Cited in AC Lawrie Shield 1995; TNA AIR27/1444
156. Cited in unpublished *A War Time Diary* 1944 of James 'Jimmy' Rodgers
157. ibid
158. ibid
159. Cited in unpublished diary for 1944 of Wing Commander John Yonge
160. PR Russell Family Estate, Marble Arch London Logbook 14/08/1944
161. Cited in unpublished *A War Time Diary* 1944 of James 'Jimmy' Rodgers
162. PR Bill Atkinson, son of the late Wing Commander
163. *A War Time Diary* 1944 of James 'Jimmy' Rodgers; AC 1996
164. PR Anne Orrock, wife of the late Air Commodore. (2003)
165. PR John Sise, son of the late Group Captain. (2017)

Chapter 5: Flight Lieutenant Denis Healy DSO NWC

166. Abingdon School Archive Healy/Dennis (2016); Healy Papers from Giles, and Peter Healy (2017)
167. Papers of Dennis Healy Abingdon School Archive Sarah Wearne, Archivist (2016)
168. Healy Papers from Giles, and Peter Healy (2017)
169. Ernest Schofield & Roy Conyers Nesbit, *Arctic Airmen*, p. 32
170. ibid
171. ibid p. 33
172. Mitchell Papers, Tyne & Wear Archives
173. Ernest Schofield & Roy Conyers Nesbit, *Arctic Airmen*, p. 34
174. ibid p. 34
175. ibid
176. TNA H47/MR cited in Charles Usher's handwritten notes.
177. Cited in Ernest Schofield & Roy Conyers Nesbit, *Arctic Airmen*, p. 50
178. ibid
179. Alexander Glen, *Footholds against the Whirlwind*, pp. 91-3
180. ibid p. 94
181. ibid p. 96

182. ibid p. 71 and RAF Accident Report Card RAFM
183. Cited in original handwritten account by Ernest Schofield via John Healy
184. Alexander Glen, *Footholds against the Whirlwind*, p. 100
185. Dennis Healy, in original handwritten account by Ernest Schofield via John Healy
186. Cited in Ernest Schofield & Roy Conyers Nesbit, *Arctic Airmen*, p. 76
187. TNA ADM 239/177
188. TNA AIR27/1721
189. Cited in Ernest Schofield & Roy Conyers Nesbit, *Arctic Airmen*, p. 100
190. Healy Papers from Giles, and Peter Healy
191. TNA ADM199/730
192. TNA ADM199/758
193. Bradfield College Archive
194. Cited Dennis Healy, in original handwritten account by Ernest Schofield via John Healy
195. Cited in George Adamson diary
196. House of Lords Select Committee on the Arctic 2017 Paper

Chapter 6: Lieutenant Colonel Jean Maurice Guedj DSO DFC*

197. Armee de la L'Air Service Hitorique Archive Paris, France 2016
198. AC Madam Marie Guedj via her daughter Sarah Dars 2017
199. Maurice Guedj Papers Armee de la L'Air Service Hitorique Archive Paris, France 2016
200. Felix Guedj Papers Armee de la L'Air Service Hitorique Archive Paris, France 2016; Maurice Guedj Papers Armee de la L'Air Service Hitorique Archive Paris, France 2016
201. London, French Embassy, Air Attaché Colonel Patrice Hugret and Armee de la L'Air Service Hitorique Archive Paris, France
202. Cited in Charles Corder correspondence on Guedj 1993 to 2003
203. Cited in Maurice Guedj Papers Armee de la L'Air Service Hitorique Archive Paris, France 2016
204. Cited in Charles Corder correspondence on Guedj 1993 to 2003
205. Edouard Pinot Papers Armee de la L'Air Service Hitorique Archive Paris, France 2016
206. Maurice Guedj Papers Armee de la L'Air Service Hitorique Archive Paris, France 2016
207. Cited by Roger Morewood 2010
208. 1911 Census
209. Old Palmerians Association Archive 2016

210. TNA AIR27/1496
211. Maurice Guedj Papers Armee de la L'Air Service Hitorique Archive Paris, France 2016
212. Cited in taped interview by Inniss via James Inniss 2014
213. TNA AIR27/1496 and Maurice Guedj Papers Armee de la L'Air Service Hitorique Archive Paris, France 2016
214. ibid and cited in Charles Corder correspondence on Guedj 1993 to 2003
215. RAF Accident Report Card RAFM
216. Martial Valin Papers Diary unnumbered page Armee de la L'Air Service Hitorique Archive Paris, France 2016
217. From a letter from Montague-Smith to Valin Maurice Guedj Papers Armee de la L'Air Service Hitorique Archive Paris, France 2016
218. Cited in Maurice Guedj Papers Armee de la L'Air Service Hitorique Archive Paris, France 2016
219. Cited in unpublished diary for 1944 of Wing Commander John Yonge
220. TNA AIR27/1496
221. Cited in 'Bill' Parfitt's AC 1991 to 1997
222. Cited in Henry Hector Bolitho, *Task for Coastal Command*, p. 124
223. Cited in 'Pat' Ross's AC and AI 1990
224. TNA AIR28/49
225. TNA AIR27/1496
226. Bird, *Separate Little War*, p. 51
227. TNA AIR28/49
228. *Some One on My Shoulder* (Eric 'Sam' McHardy 1991); TNA AIR27/1444
229. TNA AIR28/49
230. Cited in Narrative of Operations Orange Form DAL/03/11th Jan 1945
231. ibid and TNA AIR27/1786
232. PR Russell Family Estate, Marble Arch London Logbook 11/01/1945
233. TNA AIR27/1786 and DAL/03/11th Jan 1945
234. NAA A8231
235. Cited in Donald Clause AC 1997
236. NAA A8231
237. P/P75 RAAF (RAF Form 1580) within NAA A8231
238. AI Thames Masonic Lodge 1993
239. Cited in Philip Davenport authors interview BBC Studios VE-Day Special 2005; cited in author's correspondence with Own Burns former 235 Squadron Blenheim pilot 1995

240. TNA AIR28/49 and AIR 15/481
241. Cited in author's correspondence with Joyce Sherlock nee Trovey WAAF 1992
242. TNA AIR27/1496
243. Cited in diary page of Donald Clause for 11 Jan 1945 AC 1997
244. NAA A8231
245. Cited in diary page of Donald Clause for 11 Jan 1945 copied to author 1997
246. TNA AIR27/1732
247. Cited in author's correspondence with Rudi Artner, Austria
248. Cited in diary page of Donald Clause for 15 Jan 1945 AC 1997
249. ibid
250. PR Ellis Family logbook entry 15 Jan 1945 2016
251. Cited in 235 Squadron magazine July 1945 edition
252. PR cited in letter from son of 'Jock' Couttie 2002
253. PR Maria Guedj aged 102 via her daughter Sarah Dars 2017

Chapter 7: Wing Commander Roger Morewood MID

254. Cited in Eulogy for Roger via Andrew and Rowena Buck
255. Cited in papers of Alice Percy Cheltenham Ladies College, Mrs. Rachel Roberts Archivist
256. ibid
257. Eulogy for Roger via Andrew and Rowena Buck
258. Cited in papers of Roger Morewood Abingdon School, Sarah Wearne, Archivist
259. Eulogy for Roger via Andrew and Rowena Buck
260. The University of Edinburgh - Alumni Officer, Cara Christie
261. Eulogy for Roger via Andrew and Rowena Buck
262. Cited in papers John Roysse Lodge (no. 7957)
263. ibid
264. Cited in HC Deb 25 June 1935 vol 303 c955W
265. Cited in AI 2010
266. 56 Squadron Association
267. TNA AIR27/527 and cited in Roger Morewood's logbook
268. ibid and cited in 248 Squadron Line Book 1939 – 1941 p.1
269. RAF Hendon construction papers RAFM
270. ibid
271. Cited in Aircraft Movements Card – Miles Magister R1832 RAFM
272. Cited in TNA AIR 28/64 and AIR28/603

273. PR Sharman Family and Ancestry site
274. Cited in 248 Squadron Line Book 1939 – 1941 p.2
275. Cited in AI 2010
276. Canadian Armed Force Archive Ottawa, Canada
277. Cited in Bird, *Coastal Dawn*, p. 65
278. Cited in AC with Rodney Murry-Steele 1995
279. Cited in 248 Squadron Line Book 1939 – 1941
280. ibid
281. TNA AIR27/1496
282. PR Sue Kenworthy
283. Cited in 248 Squadron Line Book 1939 – 1941
284. ibid
285. Cited in papers at Durham University
286. *The Surrey Advertiser* March 1935
287. PR Robert 'Bob' Harwood
288. TNA AIR27/1496
289. Cited in Roger Morewood's logbook
290. ibid
291. Roger Morewood cited in AI 2010
292. ibid
293. TNA AIR27/1496
294. Roger Morewood cited in interview with author 2010
295. ibid
296. Cited in Roger Morewood's logbook
297. TNA AIR28/445
298. ibid
299. Cited in Roger Morewood's logbook
300. TNA AIR28/445

Chapter 8: Flight Lieutenant Allan Triggs MBE DFC and Flying Officer John Watson

301. TNA AIR 27/1105/1
302. ibid
303. Cited in NAA: A705 163/59/73
304. Cited in NAA: A705 163/156/103
305. John H. F. Watson Statement of events 18/8/1942 ibid p. 27
306. ibid
307. AVM Peter Cracroft cited in NAA: A705 163/156/103
308. Ms Alice Bolter, AI 2016

309. TNA AIR 27/1105/5
310. TNA AIR 27/1912/3
311. http://cornishmuse.blogspot.com/2013/01/barbara-tribe-sculptors-life
312. Cited in papers of sculptor Barbara Tribe, Australian War Museum, Canberra
313. Cited in NAA: A9186, 48
314. ibid
315. ibid

Selected Sources

Chapter 1: Wing Commander 'Jack' Davenport AC DSO DFC* GM – 455 Squadron

Author's Interview with Phil Davenport in 2005 at the BBC Studios.
Author's Correspondence with Stevie Davenport, 2012 – 2017.
Author's Interview Ronald with 'Ron' Day, 2005 BBC Studios
Norwegian NRK interview between author, Phil Davenport and Ron Day, 2005 BBC Studios.
Davenport Rescue Papers and Award Citations via Australian Government Archive, Canberra.
No. 455 Squadron ORB via Australian National Archive, Canberra.
Royal Australian Air Force Historical Branch, 2016.
Royal Australian Air Force Air Attaché, Australian Embassy, London.
RAF Museum Archives London.
Author's Correspondence & Interview with MRAF Sir Arthur 'Bert' Harris, 1st Baronet, GCB, OBE, AFC 1977-1983.
Joint Forces Command Archive, Northwood, Middlesex.
Sholto Douglas Papers.

Chapter 2: Wing Commander Edric 'Sam' McHardy – Someone on My Shoulder

Author's Collection: *Some One on My Shoulder*, unpublished By Sam McHardy, 1991.
Author's Interview with Tom McNeil, 'Early Days' Duxford, 2012.
Markby, Jack Eugene, F/O –killed 30 October 1931 at Hucknall in a Tutor of No.3 Flying Training School, Grantham. Member of 504 (County of Nottingham) Squadron. He was pilot of the aircraft.

McHardy, Louis, F/O – killed 30 October 1931 at Hucknall in a Tutor of No.3 Flying Training School, Grantham. Member of No. 504 (County of Nottingham) Squadron.

RAFMA 5 March 1940, Flying Accident Card Form 1180 Blenheim IV 4829.

Stab I./KG30 Junkers Ju 88A-1. One engine damaged by AA fire and cockpit hood lost during attack on HMS *Southampton* in the Firth of Forth. Finally engaged by Blue Section of No. 602 Squadron (S/L A. McKellar, F/Lt G. Pinkerton, and F/O P. A. Webb) and ditched in the sea off Crail 2.45 p.m. (Ff) Hptmn Helmut Pohle (Gruppenkommandeur) rescued – badly injured face in landing. (Bs) Gefr August Schleicher rescued badly wounded - later died, (Bf) Uffz Kurt Naake killed, and (Beo) Fw Werner Weise missing. Aircraft 4D+AK 100% loss.

Some One on My Shoulder, p.18: 'Woods remarked that there was a pair of Hawker Hurricanes escorting them – within a few minutes their Blenheim was in the sea having been shot down.'

Maurice Baird in conversation with Sam McHardy in 1945 and 1946 about the ditching of his Blenheim fighter.

Flight Lieutenant Kenneth Kershaw Hay-Roe RCAF reported for flying duties on 2 August 1941 to 404 Squadron from 400 Squadron RAF Odiham. 'No Flying' given on Blenheim between 5 and 7 August, sent off solo that afternoon.

Pilot Officer John 'Johnnie' Day navigator and bomb aimer underwent extensive surgery, and the medical team had to amputate a leg. With a prostatic leg Day would take on a ground role before going back to fly missions.

Sergeant Alexander Ascroft Waldie the 29-year-old from Jedburgh, died on 12 August 1942 whilst on a mission against targets in Le Harve.

Sergeant Reginald Neville Smith Plumtree School Rhodesia 1933-1938 Record: House Prefect, 1937; Head of Lloyd House and School Prefect, 1938; Sergeant in Cadet Corps; Bisley VIII, 1936, 1937, 1938; Rugger 1st XV, 1937-38 (Colours); Swimming Captain and Colours, 1937; Cricket 2nd XI.

Reginald Neville Smith letter to Headmaster Plumtree School Rhodesia, January 1942 *Plucked to Safety* gives a time of in the water as 40 minutes before being rescued.

Lieutenant Kennedy Brown presented Reginald Neville Smith with a Naval Whistle in case he needed to be rescued again. One of the recommendations from this first combined operation was that all RAF and Naval aircrew be issued with a whistle. This was adopted by Fighter, Bomber and Coastal Command.

Kenneth Illingworth Family Notes, County Archive, Yorkshire.

Australian Government Archive File A705, 163/55/151 – John Worrall Roche RAAF (402191) 26 combat missions flown: Shot down into the sea by Me109 on Vågsøy raid.

Author's Collection, Roderick McConnell Diary, entry December 1941.

Wing Commander George Bernard-Smith entered dense cloud. The forty-year-old, former Sherborne pupil and civil pilot, misread the altimeter and flew into the ground at Dykes End Forfar, on a flight to Dyce.

AC1 David 'Dave' Clarke and AC2 Norman Leitch Statutory Death Notice indicates cause of death due to gunshot wound by enemy action.

Chapter 3: Flying Officer Lloyd Allan Trigg VC DFC – Consolidated Courage

Whangarei Boys High School, Whangarei, New Zealand.

Royal New Zealand Air Force Museum Archives.

Royal South African Air Force Archives.

Day Ops Secret Form Orange Negative, 11 August 1943 typed dialogue via SANDFA.

South African National Defence Force Archive.

Auckland Museum, Auckland New Zealand.

Auckland Museum Cenotaph.

Auckland Library, Auckland New Zealand.

U-boat Museum Cuxhaven.

Flight Sergeant Thomas 'Tommy' Cater Sunderland *H-Harry* memories August 1943.

490 Squadron: 11 August 1943 Wing Commander Douglas Baird: the U-boat attacked was *U-757* (Kptlt Friedrich Deetz), which reported an unsuccessful attack by a flying boat in naval grid EK7829 (approx. 11°09'N/18°27'W) at 12.32 hrs on 11 August 1943. The U-boat was not damaged by the depth charges that fell 50 meters astern. It escaped by crash-diving after keeping the aircraft at a distance using the AA guns for 20 minutes.

Short Sunderland: German nickname *'Fliegendes Stachelschwein'* (Flying Porcupine)

Edward Campbell Lacy Day.

Commodore James Powell DSO Rear Admiral.

Ancestry.com.

RAFMA.

IWM London.

Pilots Notes – Liberator.

Wing Commander William Ingle family papers via Ancestry.com.

ORB AIR27 1174 01.
ORB AIR27 1174 02.
ORB AIR27 1174 09.
ORB AIR27 1174 15.
ORB AIR27 1174 16.
New Zealand Newspaper Archive
London Gazette, Tuesday 2 November 1943.
Find-my-Past.com
Dudley Peyton-Ward notes *Coastal Command at War 1946* for MRAF Sholto Douglas.
C.B. 04051 (85) *U-468* Interrogation of Survivors – October 1943 RN Intel Div., via uboatarchive.net.
Lloyd Trigg Pilot's Log Book entries via Royal New Zealand Air Force Museum Archive.
Lloyd Trigg entry for flight from West Africa to Nassau for Liberator training, gave initials of 1st pilots during flights. Air Force Historical Research Agency, Maxwell AFB USA supplied logs for time period at Nassau revealing first and surname.

Chapter 4: Wing Commander 'Bill' Sise DSO* DFC* – Ship-Buster

BBC Archive Caversham, Berkshire, typed broadcast script dated 22 November 1942.
Aircraft Restoration Company, Duxford.
Harold Victor Charles Hoskins, unpublished memories.
Leonard Murphy Logbook.
ORB AIR27 1514 17 and 1514 18.
ORB AIR27 1514 25 and 1514 26 reference, 1 January 1941.
ORB AIR27 1515 15 reference McConnell, August and September 1942.
Alwyn Bonnett Papers RCAF Ottawa.
The *Guardian* Archive
Commander Christopher Montague Vernon Francis Dalrymple-Hay DSC, RN
Brigadier General R. M. Groves, C.B., D.S.O., A.F.C., who was born in 1880, served in the Mediterranean 1912-1914, went into the Royal Naval Air Service in 1915, became commander of the No. 1 Wing.
Flight Sergeant Roy Bartolotti died on 3 March 1943 whilst on a mission with 521 Squadron as navigator aboard a Mosquito damaged by Fw. 190. He bailed out 30 miles off Yarmouth and unfortunately drowned.
Hector Bolitho Papers University of Texas, Austin USA.

Warrant Officer Angus McIntosh DFC Logbook entry, 20 November 1942.

Group Captain Raymond Price DFC Memories of 254 and 248 Squadron 1941-1945, interview August 2015.

Flight Sergeant Walter Yaholnitsky (RCAF) a Canadian Ukrainian born September 1912 died on 9 April 1943 aged 30, defending the besieged Island of Malta.

Flight Sergeant Walter Yaholnitsky (RCAF) Papers Ottawa.

Mark Bateman of 236 Squadron managed to take off at 15.05 hours.

Pilot Officer Alfred Treadwell family letter about the death of his pilot.

Squadron Leader's Geoffrey Edney did not see his baby daughter Ann Maris Edney born on 2 February 1943. She herself died in 2006.

Uffz Otto Schmid of 5./JG 1 claimed a Beaufort at 16.08 hours 75 km west of Zandvoort.

Captain Dudley Peyton-Ward, hand-written notes for MRAF Sholto Douglas, 1946.

George Blackwood, personal tribute to Howard Fraser.

John Fraser.

Wing Commander Edward Hutton, IWM Papers.

Henry Neil George Wheeler, Kings College Papers.

Group Captain 'Bill' Sise DSO* DFC* Logbook, various entries via John Sise.

Australian, Flight Lieutenant Vyse Millard DFC, former Captain in the Essex Regiment and Lieutenant in the Royal Air Force, awarded DFC Gazetted on Tuesday 2 July 1918. Purchased Bury Mill, Amersham, in 1928 and opened Vyse Millard Antiques Emporium. Rejoined the RAF in September 1939 in the Administrative Branch.

Elizabeth Vivienne Esnie Parsons memories: died January 2007 a widower, Norwich, Norfolk.

Flight Lieutenant Frans Josef Antonius Lutz information via ancestry.com.

Canadian Armed Forces Archive, Ottawa, Squadron Leader 'Bill' Sise letter dated 22 June 1944.

Wing Commander Robert James: Coastal Command's Air Crash Investigations Officer.

James 'Jimmy' Rodgers unpublished memories, *A Wartime Diary 1944*.

German Minesweeper M370, 8 Minesweeper Flotilla.

German *Navy News Chronicle* 1939-1945, 12 August 1944, M370.

William Watson Millar Debriefing Report via James 'Jimmy' Rodgers 1991: Flight Lieutenant Lancelot Dobson his seat and GEE box had all disappeared through a hole in the floor!

William Millar, Truro Hospital, 'Both ankles completely broken: Able to walk within five to six weeks.'

Correspondence with Lawrie Shield.

Correspondence with Tom Armstrong.

Correspondence with 'Bill' 'Puppy' Calder (RCAF).

Correspondence with Angus McIntosh.

Noel Russell DFC Logbook – Copies of entries, August 1944.

Hector Bolitho Papers, Austin, Texas.

Group Captain Raymond Price DFC Logbook entry - HMS *Lord Essenden* FY218

Author's copy of Wing Commander John Yonge's diary, entries for 1944.

Felicity Cuttle.

Author's correspondence with Lord Beaverbrook, 1991.

Chapter 5: Flight Lieutenant Denis Healy DSO, NWC – High Arctic Flight

Giles Healy.

Peter Healy.

Ian Fleming (1908-1964) Miscellaneous uncataloged materials The Lily Library, Bloomington, Indiana USA.

Edward Hutton Letters and Memorabilia.

Sarah Wearne, Abingdon Boys School Archivist.

Abingdon School Magazine.

BBC Archive Caversham, Berkshire.

ktsorens.tihlde.org/flyvrak website material used by kind permission of Kjell Sørensen

Leicester Daily Mercury, 28 April 1939.

Flight Magazine, Newcastle upon Tyne Aero Club: Howard Mitchell Passed Instructors Course 1938.

Derby's municipal secondary school, Bemrose School.

Flying Officer George Victor Kingett DFM, from 1 May 1943 extended service under Air Ministry Scheme 775/45 Scheme B, whereby Kingett retained his existing rank under wartime rules for four years thereafter.

Desmond Hawkins left Bancroft School, Kent, and before he reached twenty walked 2,000 miles across Europe.

23 March 1942: Ernest Schofield gave Kingett at thirty minutes intervals fresh positions throughout the flight so that he could send an immediate distress signal should an emergency arise.

Muckle Flugga lighthouse was originally called North Unst lighthouse until 1964.

Alexander Glen, Fettes College Archive.

240 Squadron Catalina Serial No Z2143.

Dennis Healy's usual plane 'N-Nuts' AH599, initially replaced by a Catalina Mark I serial W8428 that had flown hundreds of hours with No. 209 Squadron before being refitted for 'Arctic Flying' at Greenock by Scottish Aviation.

Scottish Aviation configuration for three fuel tanks holding 500 gallons with sundry equipment for the Catalina was designed chiefly by Robert McIntyre.

RAFMA.

Ancestry.com.

Catalina Society.

Chapter 6: Lieutenant Colonel Jean Maurice Guedj DSO, DFC* CdeG – Legacy of Valour

Author's correspondence with Maurice Guedj daughter.

London Gazette

French Embassy, London Air Attaché: Col. Patrice Hugret.

Armee de la L'Air Service Historique Archive, Paris.

2nd Regiment of Zouaves – 2nd Regiment of Light Infantry based at Meknès in northern-central Morocco.

Archive of Louis Majorelle Art Nouveau, cabinet-maker of Nancy.

Free French Air Force Training School, Major Lionel de Marmier Sywell, Commandant during the First World War started as air mechanic to French aviator Georges Guynemer.

Maurice Guedj Papers Armee de la L'Air Service Historique Archive, Paris.

Félix Guedj Papers Armee de la L'Air Service Historique Archive, Paris.

RAFMA Beaufighter VI.C JL563 WR-W.

Letter dated 26 March 1942 to Commissariat National à l' Air, French Institute, Queensberry Place; Arrived 27 March 1942, No. 2176 – Dispatch returned at 15:00 hours to Air Ministry.

Copy from Armee de la L'Air Service Historique Archive, Paris.

Author's interview with Charles Corder 1993, 1995, 2003.

Taped Interview with Aubrey Inniss, 1990.

Air Commodore Graham Pitchfork.

Unofficial Portreath Wing Diary 1944.

Letter dated 14 April 1942 to Commissaire National à l' Air, French Institute, Queensberry Place; No. 3732.

Copy from Armee de la L'Air Service Historique Archive, Paris.

Author's interview with Donald Clause, August 1997.

Frederick Bentley RCAF 279 Squadron Papers via Canadian Armed Forces, Ottawa, Canada.

RAF Coastal Command Narrative of Operations Orange Form DAL/03/11th (January 1945).

RAF Coastal Command Form Green RO/G5/11th (January 1945).

Form P/P75 Australian Air Force (RAF Form 1580) Airman's Record Sheet (Active Service – Overseas) Australian Government Archive.

Waverley Harris Papers, Australian Government Archive.

Author's interview with Donald French, Thames Masonic Lodge Meeting, 1993.

Phil Davenport on brother Jack Davenport's Operational Planning for 15 January 1945 mission, interview in 2005.

Author's Correspondence with Flight Lieutenant Owen Burns former 235 Squadron Blenheim pilot 1995

Author's Correspondence with Corporal Joyce Trovey WAAF, 1992.

Tony Mottram, Warwickshire tennis player and 489 Squadron pilot, who flew Hampdens, and later a flight commander of 272 Squadron before joining the Banff Wing. Mottram dominated post-war British tennis, representing his country in 56 Davis Cup matches and reaching the Wimbledon doubles final in 1947; he later became an influential coach.

Australian Government Archive 143 Squadron, Food Complaint, RAF Coastal Command Eastbury Park, Northwood.

AIR 28/289 RAF Station Fraserburgh Weather on Patrol – 26 Knots.

Author's interview and preflight meal Donald Clause, August 1997.

Author's interview briefing from Donald Clause August 1997.

General Conduct Form P/P – (RAF Form 120 and 121) Australian Government Archive.

Félix Guedj died from punishing beatings and water treatment received at Port Lyautey, where Félix had been imprisoned for his open sympathies with the Gaullist cause that his son had joined in September 1940.

Author's interview 'Crossing the North Sea', Donald Clause, 1997.

Werner Gayko Born 22 May 1922 in Wehlau, Germany; total of 14 air victories. After the Second World War he served with the Bundeswehr, retiring with the rank of Oberst.

333 Squadron pair lost: Kåre Oscar Sjølie and Sjt. Ingvar Sigurd Gausland R-Robert – HP904

Author's correspondence with Leslie Parker 'Sortie on January 15 1945', 1996.

Author's interview and correspondence with William 'Bill' Clayton-Graham DFC, 1990-1997

Author's interview and correspondence Luftwaffe Ace Rudi Artner, JG5.

Air Historical Branch, RAF Northolt - 18 Group Ops Day Secret Form Orange Bnf/01/15.

Author's interview with Sir Christopher Foxley-Norris GCB, DSO, OBE, FRSA and his wife Lady Joan Foxley-Norris.

Author's interview with Flight Lieutenant Noel Russell DFC relatives, 2016.

Author's copies of Noel Russell Pilot's Logbook, March 1944 to May 1945.

Author's interview and correspondance Tom Armstrong DFC 1989-1996.

Chapter 7: Wing Commander Roger Morewood MID

Rowena and Andrew Buck.

Sarah Wearne, Abingdon Boys School Archivist.

Eulogy for Roger Morewood.

Abingdon Boys School Magazine.

University of Edinburgh - Edinburgh College of Art.

London Gazette.

Air 20/22 RAFMA.

56 Squadron History – *The Firebirds.*

248 Squadron Line Books 1939 to 1941.

Edric 'Sam' McHardy.

RAFMA Miles Magister R1832.

Malcolm Leslie Wells surname was occasionally spelt Welles on paper records.

10 May 1940: Robert Patterson, Reconnaissance Texel to Borkum in Blenheim IVF N6193 *N-Nut.*

Pilot Officer Curran 'Smiley' Robinson's Blenheim shot down at 19.10 hours, by S/Lt Jacquenet, Adj Marchais, and Sgt Dietrich of GC II/8 who mistook the aircraft for a Heinkel 111.

Some One on My Shoulder.

Author's copies of Roger Morewood Pilots Log Book.

Battle of Britain Monument website.

Victor Ricketts died when flying a De Havilland Mosquito on a Photographic Reconnaissance flight to Strasbourg and Ingolstadt on 12 July 1942 with his navigator George Boris Lukhmanoff DFM of San Francisco, California, U.S.A.

Author's correspondence with Chris Ashworth, 1989.

Air Marshal Sir Philip Joubert de la Ferté, Private Papers.

Bob Harwood – Sergeant James 'Jim' May.

The Bishop of Durham was christened Herbert Hensley Henderson aged 14, but commonly just used his middle name of Hensley.

Whilst CO of 248 Squadron, Hyde took the lead role in the Ministry of Information Film entitled *Coastal Command* with Hyde flying Sunderland

T-Tommy, he emploed 248 Squadron in the aerial battle scene with McHardy, Morewood and Maurice Guedj flying the Beaufighters.

Linz Druce Air Raids on the *Tirpitz* Spring 1942.

Mention in Despatches, Roger Morewood.

Chapter 8: Flying Officer Allan Triggs MBE, DFC and Flying Officer John Watson – The Sea Shall Not Have Them

Position of 172 Squadron Wellington ditching was 4806N 0739W.

Air Accident Form 172 Squadron, Wellington *D-Dog*, partially completed.

Eria Buckland-Jones WAAF via National Archives of Australia.

London Gazette

John Watson Papers via National Archives of Australia.

235 Squadron Unofficial Diaries, circa 1942.

Ralph Barker *Down in the Drink*; author's notes via John Davis, Grub Street Publishing, London.

National Archives of Australia.

Women Artists in Cornwall, Barbra Tribe; *A Sculptures Life*, by Helen Hoyle, 2013 blog. cornishmuse.blogspot.com.

Australian War Memorial. Accession Art 27651.

National Portrait Gallery, Barbara Tribe, 1913-2000.

National Gallery of Australia, Barbara Tribe.

The Bloomsbury Archives, Sussex University.

Chapter 9: Wing Commander Ken Gatward DSO, DFC* AE and Sergeant Gilbert 'George' Fern DSM – Operation Squabble

Palmers Green School Records.

St George's College, Weybridge – Gatward may have attended the college but not all old records exist in the archive started 15 years ago due to past administrations skipping of old records.

National Newspaper Archive.

1911 National Census.

Gatward Baptism Records, Camberwell, Christ Church, 1914.

Illustrated Police News – Police Archive London.

Tottenham Hotspurs' Football Club Archive

Electrol Role 1928 and 1929.

British History on Line, *Hornsey, including Highgate: Growth from the mid 19th century*, pages 111-122.

National Newspaper Archive.

National Army Museum Chelsea, London.

Air Commodore Graham Pitchfork, obituary by Dick Maydwell, January 2006.

Berkshire Aviation Museum, Woodley, Berkshire.

Ancestry.com.

Pilot Officer William Peter Bruce Cleary failed to reach the required standard and was transferred to non-flying duties after his flying training was abruptly terminated on 13 September 1939. On 9 November, that year he was granted a commission on probation. 1942 saw Cleary become one of the first RAF liaison officers at the 8th Air Force headquarters at Bushy Park.

Charles Roy Bush (42691).

John Neale Bethell (42689).

John Mallon attended Bell Block Primary School and then New Plymouth Boys' High School.

Arthur Thomas Shackleford joined the Inland Revenue in 1930 as a tax clerk, and six years later was a Customs and Exercise officer.

Pilot Officer George Newton Quarterly Coastal Command Magazine 1942, via RAFMA.

'Battle of the Barges' also included attacking Dutch, French airfields and other strategic installations.

John Maguire married Mary Shaw in the summer of 1940, worked as a Shorthand Secretary Typist at Avro.

RAF Form 1180 Flying Accident Card, Bristol Blenheim Mk IV L9043

Pilot Officer John Mallon, *Manchester Evening News* 'Killed on Active Service.' BDM Section.

Harold Milne Aspen had joined the Army in 1915 and transferred to the Royal Flying Corps on its amalgamation with the Royal Naval Air Service in April 1918. Aspen served a further twenty-five years working his way from Aircraftsman to a Non-Commissioned Officer before being granted a commission as a Flying Officer on 27 July 1939 and aged 45-years-old was posted to 53 Squadron as the Signals Officer. He was known affectionately as 'Pop' or 'Morse' amongst the men.

Mary Abraham, formally Aspen via High Wycombe Chronicle Archive.

The Scotsman 11 October 1940, confirmation that Arthur Shackleford had died in France.

Papers of Marshal of The Royal Air Force Arthur Harris, RAF Museum Hendon, London.

RAF Coastal Command 16 Group memorandum, Australian National Archive, Canberra.

Papers of Hector Bolitho, Austin, Texas, USA.

Flight Lieutenant Richard Warren Denison emigrated to Canada, joining the Royal Air Force in 1935. After being commissioned as a pilot he was posted to 213 Squadron at Church Fenton. The squadron re-equipped with Hawker Hurricanes at Wittering, before being assigned to 236 Squadron during the Battle of Britain.

Papers of Richard Warren Denison, British Columbia, Canada

Author's correspondence with Flight Lieutenant Stanley Nunn, who was posted to 3 School of Ground Reconnaissance in Blackpool 1995.

Bristol Aeroplane Company Graph, December 1941, RAFM Hendon, London.

12th Course from 2 OTU Catfoss started 18 November 1941. Aircrew advised that they had been posted to 236 Squadron on 19 February 1942 whilst on seven days' leave, joining the unit at Wattisham on 21 February.

Papers of Wing Commander James Pike (mentioning Jack Hannaford in buoyant mood, 15 March 1942).

Air Ministry March 1942 Report, Aircraft Lost Dutch Coast 15 March 1942, via Royal Air Force Museum.

Feldwebel Helmut Baudach of I./JG 2 – 236 Squadron *U-Uniform* was his sixth combat kill and second on 20 March, having earlier shot down Wg Cdr J W S Forbes in Spitfire X4503 of 1401 Met Flt at 14.03 hours.

National Archives of Australia File Code 5534390, papers Jack Coulson Hannaford.

Mary E. Fern (nee Hawkins) married September 1941 in the Forest of Dean to Sergeant Gilbert Fern.

Group Captain Alfred 'Fred' Willetts' Air Support Plan ,also see McHardy chapter for Vågsøy Operation Archery raid and Willetts involvement.

Jonathan Gatward.

Gilbert 'George' Fern Flying Log Book Operation *Chariot*, via widow Judith Fern.

Papers Group Captain 'Bill' Sise, Operation *Chariot*.

Papers Guy Sayer R.N.

Ronald Rankin in 1939 was en route to Britain with the Wallabies rugby team when war was declared and volunteered for the Air Force. After beginning training in Australia, it was to Canada that he was sent to complete his pilot training. In early April 1941, with his wings on his tunic and a commission, after crossing the Atlantic to Liverpool he found himself playing in a Rugby XV fixture. Rankin represented New South Wales (capped twenty-two times) against Queensland (1935-38),

Victoria (1936), South Africa (1937), and New Zealand (1938), and played for Australia (capped seven times) against New Zealand (1936, 1938) and South Africa (1937).

Papers Robert Ryder VC.

National Archives of Australia File Code 402417, Papers of Archie William Taylor.

UK National Archives, Kew, HW 13/26: CX/MSS/EX SALU, Nos. 1–30, 5/4/42–12/1/44.

Papers of Harold Kent, Flying Log Book Operation *Chariot*, via Australia.

Sergeant Maxwell, *Addess Jewish Chronicle* and Ancestry.com.

Sergeant Bryan Lane, *Maidenhead Advertiser* and Ancestry.com.

Pilot Officer Vincent George Desourdy joined the Royal Canadian Air Force on 24 October 1940. During training he frequently scored above average at his initial training wing in Canada. He was commissioned on 27 July 1941 and posted to 236 Squadron ten months later. On 17 May 1942 Desourdy, together with navigator Eric Lee, were transferred to 235 Squadron and posted missing on 26th after a mission to southern Norway.

Sergeant Eric Geoffrey Lee, Stroud Chronicle Archive.

National Archives of Australia, Harry Daish Papers.

The Guardian Newspaper Archive, 1937, Daish and Ireland (Birth, Deaths and Marriages).

Squadron Leader William 'Bill' Jay AHB Northolt, London.

Birds & Fishes, by ACM Sir Philip Joubert de la Ferte, Hutchinson, 1960.

Papers of Dudley Peyton-Ward via Sholto Douglas Archive, RAF Coastal Command resumé 1942-1945.

Life Magazine, 'Paris Under The Swastika'.

Benjamin Hodkinson Cowburn, though of British parentage, had been ferried across to France by his mother Margaret and brought up in a Parisian suburb, Boulogne. As a schoolboy with the advent of the First World War he became interested in mechanical and electrical mechanisms and in the late 1920s became a petroleum engineer. Escaping France during the *Blitzkrieg* in the summer of 1940, having gone to 'a decent school,' became a member of the SOE, set up to resist and sabotage in German occupied territories and became one of F Sections agents.

Guillaume Fonkenell, Curator Department of Sculptures and museum historian, Musée du Louvre.

Travelling to Paris September 1941, Ben Cowburn interrogation report 30 March 1942, Baker Street, London.

Gestapo Headquarters, Avenue Foch Papers, via Chemins de Mémoire. Ministère de la Défense, 60 boulevard du Général Martial Valin - CS21623 - 75 509 Paris Cedex 15.

Life Magazine, 'British Take a Look at Paris', 17 August 1942.

British Newspaper Archives – *Tatler* Magazine Editorial.

Coloroll was started in the early 1970s as a printed paper bag manufacturer and owned by the Gatward family.

Select Bibliography

Alexander, Kristen *Jack Davenport Beaufighter Leader* (Australia: Allen & Unwin, 2009)

Bird, Andrew D. *A Separate Little War* (London: Grub Street, 2003, 2009)

Bird, Andrew D. *Coastal Dawn* (London: Grub Street, 2012)

Cowburn Benjamin *No Cloak No Dagger* (Yorkshire: Frontline Books, 2009)

Cremer, Peter U-333 (London: Grafton Books, 1986)

Docherty, Tom *Ours To Hold – RAF Aldergrove At War 1939-1945* (Lincoln: Old Forge, 1995)

Foot, Michael Richard Daniell *SOE in France* (London: HMSO, 1966)

Gardiner, Juliet Wartime Britain 1939 – 1945 (London: Headline 2004)

Glen, Alexander *Footholds Against a Whirlwind* (London: Hutchinson, 1975)

Gordon, Ian *Strike and Strike Again 455 Squadron RAAF* (Australia: Banner Books 1994)

Holland, James *The War in the West – A New History Germany Ascendant 1939 – 1941* (London: Corgi 2016)

Joubert de la Fertè, Sir Philip *Birds and Fishes – Story of Coastal Command* (London: Hutchinson, 1960)

Lush, Peter *Wing Chariot* (London: Grub Street, 2016)

Lyman, Robert *Into The Jaws of Death – The True Story of the Legendary Raid on Saint-Nazaire* (London: Quercus, 2014)

Macaulay R. H. H. *Beaufighter – The Aircraft in Defence and Offence 1940 – 1944* (Aldershot: Gale & Polden 1944)

Rawlings, John D. R. *Coastal, Support and Special Squadrons of the RAF and their Aircraft* (London: Janes, 1982)

Scholfield Ernest & Conyers Nesbit Roy *Arctic Airmen* (Kent: Spellmount, 1987)

Walbank, Frederick Allan, Wings of War (London: B. T. Batsford, 1942)

Warner, Graham, The Bristol Blenheim -An Illustrated History (London: Crecy, 2002)

Wilson, Michael & Robinson A. S. L., *Coastal Command Leads the Invasion* (London: Jarrolds, 1945)

Journals

Bolitho, Hector H. *Coastal Command Review Vol. 1 to Vol. 4* (1942 – 1945) via RAFMA

Bolitho, Hector H. *Coastal Command Quartley Reviews* (1942 – 1945) via RAFMA

Acknowledgements

Having worked on some of the high profile genealogy programmes, there is no doubt that interest in family history is at an all time high. This new book hopes to retell stories through those who served in Coastal Command between 1939 and 1945. The people chosen for the book, are not well known characters; I always try to bring in fresh material for every book I write so the men here are diverse and I have tried whenever possible to draw on contemporary sources – letters, diaries, as well as official documents, supplemented by a wide range of people who have enabled me to prepare this work especially the stalwart hearts of those families who, understanding the importance of their loved ones' testimony, added riches to the stories within.

I was dependent upon the time, patience and goodwill of Katharine Campbell, Stevie Davenport, Sally Goldsworthy, Mrs Judith Fern, Felicity Cuttle, John Sise, John Fraser (son of Wing Commander Duncan Fraser OBE), David Crowe, Rowena and Andrew Buck, Sue Kenworthy, Sally Hedley, Jonathan Gatward, Giles and Peter Healy, Katie Gordon, Peter, Henry, George and Tom Meakin (sons of Wing Commander 'Jack' Meakin DFC*, MiD), Edward McManus, Bob Harwood and Robert Letcher. I am also profoundly grateful for Madame Maria Guedj aged 102 years-old and Sarah Dars for their time, for which huge thanks.

I'm especially indebted to Air Commodore John Meier, Director General History and Heritage – Royal Australian Air Force for his very generous forward. I hesitated to ask this most accomplished and busy man to under take this task. Flight Lieutenant Julie Dryden, Senior Research Officer from the Directorate of History – Air Force, Martin James Historian Royal Australian Air Force and Simon Moody, Research Officer at Air Force Museum of New Zealand. Peter Devitt of the RAF Museum Archives and Library in London who was unfailingly helpful. The Heritage Collection Librarian, Lorraine Johnston of Dunedin Public Libraries for her patience, professionalism and courtesy during my researches from afar.

I'm grateful to Maeve Waggott, and Sarah Wearne, for sight of tattered journals and reports in school archives, and Jane Robertson at The Australian War Memorial Canberra, for the papers on Australian sculptor Barbara Tribe and one of her sitters Flight Lieutenant Allan Triggs. My thanks to Bas Maathuis and Jac Baart of the Dutch Air War Study Group their enthusiasm for the project and their knowledgeable insights and observations on the maritime war in the North Sea and air-war over the Netherlands. Also special thanks to military historian and fellow author Dr. Rob Lyman for his help on the Saint Nazaire mission, and Peter Lush's knowledge and resources.

Thanks too once again, to the staff of the Imperial War Museum, the National Archives, and the Deutsches U-Boot-Museum in Cuxhaven, which pointed me in the direction of Kapitänleutnant Peter Cremer *U-333 Story of a U-boat Ace* for background material on Oberleutnant zur See Klemens Schamong. Despite my best efforts it is possible that some errors have been over looked. If this is the case I alone remain responsible. If they are brought to my attention I will endeavour to correct them in subsequent editions.

I have received considerable assistance from Kjell Sørensen, with his Second World War Air Force and Luftwaffe crash sites portal Flyvrak and the French historian Frederic Henhoff. Finally, the support of my family, and of Martin Mace and his wonderful crew at Frontline Books, has made this endeavour not just possible, but immensely pleasurable. Thank you all.

Index